D1713685

Drinking the Waters

Drinking the Waters

CREATING AN AMERICAN LEISURE CLASS AT
NINETEENTH-CENTURY MINERAL SPRINGS

THOMAS A. CHAMBERS

Smithsonian Institution Press
Washington and London

Editor: Ruth G. Thomson
Designer: Brian Barth

Library of Congress Cataloging-in-Publication Data
Chambers, Thomas A.
    Drinking the waters : creating an American leisure class at
nineteenth-century mineral springs / Thomas A. Chambers
        p.   cm.
Includes bibliographical references (p.) and index.
ISBN 1-58834-068-6 (alk. paper)
    1. United States—Social life and customs—19th century.
2. United States—Social conditions—19th century. 3. Leisure
class—History—19th century. 4. Upper class—United States—
Social life and customs—19th century. 5. Health resorts—
United States—History—19th century. 6. Springs—Social
aspects—United States—History—19th century. 7. Saratoga
Springs (N.Y.)—Social life and customs—19th century. 8.
White Sulphur Springs (W.Va.)—Social life and customs—19th
century. I. Title.
E166.C43   2002
306'.0973'09034—dc21   2002021788

British Library Cataloging-in-Publication Data available

Manufactured in the United States of America
09 08 07 06 05 04 03 02   5 4 3 2 1

⊗ The paper used in this publication meets the minimum re-
quirements of the American National Standard for Information
Sciences—Permanence of Paper for Printed Library Materials
ANSI Z39.48-1984.

For Anne E. Ward

and in memory of
Virginia Ward Chambers
4 December 2001

Contents

Acknowledgments

*I*t seems inconceivable that I began this project nine years ago. Since that time I have accumulated a store of debts that I wish to acknowledge. From my first day of graduate school, Robert A. Gross has been an enthusiastic, dedicated, rigorous, and positive influence on my work. Those who know Bob will see his imprint on this book, and I thank him for making it better. Likewise, Carol Sheriff offered encouragement, advice, and a keen critical perspective throughout the project; again, the book is much better for her involvement. Each is an ideal model of an outstanding teacher, scholar, advisor, mentor, and friend. At Smithsonian Institution Press Mark Hirsch deserves an extra note of thanks for taking up this project and backing it enthusiastically, and Ruth G. Thomson has been a friendly, outstanding editor.

Others who generously offered to read and comment on the project along the way include Barbara Bellows, Chandos Brown, Dona Brown, Field Horne, Laura Croghan Kamoie, Michael Lynn, Greg Pfitzer, Marcy Sacks,

Gavin Taylor, James A. Ward, Nick and Virginia Westbrook, and anonymous readers for Smithsonian Institution Press. Charlene Lewis set the bar quite high and provided the solace that someone else toiled in the field of mineral springs history, and Jon Sterngass offered a useful example of exactly what Saratoga Springs was not. The complements and contrasts between these two scholars' work and my own proved especially fruitful. Moral support and scholarly encouragement came from Mary Lynn, John McCardell, and the history faculties at Emma Willard School, Siena College, and especially Albion College. Research assistance from Jim Nida, Erin Silverman, and Annelliott Willis also helped this project in its early stages. Ralph Houghton of Albion College's Department of Instructional Technology provided invaluable help with digitizing illustrations and other computer matters, and Tom Stock provided expert photographic services.

Of course, this work would not have been possible without the outstanding staff at a number of research libraries. Bob Conte at The Greenbrier, Margaret Cook at the College of William and Mary, Ellen deLalla at the Saratoga Springs Public Library, Field Horne at the National Museum of Racing, Lisa McCown at Washington and Lee University, and Martha Stonequist at the Saratoga Springs City Historian's Office were especially helpful in opening their archives to me and providing useful insights. The Colonial Williamsburg Library, Duke University, Historical Society of Saratoga Springs, Library of Virginia, Maryland Historical Society, New-York Historical Society, New York State Historical Association, New York State Library and Archives, Saratoga County Historian's Office, Southern Historical Collection, South Carolina Historical Society, South Caroliniana Library, University of Virginia, and Virginia Historical Society all provided professional and generous service in their archives. Interlibrary Loan staffers at Albion College, Emma Willard School, Siena College, and the College of William and Mary tracked down obscure and esoteric sources.

I especially appreciate financial assistance from Albion College, the College of William and Mary, the Virginia Historical Society, and the Stonewall Jackson House that supported several research trips. Friends and family who provided accommodations during my research forays include Jim and Joanne Chambers, John Chambers, Scott and Lynn Krugman, Jim and Roberta Ward, Jeff McMahan and Heather Ross, Annelliott Willis, and Kyle and Tisha Zelner.

On a more personal note, Anne Elizabeth Ward deserves as much credit for this book as I do. She spent vacations in various archives, proofread countless drafts, listened to my rambling theories, provided financial and emotional support, and reminded me by her presence that there are more things in life than this book. Were it not for her and Archibald Rockbridge Ward, I would not have completed this project or made it what it is. Of course, only my stubbornness is responsible for any remaining errors that she and others did not convince me to eliminate. Heartiest thanks and love.

Introduction

*It is an old story that in this
country we have no "leisure class."*

—HENRY JAMES, "SARATOGA"

uring the early nineteenth century, few public places offered the opportunity for men and women from the different sections of the United States to meet. Great cities like New York, Philadelphia, and Washington (while Congress was in session) and vacation resorts like Newport, Cape May, Nahant, and Long Branch provided some chance for mingling. But at the mineral springs resorts of Virginia's western mountains and at Saratoga Springs, New York, an intensive brand of social mixing transpired. At these springs Americans from North and South, East and West, gathered for a few weeks or months of relaxation, recuperation, and re-union. If, as Carl Bridenbaugh suggested over a half-century ago, the springs served as the rendezvous for America's fledgling aristocracy, they also functioned as a laboratory for the new nation and a site of unification during the late nineteenth century.[1] Here the nation's social and political leaders experimented with the idea that they formed a coherent culture and an elite class. Brought together by a desire for health and amusement, Americans discovered that they shared much in common at the springs. There the boundaries of class and section were defined, tested, solidified, broken, and eventually repaired.

The springs were, above all, a heterogeneous place. Extant hotel ledgers from several New York and Virginia establishments include visitors from thirty-three different states and ten foreign countries. The presence of so many "gay and fashionable" people from around the nation and world lent an air of cosmopolitan sophistication to the resorts that was unattainable elsewhere. Drawn mostly from "the wealthy class" of Americans, ladies and gentlemen could be seen "mingling harmoniously" at the springs. During the fashionable season of July and August, "the whole *elite* of the Union" assembled there.[2]

Descriptions like "elegant and select," "the most genteel and orderly," "highly respectable," "very select and agreeable," and "the most elegant + refined of the Southern Country" characterized visitors to the Virginia springs. In 1816 congressmen such as Henry Clay of Kentucky, numerous judges, military officers, and notables such as James Kirke Paulding mingled with leading Southern families: Anderson, Boykin, Branch, Carrington, Chesnut, Coalter, Coleman, Coles, Dandridge, Ellis, Giles, Gilmer, Gordon, Hairston, Harrison, Maury, Meade, Nicholas, Payne, Randolph, Robertson, Skipwith, Stewart, Stith, Taylor, Thornton, and Wilson. Saratoga Springs attracted a socially mixed crowd, but "the most wealthy, educated, and refined" Americans still set society's tone. Visitors in 1825–26 included leading New York names such as Bayard, Clinton, Corning, DePeysters, DeWitt, Fish, Geddes, Hone, Irving, Kent, Knickerbocker, Lansing, Low, Ludlow, Montgomery, Morris, Nott, Roosevelt, Spencer, Stuyvesant, Thacher, Tibbitts, Trask, Van Buren, Van Cortlandt, Van Rensselaer, and Yates. The names of military officers like Gen. Alexander Macomb, later the commander of the United States Army, former governor of New York Joseph C. Yates, and foreign dignitaries like Joseph Bonaparte jump out from hotel ledgers, as do an equally impressive list of Southern names: Hayne, Manigault, Middleton, Moncure, Pinckney, Rutledge, and Tillman from South Carolina, Lee and Tayloe from Virginia, Slidell from Louisiana, and Tallmadge from Georgia. Typical visitors in both regions were "people of the first rank in the United States; they are people of fashion, as well as great wealth; they are mostly from the seaports and great towns." These impressive names demonstrate the powerful collection of people at the springs, a group that represented the raw materials for creating an American elite.[3]

Because they gathered wealthy Americans together, the springs served as a testing ground for the idea that America composed a single nation with a coherent ruling elite and single national culture. In the early years of the new republic, the remnants of the colonial gentry made a conscious effort to maintain social order and to establish their hierarchical rule. According to this largely Federalist outlook, only a well-ordered society with authority and influence emanating from the upper levels could function as a proper republic. But, as Robert Wiebe and Gordon Wood have demonstrated, this attempt to impose a European model of social order failed by 1815, when the victory over Great Britain ensured American independence and weakened the claims of those who sought to imitate the colonial parent's social system. Indeed, the prevailing political values of the new nation attacked the idea of an American aristocracy.[4] Although Wiebe and Wood are correct in their assertion that the elite faded from the national political scene, especially after the political triumph of the frontier everyman Andrew Jackson in 1828, they wrongly posit that attempts to form a national elite disappeared after 1815. Instead, Americans continued their efforts to solidify a national aristocracy throughout the nineteenth century, especially at the springs.

These attempts were most successful in individual cities, where local or regional aristocracies developed. Boston, New York, Philadelphia, and Charleston included particularly powerful and exclusive elites who thwarted the claims of egalitarianism made by many citizens of Jacksonian America. But the parochialism of these fledgling elites, as well as the competition among them for overall prominence in culture and commerce, limited their national importance.[5] Only after local and regional elites traveled beyond the physical boundaries of their own urban centers could anything resembling a national elite begin to take shape.

One of the few national gathering places during the early republic was the country's capital at Washington. Its location at the geographic center of the nation was designed to unite America, but the nascent city's residential patterns, where congressmen from different sections of the country lodged in boardinghouses with men from similar areas, limited the possibility of cross-sectional cohesion. Before the genesis of the Jacksonian party system, Washington looked and acted less like a national capital where people coalesced into a national elite than "a series of sectional enclaves." Philadelphia, accepted by most Americans and foreigners as the premier cosmopolitan American city during the early decades of the nineteenth century, fared marginally better as a national center. Many Southerners sent their sons and daughters to colleges or finishing schools there, where the next generation developed relationships with their Northern counterparts. Some families even established temporary homes on Philadelphia's Spruce Street, also known as Carolina Row. These families sought the social and cultural sophistication that they lacked on their plantations, or even in Southern urban centers like Charleston or Mobile, as well as enhanced marriage prospects for their daughters. Although the group of families in Philadelphia was not large enough to constitute a national elite, upper-class intermingling signaled the possibility of constructing an American aristocracy. Similarly, major Northern colleges such as Princeton, Yale, and, to a lesser extent, Harvard attracted Southern gentlemen but failed to produce an easily identifiable national elite. Even such ostensibly national institutions as the army, navy, and military academies could not overcome the prevailing regional identifications of most Americans. Only later in the century, when New York City dominated the nation's financial and social scenes, was there any single locus of national power, culture, and business.[6]

What the new nation lacked were the cultural centers of high civilization. Looking back on the "extraordinary blankness" of Nathaniel Hawthorne's writings, Henry James wondered what was left to compose American culture. In James's estimation, Hawthorne's America possessed

> No State, in the European sense of the word, and indeed barely a specific national name. No sovereign, no court, no personal loyalty, no aristocracy, no church, no clergy, no army, no diplomatic service, no country gentlemen, no palaces, no castles, nor manors, nor old country-houses, nor parsonages, nor thatched cottages nor ivied ruins; no cathedrals, nor abbeys, nor little Norman churches; no great Universities nor public schools—no Oxford, nor Eton, nor Harrow; no literature, no novels, no museums, no pictures, no political society, no sporting class—no Epsom nor Ascot!

James concluded "that if these things are left out, everything is left out." The American effort to create a self-conscious elite would have to overcome the paucity of national centers noted by James. Where in England the aristocracy relied on the many institutions that James cataloged, Americans would have to fashion their upper class from whole cloth.[7]

But James erred in his claim that there was "no Epsom" in America. As did Georgian English spas at Bath, Cheltenham, Tunbridge Wells, and Epsom, Saratoga Springs and its Virginia counterparts served as gathering places for those attempting to form an American aristocracy. Taking the waters had been popular among America's upper classes since the late seventeenth century, when Bostonians visited nearby Lynn Red Springs and William Penn noted the discovery of springs around Philadelphia. In the two decades before the Revolution, Bristol Springs and Yellow Springs attracted Philadelphia's wealthy citizens; Stafford Springs, Connecticut, drew such notables as John Adams; and George Washington visited Berkeley Springs in northern Virginia. By the mid-nineteenth century, mineral springs dotted the American landscape, but Poland Springs, Maine, Sharon Springs, New York, and even Hot Springs, Arkansas, lacked sizable hotels until at least the late 1840s. Although the water-cure movement, Grahamite diet, and other health reform efforts influenced American culture, no single movement or establishment challenged the Virginia springs or Saratoga Springs as the social centers of America's leisure class. By the late nineteenth century, Newport or Bar Harbor might make that claim, but the springs continued to serve a similar function to English spas—the gathering place for the national aristocracy.[8]

But Americans failed to realize, as Henry James did later in the century, that the English spas were one of a number of cultural institutions that helped to coalesce a national elite. If Americans were to create a coherent upper class, they would have to do so without the aid of significant national cultural institutions. Their imagined community would be based on the shared interests of leisure activities, class consciousness, and the temporary unity developed during a few weeks at the springs. James's 1870 claim that there was "no 'leisure class'" in America seemed less and less credible as the nineteenth century progressed.[9]

In attempting to create a national leisure class, the springs attracted people from around the nation and, ironically, across the social spectrum. The hyperactive socializing that ensued revolved around the desire for status, whether as ratification of or elevation from one's position. Americans in the early nineteenth century were, as Alexis de Tocqueville described them, a restless bunch, "forever brooding over the advantages they do not possess." When "ambition, *in some form*, is the motive that actuates a large portion of visitors at fashionable watering-places," there was bound to be trouble. The naked ambition of social climbers, as well as the futile efforts of the established elite to limit mobility, created a competitive climate in which everyone clambered for the power and privilege of social superiority. At the springs, social mixing between the classes reduced cultural boundaries and created a society with uncertain distinctions of rank.[10] Gentlemen and ladies who had once based their claims to authority and power on economic position, land holding, and the family name could not assume that others would defer to their status. By lowering themselves to intermingle with their social inferiors, the elite may have gained the middle class's esteem or their anger at the condescension. In either case, interclass social mixing created tension.

Again, Tocqueville summarized the conflict: "as men differing in education and in birth meet and mingle in the same places of resort, it is impossible to agree upon the rules of good breeding." At the springs status itself seemed open to negotiation and competition. The old gentry emphasized its own refined manners and republican virtue in an ultimately futile effort to avoid competition with the nouveau riche of merchants, professionals, and small landowners. Wealth alone did not equal status; refinement was required as well. From this background a fledgling aristocracy arose, "based on principles that could be learned and were superior to those of birth and family, and even great wealth." These new leaders reconceived themselves through economic success and moral and cultural superiority, which they no longer based solely upon land holding and ancient lineage. Hierarchy still existed, but it derived its legitimacy from the virtue and character of rulers and citizens. The new pseudoaristocracy claimed to be merit based. In an era when the rising middle class was threatening the position of the wealthy, gentility lent legitimate social power to its practitioners and supported class authority. Pretenders might copy the manners and dress of gentility, but they could never truly attain refinement, an unlearnable internal quality. Gentility answered the challenge from the middle classes because it "deepened the division between rich and poor, adding a moral dimension to differences in wealth."[11]

Here then was the central tension of life at the springs: a contest for social and cultural authority between old and new money. The fledgling American aristocracy perished in the Revolution, but traces of class rivalries and animosities persisted "in the midst of the democratic confusion that ensue[d]." At the springs men like Clement Clarke Moore, a New York City Federalist, the author of "A Visit From St. Nicholas," and a landowner who railed against the advance of urban commerce, mixed with social climbers like Thomas J. Jackson (later known as "Stonewall"), the son of a hardscrabble family from western Virginia. Jackson tugged hard enough on his bootstraps to graduate from West Point, to serve with distinction in the

Mexican War, and to secure a professorship at the Virginia Military Institute. Both men, despite the claims of some commentators that middle-class gentlemen like Jackson could not afford the trip, frequented the springs but differed in almost every part of their background and character. Moore probably would have placed Jackson among the people he described in his poem "A Trip to Saratoga":

> Now, rough mechanics leave their work undone,
>   And, with pert milleners and prentice youth,
> To some gay, throng'd resort away they run,
>   To cure dyspepsia or ennui, forsooth!

The scarcely concealed point of Moore's poem is that the middle and lower classes did not belong at places like Saratoga Springs and ruined it for members of the elite like himself. That an aspiring gentleman like Jackson went there as well only furthered the problem: now Moore had to deal with people who seemed to be refined, even if they were not from the most select families. Moore and Jackson, though they never met, symbolized the culture clash between established families and the new middle class that drove life at the springs.[12]

This book addresses two important areas of historiography—the creation of an American elite and nineteenth-century sectionalism. Each has a broad and rich literature, but few—if any—studies have combined the two areas of inquiry. My goal is to investigate the mineral springs as a cultural phenomenon and location where Americans negotiated and defined class and section. Leisure provides a window into the structures and values of nineteenth-century America. The springs in particular offer a unique opportunity to witness Americans at their socially weakest; thrown together in geographically distant and isolated resorts, they had to construct communities, class, and social systems. By analyzing these processes, we learn much about what divided Americans and what united them, eventually, in a common culture.

In completing this book, I have made several intellectual assumptions. First, I view class as a lived as well as a material condition. More than wealth, class includes beliefs, actions, and experiences; in short, class is defined by culture. To quote E. P. Thompson, "class is defined by men as they live their own history." The subject of this book is the leisure class, a group that defined itself both by its abstention from work and by its adherence to codes of manners that Thorstein Veblen called "expressions of status." The processes of forming the leisure class and articulating its ideology compose much of this book's content.[13]

Second, I am writing in the context and wake of a number of insightful studies in a new subdiscipline, the history of tourism. Recent works by Cindy Aron, Orvar Löfgren, and Lynne Withey, as well as slightly older but equally important studies by Dona Brown, John Sears, and Dean MacCannell, have examined tourism within its social and cultural context. Tourism's role in the construction of class identity and the conflict between work and leisure seem to be issues that exist in a variety of places, times, and cultures. Similarly, more detailed studies of the springs by Charlene Lewis, Margaret Gail Gillespie, Jon Sterngass, and Theodore Corbett offer useful perspectives and perceptive analyses of the springs experience in Virginia and New York, although none does so comparatively. This work seeks to combine the best aspects of all of these studies and the larger historiographies of tourism, class formation, and sectionalism to offer a fresh perspective on nineteenth-century American society and culture. It articulates an alternative narrative to the "irrepressible conflict" interpretation of the Civil War era.[14] Throughout the nineteenth century—during the early republic, the Jacksonian and antebellum periods, the Civil War and Reconstruction, and the late nineteenth century—people at the springs attempted to form a common, national culture. In terms of business practices, landscape aesthetics, medical therapeutics, social structure, and gender relations, Northern and Southern springs were more alike than they were different. By looking at the springs as a cultural phenomenon complete with its own distinctive leisure class, rather than as resorts characteristic of regional distinctiveness, this book demonstrates the remarkable similarity of nineteenth-century American culture, North and South.

This book is organized thematically with a roughly chronological substructure. Chapter 1 analyzes the common business practices of springs proprietors before the Civil War, with an emphasis on the springs' integration into the national market. Chapters 2 through 5 include analysis of the entire nineteenth century but focus on the pre–Civil War period. Chapter 2 discusses the cultural assumptions behind springs architecture and landscape scenery and their use in attracting culturally elite visitors, as does the investigation in chapter 3 of medical practices and the contest for medical authority. Chapters 4 and 5 complement each other in describing the conflict over class and culture at the springs by looking at society and gender roles, respectively. These chapters are the heart of the book, as they illustrate the nearly constant process of social display, class construction, and the negotiation of gender across geographic sections. Chapter 6 provides a focused discussion about sectional rivalries and the attempt to create a national elite, especially in the antebellum period. Despite people's efforts to unite wealthy Americans from the North and the South, political divisions brought about the Civil War, yet the common springs culture persisted. Chapter 7 treats the springs during and after the war as a thematic whole, uniting the earlier chapters' topics in a concluding section that traces the reemergence and renaissance of the springs as the site of a national culture based on shared class assumptions. This book contends that there was a national American culture—at least at the springs—throughout the nineteenth century and that members of the variously strong and weak national elite defined themselves at these cultural sites.

Chapter 1

COMMERCIALIZING LEISURE

*J*ames Calwell and Gideon Putnam shared the same dream: each wanted to build a grand hotel and to develop successful resorts based on the mineral waters at White Sulphur Springs, Virginia, and Saratoga Springs, New York, respectively. Hoping to capitalize on the emerging tourist trade, both men chose isolated spots to seek their fortunes; at the beginning of the nineteenth century neither White Sulphur Springs nor Saratoga Springs could claim more than a seasonal population or a meager reputation as a spa. But Calwell and Putnam and their heirs transformed their resorts into the ultimate springs businesses in the antebellum South and North. Both men adopted innovative business practices and took risks on their way to success. Although they both catered to an exclusive clientele of wealthy tourists, they followed divergent business routes because of the different economic and social circumstances in their respective regions. Practice, not principle, separated their efforts to build the mineral springs industry. Both Calwell and Putnam helped initiate the springs boom, which was part of a larger growth in American tourism and elite leisure culture. Imitators in Virginia or New York State looked to these entrepreneurs for inspiration and models. Whereas in 1790 Virginia boasted only five mineral springs resorts and Saratoga Springs looked to nearby Ballston Spa's rustic taverns as a prototype resort town, by 1860 at least fifty-three springs establishments dotted western Virginia and ten large hotels lined Saratoga Springs' avenues.[1] James Calwell, Gideon Putnam, and their descendants and imitators employed clever promotional tactics to help launch the American tourism industry, to spur the commercialization of leisure, and to attract elite visitors. Operating at the forefront of early nineteenth-century capitalism, they captured the tourist trade but remained on shaky financial footing. The economic realities of the North and South limited the springs' success, even as promoters embraced the market forces that created and sustained their wealthy clientele.

Calwell and Putnam knew a good business opportunity when they saw one. Nearby resorts, as well as others in the United States and Europe, offered examples of successful spas. A few miles north of White Sulphur Springs, the much older Hot Springs hosted invalids in a rustic inn and bathhouse as early as 1766, and neighboring Warm Springs was offering similar accommodations by 1761. A few miles south, Sweet Springs attracted scientific interest in 1774 and visitors shortly thereafter. Each springs enjoyed considerable success as a resort for a small number of invalids willing to suffer spartan accommodations and dull company for the prospect of a cure. But they were not the wildly popular springs resorts that American entrepreneurs dreamed of building. Likewise, when Gideon Putnam could ride seven miles south from his home in Saratoga Springs and see a growing resort at Ballston Spa, where four taverns and guest houses catered to hundreds of annual visitors in 1792, he envisioned something grand for his fledgling town. By the early 1800s, Ballston Spa had become the premier resort of American gentry from both North and South, and Putnam envisioned his resort as its rival.[2]

American spas, however, constituted part of a larger transatlantic social endeavor. In England resort towns like Bath helped initiate the commercialization of leisure in eighteenth-century England, a process that became the model for American spas. The imitation of England's premier mineral water resort composed a key ingredient of America's early springs establishments. When during the late 1760s Stafford Springs, Connecticut, attracted New England's sick and fashionable in great numbers, pundits termed it "the New England Bath."[3] And when the South's most famous resort, located in northern Virginia, boomed in the 1780s, promoters dubbed it Bath. Residents of the fledgling Hot Springs and Warm Springs continued the trend by naming their region in the Virginia mountains Bath County. By borrowing the famous spa's name, they hoped to imitate its success.

Naming American resorts after famous English spas constituted a conscious attempt to duplicate English models and to attract business. During the Revolutionary era, many wealthy Americans visited European resorts as well and compared them with their colonial-style counterparts. Whether at Bath or a continental spa like Baden-Baden later in the century, Americans deemed the European spas superior to their own: "the grounds are much more improved and the country all around highly cultivated." That Americans visited England's spas during the Revolution is striking—but that these Americans came from the upper echelons of Anglo-American society and possessed both the means to travel abroad and the political connections to do so during wartime is not. Consider Gabriel Manigault, a Charleston merchant, planter, and politician, whose business and cultural connections with England included trade and a son practicing law there. Or the New Yorker Elkanah Watson, who after carrying American diplomatic dispatches to France during the Revolution established himself in business, only to fail and return after the war to America, where he again prospered. These men visited spas on both sides of the Atlantic and belonged to an Anglo-American elite that shared a leisure culture.[4] They, and other wealthy Americans like them, cultivated the same cultural values and standards as the English gentry. Developing an American spa culture helped define the American national elite and its place in the Atlantic world. If their cultural institutions equaled those of England, then men like Manigault and Watson could begin to feel that they belonged to a transatlantic, cosmopolitan elite.

In this context Americans constantly evaluated their springs based upon European models. The earliest American spas resembled "the State of Bath in Eng'd in the barbarous days." Lacking the cultural inferiority complex of many Americans, some British travelers found the rusticity of American springs quaint and devoid of the social excesses of English spas. Other European visitors even questioned the mania for imitation. When the spa at Warm Springs changed its name to Bath, because the proprietors "wished to give more importance to their warm spring by honoring it with a name which came from the former mother country," the French visitor Ferdinand-Marie Bayard objected. The resort did not need the name, he argued, because America possessed enough natural beauty and cultural sophistication to prosper "without seeking outside of your native land borrowed ornaments." But Americans, especially the conservative, largely Federalist group at the springs, continued to look to England for cultural models. Only by equaling the European spas could American springs earn the cultural legitimacy that the elite demanded. And American springs did so at a remarkably fast rate. Just fifteen years after his initial visit to Saratoga Springs, Elkanah Watson revised his earlier criticism. Saratoga Springs might "become eventually the Bath of America."[5]

Achieving such a distinction required constant promotional efforts that place the springs within the larger history of American commerce. According to the historian Barbara Carson, the springs were "the first and most important destinations" in "the commercialization of leisure" that created a larger tourist economy during the early nineteenth century. Promoters built resorts and destinations to attract travelers, who expanded from an elite few in the late eighteenth century to a relatively heterogeneous multitude by the 1820s. New York State's Hudson River valley became the first commercial tourist region, as efficient travel networks allowed tourists to reach historic sites along the river, the resorts at Ballston Spa and Saratoga Springs, and historic ruins like Ticonderoga on Lake Champlain, Montreal and Quebec to the north, and Niagara Falls to the west. In Virginia promoters imitated the earlier development of New York's Northern Tour by encouraging travelers to visit Natural Bridge, the Peaks of Otter, and Hawk's Nest and to make "a complete circle of travel to all the great Springs of Western Virginia." Both regions' new tourists consumed scenery, accommodations, transportation, and the experience itself—all part of an emerging commercial industry centered around tourism. The springs constituted another aspect of the Market Revolution, a term historians use to describe the late eighteenth- and early nineteenth-century transformation from local, primarily agricultural economies based on mutuality to much broader regional and national commercial networks centered around towns and cities where industry produced goods and merchants exchanged them for profit. Illustrating the ways in which those networks broke down geographical boundaries and innovated transportation systems and business practices, the springs and tourism represent two of the most radical sectors of this economic revolution.[6]

By promoting their establishments, springs proprietors enthusiastically embraced the market. One key to the springs' success was the larger transformation in advertising and publishing. Springs businessmen carefully sought and cultivated the business of travelers by using print to construct an image of their resorts that appealed to the reading public, in part the same class as fashionable tourists. Travel accounts of people's visits to the springs had long been popular, whether published or circulated privately, but the emergence of the Northern Tour in New York State during the 1820s and the Virginia springs circuit in the late 1830s triggered the publication of a new literary genre: guidebooks. These guidebooks kept their contents simple and direct, offering information, advice, and descriptions of the leading attractions. The most popular northern guidebooks covered a variety of locations, whereas Virginia's travel books focused on the most popular springs and a few natural landmarks. These books played a leading role in creating the springs boom during the second quarter of the nineteenth century. When they proclaimed, as did one Saratoga Springs guidebook, that "the day is not far distant when the present accommodations at Saratoga will be of necessity doubled to accommodate the immense numbers who will continue to make it their place of annual resort," they were both announcing and causing a trend.[7]

Perhaps the first guidebook to deal specifically with American mineral springs was Gideon Miner Davison's *The Fashionable Tour: Or, A Trip to the Springs, Niagara, Quebeck, and Boston, in the Summer of 1821*. Published in Saratoga Springs by Davison's printing office, the book sought to aid travelers by providing brief descriptions of notable stops along the tour, distance tables, and prices. By assembling a mass of disparate information, such as the names of hotels and their rates, Davison enabled someone with no knowledge of the area to embark on a journey about which others raved. Perhaps even more important, he compiled this information in an accessible, portable format: measuring only 3.75 by 5.5 inches and .75 inches thick, the 165-page volume was easily carried on a stagecoach, steamboat, or even horseback, fitting neatly inside a gentleman's coat pocket or a lady's reticule. "Designed as a pocket manual and guide," Davison's book appealed to tourists wealthy enough to afford a volume beautifully bound with leather and marbled paper and elaborately decorated with gold lettering on the spine and cover, to follow its itinerary, and to have someone else care for their baggage as they thumbed its pages.[8]

But Davison's was not the only guidebook. Recognizing "the great increase of traveling on the northern fashionable routes," other authors followed Davison's lead. Titles like *The Northern Traveller*, *The Tourist, or Pocket Manual . . .*, and *The Travelers' Own Book* appeared over the next two decades. These publications, along with their successors and imitators, shared the compact size and common purpose of Davison's work: "to be brief, and yet sufficiently explicit; to furnish statistical information without being tedious; and, in short, to give much in little on every subject that presents itself to the intelligent tourist." Rather than go into detail on every locale, the guidebooks aimed to point out "as [the tourist passes], objects which most deserve his notice and regard."[9] Notably, these guidebooks seem aimed at a specific audience. The "intelligent tourist" knew how to discriminate between ordinary sights and those that "deserve" attention. Such readers came from a culturally sophisticated background and desired a distinctive tourist experience.

According to their authors, the guidebooks sold well. Prefaces in subsequent editions referred to "liberal patronage" and "ready sale" of earlier editions, as well as changing information (new hotels, better routes, evolving fashion), as the reasons for additional printings. Publishers certainly welcomed this kind of puffery to increase sales, and the publication histories of several titles suggest that the authors may have been correct. Standards like Davison's *Fashionable Tour* went through as many as eight editions (and several titles) by 1840, and the publisher of the second guidebook on the market, Theodore Dwight's *The Northern Traveller,* printed six editions by 1841.[10] Dozens of other guidebooks appeared under a variety of titles throughout the 1840s and 1850s as Saratoga Springs boomed.

Although not as prolific as northern guidebooks, a series of publications describing and promoting the Virginia springs emerged by the late 1830s. The first, Henry Huntt's *A Visit to the Red Sulphur Spring of Virginia,* read like a travelog and offered a long list of Red Sulphur Springs' medical advantages. Though not a guidebook per se, Huntt's volume initiated the publication of works designed to attract visitors to the Virginia springs. Its successor, Mark Pencil's *The White Sulphur Papers,* explicitly attempted "to meet" what Pencil considered "the general wish so often expressed . . . for some descriptive guide of the localities and attractions" of the springs region. Amid sketches of the social scene, Pencil described the major springs without going into much detail. Apparently the "general wish" he cited was not very specific. Only when William Burke published his *Mineral Springs of Western Virginia* in 1842 was a comprehensive guide to the Virginia springs available.[11]

Burke and John J. Moorman, the resident physician at White Sulphur Springs and a prolific guidebook author, dominated the trade, publishing a combined total of nine editions of their works over the next two decades. But it was not until the late 1840s, when Moorman included information on other springs, that a definitive guide to *all* of the springs emerged. But even though Moorman claimed to "present such an account of the neighbouring *Springs,* as to enable the public to understand something of their general character," he continued to maintain that "the main design of the present volume . . . is to bring the waters of the White Sulphur Springs . . . in a condensed view before the public." Only one of the six other pre-1860 publications about the Virginia springs, Robert Cowan's *Guide to the Virginia Springs,* pretended to be anything but a promotional tract for a particular resort. Cowan echoed Davison and Dwight in declaring his intentions to publish "some Guide to the Virginia Spring, of portable dimensions, and nothing of the sort having yet appeared, we have been induced to compile [one]."[12]

The fact that Cowan could claim that no comprehensive guide to the Virginia springs existed speaks to the fundamental business difference between the two springs regions. Saratoga Springs residents viewed their resort as a cooperative economic entity where the efforts of one publisher or hotel proprietor to boost business improved the prospects of the entire community. But Virginia's springs proprietors operated individual establishments that suffered when a competitor attracted more attention to himself and away from them. Visitors to Saratoga Springs could choose to stay at any of a number of hotels, and the town as a whole benefited from their business. But Virginia's springs were separated into several autonomous establishments spread across a vast distance. If guests chose to stay at one spring over another, or to extend their visits at one establishment to the detriment of a competitor, the business of the slighted spring suffered. Virginia guidebooks emphasized the superior quality of one resort over others in almost every instance, whereas Saratoga Springs' guidebooks played up the entire town, with an occasional nod to a favorite hotel. Virginia's guidebooks focused on gaining an advantage in the competition for business above all else. As one perceptive visitor noted, "If you take the word of the *proprietor,* each spring is *best* & none *good* but *his.*"[13] Enjoying a proximity to major cities and the Northern Tour route, hotels in Saratoga Springs divided their share of wealthy travelers, whereas the Virginia springs fought over a much smaller number of elite visitors.

James Calwell and Gideon Putnam seized upon the springs phenomenon and built their resorts into sizable industries. Neither man possessed a background in promoting mineral springs or managing hotels—but each possessed a keen business mind. They also diverged in their approach to operating their establishments: Calwell sought to consolidate his holdings, whereas Putnam envisioned his hotel as one of many in a thriving resort town. Both men readily embraced the Market Revolution and its potential for both creating and expanding wealth. Calwell and Putnam benefited from the market personally in the form of increased profits and professionally from the growing number of visitors. These tourists had prospered as a result of the Market Revolution and had both the means and the cultural impetus to visit the springs.[14]

Building the springs trade required more than the right cultural and economic conditions, however. Although Calwell and Putnam followed slightly different routes to the springs, they both learned from previous failures and used their creativity to make the springs viable businesses. Calwell began his career by speculating, with limited success, in merchant vessels based in his hometown of Baltimore. His marriage to Polly Bowyer in 1797 brought him into the family that owned White Sulphur Springs. Upon the death of Polly's father, Michael Bowyer, in 1808, Calwell suddenly found himself part owner (along with Polly's six siblings) of a struggling springs resort. Gideon Putnam came from a less affluent farming family in Connecticut and saw few prospects for prosperity there. After marrying Doanda Risley, Putnam left his birthplace in Connecticut to buy cheap land in Middlebury and Rutland, Vermont, where he failed as a farmer. The Putnams then moved to Bemis Heights, New York, the site of the pivotal Battle of Saratoga during the Revolution, but a 1789 flood forced them from the banks of the Hudson River to the inland settlement around High Rock Spring.[15]

Both Calwell and Putnam faced a difficult task in turning the springs into thriving businesses. "Rustic" best describes the early conditions at White Sulphur Springs and Saratoga Springs during the last quarter of the eighteenth century. Long visited by local Indians, the springs attracted European settlers on a seasonal, sporadic basis as early as 1778 in the case of White Sulphur Springs and by 1771 at Saratoga Springs. Visitors pitched tents, found a place to sleep in the "miserable cottage or two" near the springs, or bedded down in their wagons. Elkanah Watson found "excessively bad accommodation" in "a wretched tavern" during his 1790 visit to Saratoga Springs. He counted only a dozen people congregated at the springs that summer. In his opinion, Saratoga Springs was "enveloped in rudeness and seclusion, with no accommodations appropriate to civilized man." He and

"Vue de la Source Minérale Union á Saratoga," 1845. The fence surrounding the spring *(left)* was designed to keep cattle *(right)* from drinking and muddying the waters. Courtesy of the Saratoga Room, Saratoga Springs Public Library.

the other campers climbed over logs and through brambles to reach the High Rock Spring, where a wooden spout jammed into a crevice in the rock spurted water into their glasses. When not frequented by people, the springs were places "where cattle and sheep are fond of licking and geese and pigeons delight to resort." The handful of humans bathed in "an open log hut, with a large trough, similar to those in use for feeding swine, which receives the water from the spring. Into this you roll from a bench." Life at the Virginia springs was not much better. As at Saratoga Springs, a "Bason hollowed out for bathing" served the patients, and mineral deposits covered the wooden trough that conveyed water from the spring. As Thomas Jefferson described it, the springs offered "total want of accommodation for the sick."[16]

James Calwell wasted no time in improving these accommodations, immediately urging that a manager be hired to oversee the springs and that new buildings be added. He continued to operate his Baltimore shipping business but gradually bought up the White Sulphur Springs shares held by his wife's siblings. During the War of 1812, he suffered a series of unrelated business failures, which induced him to become more involved with White

Sulphur Springs. After a fairly successful 1815 season, the summer of 1816 brought more guests and an overcrowded hotel, boosting Calwell's hopes that White Sulphur Springs would "take the head of all the springs say double the number of any other." The end of the War of 1812 increased American economic surpluses and cultural confidence; now the elite possessed both the money to visit the springs and the desire to patronize a distinctly American resort. By 1819 Calwell controlled five-sevenths of the Bowyer estate and provided the guiding force behind the growth of the resort. That same year he constructed a springhouse as the spa's symbolic center and permanently relocated to White Sulphur Springs, resolved that his fortune would come from the mineral waters of western Virginia.[17]

Gideon Putnam began not in the hotel business but in lumbering. In 1789 he leased 300 acres south of High Rock Spring and began felling trees, from which he produced sheaves and shingles that he floated down the Hudson River to New York City. From the profits of their sale, Putnam purchased his 300 clear-cut acres and built a sawmill, eventually amassing enough capital to construct a two-story tavern in 1802 near the recently discovered Congress Spring. By 1805 his tavern profits allowed him to purchase an additional 130 acres and lay out what would become the village of Saratoga Springs. Town lots sold rapidly in 1811 and 1812, and Putnam's venture seemed to be thriving. He excavated three new springs and channeled their flow through wooden tubes during the first decade of the new century. By christening them the Washington, Columbian, and Hamilton Springs, as well as naming the streets Congress, Federal, Saratoga, and Bath, Putnam hoped his Federalist and Anglophilic nomenclature would please Saratoga Springs' elite, conservative visitors from New England and New York. Hoping to drain more business from nearby Ballston Spa, in 1811 he began building Congress Hall on a scale to eclipse Ballston's palatial Sans Souci. Putnam would not see his dreams reach fruition, however; a fall from construction scaffolding broke his ribs, and resultant inflamed lungs killed him over a year later.[18]

Despite their early successes, Calwell and Putnam represented only the first phase of springs entrepreneurship. Their families continued to operate the springs for many years, but they and their successors and counterparts faced even more daunting obstacles than the pioneering generation had conquered. The mineral springs business, because of its seasonal and precarious nature as a tourist economy, remained an unstable and highly competitive industry. Resorts stayed open for the summer months and depended on revenues from a two-to-three-month season to sustain the enterprise over the lean winter months. Seasonal hotels in Saratoga Springs needed cash so desperately that each winter several mortgaged their furniture, kitchen supplies, and general inventories in attempts to stay afloat. In addition, most visitors stayed only a short time at any single establishment, which exacerbated proprietors' need to extract as much cash from their guests as quickly as possible.[19] In this unstable, seasonal business climate, springs proprietors struggled constantly to keep their establishments profitable and to ensure their long-term viability. They moved toward commercializing their establishments as much from desperation as from ideological adherence to the market. Four key areas—improved transportation networks, capital sources, increased revenue, and labor costs—were vital to the survival of springs businesses. Proprietors watched these key areas with an eye toward attracting and tapping the emerging class of wealthy tourists. In every case, the proprietors' efforts and results seemed barely adequate.

The involvement of springs proprietors in transportation improvements came from their immediate need to ease and to facilitate the guests' journeys to the springs. From their earliest pilgrimages, mineral springs visitors in both Virginia and New York State faced rudimentary—even difficult— traveling conditions. "Very few people visit these springs," James Kirke Paulding wrote from Virginia in 1817, "remote and difficult of access as they are." Abigail May suffered five bone-rattling days aboard a stagecoach traveling from her Boston home to the Saratoga Springs region during the summer of 1800. Travelers complained constantly of the poor road conditions, at least one of which was "beyond description for roughness & Steepness—it was nothing but loose stones & rocks without anything having been done to it—indeed the track in Some places was Scarcely discernible." On more than one occasion, stage coaches collapsed, broke a wheel, or snapped an axle. To save the equipment and horses, drivers frequently asked their passengers to walk up steep hills and down descents. In addition to the perils of stages, high costs—turnpike companies charged tourists' carriages several times the rate for wagons—discouraged frivolous travel. Many potential tourists reached the same conclusion as Mary Thompson about traveling to the springs: "I think that I am not going there, to be jolted half to death in a stage coach by the way."[20]

Citizens of western Virginia's springs towns led the effort to build roads and to expand the springs business. As early as 1768 they requested a road to "facilitate [travelers] on the south Side of James's River, in their Attempts to visit our Waters," and continued the effort into the next century. Of the 653 turnpike, road, and plank road companies incorporated by the Virginia General Assembly between 1776 and 1861, some forty-four (6.7 percent) began or terminated their routes in spring towns. Funding came from state aid, stock sales, and local investment, like James Calwell's granting of a roadway easement across his White Sulphur Springs property. The springs region of western Virginia paralleled the broader Southern economy. Sixty springs road companies were incorporated from 1829 to 1861, mostly in the cotton boom years of the early 1830s, the late 1840s to the mid-1850s, and the three years before the outbreak of the Civil War.[21]

Despite these efforts at road building, the Virginia springs remained difficult to reach. Steamboat travel on the Mississippi and Ohio Rivers shortened the distance between the Delta and the springs but still took more than a week. By 1840 the James River and Kanawha Canal wound 146 miles from Richmond to Lynchburg at the base of the Blue Ridge Mountains, but travel on this route proceeded at a rate similar to stagecoach travel—four to six days to the springs. Of the thirty-four canal companies chartered by Virginia, none penetrated the mountainous springs region. Besides geographical and technological limitations, canals in Virginia suffered from lack of capital. Flush times, state economic assistance, a growing springs region, and the desire to link with the South fueled Virginia's 1850s railroad boom as overall Southern track mileage tripled during the decade. But even as the Virginia Central Railroad gradually crossed the Blue Ridge, ran down the Shenandoah Valley, and traversed the Allegheny Mountains, the line stopped twenty miles short of White Sulphur Springs, leaving only a dotted line signifying a railroad "in progress" on guidebook maps. Although railroads never reached the long-established Virginia springs in the years before the Civil War, the expanding network of rails in the eastern portion of the state and along the southern and northern stretches of the Valley of Virginia both improved travel from distant points to the springs and presented new opportunities that springs proprietors quickly manipulated to their advantage. New springs appeared along the railroad lines and attracted a clientele that ventured no farther than a few miles from a railway line. Montgomery White Sulphur Springs stood only one and one-quarter miles from the Virginia and Tennessee Railroad line near Christiansburg, and guests rode "the SPRINGS COMPANY'S CARS" from the main track to the hotel porch. Railroads, turnpikes, and canals eased travel for visitors from distant markets, improved business, and fostered the growth of Southern capitalism.[22]

Although the lack of an efficient transportation network delayed the expansion of the Virginia springs beyond a few elite resorts until the 1850s, the excellent location of Saratoga Springs near the head of navigation on the Hudson River and its proximity to some of America's earliest canals and railroads spurred Saratoga Springs' growth into the nation's largest American mineral water resort. Still, as in Virginia, early travelers complained of the rough roads and jarring stagecoach rides. But complaints quickly vanished as Saratoga Springs integrated itself into the highly efficient transportation network of upstate New York.

With little involvement from springs boosters, the development of steamboats on the Hudson River revolutionized travel to Saratoga Springs. After Robert Fulton demonstrated the commercial feasibility of Hudson River steamboat travel in 1807, travelers steamed up the river and caught a stage for the last thirty-seven miles from Albany to Saratoga Springs. The return of prosperity after the War of 1812 made Fulton's company so successful that others soon challenged his domination of steamboat travel in New York State. After the state removed restrictions on competition in 1825, various companies offered steamboat travel on the Hudson River. By 1838 three firms with a combined total of nine boats plied the New York–Albany route, leaving New York City twice daily and arriving in Albany ten hours later, which was a great improvement over earlier modes of transportation. But the nation's most striking transportation innovation, the Erie Canal, carried few people destined for Saratoga Springs. The locks—nearly one for each of the twenty-eight nautical miles from Albany to Schenectady—actually increased the journey: canal boats took six times longer and traveled thirteen miles more than stagecoaches on the route to Saratoga Springs.[23]

Just as the Hudson River region served as the laboratory for early steamship and canal navigation, so too did the route from Albany to the springs witness some of America's earliest efforts at railroading. Plans for a railroad between Albany and Saratoga Springs soon followed the 1828 launch of the nation's first important commercial railroad, the Baltimore and Ohio. Promoters hoped to connect the springs to the Mohawk and Hudson Railroad, which promoters claimed would reach from Albany to Schenectady and avoid the plodding Erie Canal route. To complete the rail connection to the springs, the Schenectady and Saratoga Railroad carried its first passengers on 12 July 1832 and reached Saratoga Springs in 1833, making it the second railroad in New York State after the Mohawk and Hudson. Public enthusiasm for the railroads and prospects for profits convinced investors to launch a second, rival line, the Rensselaer and Saratoga Railroad, six miles up the river from Albany and at the head of steamship navigation. The benefits of this new transportation mode appeared immediately. A ride that formerly took an entire day now lasted only two hours. The completion of the Hudson River Railroad between Troy and New York City in 1851 only further shortened the trip. A traveler could complete the entire journey from New York—America's largest city, transportation hub, and gateway for Southern tourists—to the springs entirely by rail.[24]

Travelers enjoyed the shorter and easier trip, but springs proprietors reaped greater benefits. During the Schenectady and Saratoga Railroad's first summer of service to Saratoga Springs in 1833, it carried over twenty-one hundred passengers during May and as many as forty-one hundred during one week in August. Only a little over one thousand tourists had visited the springs in the 1820s, before the railroads eased travel. By the 1840 and 1841 seasons, more than thirteen thousand tourists arrived at Saratoga Springs, the vast majority by rail.[25] From the perspective of hotel owners trying to fill their rooms, the railroad was an unmitigated success.

But the concept of rail travel served more than a commercial purpose. Simply riding the railroad became an amusing part of a trip to the springs and a cultural experience that marked one as a sophisticated traveler. Passengers joined springs proprietors in praising the benefits of the commercialization of leisure, expressing "unbounded" astonishment at the rapid rate of travel. A rail trip constituted "one of the greatest sources of novelty and pleasure in a visit to" Saratoga Springs. Riding the train offered more than convenience; it was novel and fashionable. Traveling by rail became a status symbol. To complete the train-riding experience, many tourists went to Saratoga Springs by one direction and returned along the other track, "thus changing the scenery" and increasing their enjoyment.[26]

Saratoga Springs belonged to a broader tourist circuit known as the Northern Tour. The springs' entrepreneurs recognized the benefits of a regional tourist economy and saw transportation improvements as part of a larger project to develop their businesses. When leading Saratoga Springs businessmen such as the publisher Gideon Davison, the landowner and banker Washington Putnam, and the hotel proprietors Thomas and James Marvin sat on the Saratoga and Washington Railroad board of directors and approved the construction of a rail link with Lake George—on the Canadian leg of the Northern Tour—they acted to serve their resort. Although Virginia's promoters attempted to provide transportation links to Tidewater cities, the booming Mississippi Delta, the Ohio River valley, and "the lower country" to the south, the Virginia springs developed as individual destination resorts rather than an integrated, cooperative springs region.[27] Saratoga Springs' promoters envisioned a fast and efficient tourist circuit with multiple stops. The difference lay in practice, not philosophy. Springs promoters in both regions believed in the potential of transportation improvements to strengthen their businesses.

The springs' involvement in developing a transportation network to con- nect them with their guests and the rest of the nation highlighted the dispar- ity in market involvement. Both Northern and Southern mineral springs ac- tively promoted turnpikes and railroads, but Saratoga Springs quickly reaped the rewards of an efficient, convenient transportation system, while the Vir- ginia springs continued to founder in a spiderweb of turnpikes, rail spurs, and canals until the 1850s. In both Virginia and New York State, mineral springs proprietors stood at the forefront of efforts to improve internal trans- portation networks, and their resorts became key points on the newly devel- oping turnpikes, river networks, canals, and railroads of early nineteenth- century America. Because their business relied so heavily on the efficient, speedy movement of people and products from urban areas to rural re- treats, springs promoters adhered to the "culture of progress" that equated transportation improvement and economic growth with social and moral betterment. In terms of transportation improvements, they eagerly joined the Market Revolution. Virginia, unfortunately, did not enjoy Saratoga Springs' advantages in location and ready access to capital.[28]

Perhaps the largest impediment to operating a springs business was raising the capital necessary to establish a hotel, improve the spring itself, construct a bathhouse, hire (or purchase) workers, procure supplies, and advertise the new venture. So springs entrepreneurs looked for innovative ways to raise capital. When lotteries failed to gain enough subscribers, springs propri- etors often borrowed from wealthy guests. James Calwell initially borrowed $20,000 from fellow Baltimore merchants to buy out his remaining relatives and to improve White Sulphur Springs. Having exhausted these funds by 1825, he turned to Col. Richard Singleton of South Carolina, a frequent guest and arbiter of springs society. Basically, Singleton purchased Calwell's mortgage for White Sulphur Springs to rescue the establishment from debt and quickly became its most reliable source of income. When Calwell fell several thousand dollars short of his obligations in 1827, he asked Singleton for money in almost plaintive terms: "I beg you to believe that nothing but the urgency of the call would again make me approach you at this time." The plea worked temporarily, but eventually debts overwhelmed Calwell, and he signed the mortgage to White Sulphur Springs over to Singleton. But Calwell remained optimistic. In 1831 he hopefully told Singleton of a plan to improve the springs "to what it ought to be," if only Singleton would renegotiate the terms of their initial loan and help with some other debts. Relying on familiarity, the only bargaining point he retained, Calwell wrote Singleton: "I cannot express to you the sensibility felt on the rec't of your letter for the kind remembrance of me and I pray you to believe the grateful esteem I shall always feel for so worthy a friend." Singleton's love of White Sulphur Springs, his already deep financial commitment, and the claim of mutual social status secured Calwell well over $30,000 in additional loans from his friend.[29]

But White Sulphur Springs continued to run a deficit, and its proprietors eventually looked elsewhere for financial relief, having exhausted the patience and wallets of their friends. Springs owners attempted to remedy their lack of capital by seeking a corporate charter from the state, citing "the inadequacy of means" as an impediment to "enlarging the benefits + extending the accommodations" of the springs. Investors were attracted by the potential of a good return on their investment and the social status that came from owning part of a fashionable institution like a mineral spring. But joint stock companies also offered several legal protections that provided additional allure: the ability to pass shares on to heirs, limited individual liability, and the rights to pursue delinquent investors and to restrict dividends. Incorporation offered enough financial and legal benefits to trigger a springs boom: forty-nine different Virginia springs companies incorporated between 1834 and 1861, with average proposed capital of over $200,000.

The mere fact that springs businesses seized the right of incorporation, established in 1831–32, speaks to their financial acumen and political pull. Each incorporation required passage by the legislature, many of whose members frequented the springs. But even with these advantages, companies faced restrictions that hindered the effectiveness of incorporation. Before a corporation could gain full legal status, it had to completely raise its proposed capital while limiting a single shareholder to two-fifths of all stock, all in three years' time. Faced with these requirements, several springs tried incorporation two or three times, often with lower capitalization.[30]

Even the popular White Sulphur Springs proposed three different incorporations and stock sales over twenty years but failed each time. The most likely purchasers of the stock, the wealthy Southerners who possessed enough surplus cash to travel to the springs, had already been tapped dry. Familiarity had its financial limits.[31]

Optimistic backers of the Virginia springs continued to believe that they could raise sufficient capital to build sophisticated resorts. But in an era when Southern private capital was invested in slaves and land, springs proprietors found themselves caught in this shortage of liquid capital, a situation that was not restricted to the tourism industry and existed in other sectors of the Southern economy. The South's reliance on slavery and the subsequent concentration of its already scarce supply of capital in chattel and land created disincentives to invest in other forms of property such as railroads or industry. Unproven and unprofitable leisure-based ventures such as mineral springs resorts garnered little of the South's already limited capital supply, even if wealthy Southerners might have invested for personal, social reasons. By keeping labor costs high—in the form of slaves who had to be purchased—and preventing large-scale population influxes or intraregional movement, Southerners stunted local economic development. A staple-crop economy that relied on slavery as its labor source would never create the population growth and economic development seen in the North. Simply put, slavery limited the Southern economy's growth rate.[32]

The story was somewhat different at Saratoga Springs, where the more diversified and commercial Northern economy provided ready access to capital. Saratoga Springs' hotel proprietors avoided the need to sell stock by relying on local investors. By mortgaging hotel furnishings to the town's wealthy patrons and bankers, proprietors raised additional cash to make improvements or to meet everyday expenses, often for amounts as small as a few hundred dollars.[33] The growth of nearby Albany and Troy as centers of commerce, manufacturing, and transportation, especially after the completion of the Erie Canal, increased trade across upstate New York and created excess capital on which springs proprietors could draw. In addition, the merchant capitalists from New York City and Boston who frequented Saratoga Springs possessed investable funds that Southern planters did not. These wealthy Northerners invested in Saratoga Springs not simply as a resort but also as a town. Saratoga Springs' economy relied on more than one enterprise; it was a resort town and a commercial center composed of numerous businesses. Ironically, Saratoga Springs, the more commercial and market oriented of the two springs regions, depended less on the market for its capital needs. Because of the development of Saratoga Springs' local economy, its hotel owners could call on merchants and businessmen for capital, whereas the owners of Virginia's springs resorts were forced to look beyond their local and familiar networks for investors. Saratoga Springs' more extensive commercialization of leisure thus allowed a greater degree of local control over springs business than at the more isolated—both commercially and geographically—Virginia springs.

Both springs regions still faced the difficult task of meeting their bottom lines. Seasonal incomes and narrow profit margins forced springs proprietors to search for innovative sources of revenue. Some older resorts, like Warm Springs and Sweet Springs, Virginia, as well as Ballston Spa, New York, became county seats. The reliable business of county courts and offices maintained the towns when visitors failed to fill the eponymous mineral springs hotels. Early town formation relied on the springs and county court businesses to thrive, but at some point these towns had to choose either to remain dominated by a single industry (the springs) or to diversify into a more general commercial and manufacturing center. Warm Springs chose the former path, whereas Ballston Spa, forced in part by the drying up of its springs in the late 1820s, prospered as the governmental, manufacturing, and mercantile center of Saratoga County.[34]

But the majority of mineral springs could not draw on the business of county government and looked for other sources of revenue. Once again, they sought to commercialize their operation and to enter the market to strengthen the springs business, starting with their main commodity, water. Saratoga Springs began bottling its Congress Spring waters as early as 1810, and by 1811 town father Gideon Putnam issued a set of rules stipulating that "Every person putting up or bottling water, at said Spring for Transportation who shall not render an account + pay for the same 12½ cents a dozen will subject himself to immediate prosecution." By asserting his rights as the owner of Congress Spring to control its sale, Putnam ensured that profits from the waters were to be his alone. Congress Spring water faced competition from other sources; soda fountain entrepreneurs such as Yale College chemist Benjamin Silliman and Dr. John Clarke had operated soda water fountains in New York, Philadelphia, Baltimore, and other major cities for almost a decade. But few customers favored the iron-tinged flavor of artificially recreated mineral water, much to Silliman's financial distress. The chemical composition, flavor, and carbonation of Saratoga Springs' waters somehow worked better at the springs, and the Putnams could not bottle enough water—or keep it from spoiling—to satisfy consumers. Instead, Putnam's sons leased Congress Spring's bottling rights to Clarke and his partner, Thomas Lynch, in 1823. They perfected the bottling of Saratoga water and capitalized on its fashionable appeal.[35] Bottled Saratoga Springs water quickly replaced the artificial variety.

Clarke and Lynch completed the vertical integration of their mineral water business by controlling the production, distribution, and sale of Congress Spring water. They ensured their success by bottling water only between early November and June, when commercial production would not deplete the spring's flow for tourists. The effort to commodify Congress Spring water succeeded to the point that by 1856 one Saratoga Springs booster could claim that "there is scarcely a town in the United States of magnitude that is not supplied with it, nor a vessel destined to any distant port that does not enumerate the *Congress water* in the list of her sea stores or her freight." The firm of Clarke and Lynch continued selling water until the Civil War, employing dozens of workers and making "handsome" profits of as much as $20,000 per year.[36]

Similarly, Virginia's mineral spring owners recognized the commercial potential in selling their water to distant markets. By 1839 both Red Sulphur Springs and White Sulphur Springs announced the availability of bottled water in "any part of the Union." White Sulphur Springs' successful bottled water business (sales constituted 5 percent of the springs' gross income) forced its competitors to either begin their own bottling efforts or find alternative ways of maintaining their businesses. Many smaller resorts also advertised their water for sale by merchants in Virginia's major and regional cities. Newly established resorts like Rockbridge Alum Springs could gross over $9,000 in sales, 75 percent of which was pure profit, "a considerable revenue to the proprietors."[37] Many smaller establishments could not rely on the annual crush of fashionable visitors that frequented White Sulphur Springs and the hotel revenues such crowds created; mineral water sales may have played a vital role in the smaller springs' financial health. These springs alleviated their problem of unsteady revenues by promoting the year-round consumption of their product. When visitors stayed away from the springs, cash still arrived at the hotels. Springs proprietors commercialized their mineral water out of necessity.

These efforts secured the springs' most valuable commodity—their water—for the consumption of tourists, who would long for the refreshing, health-giving liquid both at the springs and upon their return home. Entrepreneurs in both regions extended the springs business from a few months to a year-round enterprise, from a place to a product. White Sulphur Springs regularized distribution and prices by appointing official agents in nine cities "who will keep the water constantly on hand, for the supply of the *public generally,* and *for all* DEALERS *who may wish to purchase the water to seli again."* Reliance on the agents listed in the pamphlet assured buyers of "getting the *genuine White Sulphur Water"* and not any of its many imitators. By establishing its own system of dealers, White Sulphur Springs added exclusivity and perceived luxury to its bottled water. Selling bottled water developed what modern marketers call brand identity, something Saratoga Springs' bottlers did by literally branding all bottle corks with the company logo.[38] If consumers drank White Sulphur Springs or Saratoga Springs water in January, they might prefer to attend that resort and drink that same water, only fresher, in July.

Springs promoters in both regions created an image and distribution system that made it seem as if everyone, or at least anyone who merited mention in exclusive social circles, drank their mineral water. A bottle of White Sulphur Springs water connoted the luxury, ease, and good health that people enjoyed while visiting the springs—an image people readily consumed. Selling in the South's major cities meant that the waters became available to some of the wealthy clients the springs hoped to attract—including planters who owned city homes or frequented urban centers for business or politics. Saratoga Springs' bottlers also guaranteed their product's exclusivity and profitability by restricting the sale of Congress Spring water and by shipping it only in bottles, not in barrels. That way, Saratoga Springs could claim to be the only resort to offer the vaunted Saratoga Springs waters on tap, a boast that competitors for wealthy tourists like Niagara Falls, Long Branch, Nahant, the White Mountains, or the Catskill Mountain House could not equal. In an age of temperance and health reform, the bottlers had discovered an ideal product. Its natural carbonation provided refreshment, and its tonic effects were believed to invigorate the digestive system, both without the debilitative effects of alcohol. Drinking the waters separated refined, sober members of the elite from the drunken riffraff of Jacksonian society. Bottled water became a luxury item in northeastern urban markets and among the Southern gentry, the same clientele that dominated the springs.

Table 1

Cost Items from Virginia Springs Account Ledgers

Item	Mean	Sum	Percentage of Total Revenue	N[a]
Bar	$1.49	$428.68	1.1	287
Bathing	$1.66	$246.40	0.6	148
Horse Care	$7.27	$6,438.13	16.9	885
Laundry	$1.28	$498.55	1.3	388
Room/Board	$19.61	$28,711.60	75.4	1,464
Mail	$0.97	$159.30	0.4	165
Meals	$16.95	$627.20	1.6	37
Misc.	$3.58	$807.46	2.1	225
Total	—	$38,077.64	100.0	3,599

Sources: White Sulphur Springs Day Book, 1827, GBA; Hot Springs Ledger, 1829–31, 1833, Daggs Family Business Records, LoV; Bath Alum Account Book, 1852, SWM.

[a]N = 1,501 cases.

Yet even as springs proprietors cultivated wealthy customers, they looked for more subtle ways to empty those customers' pocketbooks. Account books kept by various springs companies reveal an inventive list of fees and charges levied against hotel guests. Receipts from room and board accounted for three-quarters of total revenues, but hotel managers discovered several other categories of assessment to boost the resorts' income. Bar tabs, postage fees, surchages for using the baths, stable fees for horses, laundry charges, and any other miscellaneous assessments the proprietors could tack on provided the margin between profit and loss. Although few people incurred these additional charges, they amounted to one-fourth of total receipts. With half of all guests staying less than a week and with half of all bills amounting to just over thirteen dollars, proprietors needed these additional sources of revenue. They astutely noticed that over one-third of guests brought horses with them and set fees high enough that income from horse care and stabling ranked second only to room and board charges in gross receipts (see Table 1). Amidst such inflated charges, settling accounts was difficult at best, and many people began "to have long faces at the thought of the arithmetical combination impending over them in the financial department." One guest at Saratoga Springs "foolishly" wondered how Gideon Putnam figured his bill: "He charges only $3 a week for board, and how he got my bill up to $12, I do not know." In the end guests usually agreed to pay, but one account at Hot Springs was closed in 1829 "by cash throne down."[39]

Hotel proprietors paid little heed to guests' complaints and continued to look for ways to maximize profits. Additional charges mounted exponentially, rooms were overcrowded, and the food seemed barely edible. White Sulphur Springs' efficient manager, Maj. Baylis Anderson, was sarcastically praised by one guidebook for "making four hundred people comfortable, in quarters calculated for half that number." He earned the title "Metternich of the Mountains" from disgruntled guests by haughtily refusing to lodge some potential guests, lying about vacancies, and forcing the South's leading families to beg and plead for rooms. In essence, Anderson created demand at the already popular White Sulphur Springs by reducing the supply of rooms. Guests had little recourse against such insults, as "the immense crowd of last season might well have convinced [the staff] of their freedom from all dependence on public opinion."[40]

As if Anderson's attempts to create extra revenue were not enough, the kitchen reduced costs with little regard for public opinion. Guests who complained of sour milk were dismissed with the alibi that the cows had eaten mushrooms. In response to grousing about the atrocious board, the proprietor James Calwell coolly replied: "Why sir, I charge you nothing for your board, but $10 a week for the use of the water, and if you consider this unreasonable, you are at liberty to depart when you please." Some guests saw through the ruse and insisted that the Calwells cheated their guests because they "are so much in debt that they have no credit with the country people to purchase good provisions." Virginia's springs proprietors got away with it only because the South's leading families enjoyed the company of their fellow members of the elite more than they disliked the conditions at the springs. The proprietors had created something desirable.[41]

Even with these additional contributions to hotel balance sheets, proprietors cast about for more revenue. James Calwell hit upon an ingenious method of extracting even more cash from his customers at White Sulphur Springs by selling them exclusive rights to one of the "cottages" on the hotel grounds, the equivalent of modern time-shares. Although owners enjoyed the right to stay in their cottage, they were required to leave the keys with the proprietor, to give ten days' notice before their arrival, and to allow the hotel to lodge other guests there when the owners were not present. But cottage owners still paid the same lodging fees as regular guests. The allure was twofold: first, rather than fighting with the crowds and taking one's chances,

Greenbrier resort daguerrotype, ca. 1845. Note the cabin rows, paths, and visitors at the center of the image. This may be the earliest known photographic depiction of the Virginia Springs. Greenbrier Resort Daguerrotype (no. 11531), used by permission of the Albert H. Small Special Collections Library, University of Virginia Library.

the cottage owners obtained guaranteed lodging at White Sulphur Springs; second, owners enjoyed the status of holding a permanent place at the summer gathering place of the South's leading citizens. After a hesitant start in 1832, by the 1850s time-shares had become so popular and lucrative that the cost of cottage privileges reached as high as $5,000, with plenty of buyers. By selling cottage privileges, Calwell financed the construction of additional lodgings and assured himself a steady income—whether the owners or other guests paid for the privilege of staying in the cottages. At the same time he created a greater sense of exclusivity and desirability at White Sulphur Springs. Planters from Louisiana, Virginia, and Mississippi mingled under the porches' eaves, and prominent families including Virginia's Carters and Capertons, South Carolina's Singletons, and Louisiana's Rouths and Starkes owned cottages at the springs.[42] Purchasing cottages guaranteed membership in this exclusive club and marked one as a member of the Southern elite. In the case of time-shares, the social interests of guests intersected with the business interests of springs proprietors.

The resort's workforces constituted another junction between hotel proprietors' business needs and their guests' social expectations. Because salaries for employees and, at Southern springs, costs for hired slaves composed a significant percentage of hotel expenses, businessmen in New York State and Virginia seized every possible opportunity to keep their labor costs low. Yet their tactics were quite different: Virginians depended upon leased slave labor, whereas New Yorkers hired free blacks and immigrant women. Visitors observed "hordes of Irish servant girls in attendance on the Hotels" at Saratoga Springs, while a nearly equal number of free blacks served the guests as waiters. The French-Canadian and Irish women, as well as a few Yankee farm girls, who worked as maids, laundresses, and kitchen helpers were mostly young and single, whereas the black waiters and coachmen were mostly older and married. These women and men shared a common place at the bottom of the social scale, which prevented them from demanding high wages and saved money for Saratoga Springs' hoteliers. But perhaps more important, these workers occupied the social station expected by Saratoga Springs' wealthy visitors: poor women and African Americans existed to serve, and tourists preferred to avoid unfamiliar and uneasy social class settings while on vacation.[43]

Hotel operators at the Virginia springs also pared labor costs where they could, but with more difficulty than their competitors in Saratoga Springs. Local labor was scarce and insufficient to meet the springs' seasonal and specialized needs, even when they hired skilled laborers from regional towns and major Southern cities. When one hotel attempted to negotiate a lower price for its musicians' services, band organizers insisted on perks such as subscription concerts because the musicians, "who are the best players in Baltimore, cannot afford to come for the pay, without those privileges, they being able to command more to go to other springs." Proprietors soon discovered that these white laborers could demand and receive high wages because of their skill. Needing a band to entertain fashionable guests, springs proprietors acceded to most musicians' demands.[44]

To reduce this cost, Virginia's springs proprietors turned to the backbone of Southern labor, enslaved African Americans. These proprietors soon discovered that limiting labor costs with slaves was much easier than with white workers. Specifically, many springs preferred black slave musicians to white urban bands. But because of the seasonal nature of the springs business and its already high capital requirements, few resorts owned more than a handful of slaves. Instead, the springs encouraged guests to bring their own personal slaves with them by charging slaveowners half price to lodge and feed their "servants." But only 32 percent of guests arrived at the springs with their attendants, forcing proprietors to lease slaves from plantations in the Virginia Piedmont for service work. Contract negotiations for the summer season began as early as December, when one hotel manager remarked, "The most important matter at present is the hiring of hands." He faced a perpetual shortage of labor in the sparsely settled mountains of western Virginia, far from the eastern plantations that teemed with slaves. Even so, most springs managers leased slaves at reasonable terms, maybe even to the slaveowner's advantage. Believing the waters would cure her slave William's eye complaint, Virginian Helen Grinnan offered his services in exchange for lodging. This arrangement benefited springs proprietors by lowering their labor costs and either improved a slave's health or added income to the slaveowner's budget. Even if leasing slaves weakened the concept of a slave as property and transformed the slave into a labor resource, the social hierarchy of Southern society remained unchanged. As at Saratoga Springs, the Virginia springs' visitors found comfort and familiarity in those who served them at the springs.[45]

Although the springs as an industry and tourism in general thrived, the efforts of James Calwell and Gideon Putnam to establish mineral springs resorts ended very differently. White Sulphur Springs remained in the possession of the Calwell family until the 1850s and was always operated as a family-owned proprietorship. But James Calwell continued to sink into debt and to teeter on the verge of bankruptcy; he owed nearly $400,000 when he died in 1851. Roundly condemned as a "reckless proprietor" and "a man of simple, indolent, and inactive character," he and his seven sons were said to be "good for nothing. They all live here and do nothing but ride about and hunt." Most observers believed that the business "might be made a mine of wealth" by a better manager, with profits easily doubled. The Calwells continued to run White Sulphur Springs into the ground and in 1855 finally sold the establishment to a joint stock company that pledged to undertake significant improvements and to increase business. Yet even under new ownership, which the manager considered "very popular," White

Sulphur Springs failed to turn a profit. Despite the efforts of the Calwells and other springs proprietors, Virginia's establishments never achieved the success of their northern rivals at Saratoga Springs.[46]

There, Gideon Putnam's eight children took over the family business after their father's death in 1812 and developed both the town and their own prospects. Whether as hoteliers, landowners, real estate brokers, bankers, insurance executives, or railroad board members, they sold off portions of the estate and developed their inheritance to become one of the wealthiest families in the county. Despite the fact that Gideon Putnam's children and several other influential entrepreneurs deserved much of the credit for Saratoga Springs' successes, commentators looked backward and praised the patriarch for his vision and business acumen. In the opinion of one gushing promoter, "He possessed a will which no ordinary obstacle could long withstand, and by his own exertions the din and hum of civilization soon took the place of the deep and solemn murmur of the primitive pine forest." As firm believers in the culture of progress, Putnam and his fellow springs promoters viewed the bustling town that sprung from the forest as an absolute success. Richard Allen, himself a highly successful physician and springs promoter, declared: "It is to Putnam that the village is indebted, more than to any other individual, for improvements at the Springs. . . . He was, emphatically, the man of his day in the locality; and he made such an impression on the place of his choice, that his name must co-exist with the history of the village which his energy did so much to develop."[47]

Putnam's descendants improved upon and expanded the business they inherited, while Calwell's sons frittered away the wealth of White Sulphur Springs. One family imitated the merchant capitalists visiting its resort, while the other adopted the gentlemanly leisure of its planter guests. But both families and both springs regions in general pursued opportunities to engage in market exchanges and to commercialize their businesses, all in an effort to attract the new class of fashionable tourists. Virginia's other springs resorts followed Calwell's example and operated as family-owned and later corporation-owned enterprises that competed with other establishments in the region. Saratoga Springs' hotels, however, belonged to a single economic entity, the village, that depended upon a long-term view of development and a basic level of cooperation between the various businesses. The carefully designed village, composed of a variety of competing enterprises focused around mineral water tourism, differed from the diffuse scattering of stand-alone Virginia hotels with limited economic diversity.

Basically, there were distinctly Southern and Northern models for the springs business. One followed the plantation model of a centralized, independent entity that produced a commodity—in this case water, scenery, and society—for consumption by consumers. The other adhered to a developmental model that relied on individual entrepreneurship to open the enterprise to others, who in turn cooperated in the resort's advancement. The Southern pattern, with its readiness to adapt innovative business practices like time-shares and especially incorporation, was actually more progressive and market oriented than the Northern model, which continued to rely on individual ownership and locally raised capital to expand its business. Ironically, in spite of the less progressive business practices of Saratoga Springs' community-oriented hotels, that resort fared much better than the highly innovative Southern springs, owing in large part to the scarcity of Southern capital.

Despite the mixed records of these two springs regions and the families that led their expansion, in building the springs Calwell and Putnam helped create a dynamic leisure industry and tourist economy. Where once a few rustic taverns catered to invalids, by 1859 there were "not less than two hundred fashionable resorts, large and small, throughout the Union, whose profits probably amount to ten millions of dollars."[48] Calwell and Putnam's faith in the market and the commercialization of leisure facilitated the mineral springs' success. But the booming new business of tourism relied on more than effective promotion, improved transportation networks, new sources of capital, better business practices, cheap labor, and enthusiasm for the market. Important cultural and social changes enabled the springs and tourism in general to prosper.

Chapter 2

SELLING THE SETTING

*S*prings promoters such as James Calwell and Gideon Putnam relied on more than innovative business practices and shameless promotion to make their businesses prosper. In searching for new ways to advertise their resorts, Southern and Northern mineral springs proprietors capitalized on some of the important cultural trends in nineteenth-century America. Their "development of new and highly interesting natural scenery," wrote one promoter, "greatly augmented the number of tourists" traveling to the springs.[1] By developing and promoting their scenery as an improvement on nature, imitating the architecture of the ideal Southern plantation or Northern village, and invoking Indian legends or historical fables, springs promoters sought to identify their establishments as something other than isolated watering holes. Advertising the springs as sites of cultural sophistication amid rural splendor allowed springs proprietors to increase their business and to contribute to the formation of a national culture.

Calwell and Putnam represent a larger cultural trend in early nineteenth-century America. During this time Americans confronted the contradiction between the sublime power of wilderness and the potentially corrupting influence of civilization. They attempted to "improve" nature by removing the dangerous aspects, smoothing the rough edges, designing landscapes, and in general domesticating it. The traditional dichotomy between the sublime and beautiful that dominated eighteenth-century aesthetics meant little in early nineteenth-century America, where the new ideal of the picturesque— an eclectic melding of art and nature—created a preference for "genteel" landscapes. The emergent "middle landscape" allowed the conflicting ideals of nature and civilization to coexist harmoniously. In the process of defining their landscape aesthetics, Americans developed two regional springs landscapes, one Southern and one Northern. Yet both emerged from the same cultural desire to improve nature by human design. The landscapes, historical legends, and architectural styles of Southern and Northern springs were created to boost business and to aid in cultural nationalization but failed in two respects: the pastoral idyll rarely equaled the ideal established by cultural arbiters, and the recurring conflict between civilization and nature remained unresolved.[2] But people still came to the springs, looking for more than pleasant scenery.

Springs promoters cultivated the public's desire for landscapes by publicizing the natural scenery and romantic setting of their resorts as a calming antidote to society's tensions. If the sanguine accounts of Virginia guidebook authors were true, "beautiful and magnificent" mountain scenery was visible from nearly every Virginia spring. The location of many resorts in narrow valleys between mountain ranges only reinforced the image. In fact, one author described each of the springs pictured in his album of views as located in either a "beautiful," "delightful," or "lovely" valley, sometimes using a combination of all three terms. Proprietors of individual enterprises such as Montgomery White Sulphur Springs seized on the desire for scenery by declaring that their resort was "one of the MOST ROMANTIC AND PICTURESQUE" springs in southwest Virginia. But Montgomery White Sulphur Springs was not the only claimant to the title; almost every spring held pretensions of scenic perfection. "The variety of scenery" in Virginia's springs region attracted the attention "of every traveller of taste," according to one overly enthusiastic guidebook. Writing about the original White Sulphur Springs, another booster declared that "nature has scattered beauties with a

Greenbrier White Sulphur Springs hotel and grounds. The large hotel building
to the right opened in 1858, two years after the artist completed his paintings;
he worked from advance plans of the improvements provided him by the hotel's
architect. From Edward Beyer, *Album of Virginia*. Collection of the author.

most lavish hand around this spot." If nature fell short of perfection, springs
proprietors could call on artists such as Edward Beyer, whose folio-sized
Album of Virginia featured hand-tinted plates of landscapes of sixteen mineral springs hotels and descriptions of each scene. Beyer noted that he "obtained access to the future and proposed improvements" at five springs and
included "in advance the correct style of architecture, plans, locations of
fountains, &c. prepared by the proprietors and their architects."[3] By including this information, Beyer provided free advertising for the proprietors of
the five mineral springs and an idealized depiction of their landscapes.

Promoters did not hesitate to manipulate their public image and played
to tourists' preference for natural scenery at Virginia's springs to increase
business. But the springs also satisfied a desire among many Americans to
escape the unhealthy conditions of their urban homes or lowland plantations. In contrast to the stagnant miasmas of the Tidewater, the springs'
mountain climate earned the sobriquet "salubrious" from medical experts
and springs promoters. Virginia's "pure, bracing, and exhilarating" mountain air offered a respite from the stale atmosphere of cities and coastal
areas. Fresh mountain air could "invigorate the enervated constitution, raise

the drooping spirits, calm the agitated mind, inspire elasticity and strength to the moral and physical powers." The springs appealed to "the visitor weary of the glare and turmoil of cities" with a "landscape beauty" that "no doubt . . . enlivens the spirits and freshens the faculties of enjoyment."[4]

The appeal of fresh air worked beyond the South; one hotel in the decidedly unmountainous Saratoga Springs boasted that it "command[ed] a cool and healthy location and a delightful prospect." The advertisement continued to claim that "those who, while they enjoy the pleasures and restorativeness of our waters, would secure the bracing effects of mountain air, and the quiet of a country residence, will find at this establishment and locality all that they require." An invocation of the pastoral sensibility could not be much more direct. A local poet, Reuben Sears, continued the theme in a poem that reads more like a promotional tract than a literary work. He urged city dwellers to flee the "dust, and smoke, and exhalations foul," as well as "summer's oppressive heat." They should

> Come to these rural seats, where the sweet air
>   Of purest heaven you'll breathe, where unconfin'd
> The cooling breezes play, and from th' effects
>   Of nerve relaxing heat these Springs supply
> A kind restorative, not known elsewhere.

At Saratoga Springs the fashionable life could be set aside for "the simpler elements of rural life." One newspaper commanded, "Go, O empty-headed pleasure-seeker, to Saratoga in a pure and healthful spirit, *seeking the country and not the town,* and you may enjoy it, not for a day, but for all time!"[5]

Saratoga Springs' appeal, then, resembled Virginia's: leave the stifling summer heat and enjoy the bucolic scenery and fresh air. But unlike the Virginia springs' mountain setting, Saratoga Springs rested on the sandy plains at the base of the Adirondack foothills, and mountain scenery lay far off in the distance. Yet the town still promoted its pleasant surroundings. What distinguished Saratoga Springs was not its romantic scenery but its contrast to the urban homes of so many visitors. Although boasting the amenities and architectural style of a well-ordered town, Saratoga Springs still enjoyed a rural setting. Tourists came from New York, Boston, Philadelphia, and nearby Albany, as well as Southern cities and plantations, to enjoy Saratoga Springs' trees, fields, proximity to farmland, and cool air—in short, "a rural appearance not often met with in large towns."[6]

More than simply an advertising ploy to boost business, the springs' pro-motion of fresh air and scenery appealed to wealthy Americans. During the early nineteenth century, an interest in romantic landscapes pervaded the Anglo-Atlantic world. Writers such as James Fenimore Cooper and the New England transcendentalists, as well as European Romantics, praised the beauty and power of America's scenery, while Thomas Cole and other artists developed a school of landscape painting based upon the scenery of New York State's Hudson River valley. Besides offering pleasant views, America's scenery became an integral part of the developing tourism industry, even composing the main attraction at locations such as Niagara Falls, New Hampshire's White Mountains, or the Peaks of Otter in Virginia. Searching for sublime and beautiful views became an obsession for many American tourists and a mark of membership in the elite national culture.[7]

The desire of many upper-class Americans, whether Northern or South-ern, for natural scenery spoke to a cultural need. Americans viewed nature as a refuge from civilization's ills and as the repository of society's positive values. Simply contemplating nature, wrote the painter Thomas Cole, pro-vided "a source of delight and improvement." Nature served "as an antidote to the sordid tendencies of modern civilization." Looking at and thinking about landscapes separated wealthy Americans from their baser, more util-itarian countrymen. American travel narratives, which constituted one of the nation's first attempts to interpret its landscape, described scenery as a montage of American culture. Promotional materials that spoke of "views of the picturesque, the beautiful, and the grand, sufficient for every taste" invoked the vocabulary of scenery that elite Americans understood.[8]

In addition to viewing landscapes, sketching and painting made enjoy-ing scenery a participatory activity. On an 1816 side trip from Saratoga Springs to nearby Glens Falls, James Skelton Gilliam reported that a caravan of ladies "were all quite anxious to see the sketch I was making, + got out of their carriages to see that + the romantic scenery around." Yet his was not the first encounter with amateur artists at the springs. A few years earlier Abigail May and her friend Mr. French "took a walk. He led the way to the Bridge and when there produced paper and pencil—urging my taking a view so beautiful—it was vain to refuse." By sketching the scenery, Gilliam and May were participating in the aesthetic of romantic landscapes and demonstrating their own cultural sophistication. Springs promoters recog-nized the popularity of viewing and interpreting scenery and incorporated landscape images into promotional materials. Dozens of springs visitors imitated these depictions by attempting sketches, watercolors, or elaborate paintings of the surrounding landscape, some of which made their way into print. The artistic renderings that appeared in guidebooks and newspaper accounts complemented personal sketches and paintings. In the middle of the emergence of American landscape painting led by the Hudson River school, amateur artists, guidebook authors, and professional artists advanced the popularity of landscapes and the springs. In the process, scenery became a commodity produced and consumed by tourists, as were other parts of the springs experience.[9]

Promoters looked to more than scenery to attract visitors to their resorts. By coupling scenery with local springs lore, springs proprietors created a sense of nostalgia and cultural legitimacy at their resorts. Historical associations proved especially appropriate at Saratoga Springs, where the scenery left many visitors unimpressed. Although Saratoga Springs' landscapes proved to be mundane, the very name *Saratoga* evoked memories of patriotic glory, especially of the Revolutionary War victory over the troops of the British general John Burgoyne at nearby Bemis Heights. Early guidebooks emphasized the "turning point of the Revolution," devoting almost as many pages to battle recapitulations as to the waters' medical efficacy. Even British tourists felt compelled to visit the battlefield, although their reactions lacked the exuberance of most Americans' joyful epistles. In addition, other forts and battlefields of the Revolutionary War and Seven Years War were only an overnight excursion away at Lake George and Ticonderoga. These sites witnessed some of the crucial struggles for American independence, and pilgrims to the shrines expressed their affinity for these icons of American culture. By visiting Revolutionary War battlefields, Americans announced their cultural independence.

But Saratoga Springs' most mentioned and most culturally useful historical moment was its discovery. Local tradition held that Sir William Johnson, the mid-eighteenth-century British liaison to northeastern Indians, was the first white man to visit the springs. He suffered from a seemingly incurable leg wound sustained during the 1755 battle against the French at Lake George. Johnson's Indian allies reportedly carried him to Saratoga Springs' High Rock Spring in August 1767. After taking the waters for several days, Johnson recovered enough to walk over thirty miles to his estate at Johnson Hall and never felt pain in the leg again. The romantic story provided a compelling tale about Saratoga Springs' early history. Johnson's stature and his miraculous cure spread the fame of Saratoga Springs, helping it develop into a major resort. The only problem with the story was the fact that John-son did not visit Saratoga Springs until 1771 and probably received his cure at one of Saratoga Springs' early competitors, Lebanon Springs, which lay well to the east on the Massachusetts border. But the tale served its purpose in the early nineteenth century and helped Saratoga Springs grow. The util-ity of the Johnson legend, as well as other Indian tales, lay not in the verac-ity of the visit but in the romantic image of Indians drinking at a spring later discovered by a British-American hero. During the early nineteenth century, as Americans struggled to create a national culture distinct from that of their colonial parent, Great Britain, memories of the Revolutionary era and the idealized image of the noble savage became increasingly important and prevalent cultural symbols. Both were distinctly American.[10]

Similar tales existed at the Virginia springs, where proprietors also called upon Indian legends to stir visitors' imaginations. Warm Springs lore told of an Indian warrior traveling from beyond the Allegheny Mountains to the council fires of the eastern tribes. Weary and dispirited from his hard jour-ney, the "Young American Leopard" took refuge in the base of a valley and stumbled upon the "Spring of Strength." He plunged in and "a new life in-vigorated his wearied spirit, new strength seemed given to his almost rigid nerves." The next morning he awoke refreshed and continued his journey to the council fires, where he proved "more graceful in address, more com-manding in manner, more pleasing in look, and more sagacious in policy" than any other present.[11]

"Young American Leopard" represented the "noble savage," who had ex-isted in the wilderness around the springs before the arrival of European-American civilization. This image helped Americans define themselves in opposition to the "uncivilized" tribes they had recently expelled from the re-gion. During the Jacksonian era, when few Indians remained east of the Mississippi River, Americans created a nostalgic image of Indians that em-phasized aristocratic qualities. This Indian stood completely divorced from contemporary Native Americans, as well as the economic and social ten-sions of modern society. The "noble savage" allowed Americans to imagine themselves as part of a more virtuous time.[12] In this tradition, proprietors of springs resorts invented, adopted, and promoted their own histories in hopes of attracting travelers who shared these ideals of a romanticized past.

Springs promoters looked beyond Indians for historical legends. Another, less romantic, Saratoga Springs tale told the story of Crazy Jake, a métis who inhabited the Indian camp at the High Rock Spring in 1787. Inexplicably de-

Native Americans carrying Sir William Johnson to High Rock Spring, Saratoga Springs. From Henry McGuier, *A Concise History of High Rock Spring*. Courtesy of the Saratoga Room, Saratoga Springs Public Library.

mented, he kidnapped a young woman and terrorized seasonal visitors. Only with the aid of friendly local Indians were the story's heroes, guests of local patroon Philip Schuyler, able to rescue the young woman and eventually dispose of Crazy Jake. As in most sentimental fiction of the time, the female and male protagonists married in the end. Although not a literary masterpiece, the story called forth images of past glories at the springs and reminded visitors of the wilderness that once had existed where now "the same spot is a rich and cultivated lawn." Americans did not need to wander "too far into the regions of romance" to remember that "on the very spot where beauty, taste, and fashion now strike the keys on the piano, or mingle in cotillions, the tawny children of the forest once raised the song, or joined in the festive dance."[13]

Virginia's White Sulphur Springs promoted its own romantic legend, which told of the "monster wolf," Banco, who guarded the spring and devoured the fairy-like sylphs who tried to drink its waters. Banco slept only once a year, and during one of his naps a particularly beautiful sylph crept near the spring. She seized Banco's magic wand and opened the spring, sending a tide of water cascading on the sleeping wolf, who temporarily escaped the flood by climbing a nearby mountain. But the waves, ridden by the specters of Banco's sylph victims, eventually engulfed him. The memory treasured by most antebellum visitors was not of Banco but of the

> . . . *fair Sylph who perill'd all;*
>   *Who gave a life made up of bliss*
> *To freshen ours with joy like this.*[14]

The tale appealed to those who sought an idealized golden age at the springs, an era of virtuous maidens, brave warriors, and personal sacrifice.

These legends contributed to the developing American culture that looked to native histories and local scenery for meaning. At the springs, Americans heeded Thomas Cole's insistence that America should not feel inferior to Europe because it lacked ancient ruins but instead should recognize the unspoiled beauty of its natural scenery. One early guidebook author extended Cole's nationalism by criticizing Europe's "marks of ancient ignorance" and "remnants of former barbarism blended with tyranny." Instead of viewing such scenes, the author opined, Americans should recognize that "our own country presents a fairer and nobler scene." Most visitors, another guidebook suggested, would rather relax in the rural splendor of America's resorts while imagining scenes from romantic authors such as Sir Walter Scott and Frank Tyrrel than tangle with the crowds in coastal cities or handle the supervisory duties of a large plantation, much less wrestle with their own cultural inferiority complex while in Europe. In essence, the springs offered an antithesis to the world of early nineteenth-century life; their cultivated landscapes provided a stage on which Americans invoked narratives of their imagined past and idealized future. Visitors preferred these imagined, ideal societies to the tawdry, mundane reality of their everyday existence. Springs promoters encouraged their visitors' imaginations, and Northerners and Southerners made equally nostalgic efforts to evoke a golden age. By doing so, they could identify themselves as part of a cosmopolitan, national elite.[15]

Springs proprietors recognized this trend toward longing for pleasant landscapes and a romanticized past. They made every effort to create, in the spatial organization of springs resorts, a physical expression of the ideal society. In the process, two distinct regional architectural styles developed: Virginia's springs followed a model of a rural, carefully organized plantation, whereas Saratoga Springs resembled a quaint but developed village. Virginia's mineral springs resorts operated as single entities spread across

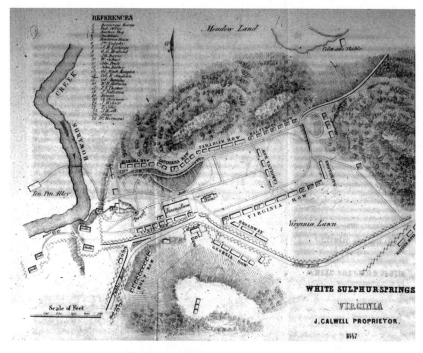

White Sulphur Springs layout, 1847. Cabin row names designed to appeal to Southern visitors include *(clockwise from center-left)* Alabama, Louisiana, Paradise, Baltimore, Carolina, Virginia, and Georgia. The "great house" is at the left (labeled "Dining Room"). From John J. Moorman, *The Virginia Springs.* Courtesy of Swem Library, the College of William and Mary.

the state's western reaches yet followed a common architectural style. Whether nestled on the floor of a narrow mountain valley, pressed so close against the mountain walls as "to afford only room enough for the erection of the buildings," or on a broad alluvial plain near a mountain stream, the Virginia springs imitated the layout and appearance of a Southern plantation. They featured long rows of connected, single-story cabins with covered porches centered around a multistoried, colonnaded structure fronted by a grand porch in the "Gothic style." The cabin system, the distinctive feature of the Virginia springs, lent the springs their rural character and quaint charm; the springs were inventing their own regional architectural style. By naming the rows after various Southern states and cities and omitting Northern names, the springs' proprietors enhanced their regional distinctiveness. But what truly identified the cabins as Virginian, according to promoters, was the way they "harmoniz[ed] in general appearance" with the other buildings. Although the individual rows appeared "beautiful and imposing," the grounds as a whole displayed what one viewer termed "a good deal of taste."[16]

Buildings were arranged in what reviewers called "a hollow square," a sweeping arc, or "as near a parallelogram as the nature of the ground will permit." Inside this semisquare sat the principal buildings of the springs, including the main hotel, dining room, ballroom, kitchen, various "rows" of small cottages for housing guests, and the mineral spring itself. By one contemporary estimate, the land enclosed within the square at White Sulphur Springs approximated the area around a typical Virginia courthouse, roughly two hundred square yards.[17] The comparison reveals the extent to which Virginians sought to duplicate the spatial and social organization of their cultural institutions, as well as the similarity evoked by the springs' appearance.

Proprietors used "convenient and judiciously planned" walkways that crisscrossed each resort's lawn to create a lovely setting for socializing. The lawn, "enameled with a rich coat of verdure," appeared to be "rolled out like a carpet." Undulating across the landscape and "overshadowed by numerous majestic sugar maples" and oaks, the lawn gave "the whole place a grove-like appearance." The organization of the lawn and buildings made, in the opinion of one guidebook, "the premises picturesque . . . and beautiful." The vast majority of guests agreed with this estimation, calling the springs "some fairy scene or some delightful dream" or "a monument to a Sylvan." This was a pastoral scene, but a carefully composed one of neatly arranged and designed buildings. Even the manicured lawn and well-distributed trees belied the planned natural setting. It was a "grove" in the sense of a cultivated orchard of trees, not a wild, untouched forest. Creating scenery was part of a larger cultural project to "civilize" America by applying the standards of refinement to the landscape.[18]

The resulting "middle landscape" at the Virginia springs looked "like quite a city" to one visitor. Another compared the scene with a deserted village, complete with well-organized buildings and pathways. Ironically, these conflicting images did not contradict the rural ideal of antebellum Virginia. Because the impulse to improve nature originated in coastal, urban areas where people rarely faced unaltered nature, many of the springs' wealthy Southern visitors found the cultivated settings perfectly acceptable and in accordance with their construction of nature. They wanted not wilderness but a managed landscape. The "city" was not an overcrowded, hectic, and disordered metropolis but a carefully planned and neatly organized collection of buildings and parks, much like the organized upper-class neighborhoods of contemporary American cities. No ramshackle assemblage of crowded streets and bustling commerce, the springs celebrated order and graceful composition. The rows of single-story cottages, manicured lawns, and grand central buildings followed a style of elegant simplicity. The park-like setting, with scattered buildings centered around a large white "big house," reminded visitors of their homes on large plantations. The spatial arrangement of the various springs illustrated the cultural ideal of antebellum Virginia—the graceful simplicity of nature, or at least nature improved by the creature comforts that springs hotels provided—as reflected in the perfectly ordered plantation. Presumably, springs proprietors figured more Southerners than Northerners would visit the springs to view the perfection of Southern society.[19]

This effort continued in the postwar period. Southern travel writers and promoters realized that their resorts still possessed romantic associations with a vanished past—that of rural plantations—and used these associations as a key selling point. Traveling south aboard a train, "the Lover of Nature will be roused to ecstasy" upon crossing the Blue Ridge Mountains. "At times the train seems to cling precariously to the mountain side," one writer noted, "and you look down upon the beautiful and fertile valley of Virginia, with its snug farm-houses, meandering streams, clumps of trees, and broad fields of grain and tobacco." Once travelers reached the springs, they stood "face to face with nature, and nature in her aspect of greatest picturesqueness, her most wooing attraction." This scenery was the kind "with which art has had little or nothing to do." Instead, the Virginia springs represented the ideal form of nature—one with pleasing scenes but no threats of danger. At these resorts, "any attempts at mere art decoration would seem lost folly, if not desecration." Rather than cultivating an image of the plantation idyll, Virginia's promoters pared the image down to its barest essentials and advanced a landscape that North and South could agree on: the quiet, pleasant, rural retreat.[20]

A distinctly different regional architecture and natural aesthetic prevailed at the North's main resort, Saratoga Springs. When Gideon Putnam designed his town in the early 1800s, he focused it around a central 120-foot-wide artery. Individual hotels fronted by columned piazzas displayed a more urban architectural style in the Greek revival and Gothic traditions. The most remarkable, as well as functional, portions of the large hotels were the grand porches that faced the town's main thoroughfare, Broadway. Many hotels placed their steps to the side of the building, rather than the front, lest the sense of size and grandeur be lessened. No matter that the "high flight of stairs" at the United States Hotel "render[ed] it very inconvenient" to some travelers, the sine qua non was an imposing facade. This pattern of hotels constructed almost atop the street itself, with little room between the structure and the road, focused visitors' attention on the hotels and the image they presented to the public. The architecture was intended to produce awe, and for the most part it did. Visitors commented that Saratoga Springs' hotels, "exhibiting a very handsome and imposing appearance, give an air of importance, of gracefulness, and animation." Saratoga Springs' architecture sought to impress its wealthy urban visitors with its grandeur and sophistication rather than to please them with order and simplicity like the Virginia springs. When local boosters declared the United States Hotel "probably the largest and one of the most expensive of the kind in the United States," they viewed size as a positive attribute. They were trying to achieve the "improving aspect" Elkanah Watson had mentioned years before. Improvement meant bettering nature and shaping an ideal scenery of impressive buildings and cultivated gardens. Entrepreneurs were stripping nature of its dangerous elements and creating a safe, domesticated landscape reserved for those who could afford to pay to see it. They hoped to attract more visitors, especially those from the wealthy and fashionable class, by creating a better, more perfect version of Northern society.[21]

But for all of Saratoga Springs' impressive architecture, the town lacked the natural scenery that Americans demanded at their resorts. One early visitor termed the surroundings "peculiarly wild and rude," concluding that "Nature indeed has not done much to beautify this spot—in truth tis dreary—and nothing to recommend it." This comment, made by an American in 1800, that nature was insufficient reveals the early presence of cultural assumptions on the proper appearance of landscape and a willingness to improve nature to achieve that goal. Yet despite Americans' scorn for Saratoga Springs' landscape, some of the harshest evaluations came from English visitors—the people whose scenery aesthetics Americans were attempting to imitate. These commentators, accustomed to a higher standard of refined landscape in their own country, found it odd that Americans flocked to a place that presented "such a neglected appearance." They claimed to have "seen no resort in the country so poor in natural beauties."

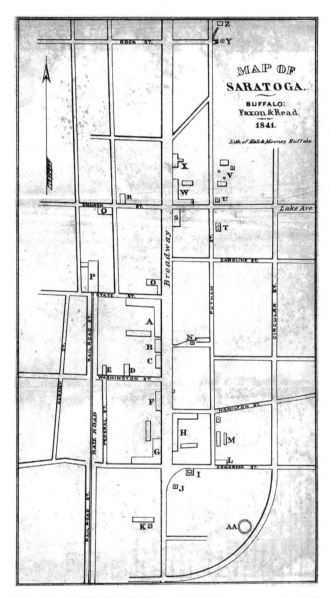

Saratoga Springs street layout. Broadway runs north-south in this depiction, with Congress Park at the southern end of the street (the block containing *I*, *J*, and *AA*, the circular railroad). Major hotels include the United States *(A)*, Union Hall *(G)*, and Congress Hall *(H)*. From Samuel DeVeaux, *The Travelers' Own Book.* Courtesy of the Saratoga Room, Saratoga Springs Public Library.

Americans criticized Saratoga Springs' appearance as well, calling it, even in the 1840s, an "immense wilderness of hotels—like stray cabbages in a potato patch, situated in the midst of an indeterminate sandy plain."[22]

Had the critics looked a little closer, they would have discovered that Saratoga Springs' recent development and deliberate efforts to cultivate a pleasant image contributed to its problems. "Redeemed from the forest" by Gideon Putnam's lumber business in the late 1790s, the town's main road in 1836 was still "just a clearance from the woods, with its centre cut up by the carriages, and filled with the native dust and sand, and the margins are overrun with grass." Ironically, the profits from destroying wilderness gave Putnam and his successors the means to construct a pastoral retreat. But improvements took years to perfect; the most obvious result of Putnam's clear-cutting was that Saratoga Springs seemed "destitute" of ornamental trees. Without their shade, visitors strolling the streets felt "naked . . . and exposed to the full blaze of the sun." To make matters worse, the streets lacked even rudimentary improvements like curbs and sidewalks, making it "impossible to step abroad without plunging ankle deep in sand, and without being enveloped in a cloud of dust, raised by the wind and the constant passage of carriages."[23]

This 1820 critique appeared in a local paper under the name "A Virginian," which must have upset the town fathers. They had hoped to create a pleasant destination that appealed to the cultural sensibilities of elite Americans from North and South. But the "Virginian" exposed their pretensions and threatened the patronage of Southern planters, a key Saratoga Springs constituency. So the Village of Saratoga Springs Board of Trustees attempted to remedy the problem. In the ensuing years the board passed resolutions granting highway tax reductions for property owners who built curbs along the sidewalks in front of their establishments, fined those who failed to keep the area in front of their property swept clean, and issued further highway tax rebates for planting trees along sidewalks. The board even reserved the right to approve all signs placed along Broadway. Saratoga Springs' projected image of a cultivated, refined village arose not by accident but by active governmental involvement. Creating and promoting the town's landscape was not an individual effort, as in Virginia, but a group endeavor. As a result of these improvements, visitors began noting that "the sterile and shining sand so universal in this region is becoming covered, year after year, with a loftier and denser foliage from the multitudes of ornamental and shade trees every where planted." People ceased complaining about the barren landscape and praised Broadway for being "beautifully flanked with trees for miles." One of the most striking aspects of these scenic improvements was their planned nature. The often-admired Congress Park, "delightfully varied in surface, luxuriously wooded," succeeded only because its creators had mastered "'landscape gardening'... and always kept [it] in the most dainty order." They obtained the right to construct fountains, to keep paths to the springs open, to maintain the cleanliness and purity of the water, and to regulate the bottling of spring water in the original Village Act of Incorporation. Saratoga Springs' promoters had to construct, quite literally, the scenic requirements of elite culture.[24]

Interestingly, neither the Virginia springs nor Saratoga Springs directly imitated the Georgian architecture that developed at English spas during the mid-eighteenth century. American resorts lacked the sweeping crescents, multistory apartment buildings, or central market squares of English cities such as Bath. This difference derived in part from the various origins of spa towns: English spas developed in already settled country towns, whereas American resorts sprung from the wilderness. Virginians may have expressed an affinity for English gardening forms, but they never imitated English spa architecture. Americans followed their own architectural styles that attempted to recall the virtue of antiquity in elaborate columned buildings. This preference for Greek revival styles reflected the ideology of republicanism and its emphasis on creating a virtuous nation independent of Europe's excesses of social luxury. In this context, American springs architecture contributed to the larger project of creating a unique national culture. The springs' regional styles emerged from the same desire to boost business by creating a distinctive American landscape but diverged in the vision of how that landscape should appear. Americans differed in their enthusiasm for the intrusion of civilization into nature. Many Northerners saw technology and material improvements as a positive good that could actually improve nature and embraced advancements such as Saratoga Springs' grand hotels and cultivated landscapes. Americans from other regions, especially the South, were more ambivalent about technological progress and preferred the more bucolic image of the Virginia springs. The romantic indolence of the plantation ideal allowed Southerners, and the Northerners who visited Southern springs, to imagine themselves as outside the social tensions and acquisitiveness of American society. This identification of the springs with values that contradicted the prevailing norms of American culture allowed resorts across the country to claim to be refuges from everyday life. Southern and Northern springs appealed to the pastoral ideal of the plantation idyll that authors in both regions popularized as a means to improve the springs' business. They viewed scenery and architecture — the pastoral zone where aestheticians envisioned the perfect balance between art and nature, the picturesque and beautiful — as advertisements of and appeals to the cultural ideals of their wealthy clientele.[25]

But as was often the case, these efforts failed to meet the approval of the same elite Americans they were designed to impress. Whatever the exterior appearance of Saratoga Springs' hotels or Virginia's cabins, guests readily volunteered their opinions of the accommodations. Some visitors to the Virginia springs thought quite well of the cottages, calling them "a palace" and "very commodious." Decorated with wild flowers and spruce boughs, the apartments had "an air of neatness + charming comfort." But the cabins and lodgings at the springs possessed a dubious reputation. One visitor seemed surprised to remark that "*Every* account I had read were all unfavorable. But we were most agreeably undeceived."[26]

Most guests, however, were not so charitable, especially regarding the condition of the lodgings themselves. The cabins generally were only one story and were often raised above the ground by supports or by being placed on the side of a hill. They contained several rooms, divided between bedrooms and sitting rooms, each so tiny that one visitor referred to his cabin as a "Small *Box*." Front and rear doors and windows enlarged the space, but the sparse furnishings of "three wooden chairs, a common board table, a small looking glass of 12 to 14 inches, no carpet on the floor, and a bed or mattress of husks, nearly as hard as the floor" did little to improve the comfort level.[27] The similarity to slave cabins was striking and the willingness of leading Southerners to lodge there even more surprising. No Southern accounts compared the cabins with slave quarters, preferring to find other sources of complaint. But the social inversion must have tickled the back of their brains.

Besides the accommodations' social irony, guests also endured long waits for inferior rooms. When Levin Smith Joynes could not find lodging at the White Sulphur Springs hotel, he took refuge in an inferior hotel nearby, where the Virginian "passed such a night as I have not experienced in many a year. There were five of us in one room, and I was a perfect stranger to all the rest. The room was dirty, and in all respects uncomfortable." Joynes's situation did not improve once inside White Sulphur Springs: "the pleasure of my visit was somewhat seriously impaired by my uncomfortable lodging. I

Cabin interior, Botetourt Springs, Virginia. Watercolor by John H. B. Latrobe, 1832. These are the kind of accommodations that Latrobe disparaged in his journal. Collection of the author.

was in a very old cabin, which had a very extensive *airhole* between the *logs,* right over my bed; and as the night of my arrival was *very cold,* and I had but a single blanket, I hardly slept at all, and took cold." Other less lucky families secured spaces on the parlor floor.[28] Members of the Southern elite like Joynes—a leading Virginia physician and a member of a prominent family whose father had fought in the Revolution and served in politics—found these conditions quite jarring and in stark contrast to their relatively luxurious home lives. But their criticisms seem tepid compared with those of European travelers.

During his 1843 visit to White Sulphur Springs, the British geologist and former New York estate owner George Featherstonhaugh registered similar complaints about his cabin's narrow, oblong room that proved "very inconvenient." Built against the side of a hill, the cabin had two doors: "The western one opened upon the hill, and you could step out upon it immediately; but the eastern and principal entrance was by a steep flight of broken and dangerous wooden steps." Even the furniture failed to please Featherstonhaugh, "there being only two low bedsteads coarsely put together with rough planks." His bed, a "narrow wooden frame . . . was so broken-backed that it tilted up in the middle. Finding it utterly impossible to sleep there, I had to get up again after I had laid down, and make a tolerably even surface by filling up the inequalities with articles from my own wardrobe. The mattress was full of knots, and what was in the thing that was intended to be my pillow I never ascertained." An equally disgruntled neighbor informed Featherstonhaugh that his pillow was also lumpy and composed of "a handful or two of dirty live feathers" and the heads of two chickens and a duck.[29] For a highly respected European scientist in the employ of the United States government to survey the South's geology, these accommodations simply would not do. Whatever the qualities of the natural scenery and mineral resources, Americans could not satisfy this gentleman's European standards of comfort.

But even these complaints paled next to the rants of one American, the Baltimore lawyer and railroad promoter John H. B. Latrobe, who found the cabin system at the Warm Springs most unsatisfying, with the "fleas numerous at all times." When he later arrived at White Sulphur Springs, Latrobe bunked down in a friend's cabin, but only "by dint of bribing the waiter and chambermaid." These servants provided Latrobe with "two benches, and a miserable pallet—a pillow and a blanket: sheets and a pillow case were out of the question. With these I was forced to be content for the first night, with the assurance that I was better off than any single man had been for three weeks. First, because I had got in, at all, and next, because I had secured such an admirable accommodation, the first night, for sleeping." A founder of the Baltimore and Ohio Railroad and a leader of Baltimore society, Latrobe objected to his accommodations, being accustomed to more comfortable surroundings. He probably would have agreed with a line uttered by a fellow Baltimore lawyer, Francis Scott Key: "If you want to fare well, say farewell to the Springs."[30] Yet Key, Latrobe, and thousands of others did not do so.

Eventually Latrobe's protestations and connections finagled him "a cabin in 'flea row' so called here." The room measured only fourteen by seven feet and featured a floor that, "as you walk over it, sinks under your tread, and certain planks of which, you are warned not to tread on, lest you go through." Terming the room a "nut shell," he continued to complain about his cot. "The foot is about 14 inches lower than the head, the iron pin of the lower legs having been lost; and the canvas sackens bottom has become unnailed in the middle, on one side, forming a valley into which at night, I have to cram all my spare clothes, so that my body may be on a level." A warped, rickety table and two simple chairs supplied the only furnishings. To Latrobe's surprise, "this establishment is the envy of some dozens of visitors, who are not half so well off." Francis Scott Key shared Latrobe's dissatisfaction with the fleas when he wrote

> There's an insect or two, called a flea here that stings
> The skins of the people that come to the Springs.

Flea Row shared a dubious reputation with other cabins. Guests who were "young and foolish . . . [and] those fond of noise and nonsense, frolic and fun, wine and wassail, sleepless nights, and days of headache" flocked to Wolf Row. Another less than luxurious group of cottages, Probation Row, housed families waiting for better accommodations. The least favorite of nearly every guest was Compulsion Row, thus named by a family placed in an unfinished, roofless cabin when there was no other room at the springs.[31] These names lacked the boosterism and regional pride of Alabama Row or South Carolina Row and were certainly not the choice of the hotel's proprietors; the ironic nicknames registered people's dissatisfaction with the unrealized ideal of the springs' pastoral design.

Wealthy Southerners shared these complaints, terming "the buildings generally . . . mean, and built without taste and judgment," and "exactly on a par, as it regards style and appearance, with those of any common country tavern." The rustic accommodations provoked the Virginian W. J. Nivison to wonder how anyone could spend more than a few days "amidst barrenness and desolation." Whether they were elite Southerners such as Nivison or Joynes, urban sophisticates such as Latrobe or Key, or foreign dignitaries and gentleman-farmers such as Featherstonhaugh, most visitors considered conditions at the Virginia springs unacceptable. They preferred more comfortable accommodations and failed to see the charm in the rustic setting. When Featherstonhaugh declared that White Sulphur Springs "has very much the air of a permanent Methodist camp-meeting," he expressed elite Europeans' and Americans' dissatisfaction with the springs' attainments. Just as Methodists seemed crude and unsophisticated to the more formal Episcopalians and Presbyterians who frequented the springs, so too were the accommodations and attempts at architectural design below their standards. The cultural ideals of a cosmopolitan—and partly urban— plantation elite clashed with the limited possibilities for refinement at the springs. These complaints continued well into the 1870s and 1880s, even when the food became "passably good" and "ordinary comforts and conveniences" arrived after "the late civil war."[32]

Wealthy guests deemed conditions at Saratoga Springs hotels only slightly better than those in Virginia's cabins; the hotels' imposing facades hid less than grand interiors. Called "uncomfortable raw sorts of places" and "confined, ill-furnished, and inconvenient" by one Englishman, guests' private bedrooms offered few amenities. Standard rooms measured only three feet wider than Virginia's cabins, lacked wallpaper or carpeting, and contained window glass so thin that it was "apt to break with the slightest jar." Even the grander suites, at eighteen by twelve feet, were cramped for the families that the proprietors hoped to attract. The rooms seemed minuscule even in comparison to the model middle-class drawing rooms recommended by the antebellum domestic reformers and abolitionists Catharine and Harriet Beecher, and the furnishings were quite modest. They included a wooden bedstead, one or two chairs, a dresser with a small mirror, a washstand with bowl and pitcher, a small table, and a closet of wooden shelves surrounded by a calico curtain. Rooms in the smaller, less prestigious hotels often contained only a bedstead, mattress, and washbasin, all of which resembled "those articles as seen in penitentiaries," according to one wit. The bedrooms were, in the opinion of the British commentator James Silk Buckingham, "exceedingly small, those of Congress Hall especially, scantily provided, and altogether inferior to what the scale and style of the house, in other respects, would warrant the visitor to expect." Even prestigious guests such as New York governor William Seward lacked the space to write a letter in his room; he was forced to impose on a friend for space to perform this rudimentary task. Most visitors preferred to visit their rooms only at night to such an extent that the hotel corridors became "a passage where the tread of human feet is never intermitted, from sunrise to sunset." To amuse guests, hotel proprietors built gracious piazzas and grand ballrooms below the lodging rooms, which forced guests to spend much of their time in public spaces. But even the coerced congeniality of common rooms failed to satisfy. As one British observer complained, "With all this show, there was still some want of keeping, and many symptoms of haste, in every thing, indicated chiefly by the absence of innumerable minor luxuries." Despite the hotel proprietors' best attempts at creating a comfortable atmosphere, the public spaces seemed "sacrificed to appearance." Elite New Yorkers and foreign visitors agreed that the hotels were "crowded beyond comfort, law, convenience, or conscience."[33] These Northerners and urbanites, as did their Southern counterparts, expected fashionable watering places to meet their cultural standards.

But Saratoga's businessmen found it easier to skimp on construction costs than to satisfy their guests' sophisticated tastes. So they diverted their guests' interest away from the rustic lodgings to attractive outdoor settings. Saratoga Springs' planners astutely cultivated a parklike setting of mani- cured lawns and ornate shrubbery around the mineral springs. Dubbed Congress Park after the nearby hotel of the same name, the park contained a wildly popular hand-powered circular railway and an Indian encamp- ment. Realizing the benefits of providing a bucolic setting for passing the time, hotel proprietors expanded on the model of Congress Park and erected formal gardens. Located within a hotel's plot of land and sur- rounded by the building's wings and outbuildings, these gardens provided a setting where guests could stroll, talk, and appraise the society about them. This created scenery worked well enough for one visitor to remark that "the grounds are kept in such beautiful order, that it is a pleasure to walk thro' them." Even in Virginia, where the lodging deficiencies were much more glaring, the unhappy John H. B. Latrobe admitted that White Sulphur Springs' efforts at cultivating scenery "makes up in picturesque effect" for the atrocious cabins.[34] Elite Americans from both North and South desired a carefully constructed and managed nature that they could observe in comfort. Their cultural ideal was Thomas Cole's Hudson River valley, not Lewis and Clark's savage West.

Always looking for ways to attract more guests, springs proprietors proved eager to appeal to these aesthetic standards. They used the design of the mineral springs, often placed at each establishment's geographic center, to advertise their resorts' sophistication and cultural exclusiveness. White Sulphur Springs featured "a classical looking octagonal marble dome sup- ported by columns below which is 'the fountain' in a large octagonal marble case," complete with benches around the perimeter for the comfort of im- bibers. Marble basins also caught and contained the waters at Blue Sulphur Springs, as well as at Red Sulphur Springs, where the canopy was supported by twelve "Ionic" columns.[35] Saratoga Springs' builders adopted a similar style of columned porticos, iron or wooden railings, and marble curbing surrounding the springs.

Statuary atop fountain pavilions embodied the cultural pretensions and assumptions of springs society. Some resorts chose to emphasize their wilderness settings; for example, Red Sulphur Springs placed "a set of huge

elk-horns" above the springs pavilion. But most Virginia resorts complemented the Greek revival architecture of their springs pavilions with a
marble statue of Hygeia, the Greek goddess of health. Again, White Sulphur
Springs defined the style. Its Hygeia held a cup in her right hand, as if
preparing to drink, and in her left a bough to represent the popularity of
herbal medicine and the spring's curative power.[36] The image affirmed the
drinkers' cultural sophistication—decoding the classical imagery marked a
guest as educated and refined. Yet for all the statues, pavilions, landscaped
grounds, and historical legends, elite Americans discovered that the springs
rarely met their ideal of cultivated landscapes and improved nature. The
springs failed to achieve the cultural sophistication they symbolized, as did
the marble statue of Hygeia at White Sulphur Springs: "Full of blue spots,
she looks not like the personification of health, but a thing full of bruises.
The features are good, but the arms are of patchwork, and the drapery looks
to have been chopped out with a broad axe." This imperfect goddess, Virginia's ramshackle cabins, and the misleading facades of Saratoga Springs'
hotels contradicted the air of cultural refinement and social grace that the
springs projected. Daily life at the springs complemented their bucolic settings only part of the time. At Saratoga Springs "the roominess and liberal
proportions of the Colonnade are one of those lies of architecture common
to the hotels of this country."[37] The lie was the mirage of cultural accomplishment, the elusive ideal of sophistication amidst rural splendor that the
springs promoted.

This gap between appearance and reality raises the question that *McBride's
Magazine* confronted in 1868: if the springs failed to provide a bucolic and
pastoral setting, offered miserable accommodations, and fell short of peoples'
expectations, "that people should be attracted here," that they "should deliberately visit [the springs] for pleasure, passeth all understanding." The
answer, quite simply, was that the springs "offered them, indeed—much
more than their fine home mansions could supply—health, high spirits,
and an atmosphere so delightfully cool and bracing even in the 'dog days'
that it made life a luxury." The springs provided something different from
everyday life, in spite of using everyday standards to promote themselves.
Visitors believed in the restorative power of the waters and the springs' position as cultural ideals of improved society and refined nature and therefore continued to suffer discomforts and disappointments. Roughing it was
part of the allure of experiencing nature and apparently trumped any reservations about poor accommodations or mediocre scenery. For old-line plan-

tation Southerners, the ability to withstand such hardships may have been a virtue. It signaled their carefree indolence that placed little emphasis on the creature comforts that acquisitive Yankees and mercantile Southerners valued so highly. The ability to enjoy leisure guiltlessly composed a part of the distinctive Southern identity that few Northerners shared or under-stood, even as they accepted the springs' rudimentary accommodations.[38] People tried to imagine life at the springs as sophisticated, refined, and com-fortable, but reality disagreed.

Americans, wrote the Northern social critic George William Curtis, "make it a principle to desert the city, and none less than the Americans know how to dispense with it. So we compromise by taking the city with us." Springs visitors in both regions—sophisticated, wealthy Americans from plantations and cities—refused to completely abandon their cultural stan-dards, even while visiting crude resorts based on the romantic landscapes and historical fables they idealized. Springs proprietors appealed to these ideals but failed to satisfy their clients. Yet the springs still attracted hordes of visitors each summer. As one of Saratoga Springs' confounded British visitors mused, "There must be some great attraction" to bring so many vis-itors to the springs "in spite of a hot sun, a sandy soil, and noisy hotels." From the cultural perspective of this Briton, American springs lacked the perfectly refined scenery, accommodations, and architecture of spas in his own country. But to Americans, whether Northern or Southern, the con-tradiction between untamed nature and imperfect civilization mattered little; they had melded those ideas into a new landscape aesthetic that em-braced eclecticism. Henry James never found the "elegant wilderness of ver-durous gloom" he hoped for at Saratoga Springs but instead discovered "a decidedly more satisfactory sort of place than the all-too-primitive Elysium of my wanton fancy." He wrote:

> At Saratoga civilization holds you fast. The most important feature of the place, perhaps, is the impossibility of realizing any such pastoral dream. The sur-rounding country is a charming wilderness, but the roads are so abominably bad that walking and driving are alike unprofitable. . . . There is a striking con-trast between the concentrated prodigality of life in the immediate precinct of the hotels and the generous wooded wildness and roughness into which half an hour's stroll may lead you. . . . You may resolve certain passages of Ruskin, in which he dwells upon the needfulness of some human association, however remote, to make scenery fully impressive. You may recall that magnificent

passage in which he relates having tried with such fatal effect, in a battle-haunted valley of the Jura, to fancy himself in a nameless solitude of our own continent. You feel around you, with irresistible force, the serene inexperience of undedicated nature—the absence of serious associations, the nearness, indeed, of vulgar and trivial associations of the best picturesque of great watering-places—you feel this, and you wonder what it is you so deeply and calmly enjoy. You conclude, possibly, that this is a great advantage to be able at once to enjoy Ruskin and to enjoy what Ruskin dispraises. And hereupon you return to your hotel and read the New York papers on the plan of the French campaign and the Twenty-third street murder.

James seems resigned to the juxtaposition of nature and civilization and most Americans' inability to see the conflict. He held a minority opinion yet accurately stated the resolution most Americans had reached to resolve the clash of nature and art: they went to the springs because they believed the waters would cure their ailments and because the resorts' rusticity provided an excuse to do so. In an age when Americans held different views about leisure—Southerners reveled in it and Northerners felt the need to justify it on moral grounds—the poor conditions, historical associations, and aesthetic ideals of the springs may have legitimized the experience.[39] By enduring poor conditions, Americans could insist that going to the springs was about health and simplicity, not luxury. Landscape provided them a socially acceptable cultural context and language within which to reach this compromise.

Chapter 3

THE DEMOCRATIZATION OF AMERICAN MEDICINE

edical science did its best to confirm Americans' belief that the springs contained health-giving properties capable of curing ailments and justifying visits. Steeped in folk wisdom and local reputation, springs in both New York State and Virginia gained regional and even sometimes national reputations for their medicinal qualities in the early years of the new republic. Prominent physicians and scientists, often aided or enlisted by springs proprietors, boosted these claims with analyses of the springs' mineral contents and their medical applicability. Trained at many of the same medical schools in America and Britain, these physicians attempted to forge a national medical consensus and to validate their own status as medical practitioners. Their reports conferred legitimacy on the springs and also marked an important development in medical and scientific knowledge. Physicians entered into the ongoing debate over medical respectability between the competing therapeutic sects during the first half of the nineteenth century, a debate fueled by the instability of medical authority.

But the scientific significance of springs analyses tells only part of the story. The analyses were read by a broad audience in both regions that included everyone from physician-scientists to shopkeepers and ladies, who responded to the texts in ways that might have surprised their authors. In an age of medical uncertainty and therapeutic diversity, the springs offered just one more option for invalids. Individuals took the waters with a considerable degree of caution and acted as their own physicians. They read and evaluated medical studies with the intention of making informed decisions about their own therapies. The publication of mineral springs analyses, intended at first to legitimize the waters and to solidify the medical establishment, actually democratized the cure and undermined the medical elite. Despite the efforts of leading physicians and scientists to elevate mineral springs, the waters failed to find a place at the forefront of American medicine. More refreshing beverages than powerful panaceas, America's mineral waters never attained the curative power and medical acceptance for which their promoters hoped. Instead, their unique medical context and cultural setting helped cure some of the social ailments that afflicted Northern and Southern society.

Attempts by medical or scientific men to examine the springs came as early as 1792, when Valentine Seaman set out from his home in New York City for Saratoga Springs laden with flasks, vials, copper basins, tubes, and a variety of chemicals and reagents. The twenty-two-year-old physician, a recent graduate of the prestigious and conservative medical school of the University of Pennsylvania, hoped to make his professional mark by analyzing the settlement's mineral water and validating its claims to medical utility. Seaman remembered the admonition of his esteemed professor Benjamin Rush to seek out any promising remedy in the undiscovered pharmacopoeia of the American wilderness: "'Who knows but what at the foot of the Allegheny mountain there blooms a flower, that is an infallible cure for the epilepsy? Perhaps on the Monongahela, or the Potowmack, there may grow a root, that shall supply, by its tonic power, the invigorating effects of the savage or military life, in the cure of consumption.'" But more than just flowers and roots held medical promise. Seaman extended Rush's musings to wonder why "there may not spring up a water, in some neglected valley, whose solvent quality . . . may melt down the torturing stone, or whose penetrating influence may root out the scrofula from the system?" Saratoga Springs provided an ideal subject for study.[1]

Seaman's analysis of the springs was not the first investigation of upstate New York's mineral springs. Two earlier studies preceded his, but neither claimed to be authoritative or comprehensive.[2] Seaman, however, envisioned a loftier goal for his undertaking. Lauding and attempting to imitate the work of Robert R. Livingston, a prominent New York jurist and politician, as well as the president of the Society for the Promotion of Agriculture, Arts, and Manufactures, Seaman sought to cure diseases through his research. In the early republic, science needed to be utilitarian to be acceptable; simple theoretical advances were insufficient. With this caveat in mind, Seaman employed the latest scientific techniques to analyze the waters and "to discover the nature of such mineral substances, as are often dissolved in it, and to which many waters owe their particular medical virtues."[3]

In pursuing his goal of discovering productive knowledge, Seaman incorporated the most recent scientific and medical methods of late eighteenth-century America into his dissertation. He described his experiments in great detail and justified all of his conclusions with a combination of empirical data and logical reasoning. No detail, including the water's taste and temperature, escaped his analysis. Seaman hoped, by conducting a series of experiments, to ascertain the water's exact contents and to link them to cures for specific ailments. After a series of distillations, filtrations, and evaporations, Seaman concluded that the water contained five important ingredients: cretacious acid, common marine salt, aerated lime, and small traces of mineral alkali and aerated iron. "One of the most difficult investigations" in late eighteenth-century science, identifying the water's components was a significant accomplishment.[4]

Not everyone was impressed with Seaman's work. Robert Livingston, to whom Seaman had dedicated his dissertation, published contradictory results of the chemical analysis in a leading periodical. Seaman was disturbed by the disparagement of his own research and its implications for the water's medical utility. He attempted to "settle the difference" by repeating his study and publishing its contents in the same issue of the journal containing Livingston's analysis, as well as an expanded second edition of his dissertation. More than a difference in test results motivated Seaman to write the new edition. Besides holding the eminent position of surgeon at New York Hospital, Seaman also had made important contributions in the advancement and acceptance of vaccinations. Any indictment of his reputation, even of experiments carried out years before in his career's infancy, threatened both his own interests and those of the medical profession in general. Although he repeated his experiments and made minor emendations, the text's main changes derived from increased page dimensions, print size, and margin width. Even so, Seaman insisted that his original results were neither incorrect, "nor will any experiments yet published . . . warrant us in concluding that [the waters] contain any thing else."[5]

Reviewers disagreed. Finding "an evident fallacy" in Seaman's experiments, they wished Seaman had conducted more research, "for it ought to be remembered, that mere reasoning can never decide a matter of fact." Seaman responded by attacking his critics on the same basis that they faulted him: for not meeting scientific standards and failing to act like gentlemanly scholars. Eventually the journal's editors stifled the controversy by declaring Seaman's replies "frivolous and unworthy of notice." In deviating from purely scientific matters, Seaman's "unjustified insinuations" constituted a "breach of decorum." They labeled Seaman's dissertation "worthless, so far as it relates to the analysis of the water." In this fight over scientific paradigms, standards, and methodologies, as well as reputations and egos, one faction of the quarreling New York City medical community quashed the attempts of a rival to refute its experiments and claims to authority. The controversy also exposed the bitter rivalries between scientists, the lack of a clear consensus on methodology, and the inability of the early republic's gentleman-scholars to agree on what constituted good science. Learned societies like the American Philosophical Society and the American Academy for Arts and Sciences admitted scholars, physicians, and gentlemen, so long as they exhibited an interest in knowledge. Medical schools included subjects as diverse as chemistry, natural history, mineralogy, and anatomy in their curriculum. Most chemists in the early republic actually received their training in medical school and devoted only a portion of their time to chemical inquiries. They constituted a community of generalists, scientists, and physicians who frequently crossed into each other's fields of study. In this age, the gentleman-scholar prevailed, and Seaman's amalgamation of chemistry and medicine perfectly marked him as an aspiring member of the intellectual, as well as social, elite. His rivals' attempts to deny him that status demonstrate its attainability and fragility.[6]

A few years after the Seaman debate subsided, the second phase of mineral springs studies began. Coincidentally, 1817 marked both Valentine Seaman's death and the publication of a new work on Saratoga Springs that altered the approach to studying the springs. John H. Steel's *An Analysis of the Mineral Waters of Saratoga and Ballston* reads much differently from the efforts of his predecessors and became the standard, as well as an immensely popular, medical treatise on the subject for years to come.[7] Where Seaman's generation focused on the chemical components of the springs, with short digressions into the waters' medical efficacy, the second phase of springs studies emphasized the springs' medical uses for invalids. Although earlier authors had been interested in the commercial or medical prospects of the springs, they had included such information as a corollary to their scientific studies. In the later publications, medical efficacy and tourist information moved to the foreground as science faded into the background. In two decades springs publications moved from scientific analysis to business and social information, from determining scientific authority to providing lay people with medical knowledge.

Steel's book was the first springs-related publication, aside from guidebooks, to include extensive information on the history, geology, and attractions of the general area. His goal was not to engage in a contentious scientific debate but to "enable invalids, as well as men of pleasure, to make such arrangements, before visiting the Spring, as may be conducive to their comforts and pleasures while there." He basically combined the two leading genres of springs publications, the medical study and the guidebook. In doing so, Steel did not bother to reproduce the numerous chemical analyses of the springs. Instead, he named the leading authors, assuming that "from the weight of such authority, the most scrupulous will be satisfied that the medical properties of these waters are entirely owing" to the components identified by the prominent authorities. Steel still performed a variety of experiments on the mineral water but used them as supporting evidence for his general argument rather than as the central focus of the entire work. Ordinary readers could decide on medical and scientific veracity.[8]

What set Steel's study apart from earlier works was his appeal to readers not as a leading scientist from an intellectual and urban center but as a local physician experienced in the use of the waters as a medical agent. He introduced this information on the title page of the second edition of his book, where he called himself not only "John H. Steel, M.D.," but also "Resident at the Springs, President of the Saratoga Medical Society." The two other general studies of Saratoga Springs followed the trend by identifying the authors as resident physicians. To these men, local knowledge mattered more than scientific theory. Likewise, virtually every study of the Virginia springs identified the author as at least a physician and in many cases as the resident physician of the spring under consideration. The authors used these titles to satisfy their pretensions of legitimacy and to garner the respect of their readers. Thomas D. Mütter's 1840 publication was titled simply *The Salt Sulphur Springs, Monroe County, Virginia,* but identified the author as "M.D., Lecturer on Surgery; Corresponding Member of the N.Y. Medical and Surgical Society; Fellow of the College of Physicians of Philadelphia; Member of the Pathological Society of Philadelphia; Member of the Acad. of Nat. Sciences of Philadelphia; Hon. Member of the Medical Society of Philadelphia; One of the Physicians to the Philadelphia Dispensary; One of the Council of the Historical Society, &c." Besides parading credentials to impress readers, Mütter also identified himself as a regular physician, not an adherent of one of the many medical sects that populated antebellum medicine. To stress professional medical credentials was to identify the text as conservative in therapeutics and authoritative in its conception of the physician's role. More than just honorific, a title signified the author's place in the politics of antebellum medicine. By looking at the title page of a medical work, invalids could quickly determine if the author shared their therapeutic outlooks and decide whether the tract was worth reading or buying. Those readers, not Valentine Seaman's critics, evaluated a text's utility.[9]

Steel's book marks an important change not just in content but also in publishing and distribution. As the first springs medical guidebook aimed at a general audience, Steel's work helped to create a market for and to disseminate, in print, springs information throughout the antebellum era. A significant number of the gazetteers, periodicals, newspaper stories, travel accounts, guidebooks, and broadsides that discussed the medical use of the waters included chemical analyses.[10] The proliferation of printed springs studies and the capitalization on this trend by local publishers, who issued brief, inexpensive, yet handsome editions of studies of individual springs, led to greater awareness of the waters' curative powers. Several copies of John Steel's thirty-three-page booklet on Saratoga Springs' Congress Spring bear inscriptions attesting to the gift of the four-by-five-inch hardbound booklets to "a friend" or "as a token of esteem." The small size, attractive design, breezy content, easy availability, and use as gifts of mineral springs studies marked a shift from their status as serious scientific tomes to objectified tourist commodities. Whereas the earliest springs studies were scientific tracts printed in urban centers for the medical establishment, the proliferation of print and the expansion of springs tourism after 1830 combined to form a more local, nonmedical, and easily accessible springs print culture.[11]

The net effect of the boom in publication and dissemination of medical and chemical studies was an increased understanding among lay people of the springs' reputed medical power. Springs visitors delighted in retelling the results of experiments, especially the lowering of live animals into the cone of Saratoga Springs' High Rock Spring—a test of the water's gas levels and curative power. But they also assessed the medical qualities of the springs by reading the available analyses, often noting that their or a relative's "Case is described in it & the waters particularly recommended." Recognizing the comparison, they then urged others to join them in obtaining a cure. Reading mineral springs studies also enabled invalids to differentiate between various springs and to evaluate each spring's efficacy. When an undistinguished place such as Lackland's Well in western Virginia, the site of a long-established tavern on an important thoroughfare, was "*discovered* to be a valuable mineral [spring] + people *humbuged* to go there as such" in 1842, William Bolling noted his displeasure. His objection came not from the spring's dubious medical value but from the fact that almost anyone could claim that a particular spring possessed miraculous curative powers. Once this boast appeared in print, many readers believed it, and the report became frustratingly difficult to disprove. Although Bolling, a prominent Virginian, recognized the "humbug," less well-informed people would not, especially without evaluation by credible authorities.[12]

The authority and respect that medical and scientific men once commanded seemed to be weakening under the egalitarian onslaught of print culture. David Hosack's influential book *Observations on the Use of the Ballston Mineral Waters* detailed the springs' potential medical uses with the caveat that "the directions of the physicians are indispensibly necessary." As with any other part of the *materia medica,* wrote this prominent New York City college instructor, naturalist, and pillar of the medical establishment, mineral waters were subject to misapplication and abuse by patients and should be used carefully. In this prescription Hosack was interposing his authority, and that of medical practitioners in general, between the invalid and the mineral waters. He acted to affirm the physician's position as the ultimate arbiter of medical decisions and to relegate the patient to a passive role. In 1811 Hosack's admonition may have chastened patients, but his successors faced a more difficult task in asserting their authority. By comparing the chemical compositions of the waters at European and American spas, proprietors could assert that their establishments equaled Cheltenham or Tunbridge Wells in England, Spa in Belgium, Baden-Baden in Germany, or several other European springs in curative power.[13] Besides associating American springs with the powerful and long-established medical reputations of their European counterparts, the comparisons connoted a similar level of luxury, exclusivity, and social sophistication.

That combination of medical and cultural respectability may have influenced John J. Moorman of White Sulphur Springs, author of several springs guides and medical studies, to counter the democratizing effects of print by cultivating an authoritative image. He walked about the springs wearing gold spectacles and carrying a gold-headed cane, traveled in Europe to study its springs, and remained as aloof from the patients as possible. His reputation as the long-standing resident physician led many to recommend that his latest in a series of books on the springs "should be in the hands of every invalid, comprising, as it does, most valuable directions on [the waters'] efficacy and use." Moorman may have convinced White Sulphur Springs' visitors of his knowledge and expertise, but beyond the springs almost anyone with access to a press could assert a spring's medical utility and the writer's authority. Moorman's competitor in guidebook publication and the tourist business, William Burke of Red Sulphur Springs, engaged in a running feud with Moorman over the efficacy of bottled water and each spring's curative power. Moorman attempted to discredit Burke by writing that his rival "is the *proprietor* of a would-be rival watering place; we the Resident Physician at the White Sulphur. Which, under the circumstances, we would ask, is likely to feel the deepest interest in the reputation of that water?" The invocation of professional objectivity, rather than pecuniary motive, answered Moorman's rhetorical question.[14]

Invalids, sensing the uncertainty of promoters'—and physicians'—claims, cultivated a cautious skepticism. They believed that "chemists pretend to analyze [the waters] very accurately and confidently tell us their components" in reports that informed readers often considered erroneous. By constantly "talking most *learnedly + scientifically* of the various properties of the waters" and by comparing notes on the different springs and their effectiveness in treating different conditions, springs visitors took an active role in their cures. They read the chemical studies, occasionally conducted their own experiments, and formed opinions of the qualities of the waters. These topics proved "a fruitful subject of conversation at the springs . . . not only of this day but some part of every day." By using the language and data of chemical analyses, supporters of the various springs attempted to persuade each other that their particular spring exceeded all others in medicinal power. Chemistry, considered a necessary part of a gentleman's education, became a conversational tool employed by visitors lest they be "confounded by the learning of those around [them]."[15] Every visitor could be his or her own scientist and physician. In this context, learned studies, once a mark of elite status, degenerated into ammunition for the competitive battle of social display at the springs. Scientific knowledge was losing its power not only to impress but also, more ominously, to persuade.

This trend increased with the appearance of a new genre of springs publications that focused on a single spring or resort rather than on a region. At least fourteen such publications (eleven for Virginia, three for Saratoga Springs) appeared between 1834 and 1860, a publishing boom that coincided with the release of what most contemporaries considered the seminal work on the mineral waters of the United States, John Bell's comprehensive study of the medical uses of American mineral springs. The new generation of studies had little trouble getting into print, but only if their authors left the springs for an urban publisher. All but three of the fourteen springs studies (78.6 percent) were issued by publishing houses in New York, Boston, Philadelphia, Washington, Albany, or Richmond.[16] Ironically, the forces that decentralized medicine and weakened scientific authority depended on the nation's publishing and intellectual centers, its major cities, to disseminate their claims.

These increasingly specific studies relied on two basic pieces of evidence to bolster their claims of medical utility: chemical analyses and patient testimonials. Even though chemical analyses lost their influence and occupied less space in springs publications, those analyses continued to appear throughout the antebellum period, as every mineral springs study either mentioned previous chemical analyses of the springs or conducted new experiments. Northern and Southern authors still listed key ingredients as part of the *materia medica,* a central claim in their promotional efforts. The Commonwealth of Virginia considered the springs' chemical components of such significance that it required sixteen of twenty-six springs incorporated between 1835 and 1850 to analyze their waters and to publish the results "for the benefit of the community." The state geologist even devoted a significant amount of his time and portions of his annual reports to chemical analyses of the springs.[17] From this information patients could make informed decisions as to which spring best suited their ailments, and springs proprietors could compare their water with that of their competitors. The results allowed newly discovered, smaller, or less popular springs to claim that their waters equaled those of better-known rivals, and established springs trumpeted the strength of their waters as unmatched by any other spring in the world. By the 1850s Valentine Seaman's goal of linking mineral content with a medical cure seemed complete. His idea had become part of a national consensus on the utility of scientific knowledge and the medicinal uses of spring water. The print revolution disseminated information about springs and their medical powers, but patients, not physicians, evaluated the evidence.

If the associations drawn from chemical analyses failed to convince invalids of the efficacy of the springs, patients could then consult the numerous testimonials included in most springs publications. Reports of miraculous cures appeared in the earliest springs studies, often as anecdotal accounts, such as Samuel Tenney's 1783 summaries of the Revolutionary War soldiers he treated at Saratoga Springs for skin diseases and liver ailments. The scientists and physicians who wrote the second generation of tracts attempted to systematize and to legitimize these early tales. From "intelligent men from all sections of the Union" and "distinguished medical gentlemen in various parts of the country," as well as famous politicians, springs promoters solicited "public opinion as to the adaptedness and power of this water" to cure various diseases. Letters from eminent physicians lent credibility to the claims of medical efficacy, especially if the doctors mentioned that they sent their own patients to the springs. Likewise, affidavits recounting miraculous cures and the springs' powers from prominent individuals such as United States Supreme Court Chief Justice Roger Taney or Yale professor of chemistry Benjamin Silliman were designed to impress a reader. If these important individuals endorsed the springs, ordinary invalids could benefit as well.[18] The springs identified themselves with elite Americans and hoped that potential customers would do the same.

These endorsements varied little: they began with a description of the disease and its incurability using conventional means or regular physicians and then cited the desperate efforts of invalids to visit the springs in a final attempt to restore their health. The tone of the letters turned quickly from desperation to joy as the patients related the end of their symptoms and their return to almost perfect health. Many echoed a visitor to Bedford

Alum Springs, Virginia, who lauded the usefulness of the waters and wrote the words that every invalid hoped for: "*I am well.*" Books included a large number of such testimonials, often squeezing in dozens of letters relating to every conceivable disease, occasionally filling as much as one-quarter of their pages. The majority came from men writing about their own cures or those of their wives, but a small number of the letters were written by women, especially those concerning what the authors politely termed "feminine complaints." Women suffering from uterine diseases, amenorrhea, and infertility composed a significant portion of springs business, and authors readily added information on these ailments to their studies. Whether the market was Virginia, New York, or England, springs promoters knew that both medical efficacy and business acumen justified appealing to female patients. Influencing their own cure allowed women, as well as men, an increased level of agency in their lives.[19]

While these case studies helped patients to select the spring best suited to their individual situations, they also involved physicians in dialogues with their patients. By including detailed case information, physicians hoped to engage and to solve the perplexing questions of their profession through the exchange of information with their peers. The publication of these letters also took place during a period of medical controversy and sectarian conflict when regular physicians attempted to stabilize their positions as the leading care providers. Agreement on the importance of empirical evidence in determining the best therapeutic practice blunted the critiques of those who attacked regular physicians' methods. Testimonials in mineral springs studies spoke both to invalids eager to cure their illnesses and to physicians reading for the latest news in medical advances. The publication of case studies shortened the distance between members of a scattered profession and increased their consciousness of themselves as a distinct professional group. These studies stated the therapeutic principles of accredited, reputable, regular physicians, but they also admitted lay people who read the tracts into the conversation about a particular therapy's efficacy.[20]

The dialogue between physicians and patients about the springs' medical applicabilities belonged to a larger debate about therapies in general. Few physicians received formal medical training during the early republic era, and even those who did lacked a consensus on proper practices, as Valentine Seaman's story indicates. State medical societies faced difficulty in gaining recognition and even lost government charters in some cases. Physicians lacked a monopoly on care and in the case of childbirth performed little better than midwives. This age of medical competition continued through the first half of the nineteenth century, when invalids could choose among Thompsonians, who advocated the use of herbs and other natural remedies; homeopaths, who prescribed infinitesimal amounts of medication; the heroic treatments of regular physicians; and the water-cure.[21]

Attention to specific symptoms and treatments, as well as scientific detail, set springs physicians apart from the diversity of methodological competitors. The water-cure came closest to the therapeutics of mineral springs, and the two are often confused. The water-cure, or hydropathy, relied on the external application of water to the body, as well as less extensive internal use, to relieve all sorts of ailments. Started by a German peasant in the 1830s, hydropathy became part of a larger reforming impulse during the mid-nineteenth century in Europe and America. Instead of emphasizing the role of the physician, hydropathic treatment advocated that patients take an active part in curing disease. The water-cure eschewed drugs in favor of hot and cold baths and showers, sweat baths (wrapping the body in blankets until the individual was soaked with perspiration), frequent purges, and dietary moderation. Believers in hydropathy relied on the interaction between water and either the skin or the digestive organs to achieve a cure. Unlike invalids who visited mineral springs, hydropaths refused to accept that the chemical content of water played any part in treating disease. They also emphasized liberating the patient, especially women, from the authority of regular physicians.

Invalids bathed in the springs of both regions, although not necessarily under the direct supervision of a water-cure physician, and adopted portions of the water-cure regimen, especially frequent bathing. Rather than directly challenging the springs' therapeutic methodologies, the water-cure, which became popular in the 1840s in America, can be seen as a reformist offshoot of the growing popularity of mineral springs resorts. One water-cure establishment even existed in antebellum Saratoga Springs. The simultaneous boom in mineral springs and the emergence of the water-cure grew from the same cultural impulses. Both catered to an equalitarian society becoming increasingly democratic, both in politics and culture. In addition, Jacksonian America was a particularly perfectionist society, especially in the North, and nearly every aspect of life, from politics to personal hygiene, seemed in need of reform. Both mineral springs and the water-cure catered to individuals who sought to improve their health and to perfect their lives.

But whereas mineral springs offered health as an adjunct to socializing, water-cure institutions restricted their business to healing the patients' bodies and minds. Each regimen helped popularize the other, but few antebellum Americans would have mistaken one for the other.[22]

The main distinction between the springs and the water-cure was their different therapeutic philosophies and their place in early nineteenth-century medical politics. The water-cure movement posed a direct challenge to the prevailing medical orthodoxy and created its own medical colleges that challenged traditional training and took the radical step of graduating female physicians. Mineral springs, however, remained firmly within the school of regular medicine and the emerging medical concept of specificity—the idea that each disease required a discrete course of treatment. The identification of certain diseases with particular springs was not an isolated phenomenon but part of a growing therapeutic trend. Specificity held that each individual disease and patient required a different therapy, depending on the variables of age, sex, race, wealth, moral status, and geographic region. Individual cases mattered more than universal prescriptions or theoretical bases for treatments, as principal springs physicians acknowledged by their insistence that each patient consult a doctor to determine the best course of treatment for his or her ailment. Detailed knowledge of individual patients and appropriate therapeutics increased the importance of local physicians, especially those in residence at the springs. Specificity, with its emphasis on local experience and individual circumstance, suited an increasingly decentralized, democratic society such as early nineteenth-century America and ensured the influence of medical authorities in therapeutics. But the development of specificity was not limited to Saratoga Springs or the Virginia springs. Specificity gained credence at roughly the same time at the predominant spa in the Anglo-American world: Bath, England. The publication of so many medical studies of American springs, complete with detailed recommendations for curing individual diseases, reflected this new therapeutic doctrine and the gradual loosening of the authoritarian doctor-patient relationship in the Anglo-American world.[23]

Springs studies had long alluded to the connection between the exact content of an individual spring and its efficacy in certain diseases but refused to "attribute to mineral waters of any description any very exclusive property which cannot be shown by chemical analysis." Only with the advent of more sophisticated chemical techniques and additional data from springs patients were medical authors able to make direct links between cure and spring. For instance, John Steel discovered that the numerous mineral springs of Saratoga Springs and Ballston Spa, all located within ten miles of each other, contained the same general list of ingredients but in slightly different quantities. Steel's accomplishment came from his realization that the "difference in the *quantities* of the substances common to all" determined the applicability of each individual spring to various diseases. On this basis he recommended the best uses of thirteen different springs in the area.[24]

Perhaps because of the isolation of Virginia's springs among the mountains of the western part of the state and their widespread locations across several hundred square miles, direct ties between these springs and individual diseases came more slowly. Virginia's springs, which began as local retreats steeped in folk wisdom, were slow to adopt the market-oriented dissemination of their virtues. But by the late 1830s and early 1840s, several medical guides to the Virginia springs emerged, complete with a list of the various resorts and the diseases the springs aided. This strategy often backfired, as nearly every spring could claim its power in cases of dyspepsia and bilious complaints. But only Virginia's Red Sulphur Springs could boast that it cured consumption. Three different pamphlets, more individual studies than for any other spring, promoted Red Sulphur Springs' power to clear congested lungs, lower the pulse, and act as a general purgative. Physicians determined that the specific composition of the water's red sulphurous precipitate acted as "the principal medicinal agent." Although various doctors issued caveats regarding individual cases and emphasized the need to consult physicians, they boldly endorsed Red Sulphur Springs as the best and only cure for troublesome illnesses such as consumption and tuberculosis.[25] Specificity allowed Red Sulphur Springs to use science to its business advantage. In this regard, specificity transcended region.

Therapeutic conventions at the Virginia springs adhered to the same general principles and advised the use of waters in the same set of diseases as did their Northern counterparts. The course of therapy preferred by America's early springs physicians was not radical but conformed to the practices of mainstream medicine during the early republic. Springs physicians prescribed drugs, applied blisters, and bled and purged their patients as a prelude to, or a part of, mineral water therapy, just as their contemporaries

Drinking the water, White Sulphur Springs. This scene was a daily morning and afternoon ritual at Southern and Northern resorts. Most springs served water from dipper cups on long poles, as illustrated. From *Harper's New Monthly Magazine*, August 1878. Courtesy of the Albion College Library.

did. The most basic theory on the use of the springs—that they elevated debilitated systems—agreed with the prevailing medical understanding that diseases were caused by either excited or depressed systems and that the physician's main task was to reverse the body's state and produce a cure. Such orthodox methodology qualified mineral waters for inclusion in regular medical reference books as accepted medical agents. In an age when the prevailing medical paradigm called for the physician to produce an immediate, observable effect on the patient's body, mineral waters fell within the requirements of an appropriate treatment. Drinking six to eight pints of mineral water before breakfast and as many as a dozen more during the day certainly qualified as a "heroic" therapy, especially when springs visitors made exaggerated claims that some guests quaffed as many as fifty-four glasses of water in a single day.[26] The point of such outlandish estimates was not to provide an accurate count of glasses drunk but to demonstrate the springs' adherence to regular medicine and the extremes to which invalids would go in search of a cure.

Once patients drank the water, they generally moved their bowels, a topic of frequent conversation at the springs, "in sufficient time for breakfast." For guests who ate prodigious meals at a rapid rate, defecation was not an undesired effect; it cured their indigestion. St. George Tucker's comment that "this morning I had one of the most bilious discharges I ever had in my life" indicated not only that the waters produced the desired result but also that the outcome was extraordinary. The fact that springs visitors discussed the water's effects so openly indicates a willingness to share personal medical information in hopes of attaining a cure and the active role that patients played in their cure. The springs broke down the societal taboo concerning bodily functions. By telling friends and family how well the springs worked, patients validated the waters according to prevailing medical assumptions. More than a simple laxative, the waters caused "copious discharges," which qualified them as a legitimate treatment with observable results. In the context of early American medicine, prescribing or taking the waters was not a revolutionary act that undermined the medical establishment; the waters composed part of the regular physician's arsenal of weapons used to combat disease. Taking the waters served as a less harsh alternative to the gradually fading therapeutics of heroic medicine but did not directly challenge its principles or its domination of the medical scene. Many orthodox physicians recommended the springs as a last resort, "Just when we've taken calomel enough."[27]

Doctors still sought to produce immediate changes in observable symptoms but eschewed the bleedings and harsh purgatives of a few decades earlier. This restraint was due in part to patients' reluctance to undergo such treatments. Invalids preferred to cure themselves first, and published medical guides gave them the information they needed to direct their treatment. But when these guides failed, invalids consulted physicians with alacrity. More often than not, the patients were "much indebted" for the doctors' advice. The presence of physicians, and especially resident ones, at mineral springs increased the confidence of many patients. An éminence grise such as Dr. Moorman, despite—or maybe because of—his aloof nature, reassured patients that someone at the springs was a competent and respected physician. Some guests even attributed the cure of diseases at Dr. Goode's Hot Springs "to the enlightened use of the waters under his direction." That "enlightened use" was flexible and undefined, despite what the doctrine of specificity might say. So long as patients influenced their own cure, physicians could not dictate therapies. Few doctors turned patients away because of the unsuitability of the waters to their complaint but instead tailored the course of treatment to include other therapies. Or they might act like Dr. Clarke, the owner of Saratoga Springs' Congress Spring and its profitable bottling business, who prescribed "whatever spring a person drunk of most freely."[28] Clarke and many of his colleagues readily abandoned the doctrine of specificity when it suited their commercial purposes.

The flexibility that doctors demonstrated in prescribing the waters was due in part to the uncertainties of early nineteenth-century medicine. Despite the growing influence of specificity and empiricism, alternative remedies were often as effective as regular medicine and frequently less demanding of the patient. Most patients did not regard regular physicians as infallible, however hard the medical establishment attempted to bolster that reputation. Patients, whether men or women, took a leading role in their own cures by evaluating their medical options and deciding on the most efficacious course of treatment. Some visitors even thwarted medical convention by drinking the waters after breakfast "in spite of the wisdom of those who deem it fatal to drink the water on a full stomach." Invalids occasionally challenged the wisdom of their doctors more directly, as when Edward Eccles followed the advice of Saratoga Springs' Dr. North only to discover that "I was not only not gaining anything but rather losing." Unsatisfied with his treatment, Eccles visited a competing physician, Dr. Allen, who said that "I was injuring myself" by following North's advice and prescribed a different course of treatment. After several days Eccles reported that "I am improving gradually."[29] Even though North and Allen adhered to regular medicine and their prescriptions varied only slightly, the differences were significant to Eccles. He made an informed choice among the available medical options based on his own knowledge and the results (or lack thereof) of his treatment. Although he stuck with traditional practitioners, Eccles made the key decisions regarding his cure.

The willingness of invalids to switch physicians quickly was due in part to the precarious position of traditional medicine. Regular practitioners held no monopoly over medical efficacy, as any victim of a copious bloodletting, harsh purgative, or mercury overdose could attest. But patients at the springs were not abandoning regular medicine; they manipulated physicians' lack of absolute authority to demand effective and, if possible, nonheroic cures.

However, the supply side of this equation mattered as well. Just as Americans chose from a variety of medical sects, at the springs they could also choose from a number of different physicians. Although some springs boasted their own resident physicians, no one doctor controlled the medical scene. Homeopaths, water-cure enthusiasts, quacks, and itinerant physicians frequented the springs and siphoned their share of patients from the predominant practitioner.

Springs proprietors also encouraged a diversity of medical options by granting preferable terms to doctors who stayed at their resorts. One physician, Charles William Ashby of Virginia, reported making several consultations in spite of himself during an 1860 tour of the Virginia springs. He had not intended to practice medicine on the trip, but once people heard of his profession, they deluged him with requests for advice and readily paid for Ashby's prescriptions. One springs proprietor charged Ashby only half price for his lodging, "as he thought I had been of service to him in recommending his establishment." Even at Healing Springs, where a resident physician presided, Ashby offered prescriptions without interruption. Ashby's only regret from his journey was that he "did not let it be known when I came here that I would practice." Had he done so, he might have enriched himself considerably. The situation was similar at Saratoga Springs, where no single doctor dominated the market. One of them, Cyrel Carpenter, urged his nephew to move to Saratoga Springs to continue his practice, as none of the other physicians seemed particularly adept at or attuned to the business of doctoring. While "the regular Physicians let their Patients die," quack doctors and patent medicine hucksters gained clients. In Carpenter's view, the medical community in Saratoga Springs was so inadequate that "A good physician will soon starve them all out." In this situation, the patients controlled the interaction between themselves and their doctors. One visitor to White Sulphur Springs—and there were probably many like him—would ingeniously "meet with a 'Physician' and consult him about his case, & another, &c., then with visitors, compare his situation with others & so on, until it was really amusing to see his tack to find out a Physician and to find out if he charged anything for advice."[30]

The multiplicity of therapeutic options extended beyond the springs to patients' homes. Because the waters fit so well within the prevailing therapeutic paradigm, physicians saw both medical and commercial possibilities in mineral waters and proposed recreating the waters away from the springs and establishing a new market for their curative powers as early as the 1790s. Reconstituting the waters allowed people to derive medical benefits from the waters "without the inconvenience or expense of attending at the spring." Benjamin Silliman, a recently appointed professor of chemistry at Yale College, hoped to supplement his meager income by producing artificial mineral waters on a grand scale. After initially failing to produce water in large quantities, Silliman perfected the production of waters and in 1808 opened a New York City fountain room. People enjoyed the waters, and prominent physicians endorsed their use, but Silliman realized no profits and abandoned the business after two seasons.[31]

Others were more successful. By 1820 several businessmen began bottling Saratoga Springs' Congress Spring water for transportation to and sale in urban markets. The success of this effort, as well as similar bottling operations started at several Virginia springs in the late 1830s, ended the artificial mineral water business.[32] If consumers could drink the real thing from a bottle, they had little need for chemically altered generic water dispensed from a tap, whose medical value remained untested. Consumers demonstrated less ambivalence toward the pills and powders concocted by Virginia and New York druggists that reportedly possessed "the same medical qualities" as water "taken immediately from the springs" without the high cost of bottled water or an extended stay. Springs promoters rejected such claims, stating that artificial medicines "in reality bear no resemblance, either in their effects or their properties, to the mineral water, the name of which they have assumed."[33] Whichever side was correct, the marketing of pills and powders completed the process that bottling water began. Individual patients could test the waters' curative powers far from the springs and farther still from the direction of springs physicians.

Even if invalids could obtain a cure from bottled waters or mineral-laden powders, most preferred visiting the springs. Legitimate health concerns pushed people out of the South's coastal regions and away from urban centers up and down the eastern seaboard. For Southerners, the annual onslaught of extreme heat brought uncomfortable living conditions and, more important, outbreaks of disease. Conventional wisdom held that the heat and moisture of marshy lowlands contributed to "vegetable decomposition" and dangerous miasmas that caused periodic outbreaks of cholera, yellow fever, and similar diseases.[34] The June 1834 cholera epidemic in New Orleans killed "upwards of one hundred . . . daily" and, according to one local resident, "rarely yields to any remedies." Such experiences convinced most lowland Southerners that June, July, August, and early September were a dangerous "season when half of our population have left us and the remainder dreading the Dangue [*sic*] or some other fever." Most preferred to escape the ravages of disease by fleeing to higher, cooler, drier, and healthier ground.[35]

The desire to abandon the low country extended beyond specific epidemics to a general exodus of the wealthy each summer. Overall opinion held that swampy, humid, hot, and stagnant regions were "unhealthy" and "unwholesome." Some medical experts even hypothesized that specific "Diseases of the South" existed. These ailments originated in "marshy counties" and were characterized by "languor, and disinclination to motion of any kind." By the 1840s and 1850s, Southern and national medical opinions agreed that a change in climate prevented illness and could improve a sick patient's condition. Southerners were especially interested in the salubrious effects of "the health-giving breezes of the mountains." They went not only to the mountainous Virginia springs but also to Piedmont springs, the seashore, and northern resorts. As transportation networks improved and a national tourist culture developed, some Southerners even journeyed to the refreshing air of the faraway Great Lakes.[36]

Northern guidebook authors capitalized on this trend by targeting their books to tourists from the South, who "accelerate their journey to the more salubrious climate of the north" as summer approached. These authors omitted Southern resorts since mentioning them ran counter to medical orthodoxy and their business interests. When Northerners sought to escape hot, occasionally disease-ridden cities such as New York, Philadelphia, and Boston for cooler climes, they headed north to the stops on the fashionable tour, not the Virginia mountains. Most tourists and invalids came to Saratoga Springs

> From crowded cities and oppressive heat
>   Flying, to quaff the cool delicious draught,
> Where smiling nature all around invites,
>   And free and pure, ambrosial breezes play.[37]

Besides offering an agreeable reason to visit the springs, the change-in-climate theory also appeared to realize a substantial number of cures.

Although E. M. Grosvenor was ambivalent about the curative powers of Saratoga Springs' waters, he shared few doubts concerning the change in climate: "The air strengthens my lungs, and rest and quietness do me more good than any kind of medicine." Grosvenor was not alone in his belief in the salubrious effects of fresh air; several visitors to the Virginia springs cited the cool, fresh mountain air "and the shaking of the long passage over the mountains necessary to reach" the springs as the cause of their improving health. When Charles Ellis claimed "that I feel better when I am in the stage or traveling any other way than I do when stationary at the springs," he spoke not only of his own preference for an active life but also to the significant change in lifestyle that Americans experienced at the springs. Rather than leading the relatively passive life of a Northern merchant or Southern planter, men such as Ellis suddenly filled their days not by balancing accounts or supervising work but by riding, walking, dancing, playing various games, and focusing on healthy activities. The change was even more marked for elite women, who enjoyed few opportunities for physical exertion at home. Women and men found the vigorous life so stimulating that they believed "exercise would cure almost every one."[38]

Not all tourists shared Ellis's faith in activity. In fact, a significant number of springs visitors were confirmed invalids with few hopes of recovery. They wandered gloomily about the hotel grounds, processing solemnly toward the spring at dawn each morning "as though their salvation depended upon it." Their "emaciated sallow faces, made ghastly with fever and ague," frightened away more than one votary of pleasure at the fountain. The contrast between invalids and fashionable tourists was so stark that they seldom mingled, each group keeping to its own hotel or springs. Some hotels at Saratoga Springs and Ballston Spa were known as invalid houses where visitors could escape the harried life of springs society, and Virginia's Hot Springs developed such a reputation for invalidism that some fashionable stagecoaches drove directly past the hotel without stopping. Passengers took the opportunity, however, to note that the place "seemed to be a gathering place for Disease" whose porches "were filled with invalids . . . some were limping; some were on crutches; and some were wheeled about like children." Characterized as "a sorrowful sight," places such as Hot Springs received few healthy visitors. Those few hale travelers who stopped became "quite disgusted with this place." Likewise, the constant coughing and spitting at Red Sulphur Springs, "the great rendez-vous for consumptive invalids," so pervaded the resort that, in the words of Jonathan Grimball, "one can't divest oneself of the idea of consumptive disease even at meals."[39]

Those few springs visitors who did come for their health experienced mixed results. A sampling of people's reactions to the springs reveals that 45.7 percent felt a positive improvement in their health, 29.6 percent detected either a slight improvement, no change, or a general decline, and 24.7 percent reported negative effects from the waters.[40] Although a plurality of invalids sounded ringing praise for the power of the springs, a majority withheld an absolute endorsement. Far from being the universal cure promoted by their advocates, the springs failed to prove their medical efficacy in a significant number of cases. It is in the ambivalence of many visitors that the actual therapeutic value of the springs lies.

This group of individuals is remarkable because they neither condemned the springs outright nor lavished them with praise. Their reactions sound indecisive—they received some benefits from the waters but not as many as, or to the extent that, they had hoped. If the waters cured one complaint, they failed to alleviate, or exacerbated, another. But these invalids did not despair. They resolved to "drink the waters honestly, and with as little of a wry face as possible, until it has been of some service to me, or until I see that it will do me no good." Most agreed with Robert Mackay of North Carolina, who—despite his uncertainty about the strength of the waters and the length of his stay at Saratoga Springs—declared that "having come this distance I am determined to give [the waters] a fair chance." Letters home frequently informed family members that the correspondent was extending his or her stay until the waters completely cured the patient. Invalids remained at the springs and vowed to seek the cure "even if it carries me to the last of debt."[41]

Even after several unsuccessful weeks at various Virginia springs, Thomas Joynes still wrote, "I cannot withhold my belief in [the water's] efficacy in my own case." Joynes's statement negated the logical response to science in favor of his own personal faith in the waters. Perhaps the only factor that persuaded people like Joynes to persist in their therapies was the *hope* that the waters would effect a cure. Like the sick man in Herman Melville's novel *The Confidence-Man*, invalids needed to have faith in the cure. Though Melville's herb doctor sold a remedy other than mineral waters, his words applied to the springs: "'Hope is proportioned to confidence. How much confidence you give me, so much hope do I give to you.'" Patients at the springs needed such confidence to achieve a cure, regardless of the weight of scientific and medical evidence amassed by guidebook authors.[42]

The few detailed accounts of treatment at the springs that survive today are replete with references to the patients' "hope." Often people of deep religious faith, they believed that, despite their debilitating ailments, God and the mineral waters would provide relief, if not a cure. Confronted with extremely faint chances of curing their diseases and realizing that the mineral waters were a last medical option, many invalids turned, as did George W. Munford, to familiar religious tenets for solace. Munford wrote to his sister that "there is a balm in Gilead, there is a physician there, and I have only to do as the prophet bade the Heathen—cry aloud to the physician 'for perchance she sleepeth.'"[43] This faith, hope, and determination enabled women such as Abigail May to withstand the excruciating treatment of cold showers, physical therapy, and cold wraps on her crippled hand, all of which had only limited success, with a simple declaration: "I can and will bear it."[44]

Few people required such determination, however, because invalids composed a minority of total springs visitors. The presence of a few ill visitors reminded most guests of their trips' ostensible purpose while invoking a reputedly noble therapeutic past. Commentators frequently criticized the springs for cultivating a hypersocial atmosphere of competition and display when visitors should be attending to their health, but the jeremiads fell on deaf ears. One of the earliest and most damning critiques of the springs came from Washington Irving, who wrote in 1807 that visiting the springs "originally meant nothing more than a relief from pain and sickness." But social relaxation and increased popularity turned the springs into a "careless place of resort" where invalidism mattered little.[45] If the golden age of invalids had passed by 1807, it had enjoyed a short life. Only in the earliest days of springs history before 1800, when a handful of invalids drank and bathed out of wooden troughs, did the mineral waters serve solely as a retreat for the sick.

The vast majority of visitors went to the springs for pleasure. They came "for amusement . . . and for the preservation rather than the recovery of health." For these visitors, the chief attraction of the springs was "neither the mineral waters nor the salubrious climate, as these are mere excuses for the journey." Going to the springs served little medical purpose but a significant social one: at the springs people enjoyed "pleasure and dissipation." Epicures and "dissipated men," not invalids suffering from any of the ailments the springs could cure, gathered there because the waters possessed "the remarkable quality of preventing the malignant effects of repletion." Full from the excesses of springs society and life in general, springs visitors relieved their physical complaints and, more important, restored mental harmony. Nebulous complaints of general debility, not acute medical emergencies, brought people to the springs. Visitors agreed with the poet and social critic Clement Clarke Moore:

> *That idle, pamper'd wealth should gladly haste*
> *To try the traveller's miseries, may be right;*
> *The sickly palate needs some pungent taste*
> *To cure the nausea that mere sweets excite.*

The springs became exactly what early scientists and physicians feared most: a cure for self-diagnosed, minor ailments available to many Americans without proper medical supervision. Even worse, fashionable springs society had moved so far away from curing diseases by 1860 that one visitor called Saratoga Springs "a 'watering-place' where you drink the waters without having need to."[46]

Yet springs visitors, perhaps feeling guilty about the carefree life they led, were reluctant to embrace the new order of dissipation too readily. Although Thomas Gordon Pollock initially visited the springs to improve his health, he concluded reluctantly that "there is nothing for me to do but seek my own pleasure." Resigned, he admitted that "now I see that was the actual though not the ostensible object of my springs trip." Pollock needed the veneer of invalidism to justify his visit but quickly realized that he was merely providing a psychological buffer between his motivations and what he considered a legitimate reason to attend the springs. The springs, because of their reputation for curing disease, allowed people to go there without feeling or appearing frivolous. A springs vacation carried moral import even if in reality it possessed none.[47]

For Pollock and many other Americans, going to the springs meant much more than cultivating health. A social rather than a medical complaint drew people there. According to the ever-satirical James Kirke Paulding, "the most common infirmity which brings people to watering places . . . is the disease of I don't know what." The symptoms usually appeared generally in early July, especially among women. The typical lady

> begins to complain of the intolerable heat of the town, and fans herself violently for several days. If this don't do, she begins to complain of weakness and

want of appetite and spirits; and if this don't do, the Doctor is called in; who, to get rid of a patient whose disorder he knows to be incurable, recommends a trip to the springs. After this, if the lady is not permitted to go, the husband is voted an inhuman monster at all tea-parties.

According to Paulding, these women manipulated their husbands and fathers, claiming that "the trip is absolutely necessary for her health (which never was better) and positively the last time she will appear in those parts." Their insistence on the trip grew from ennui and a desire to escape the ordinary. Despite Paulding's apparent distaste for bored women, he admitted that the ailment affected men as well. Fashionable gentlemen labored "under a sort of anti-maladie du Pays. They have become tired of the same amusements, and the same people; they have paced up and down the same fashionable promenade till every body is tired of them." With no new targets for conversation or seduction at home, they set out for the springs, hoping to "find it easier to get new auditors than new ideas." More than simply expanding their social field, at the springs gentlemen relieved "the anxiety of worldly pursuits and vexations" that troubled so many in antebellum society. Going to the springs ameliorated social diseases as much as it aided medical complaints.[48]

Many of the men and women who traveled to the springs were like Mary Lee, who suffered from general debility: a shattered nervous system, "a horror of crowded places, [and] an indisposition to make the least effort." Yet she continued to travel to the Virginia springs in hopes of curing her elusive ailment. It seemed, wrote her father, that she suffered from "a restless anxiety which renders her unhappy and dissatisfied." Only traveling and socializing cured Lee's ailments. Many Americans shared Lee's nervousness, which physicians and medical practitioners attributed to overexcitedness. This illness eluded definition, and patients resisted physicians' efforts to cure them with traditional therapies. Instead, the springs offered a pleasant, relaxing alternative and held out the promise that life's troubles could be cured with a distasteful beverage and a few weeks at a bucolic, if somewhat rustic, hotel. Only patients knew what cured their "restless anxiety," and the springs' combination of healthy living and socializing provided exactly what most invalids sought: the possibility of "total regeneration" from life's pressures.[49]

Despite the claims of springs physicians, the waters cured few patients of acute diseases yet alleviated a significant number of less serious complaints.

People visited the springs because they believed the waters could cure their illnesses, regardless of medical opinion or the eventual outcome. Springs physicians' guidebooks and medical tracts popularized the cure while simultaneously democratizing it and diminishing the physicians' own influence. Armed with detailed instructions on the utility of different springs in various diseases and directions for the waters' uses, invalids no longer needed expert medical advice; they provided it themselves. But by placing an imprimatur on the waters, regular physicians legitimized the dubious medicinal value of mineral springs, transforming them into a curative agent, fashionable social rendezvous, and badge of American cultural accomplishment.

The grand hotels of the Virginia springs and Saratoga Springs would never have achieved the degree of popularity they did without the endorsement of medical efficacy, whether for real or imagined ailments. The medical assumptions, practices, and promotional tactics were remarkably similar at Northern and Southern springs. These common elements helped create a rejuvenative society at American springs that by the late 1840s possessed only a veneer of medical purpose. But the springs provided their greatest benefit to Americans as social centers. By designating themselves as places for relaxation, recuperation, and healing, the springs filled a crucial gap in American culture: they offered a social space for focusing solely on those pursuits without the obligations of society. Yet many visitors found the same status-seeking society of conspicuous consumption and social conflict that they experienced at home. Conflicts over class, status, respectability, and authority—the battles that springs physicians and scientists waged with a skeptical and independent public—moved from the medical to the social sphere.

Chapter 4

SOCIETY OF FASHION

The worldly, fashionable, dashing, good-for-nothing people of every state, who had rather suffer the martyrdom of a crowd, than endure the monotony of their own homes, and the stupid company of their own thoughts, flock to the Springs—not to enjoy the pleasures of society, or benefit by the qualities of the waters, but to exhibit their equipages and wardrobes, and to excite the admiration, or what is much more satisfactory, the envy of their fashionable competitors.

—WASHINGTON IRVING, "STYLE AT BALLSTON"

The greatest charm of this place . . . is the delightful society which is drawn together in every agreeable variety . . . the gay, the young, agreeable and handsome of both sexes, who come to the White Sulphur to see and be seen, to chat, laugh and dance, and to throw each his pebble on the giant heap of the general enjoyment.

—PEREGRINE PROLIX, *LETTERS DESCRIPTIVE OF THE VIRGINIA SPRINGS*

*M*any early nineteenth-century visitors to America's mineral springs found the setting and society less bucolic, carefree, and refined than guidebooks and springs promoters would have had them believe. Although some visitors agreed that the springs offered "an oasis of repose in the desert of our American hurry," contrarians insisted that at the springs "all is activity, bustle, and gaiety." Instead of finding the sylvan setting or therapeutic environment advertised by guidebooks, many visitors imagined themselves "in the most fashionable street, or publick walk, of a large city, rather than in a rural and sequestered village." The illusion of relaxation proved problematic for those, such as the Massachusetts scion Robert G. Shaw, who felt "the pressure of the times, care, anxiety & over work." Faced with "a severe indisposition last autumn [that] had so exhausted me that I was literally worked out," Shaw found it "necessary as well as my duty to make an effort to recruit" while at Saratoga Springs. Similarly, at the Virginia springs Clement Claiborne Clay remarked that "after the most oppressive correspondence of Washington, together with many other labors, it is a great relief to do nothing but what promotes physical health & enjoyment." People such as Shaw and Clay flocked to the resorts at Saratoga Springs and the Virginia springs because they were supposedly places where "life is leisurely . . . and business is amusement." As did so many others, Shaw desired "fresh air, rural scenes, exercise and exciting excursions, cheerful society, total relaxation from business." But once there he and his contemporaries discovered that Washington Irving's fashionable competition, with its constant display of fashion, gentility, and class status, dominated springs society more than attempts to relax and recuperate. Historians of English springs discovered this same social atmosphere more than a century earlier at Bath and Tunbridge Wells, which American resorts consciously imitated.[1] Fashionable competition and class anxiety existed at the springs from the start and only worsened as their popularity increased, social boundaries weakened, and class animosities intensified during the early republic and antebellum period.

The geographically and socially diverse springs visitors created a lively social setting that crossed boundaries of region and class. In general, Saratoga Springs claimed a much more disparate clientele than did its Southern rivals. According to one visitor, "There is a greater diversity of character at the Springs than I was prepared to find. There are representations of every grade in our society, except the very lowest." Another found Saratoga Springs' society "composed of all nations, sexes, ages, and complexions. . . . Such a diversified gallery of portraits I have never seen grouped together." Included in the multitude were "Invalids in search of health, maidens in search of husbands, widows disconsolate, young men inclined to matrimony, [and] politicians looking after votes or characters." What distinguished Saratoga Springs was its intensive social mixing across class lines. Saratoga Springs was "the resort of statesmen, of office holders and politicians; and the great, and would be great. With these are mingled gentlemen of the turf, connoisseurs of the odd trick, and the amateurs of poker. With these too will be found the exclusives of society, whether Presbyterian, Romanist, or Churchman; the fashionable lady, and the belle of high pretension." The resort, in one diarist's opinion, represented "the world in miniature." Only at Saratoga Springs could one see a variety of aspects of "the human face. For here we find people from almost all sections of the world, possessed of all their own particular notions, & acting out themselves. There is the High & low, the rich & poor, the Healthy & lame, & the white & the black, the Serious & the gay, the man of business & the man of leisure, as well as the idle and profligate."[2]

Few visitors bypassed the opportunity to comment on the heterogeneous nature of Saratoga Springs' society, which corresponded with the crowd at other Northern resorts. Because "the most wealthy, educated, and refined" Americans and foreigners favored Saratoga Springs, the resort "as a consequence . . . attract[s] also those chevaliers who prey upon society, wherever it is accessible, lavish in its expenditure, and free in its amusements." Only at Saratoga Springs could one "see the vulgar and genteel jumbled together without distinction." No other watering place afforded a similar opportunity to see the broadest possible spectrum of American society. One New York newspaper columnist differentiated Saratoga Springs' visitors into four distinct classes: the real invalids, recognizable by "their gloomy air and cadaverous cheeks"; the fashionables— "those who go to Saratoga to kill time, and make a wake in the water"; the "busters . . . keen blades from the cities, who come out here not merely to kill time, but themselves also"; and the politicians trolling for votes. Except for "the small shopkeeper and mere labourer, every other class" of respectable society was represented at Saratoga Springs. Even those whose means failed to meet the costs of high society at Saratoga Springs' finer hotels could, "by the moderate payment of two dollars a day, . . . be seated at the same table, and often side by side, with the first families of the country." These visiting privileges extended to walking the hotel piazza, lounging in the drawing room, and dancing at balls and hops. Less wealthy and fashionable visitors could "thus, for the week or month . . . stay at Saratoga, [and] . . . enjoy all the advantages which their position would make inaccessible to them at home." These "ill-bred and obscure" visitors, "who, perhaps, by some lucky turn of trade, had got together a sufficient number of dollars for their summer amusement, without ever before having had the leisure or the means to play gentility," tarnished Saratoga Springs' luster for the select few. New money was not welcome at the springs.[3]

But even if Saratoga Springs' liberal access resulted in "much less display of pomp + wealth" than some expected, the elite still managed to elevate themselves from the masses. Hotels that aspired to a particularly distinguished clientele "displayed no small tact in singling out the fashionable." When dust from the stagecoach ride obscured the clothing of potential guests, hotel proprietors studied other signifiers of a wealthy patron: "a 'hair trunk' being seen in the baggage boot has proven fatal to several parties." The guests proved an even better deterrent to social pretenders. Those who were "inaccessible by every means as haughty, high-minded and proud" did little to encourage congenial relations between the middle and upper classes. Social segregation at the springs seemed perfectly natural. People fell "into a particular class; not one formed by any arbitrary rule, but as they are pleased to rank themselves with each other." The very idea that class lines might be crossed, that any "mutual interest could be felt by a multitude of people who had come together to drink water," appeared "preposterous" to one essayist. Despite its socially mixed population, class boundaries remained distinct, if blurred, at Saratoga Springs.[4]

Such was not the case at the Virginia springs, where a more homogeneous population and stricter behavioral code enforced social discipline. Virginians still claimed that "there is no place one may see more of human character in a short time" than at the Virginia springs. Some resorts, such as the Fauquier White Sulphur Springs, located between Richmond and Washington near a rail line, attracted a social mixture similar to that at Saratoga Springs: "Health and disease, fashion and ungentility, beauty and ugliness, old maids and maidens, little girls, boys, and stripling youths, fathers and grandmothers, the 'lately engaged,' and 'newly married,' widows and widowers, lawyers, divines, doctors, quack-dentists, writing-masters, artists and horse-jockies, merchants, students, clerks, and fops, are each represented at Fauquier." But most of the Virginia springs lay west of the Blue Ridge and Allegheny Mountains and proved harder for the less affluent to reach. Just the time required to travel to the springs, usually several days to a week, prevented those without extended leisure time from reaching the springs. Instead of drawing the mixed-class crowd that frequented Saratoga Springs, the Virginia springs' antebellum guests included more than one president, "ladies of fashion and belles from the principal cities—foreign ministers—members of the cabinet, senators—and representatives, prominent judges—officers of the army and navy, and polished private gentlemen."[5]

Terms like "elegant and select," "the most genteel and orderly," "highly respectable," "very select and agreeable," and "the most elegant + refined of the Southern Country" described visitors to the Virginia springs. Because of the highly stratified structure of Southern society, with its emphasis on the gentleman-planter, the Virginia springs attracted a much more exclusive clientele than Saratoga Springs. Typical visitors were "people of the first rank in the United States; they are people of fashion, as well as great wealth; they are mostly from the seaports and great towns." Resorts such as Salt Sulphur Springs boasted of their exclusivity: at no other spring was the society "more select, more charming, more intellectual, than it is at the Salt Sulphur." But the acknowledged leader in exclusivity and social prestige was White Sulphur Springs, which bore "the title of 'The Queen of Springs.'" In the early 1850s, one guidebook author reported that "To say that all the *elite* of the nation are annually seen here would not be true; but to say that a large portion of them, and of the learning, wit, beauty, elegance and fashion of the States is here assembled, is certainly no exaggeration." What set places such as White Sulphur Springs apart was their ability to distance people from the less genteel masses of antebellum society and, unlike at Saratoga Springs, to allow the so-called elite to "luxuriate in all the consciousness of superiority!"[6]

The homogeneity of the Virginia springs encouraged carefree socializing that seemed foolhardy at Saratoga Springs. Because of the resorts' small size and narrow social spectrum, at the Virginia springs, "there is an entire feeling of equality, a relinquishment of formality, a republican simplicity of manners, a reciprocity of kind, courteous, and unpretending civility, that renders the places peculiarly agreeable." Even at some of the smaller Virginia springs the company was "very select, + all of us *at home* with each other." Saratoga Springs' problem, according to one Virginia spring proprietor, stemmed from its accessibility "by railroads to persons in every condition of life, and at a trifling expense." Because of this easy access, "the mass of visiters [sic] is of course composed of all sorts of people. The knowledge of this fact makes men distrustful of each other's standing, and shy and reserved."

This situation lacked "the enchanting ease of manner, dignity of deportment, and air of true gentility, founded on benevolence and forgetfulness of self, which distinguishes Nature's gentleman from the mere cockney and pretender," all qualities that prevailed at the Virginia springs. It was a distinctive "calm repose, that freedom from restraint, that omission of conventional usages, which render the society of our Virginia Springs so delightful." Saratoga Springs' boosters admitted that "men of different degrees of wealth, of station, and of information, are now constantly brought together on certain terms of equality," but those boosters saw such social interaction as a positive quality. They saw the potential for improvement, rather than social degeneration, in the mixing of classes. As one Northern guidebook author noted, "The mere superiority of wealth in a railroad car or steamboat is of no avail for the time being, and reciprocal kindness becomes as necessary as it is unavoidable. Persons are here thrown together who otherwise might never meet; and while points of difference are rubbed off in the crowd, much of good, much that is worthy of imitation, is soon observed and speedily adopted." Whereas Southern promoters and elite visitors preferred social stability and exclusivity, some Northern promoters and a smaller number of visitors lauded the beneficial possibilities of social mixing. Even though people made "the most delightful and lasting intimacies," they still adhered to class boundaries in their daily machinations.[7]

All agreed that the society at both Saratoga Springs and the Virginia springs divided along class lines. The fact that some people journeyed together in groups and continued to "associate together + dance together, which impairs the sociability of the drawing rooms," only exacerbated the sense of exclusiveness that some springs visitors felt. These parties found it fashionable "to be rather exclusive, bringing gentlemen enough with the party to monopolise all the belles belonging to it," thus preventing any mixing with unknown or undesirable persons. But overflowing hotels and crowded ballrooms forced visitors to "imperceptibly form different social parties."[8] This exclusivity hindered the ability of upper-class Americans to meet a large number of their social equals and to form a national elite.

Part of the problem of exclusivity arose from the system of introductions that dominated springs society. Decorum dictated that one not strike up a conversation or press an acquaintance unless the two parties had first been properly introduced. One social critic, Nathaniel Parker Willis, even proposed a system of introductions to ease the entrance of newcomers into Saratoga Springs society. His Committee of Management would be staffed by the leading residents of a hotel, who would oversee the introductions of guests to one another while ensuring that social mixing occurred only within established class boundaries. "Any stranger who had tolerable tact and good manners . . . would find no difficulty in getting on" under Willis's system. But even those, such as the young Virginia woman who received, "without seeking them, many introductions," felt reluctant to press "them to intimacy." Social organizers at English spas overcame this hindrance by developing a strict schedule of activities that forced people to interact, but only if they met the stringent admission requirements of polite society. Beau Nash, the Master of Ceremonies (his actual title) at Bath, introduced wallflowers to other members of the assemblage. The highly ordered nature of English spas ensured congeniality.[9]

Americans lacked this kind of system, but the forced isolation at the more remote Virginia springs made it "very easy however to find people to talk to," wrote J. Mackay, "as many like myself . . . have no friends and it is inconvenient to be too reserved." This openness and congeniality made the Virginia springs "as sociable a place as you can conceive. Every body knows every body + no introductions are needed." But many people found they knew only a portion of their fellow visitors at best and needed the help of introductions. At most of the springs "a regular system of visiting from Cabin to Cabin" encouraged people to meet each other. The system worked because people felt at ease among their social equals without fearing the ignoble motives of social pretenders. In addition, "what adds very much to the pleasure of the new acquaintances we make is the apparent disposition of all to make the time of each other pleasant and agreeable." After just twelve days at White Sulphur Springs, John Rossen had "a good many acquaintances, some of them feel to us more like old friends, than new acquaintances." Even a self-described "saturnine and unsocial" visitor admitted that "the influence of the lively and brilliant company around has penetrated even my triple folds of apathy, indolence and debility and for the last two weeks I have been so metamorphosed that I hardly know myself and certainly would not be recognized by any sober minded friend."[10]

More than simply an enjoyable excursion that changed one's mood, a trip to the springs was a social statement, an expression of one's class identity. Going to the nation's mineral water resorts marked one as part of a social elite or at least an aspiring member of that group. But shaking hands, bowing and curtsying, exchanging pleasantries, and meeting new people composed only a small part of the springs' attraction to tourists. Mineral springs in both Virginia and New York State belonged to a growing touring impulse in mid-nineteenth-century America that directly imitated English models. The sons of the British aristocracy began peregrinating around Europe in the mid-eighteenth century in search of worldly experience, culture, and dalliances not permitted at home. In an effort to equal their cultural cousins, wealthy Americans joined the European Grand Tour after the end of the Napoleonic Wars in 1815 and eventually created their own version in the United States. Spurred by an interest in rural landscapes and eased along their journey by improved transportation networks, by the 1820s and 1830s more and more Americans embarked on extended summer tours to landmarks like Niagara Falls, the Hudson River valley, and the mineral springs. As one commentator wrote, "Summer in the United States is the season for travel, and it is then when all, whom inclination may lead and convenience will permit, are in motion for some quarter where health and recreation are the chief attractions for the journey; or where fashion has erected [its] temple." Americans toured even "in spite of the inconveniences extended upon collecting together in large numbers, during a season when the heat is truly oppressive." During the summer months, travelers met "with crowded stages, crowded hotels and boarding houses, crowded steam boats, and crowded drawing rooms. You see people tormenting themselves by parading in all the bondage of ceremony and full-dress amidst glare and dust, when you would naturally suppose that a cool nook in the forest, and a dress of easy and unrestrained negligence would be among the necessaries of life for the time being." Only fashion, "the goddess who can make an Oasis in every desert," could cause a phenomenon, in which "from June to September, all parts of the country pour forth their children, on the pilgrimage of fashion." People journeyed great distances and endured numerous hardships "for the sake of spending a week or two among the fashionable to see & be seen."[11]

As an integral component of the new travel impulse, each mineral spring, and especially its visitors, wanted to believe that its society surpassed all others in fashion and cultural sophistication, both signs of upper-class status. For the most part, visitors agreed. In 1813 Saratoga Springs exceeded, in one visitor's opinion, "anything for gaiety and dissipation of any establishment or watering place I have visited." Just a few years earlier Elkanah Watson had described a gathering in nearby Ballston Spa, New York, of over one hundred men and women "principally moving in the walk of high

Life." This scene was a marked contrast to his visit fifteen years earlier, in the late eighteenth century, when Watson declared that "all is rudeness + barbarism—the accommodations only fit for Indians." Many Northern travelers doubted the sophistication and quality of accommodations at Southern springs once their own region's leading spring had attained respectability. But James Kirke Paulding allayed their fears "that there is nothing refined to the south of the Schuylkill, and no watering-place worth visiting." In 1816 he found Berkeley Springs, Virginia, "as gay, as fashionable, and far more delightfully situated than any I have ever visited." The only question for travelers seemed to be how "those who have means and leisure should tear themselves away after a few days' enjoyment."[12]

This fashionable society drew the likes of the fictional Frank Meriwether, a Southern planter depicted in John Pendleton Kennedy's 1831 novel *Swallow Barn*, who journeyed to the springs late each summer "for the crowds that resort there for the same reason which operates upon him": escaping the unhealthy summer weather in the Tidewater and "for the opportunity this concourse affords him for discussion of opinions." Meriwether and his fellow "votaries of pleasure are willing to be crushed to death, to obtain a chance of laying their offerings on the shrine that fashion has set up." Southerners withstood overcrowding, poor food, and filthy rooms "just to get a glimpse of gay life at the great watering-place of Virginia." The desire or "total possession" of many fashionable Americans to visit the springs reminded one visitor to White Sulphur Springs of "nothing short of the intense feeling of the Hebrews at Jerusalem." Saratoga Springs proved equally popular as "*fashion*," wrote one visitor, makes "*some* of us restless to get into a larger crowd."[13] Dissipation, excess, fashion, and competition gave the springs their vitality. Socially conscious Americans felt absolutely obligated to attend the year's premier social gathering despite the rustic conditions in the South or the interclass social mixing at Saratoga Springs because doing so marked them as members of the fashionable elite.

But the fashion that popularized the springs also transformed them in ways that dismayed the elite. Resorts that once catered to an exclusive clientele of a few hundred visitors soon attracted thousands of guests from across the social spectrum. By 1839 the springs resembled "a general muster, under the banner of folly, to drive care and common sense out of the field." Saratoga Springs seemed particularly prone to the dangers of increased popularity. "For a time the 'select' had it all to themselves," wrote a British traveler, "but by-and-by 'everybody' began to resort to it, and on 'everybody' making his appearance the 'select' began to drop off, and what was once very genteel is now running the risk of becoming exceedingly vulgar." During the 1850s, the crowds had grown to the point that an American social critic echoed his British counterparts in lamenting that "Everybody goes to Saratoga now. . . . Merchants, shop-keepers, and tradesmen, with their wives and daughters, all mixed up together, into a kind of hodge-podge. It used to be a fashionable place of resort—but people that think any thing of themselves . . . don't go there now." Advised that their watchmaker attended the springs, one family decided to avoid Saratoga Springs that year, declaring that "genteel people will have to stay away, then, that's all." This belief—that a socially inferior and undesirable clientele was invading the springs—was the same criticism that English commentators leveled against their nation's spas at the turn of the eighteenth century. The problem was worse in early America, where, as historian Michael Zuckerman has suggested, society was too closely drawn to allow an aristocracy to develop. Repeated attempts by an insecure elite to establish its social superiority failed in the mixed society at the early nineteenth-century springs. But fashion, despite such criticism, continued to send its throng toward English and American springs each summer; the crowds grew rather than decreased. The very "uniformity" of fashion was liberating. "By its magic influence on dress and demeanor, it reduces grace and deformity, beauty and ugliness, youth and age, activity and decrepitude, talent and stupidity, to a perfect level. All are alike—all look alike, act alike, talk alike, feel alike, think alike, and constitute as it were one universal identity."[14] Fashion, by making everyone similar, allowed imitators to infiltrate the upper reaches of society. What they found was a constant display of manners, pretensions, and social status.

"Life at the springs is a perpetual festival. The people dance and drink—drink and dance,—rising early to do the one, and sitting up late to perform the other." Most visitors agreed with this guidebook description of daily life at the springs: "Amusement in all Shapes, & in high Degrees, are constantly taking Place" at both Saratoga Springs and its Virginia rivals. The nature of these amusements, a mixture of "killing *Time*—that arch enemy" and social display, shaped springs society. The wealthy Americans who visited the springs enjoyed such an abundance of leisure time that they sought ways to "kill" it. Entertainments at the springs were "continually brought forward to amuse & to pick your pockets," in pursuit of the goal of disposing of leisure time. But if these leisure pursuits developed into "a strange succession of agreeable nothings, to which we become more attached than can be well imagined at the outset," it was because they held social meaning. Everyday activities at the springs were more than simple ways to pass the day; they constituted the social competition between and display among classes that lay at the core of springs society. A "competitive community" striving for social status existed at both Saratoga Springs and the Virginia springs.[15]

The daily round began early in both springs regions. One visitor to Saratoga Springs was astonished to look out his window at dawn "to see the crowded groups assembled around, + hastening to Congress Spring," located just a few hundred feet from Saratoga Springs' largest hotels. A "constant stream of visitors flowing down the avenues" toward the fountain led one commentator to estimate that nearly all of Saratoga Springs' visitors "drink this water every morning." The day at the Virginia springs began similarly: the visitors "all turn out from their little burrows, meet in the public walks, and go down to the spring." For slow risers or those who wished to avoid the crowd, "a maid with a pitcher to carry the cooling draught to some sleeping beauty" made the rounds of the cottage rows, and some wealthier guests sent their personal slaves to fetch the water.[16]

Even at this early hour, when dew covered the grass and a light fog often obscured the view, fashion ruled. Visitors dressed simply, many "enveloped in shawls and surtouts" or "the primitive styles of *dishabille*." Some chose to display at least a touch of fashion by adding to their "loose morning robes . . . a kind of fringed hood of crochet work" over their heads. Other ladies appeared "nice and white and fresh looking, wearing all manner of head gear," a style matched by men "in every sort of summer wear." The healthy effects of the water drew only a part of the early morning drinkers, however. Many came to "walk among the multitudes" in the hour before breakfast "when the company all gather" at the spring. It was a "time for observation—where you may learn the news, survey the new comers; and where diffident men take stolen glances at beauty." Saratoga Springs' guests enjoyed walks about the manicured lawns of Congress Park "hailing old acquaintances" and making new ones. Some found drinking the waters so early in the morning "not fashionable . . . indeed vulgar." But the majority of visitors preferred to wander around the park, listen to the bands playing operas and open airs until eight A.M., and admire others' equipages.[17]

Even at this early hour, just getting a glass of water to drink involved a social competition. In both springs regions, "dipper boys" served water from long-handled sticks with attached cups. Slaves dipped the water at the Virginia springs, whereas young boys staffed the rail around Saratoga Springs' fountains, in many cases driving "a thriving trade" by charging—or coercing—a tip of one cent per glass. The dipper boys, however, distinguished the rich from the less well-to-do: "An imposing exterior is sure to procure for its possessor their services, while individuals less richly attired, or whose physiognomy indicate[s] a less liberal disposition, are often compelled to wait till it is more convenient to attend to their wants." The drinkers themselves created rivalries at the springs to "vie with each other [as to] which will swallow the most water." Staid old gentlemen and polite ladies seemed "intent upon putting an end to the Spring" and outdoing each other by draining as many as twelve glasses a morning. While doctors recommended four to six glasses at maximum, many visitors agreed that "tis somewhat wonderful to see howe [sic] much of this water can be drank without injury."[18] For some, the amount of water one could drink provided a mark of distinction.

Breakfast, the next event on the regular social calendar, paled in comparison with other meals in terms of fashion and social rivalry. Hours were flexible, with breakfast served from eight to ten "for those who dislike early rising." Enough diners assembled on the hotel portico by 7:30 to necessitate an ordered system of bell ringing to instruct guests to enter the dining room and take their seats, sometimes at a place card to prevent "rushing and crowding." Most guests attended but eschewed formal attire, for at breakfast "you may wear anything and not appear singular in such a crowd, from a ninepence calico wrapper, with the hair plain on the face up to silks + curls." One English visitor took little note of the costume or fare but was astounded by the "rapidity with which [breakfast] is dispatched" at Saratoga Springs. Slow eaters took fifteen minutes to consume their victuals, whereas the speedy needed a mere five minutes to devour breakfast. Businessmen in America's great cities needed to down their meal quickly to get on with the day's affairs, but visitors to the springs, "with the entire day before them, and nothing whatever to do," ate with the same haste as counting-house clerks. Few chewed thoroughly, and nine of ten diners rose from their chairs before finishing the meal "with the last mouthful still unswallowed, and dispose of it gradually as they walk along." Refined visitors such as James Kirke Paulding objected to this practice; he preferred "to masticate before I swallow my victuals." According to one English traveler, "Business may have originated, but it cannot always excuse the practice of fast eating; and the inmates of [the springs] were in perfect idleness."[19] At the springs Americans ate as if

Congress Hall piazza, ca. 1830. These hotel porches, often hundreds of feet long and as much as twenty feet deep, served as Saratoga Springs' social gathering places and stages. Men and women could interact freely in this public sphere. Courtesy of the Saratoga Room, Saratoga Springs Public Library.

they were late for an important meeting or had a train to catch, not as if they were on vacation. In so doing, they demonstrated a lack of refinement and true elite status.

The time after breakfast, because it preceded few major social events, often assumed a slower pace. Yet the variety of activities was astounding: lounging, promenading, taking rural walks, dancing, performing music or plays, reading, conversing casually or paying formal visits, playing cards, billiards, or nine pins, and drinking from various springs occupied most of the morning at both Saratoga Springs and the Virginia springs. But even with this diversity of amusements, visitors still searched for ways to "pass the day" or "dispose an hour or more of lingering time" during the "listless" period before dinner. The best most visitors could do was sit on the wide hotel piazzas and display "the elegance of their morning costume."[20]

In the meantime, springs visitors readied themselves for the next milestone on the social racecourse—dinner. The meal was usually served between one and three in the afternoon, but crowds gathered well ahead of time. As she arrived at White Sulphur Springs, Mary Hagner, who published under the pseudonym Mark Pencil, witnessed the company "going to dinner, and all the walks and avenues leading from the different cabins were streaming with lively forms." A band played on the hotel's porch while the prospective diners gathered. One Saratoga Springs visitor compared the group assembled outside the dining room, in parlors, and on piazzas with "a resuscitated crowd, like an ant-hill into which a mischievous boy, or an equally mischievous professor of natural history, has thrust a stick." Guests cast nervous glances at the dining room windows, hoping to beat the rush into dinner. Even though the doors remained locked, some ladies and gentlemen entered via passageways from their private rooms: "The *ignóbile vulgus,* in the interior colonnade, were kept out until the ladies and those accompanying them were seated." But once the doors opened, "in rushed, helter skelter, the eager crowd." Some "pounced" on their seats, while others scrambled about, in the era before placecards, looking for spots. It seemed that "in the *hurry scurry* of entering . . . some were leaping in at the windows."[21]

Various springs attempted to moderate the chaos by instituting a system of assigned seating. Placecards were used sporadically at Saratoga Springs, but almost every Virginia spring adopted the system. Writers agreed that the placecard system "cannot be too much commended" because it prevented the "rushing and crowding" that had previously characterized dinner. Some of the smaller Virginia springs carried the system even further by establishing a seniority system for seating similar to the model adopted at some English spas. Those newly arrived at the hotel sat at the far end of the table, whereas veterans sat farther up toward the head, where the resort's proprietor presided.[22] Proprietors hoped that the system would encourage people to develop relationships with those around them and to establish some measure of social stability. But even this innovation failed to eradicate the hectic, competitive scene at the dinner table.

Above all, dining was done on a grand scale. Tables stretched across long rooms used for balls in the evenings. Sometimes hotels crammed extra seats in by combining "three long Tables spread as long as an immense room will admit of." Diners at the Sweet Springs in 1839 found themselves crowded into a room "where over two hundred persons were struggling for elbow room at two tables only large enough for half that number." Amidst these cramped conditions, many questioned the pretense of elegance. English émigré George Featherstonhaugh could not describe "the noise, the confusion incident to a grand bolting operation conducted by three hundred

American performers" dining at White Sulphur Springs. "Almost every man at table," it seemed to Featherstonhaugh, "considered himself at job-work against time, stuffing sausages and whatever else he could cram into his throat." As at the day's earlier meals, people ate "as if they had not a moment to lose." One diner devoured his meal in eight minutes, most of the table finished within twelve, and after twenty minutes only Northern diarist C. O. Lyde remained at his table at White Sulphur Springs.[23] If the springs supposedly represented the finest in American society, then gentlemen like Featherstonhaugh and Lyde expected that table manners there would be impeccable and in keeping with the standards of elite Anglo-American culture.

But once waiters served the food, "such a clatter of dishes and a noise of knives and forks arose, mingled with a chorus of human voices, some commanding, others supplicating the waiters, as I had never heard before." Waiters rushed to and fro, occasionally crashing into each other, adding the discord of "a smash of crockery or crystal" to the cacophony. "The confusion of tongues, like the sound of many waters; the enormous consumption of food; the mingled demands for more; the cloud of black waiters passing down the sides of immense tables; the hungry, eager faces seated at them," formed, for one observer, "a most amusing subject for contemplation." Diners such as James Silk Buckingham considered the experience less comical: "The contest for the dishes is a perfect scramble; the noise and clatter of the waiters and their wares is absolutely deafening." Another writer compared the scene at Saratoga Springs with dining "Amid a din, 't would rival Babel."[24]

Many visitors attributed the confusion to the "crowd of undisciplined negro waiters" that ran the dining rooms at Northern and Southern springs. Diners in Virginia encountered black waiters carrying "dishes as if they were mulatto harmony instruments, and every one is in momentary dread of being overwhelmed with an avalanche of victuals." At Saratoga Springs "nothing can be seen, but waiter bumping against waiter, and dish rattling against dish." Yet visitors indicated that waiters delivered the food with some skill, and guests referred to serving dishes as "mulatto harmony instruments." This latter comment equates waiting tables with slaves' purported natural musical talents, a backhanded recognition of the black waiters' abilities. Even so, the Virginia springs' black waiters remained in the background as part of the romantic landscape. Saratoga Springs' African American waiters, however, achieved a high level of accomplishment and status. The thirty "colored men servants (not slaves)" at one hotel worked with "precision and order" in bringing food to the table. Interestingly, the author differentiated the term "servant," which was used as a synonym for "slave" in the South, from the latter, more blunt, term. Emphasizing that the waiters were servants, not slaves, demonstrated the author's politics and conferred a degree of social status, however servile, on Saratoga Springs' free black waiters. This high opinion of the waiters was not isolated. A British visitor described how at the United States Hotel, Saratoga Springs' largest and most prestigious establishment, 150 "negroes" waited on 600 diners, "commanded by a black maitre d'hôtel." Acknowledging that such an undertaking was "no trifling task," the visitor recognized the skill of the waiters who, "dressed in spotless white jackets, extend their hands over the [platter] covers, and, at a signal from their chief, stationed in the center of the saloons, remove them simultaneously." Even amidst the clatter of cutlery and din of conversation, as the "black troops are rushing hither and thither in hot haste, at the bidding of impetuous Southerners or less irascible Northerners," the head waiter maintained his command. "At a clap of his hands [the waiters] fall into their places, and at another all the dishes are removed." These precise maneuvers continued throughout each course of the meal. Although Virginian Jane Caroline North found the "air" of Saratoga Springs' black waiters "truly disagreeable" because of their relaxed manner around whites, even she admitted that they were efficient in their work and "very civil." The precise orders and fashionable, handsome dress of "*Mr.* Maurice," the black headwaiter, further disturbed North. By italicizing the headwaiter's title, North expressed her surprise that an African American held a position of such responsibility. Even more shocking was the social inversion that occurred at Saratoga Springs: Southern planters, used to calling their slaves, regardless of age, by first names, suddenly found themselves using titles of respect for members of a race they considered inferior and upon whom they now depended for service without the threat of violence. Southerners like North noted their discomfort with a situation where "the blacks are supreme." Ultimately, Southern reservations about the position of Saratoga Springs' black waiters mattered little. By 1850 African American waiters proved so adept that they dominated the profession in Saratoga Springs, where few whites served as waiters.[25]

Holding positions as waiters conferred a notable power on African Americans at the springs. In 1851 the head waiter at Saratoga Springs' colossal United States Hotel, Mason Morris, dispensed prize seats to guests with a quick "look over his list" of tables. "In such cases he would be compensated."

Union Hall dining room. African Americans dominated the waiting trade at Saratoga Springs, serving hundreds of diners at one sitting. From *Frank Leslie's Illustrated Newspaper*, 9 July 1864. Courtesy of the Saratoga Room, Saratoga Springs Public Library.

This "compensation" extended to the waiters, who often entered the dining room before the general public "to take possession of the most desirable places at the table" by either sitting in a chair or tilting it upward against the table for their patron. Likewise, at the Virginia springs waiters, who were described as "servants" but were almost exclusively enslaved African Americans, entered the dining room fifteen minutes before the diners and carved meats for those astute enough to realize that "without *bribing* a servant to attend to you particularly you can get no attendance except by accident." Few wanted to risk the fate of the diner who "civilly requested" various foodstuffs three times only to go unfed for forty-five minutes. He failed to realize that each of the waiters "had been bribed to wait on particular gentlemen; and if I had screamed at them loud enough to rupture a blood vessel, the knaves would have been as deaf as adders." Here was one of the few settings in Southern life where a black could refuse to serve a white or could demand payment for the privilege and not fear reprisal. The waiters exercised such a degree of power that guests at the Virginia springs soon realized that "bribery furnishes you with the best of what is to be got, and shifts the fighting at meals from the guests to their servants." Waiters were even known to engage in fistfights in the kitchens to secure a prized dish such as an apple pie for their favored grafter. This arrangement allowed guests to project an air of refinement while still getting the food and service they wanted. But to reach this compromise, white guests had to acknowledge the power of the black waiters and to accept their terms of service. Many Southern planters had often made these negotiations with their slaves, but never in the direct, monetary exchange of the Virginia springs. Even at Saratoga Springs, a Northern town frequented by whites who were less enthusiastic about slavery, guests contended with waiters who were

> *Impelled by eager thought of gain*
> *Each choicer viand to obtain,*
> *For those who wisely pay them best,*
> *But laugh and jeer at all the rest.*

Northern whites also had to negotiate with African Americans for service at the springs. Guests in both regions found the system troublesome enough to protest the bribing system. So the waiters "soon hit upon a compromise of their own" that maintained their position, "which was to take the money without rendering the *quid pro quo.*" Even so, John H. B. Latrobe concisely described the mode of living at the springs: "Bribe high, live high."[26]

Bribing had little effect on the quality of food at the springs. Some visitors enjoyed "fine eating," whereas others termed the fare "abominable." Whether the springs were "the great rendez-vous for all gastronomers" or a place that offered "no temptation to the epicure" mattered little. Social display and competition dominated the dining hour. Meals were an opportunity to show off good manners, or the lack thereof, and the latest styles. As early as 1805, Elkanah Watson described the crowd at the fledgling resort at Ballston Spa, New York, behaving "in the true french stile [*sic*] of *sans souci.*" The company included "a rich variety" of guests "and an unusual display of servants in attendance, clad in elegance." Years later at White Sulphur Springs, Roberta P. Burwell witnessed ladies wearing "as much finery as [they] choose to pack on" at the dinner table. Her own "elegant + abundant wardrobe" enabled her "to go out into the world a little."[27]

But Watson and Burwell described an increasingly rare scene. Despite the springs' reputations for high style, many visitors called them places where "there is no ceremony and little politeness observed," especially at meals.

The Englishman Patrick Shirreff felt that the party at Saratoga Springs "displayed few symptoms of refinement." A gentleman on the opposite side of Shirreff's table "deliberately folded up the sleeves of his coat before commencing dinner, planted both elbows on the table, and swallowed his food voraciously, without once looking to the right or left." Even at the supposedly refined White Sulphur Springs, "a man forgot himself so far as to walk across the table for something he wanted." John H. B. Latrobe declared, "'Look sharper, eat fast, and forget good manners,' this is the motto of the dinner room at the White Sulphur." The same was true for Saratoga Springs, where a critic decreed that "elegance of manners in such a scene as this is quite out of the question." Another wondered at the way that the "high and mighty Lords of Creations, as they call themselves—will pick their teeth and stare confidently in your face" during meals. Too many springs visitors had not yet learned proper manners and detracted from the refined atmosphere that polite guests preferred. Because the springs attracted Americans from various classes and regions, the standards of cosmopolitan, old-money guests were not necessarily met by nouveau riche Mississippi planters or Northern land speculators. Attended by people of disparate class backgrounds and varied levels of refinement, dinner time at the springs seemed to resemble

A scene of strife and empty show,
   Which folks there daily undergo,
Because, where people all convene,
   One best may see, and can be seen.

The show continued long into the afternoon. Dinner had served "as a sort of isthmus, uniting the freshness and brilliancy of the morning with the gayety of the evening." Revelers made the transition with little delay, returning to a favorite morning amusement—riding through the countryside after a short rest and wardrobe change. Carriage rides and picnics in Virginia became more than leisurely rambles; they provided elaborate entertainment. Hired stages and formal processions on horseback and in carriages ended with picnics where "the table was sparkling with wine and wit." Hours later, the typical party returned, "singing songs, duets, relating anecdotes, in fact we were as excited a set of persons as you would wish to see." When an observor noted, "We went forth in gallant style, and only wanted the hawkers, to have imagined ourselves in the reign of Queen Elizabeth on a Holyrood day," he revealed the cultural aspirations and aristocratic tendencies of those at the Virginia springs.[28]

Likewise, Saratoga Springs' denizens assembled their carriages in front of the hotel piazzas along Broadway, which were "crowded with guests" outside the hotels for daily excursions. The ride itself might prove boring, "but then it is a distinction here to ride out in one's own carriage when so many stand to gaze and admire, and envy the fortunate ones who ride, while they must go on foot." The scantily concealed social competition "bore more the appearance of a race course, than any thing I can compare it to." Display, not the destination, was the object. Long excursions and even overnight trips to historic and romantic spots such as Lake George or the Revolutionary War battlefields at Old Saratoga paled in comparison to the most popular destination. At Saratoga Springs, "there is but one drive: every body goes to the lake." But without the "delightful and extensive prospect" of a place like Warm Springs, Virginia, Saratoga Springs' guests had "nothing very delightful in scenery to make them attractive." Instead, people went to the lake to sit on the porch of the hotels that dotted its shore and to sip sherry cobblers "not certainly because they needed sustenation of any sort, but from very idleness." The contrast of a peaceful setting, where "the light is tender, the air is soft, and the lapping of the water upon the pebbly shore," to the "city gala" at the hotels enchanted many visitors. The "monotonous banks" of Saratoga Lake provided the respite from the hectic pace of resort life. It constituted a vacation from the vacation.[29]

Most guests needed to get away from the village not only because of its hectic lifestyle but also because of their hotels' rudimentary accommodations. Saratoga Springs' cramped hotels forced people into public spaces, whereas Virginia's confining cabin interiors compelled people "to seek the common room, to get out of their own . . . wretched dog-holes." The design of a single room that served as both bedroom and parlor demonstrated the proprietors' "no little ingenuity in promoting social intercourse." In early national and antebellum society, where "we Americans are not yet in that pure state of Parisian innocence that we can visit a lady in her bedroom, without considerable—trepidation," social meetings were pushed out of the cabins and onto the lawns or into the resort's public rooms, where visitors conducted "the main *life* at the Springs." Located in either the central hotel building or the outlying dining room or ballroom buildings, the parlors provided "large rooms where ladies and gentlemen can meet to exhibit themselves before dinner." Saratoga Springs' hotels reserved their first floors for a combination of dining rooms, ballrooms, and parlors. To maximize space, hotels divided the rooms with "folding doors which may be thrown open exhibiting a long and splendid area which may [be] used for dining [and] balls." Usually the chairs and tables from dinner had to be cleared from the multipurpose room before the evening's festivities could begin. Resorts in both regions featured physical structures that forced guests into the public sphere and encouraged easy socializing. Furnished with "carpeting, curtained, with two fine mirrors, the piano, tables and chairs," these parlors and ballrooms contained "a never ceasing scene of stile [sic], commotion, display + enjoyment."[30]

In the hotels' public spaces, "the gentlemen lounge about the balconies, smoking cigars, while the ladies within read, net [sic] purses, or endeavor to extract music from a jingling piano." Together, men and women played games such as checkers and backgammon and occasionally created "Tableaux Vivants" depicting a Turkish slave market, prison inmates, Lady of the Lake, Taking the Veil, or scenes from Hamlet. Plays and farces, acrobatics, ventriloquism, magic tricks, and public lectures also amused the parlors' occupants. Apparently many hotels furnished their common rooms with pianos, and guests such as Sarah Virginia Hinton frequently "went to the parlour [and] played a few pieces on the piano." The genius of putting pianos in the parlors was that they became centers for spontaneous social interaction and provided culturally acceptable amusement. John Briggs, who always carried his flute, discovered that with "the ladies, being fond of music . . . I had not unfrequently the pleasure of spending my time in accompanying" them. Even those who lacked musical talent enjoyed listening to the impromptu concerts; almost every evening during her stay at Ballston Spa, Abigail May recounted that "we had quite a concert" by the hotel guests.[31] Playing and listening to musical instruments in the parlors were favorite ways of displaying one's refinement, affirming the cultural basis of social status, and enjoying a few idle moments. The physical limitations of springs architecture forced men and women together and broke down the restrictive barriers the elite had constructed around themselves. Coerced into the public sphere, wealthy Americans both got to know their social inferiors and to make contact with their peers.

Parlors and ballrooms were both public and domestic spaces. Here women could exhibit their refinement, sensibility, and class status in front of men. When women such as Grace Fenton Hunter wrote that "while in company I was tolerable busy, with my needle," they were using fancy work not only as a show of manners but also as busy work while the real business of social interaction took place. But this work was rarely done alone or silently. Women gathered in groups, and a member "read aloud while we sewed." They created a "reading Plan" or "System" wherein different women (and occasionally men) took turns reading aloud while "the rest should be employ'd with the needle, shuttle or any thing else, and it is admissible to comment occasionally upon the work." More than just a distraction, women found that "this expedient has a very happy effect, as it draws all the best part of the company together + is productive of that social intercourse which is not often enjoy'd at these places."[32] Women, needing to maintain their socially mandated reserve, found fancy work a convenient excuse to gather and to socialize without appearing frivolous. Like the springs' medical utility, needle work allowed women to enjoy themselves while simultaneously sustaining their social virtue and displaying their cultural pretensions.

A more private but equally significant cultural activity was the time "spent in reading." Unfortunately, reading materials proved scarce at the Virginia springs, where the pseudonymous travel writer Mark Pencil advised visitors "to bring with them some amusing and entertaining books." Otherwise they might end up like James Kirke Paulding, who called his "confinement [at the springs] more irksome" once he finished reading the last novel in his satchel. St. George Tucker, who begged his wife to "send me a Fredericksburg paper + [Richmond (Va.)] Inquirer + my Whig," rued his "miserable oversight" in not bringing his own reading material "when I had plenty of room in my trunk for a dozen books + more." With "no books or papers at all to amuse myself with," he continued his plea: "Do not fail to send my papers regularly to this place."[33]

Readers at Saratoga Springs enjoyed easily available literature and periodicals as early as 1808, when the subscription Social Library began collecting dues and loaning books to members. By the early 1820s, Gideon Miner Davison, a local newspaper editor and prolific guidebook publisher, had opened his Reading Room near the town's major hotels. Davison boasted over one hundred newspapers from across the United States and Canada, as well as two thousand volumes of "well selected books for circulation, embracing the modern publication." As added enticement to lure readers to his premises, Davison kept a register of guests at the various hotels; people came to sign their names and to discover whether a friend was in Saratoga Springs or had already left. The urban atmosphere and commercial saturation of Saratoga Springs that Southern writers so enjoyed attacking provided at least one luxury that the Virginia springs lacked for many years: ready access to reading material. Not until the 1850s did Virginia springs begin to advertise "a *Reading Room,* furnished with a variety of newspapers, from all parts of the Union."[34] In their reading selections, springs visitors sought not to escape the events of the outside world but to remain connected with them, a sign of their cosmopolitanism.

Hotel proprietors realized that riding, amateur theatrical or musical productions, sewing, and reading failed to satisfy everyone's entertainment needs. In addition to these basic activities, they offered "every kind of amusement for the visitors" to fill gaps in the daily schedule. Broadsides advertised the music, ballrooms, bowling alleys, billiard rooms, and "other places of amusement" that added "to the sources of healthful and agreeable relaxation" at various establishments. Exhibitions of boxing and fencing were popular, as well as more elaborate tournaments meant to recreate medieval times and to reinforce the elite status of Southern planters. Such tournaments might elevate Southerners' opinions of their society, but outdoor games such as shuffleboard provided a more utilitarian service by relieving the "tedium" produced "by the *sameness* of the life we lead." Billiards was also a favorite pastime, as John Briggs discovered when he stumbled upon a table at Red Sweet Springs and "played for amusement an hour or two." Bowling provided another diversion but could be taken to extremes: "before breakfast we have ten pins; after breakfast, for a few moments, the graces, then until dinner ten pins.—After dinner a small touch at the graces, and from that until supper ten pins, and occasionally from supper until eleven o'clock at night ten pins."[35]

Because Saratoga Springs was an established village with a strong non-tourist commercial base, it offered its guests a much broader array of amusements than did the Virginia springs. Instead of a few hotel-organized activities, Saratoga Springs' independently owned pleasure gardens, billiard rooms, bowling alleys, and saloons provided numerous options; their proprietors pledged "that no pains or expense shall be spared to render a visit to this fashionable establishment . . . agreeable." For those who favored outdoor activities, the area around Congress Spring resembled a manicured park, with its outlying reaches containing active amusements. In one corner, a carousel "whirled [riders] around with great rapidity." Couples favored the circular railway where passengers propelled "gaily painted cars." Although "with much ease the gentleman gives power to the movement," many ladies were seen "helping their partners most vigorously." Some visitors praised the railway as "exhilarating," but others criticized it as a means "to cheat people into exercise and out of money" and as a place where "on payment of a fare, you may enjoy the privilege of toiling like a galley slave." In either case, at twelve and a half cents for three laps around the track, the circular railway's builders soon recouped their $1,150 investment in the apparatus.[36] Unlike Virginia's hotels, which provided entertainment as part of their over-all business revenue, Saratoga Springs' independent amusements were each proprietor's sole source of income. With this incentive, the proprietors made their facilities as convenient and enjoyable as possible, and visitors flocked to their establishments. The opportunity to be seen by one's peers and so-cial rivals riding a carousel, walking through gardens, playing billiards, or even powering a train car proved irresistible.

Just beyond Congress Park's boundaries lay one of the most popular and unique of Saratoga Springs' amusements, the Indian encampment. A group of Abenaki métis from northern New York State and Québec performed war dances, archery exhibitions, war whoops, and mock scalping demonstra-tions. These exhibitions appeared "sufficiently savage and strange," but the violin recital by an Indian dressed in European garb of "Scotch reels, Strathspeys, Paddy O'Rafterty, and such like civilized tunes" seemed out of place. To many Americans and Europeans, the Indians looked more civi-lized than savage. They wore spectacles and loose cotton clothing and used metal needles and scissors in their sewing. Despite this acculturation, their command of English was "confined to the subject of currency. They told me exactly how many cents made a dollar; and on my taking up a watchpocket that one of them finished while I was there, she showed me which of the pieces of silver in my purse would pay for it." The Indians' "present degraded situation" of living in cloth and leather tents, making baskets for tourists, and generally appearing "very inferior" contrasted sharply with their once exalted condition when as "Lords of the soil they roamed the forest free." Americans relegated Indians, who were no longer a viable part of society, to the role of sideshow attractions at America's summer resorts. As reminders of the springs' historic and romantic past, as well as guests' own exalted so-cial status, the Indian encampments were a culturally acceptable and profit-able amusement.[37]

Other entrepreneurs also attempted to loosen the wallets of fashionable visitors. At the Virginia springs, itinerant jewelers spread their wares on the lawns, resident physicians offered advice on taking the waters, and "tran-sient artists—dentists—and phrenologists—and a corn doctor" solicited customers. Perhaps the most popular and successful of these practitioners were the phrenologists. Skilled in measuring the bumps and crevices of a subject's head as indicators of personal traits and characteristics, phrenologists soared in popularity during the second quarter of the nineteenth century. The collection of famous, powerful, wealthy, and fashionable persons at the springs provided a perfect market for the phrenologists' readings. Mark Pencil reported in 1839 that "Phrenology thrives well at the Springs, not because it is the only head profession here—but from there being so many persons at all places like this, who are very willing sometimes . . . to be made pleased with themselves when the cost is so little." At only one dollar per reading for analyses such as that of the little boy with a "'remarkably fine head—the organs are very prominent—benevolence very large, I would say, he was a man whose whole course of a long life had been devoted to charitable objects,'" the phrenologists examined heads from dinner until dusk. As practitioners of what contemporaries viewed as a highly scientific, respectable profession, phrenologists found many customers among a self-conscious elite eager to have their egos and social pretensions flattered.[38]

Another activity maintained its popularity throughout the nineteenth century by reinforcing and ratifying people's social status. The vast majority of springs visitors held devout, traditional Protestant religious beliefs and attended religious services "when a clergyman, willing to perform here, is to be found among the guests." The more formal church setting of city or Tidewater congregations gave way to dancing rooms "consecrated to more hallowed purposes" where sizable groups of worshippers "assembled . . . and listened to a solemn and eloquent discourse" on Sundays. Some Saratoga Springs hotels, such as the Union Hall, developed reputations as "pious house[s]" populated by clergymen "where it is not considered unfashionable by the guests to spend the evening in their great room, singing hymns and praying." But as "fashion began its reign and music invaded the parlor, dancing and prayer" clashed. Instead of holding services in the hotels, guests "began to pour forth their several congregations" in the village each Sunday morning. The more settled, permanent society at Saratoga Springs supported the year-round religious establishments that the more isolated Virginia springs, with their seasonal population, could not.[39]

Ministers in both regions kept things "primitive and fraught with old associations, and recollections of by-gone times, when our fathers worshipped God without any of those striking aids to devotion, which the increasing wealth, luxury and improvements of society have established." A simple sermon and hymns sung in couplets after the words were read aloud characterized the service. The anonymous newspaper columnist Netta, who spared no ink in criticizing other aspects of springs society, found it refreshing "to see so goodly a number of visiters engaged in the old fashioned custom of singing hymns, listening to short exhortations, and joining in thanksgiving and prayer." Virginian St. George Tucker enjoyed himself "more in one hour spent in this way than in ten attending dry doctrinal preaching." This nostalgia for simple religion extended to Episcopalian, Presbyterian, and Congregational ministers drawn from the hotels' guests but had its limits. When "our pedantic, fopantic, foolantic Minister" attempted to say grace at Ballston Spa, Abigail May "tried in vain to suppress my laughter." The reverend "waits till we are all seated, and then spreading his taper fingers and rolling up his eyes, he in the most affected, simpering, yet thundering Tone of Voice pretends to address his maker." May nearly burst out laughing when the minister "turn[ed] his tune at the word *only* in such a manner" and suppressed her outburst only when she "cram'd my mouth so full of bread I had like'd to have choked." This same woman, in disparaging her own journal writing abilities, compared them with "a Methodist sermon."[40]

Springs visitors such as May paid attention to religious matters but only respected ministers they found acceptable. In the context of the Second Great Awakening, attending to spiritual matters was part of a larger piety and attention to personal piety. But worshipping also allowed elite springs visitors to say who they were not: unlettered, overly enthusiastic evangelicals from newly established denominations who placed more emphasis on the radical egalitarianism of Christianity than the social responsibilities it entailed and hierarchies it supported. There was a right and a wrong way to worship at the springs.

In this context, it is difficult to underestimate the portion of religious springs visitors. Almira Hathaway Read felt that of the hundreds at Saratoga Springs in 1826, "but few are disposed to pass an hour in divine service. The pleasure parties and balls every evening in this village engross the attention of the old and young, sick and well, and this village place I fear will prepare more souls for destruction than these efficacious waters will ever heal infirm bodies." At many Virginia springs the ballroom doubled as the chapel, a situation that caused one observer to remark, "How strange! that the same room should be used for purposes so widely variant. Six days it is used for the amusements and follies of the gay & young & one day in seven for Divine Services." Religion became something "very little thought of in this place, and surely, it ought to be made a place of prayer, where we all come in search of health."[41]

Instead, balls and hops dominated, signifiers of both the excesses of the irreligious guests and the achievements of fashionable, refined society. In these dances, the day's final and most elaborate events, visitors spared no effort in displaying their status. A typical White Sulphur Springs dance began at twilight when "the whole grounds" were "interspersed with company, promenading, laughing, chatting." Saratoga Springs' gathering places, "the spacious Collonade[s]," were "thronged with the five hundred guests of the house, who pace to and fro for an hour" before the beginning of the ball.[42]

Although dances were "the one great article in the code of fashionables to which all other amusements or occupations were subordinate," they were not a daily part of the social regimen. In Saratoga Springs, the various houses shared the responsibility for organizing the events, with the principal hotels hosting one hop and one ball each week. The term "ball" indicated a more formal affair "got up by subscription, a list being sent around to each house and the expense of refreshments &c. is paid by the subscribers in equal proportions." Hops lacked the glamour of balls and were "considered a family dance . . . confined to the boarders in the house." Others attended by invitation to augment the number of dancers and "the hilarity of the occasion."[43]

Dancers arrived to discover the ballroom lighted up to accommodate "the mirthful meeting of the young and the gay." The hotel proprietors or ball subscribers created a festive atmosphere by providing champagne, sangaree, wine, and "other refreshing beverages," as well as ice cream and blancmange. At the Virginia springs, a promenade preceded the ball proper. One woman found that "the promenade before the dance was better worth looking at than any thing I ever saw." A double archway "bound with evergreens, and stuck full of candles" divided the ballroom in half as promenaders processed through it. Into the room marched "the Lady Patroness . . . on the arm of the gentleman who has the most stock in the Bank, followed in couples by all the gentlemen and ladies who intend to dance or play wallflower." After the procession established social hierarchy, "a platform was placed under one of [the arches] for the music, and then the dancing began."[44]

House musicians played in the ballroom before the ball proper and once the dancing began. Some springs employed white musicians, but the majority of bands featured black performers. Nathaniel Parker Willis described

Formal "German" dance, White Sulphur Springs. Visitors enacted these elaborate figures for entertainment and as a sign of their refinement and status. From *Harper's New Monthly Magazine*, August 1886. Courtesy of the Albion College Library.

a scene at a Saratoga Springs ball where "The black musicians 'vex their instruments,' and keep time with their heads and heels," an image repeated at the Virginia springs, where a newspaper reported that during the ball "Cuffee nods his head and stomps his foot and works his elbow" while playing the tune. One commentator went so far as to declare that "the colored race of Virginia being born fiddlers, a musician is never out of the way." Many proprietors of smaller springs, who might not have been able to afford a full band, actually chose to employ one or two of these "born fiddlers" to provide their establishments' music. As with hotel waiters, as skilled musicians some African Americans held positions that both lent them a modicum of prestige and fit within the established social order.[45] But unlike the waiters, who extracted limited social power from the diners, black musicians only provided ambient noise for the display of style and refinement during balls. With less direct interaction with white guests, the black musicians exercised less social power. They provided service, in the form of entertainment, for wealthy white guests.

Once the actual dancing began, the center of the hall seemed alive with dancers performing a "waltz where the gentlemen whirl their partners round and round, and then as suddenly leave them and whirl away in their turn, leaving the lady to overtake them in the crowd." Individual couples separated themselves from other dancers by their superior skills. At one gala two newlyweds "whirled around exactly twice while every other couple was making one turn, and the gentleman's feet and legs had to fly with great rapidity." In an ideal figure "the beaux bow to the fair ladies, who coyly give their hand, and are led out on the floor." The ultimate goal of any dance was to earn the praise of society, as did one lady at the Virginia springs: "how neatly the little foot is pointed—how gracefully she holds forth her arms— how majestically she moves along just touching the floor over which she flies—how swimmingly she turns her rounded form!"[46]

Saratoga Springs' ladies rivaled the belles of the Virginia springs for dancing supremacy. One evening during the summer of 1800, Abigail May danced nearly "every dance but one" with a variety of partners. Another night she "called (Hob Nob) with the Doctor which was very much admired never having been danced here." May completed her performance by telling a friend that she had invented the dance. The friend "proclaimed it and it was buz'd round the room quickly—one couple stood after another to dance 'Miss Mays dance'—till at last quite ashamed and tired I begged to sit down." By introducing and calling the dance, May succeeded in displaying her style and refinement, to the envy of her competitors. For spa ladies such as May, nothing equaled the ballroom for making an impression. As one commentator noted,

> This, this is the hour, and this the scene,
>   Where MODA reigns despotic queen!
> Here is her triumph most complete,
>   Her sweetest joy, her high estate. . . .
> The ball, her highest worship claims, —
>   The ball, —her waking thoughts, her dreams!
> In this she never yields, or tires,
>   In this, alone, she perseveres.
> Such joys her highest hopes comprise,
>   And such her only paradise.
> E'en heaven itself she would forswear
>   If taught there was no dancing there.[47]

Above all, balls were a space of contested social status. During the height of Saratoga Springs' season, "the wealthiest persons in the country were there congregated, each trying to outvie the other in magnificence and costliness of apparel." Style so ruled the scene that, in one observer's opinion, "the votaries of fashion outnumber the pursuers of health." Dancers at the springs attempted to exhibit their refined manners and elevated social status in "a fine display of refinement of the *beau mond* . . . strutting round in high life + polished manners." This was not an idle observation but a sign of the growing sophistication of American society. Where once country dances, four-handed reels, and cutting in and out of dances prevailed, Elkanah Watson "was delighted to notice the progress of refined manners, the graces of Paris, taught by french dancing masters, exhibited by many elegant Ladies, + well dressed gentlemen in dancing cotillions" at Ballston Spa in 1805. At this early date the springs lacked the material conditions for refinement—elaborate hotels, grand ballrooms, tree-lined paths, manicured lawns, and ornate fountains—established by English models. But the springs already possessed the desire to be genteel, to separate the barbarous from the civilized. The standard of refinement and the ideology of politeness existed long before the springs did and provided a model of behavior that springs society tried to equal. When Virginians boasted that their glamorous balls and famous visitors lent their springs "precisely the same finery, fashion and pretension as at Saratoga," they desired not only to outperform their rivals but also to display the symbols of refinement they had achieved. No slouch when it came to style, the Virginia springs abounded with "a fashionable crowd in most of the paraphernalia of their order." In staging "a parade of finery" replete with "jewels that sparkled amid fine laces and rich silks [that] were only outshone [by] the beauty of those they adorned," Americans demonstrated that they possessed the economic means to create and to perfect a refined society, the ultimate goal of any social gathering of worth in early nineteenth-century America.[48]

Unfortunately, perfection never lasted, and neophytes constantly spoiled the accomplishments of the elite. Among the fashionable crowd at the springs lurked many unrefined visitors, especially the crowds of gamblers who marred the polite discourse of springs society. As early as 1791, the French traveler Ferdinand-Marie Bayard reported informal gambling on billiards and an efficient faro bank at Bath, Virginia. Travelers throughout the early nineteenth century echoed his description. Cards seemed to prevail at the Virginia springs, where "devious gamblers" and "black-guards" practiced their "pernicious games." Saratoga Springs offered many diversions other than gambling, but bets on bowling, faro games, dice, roulette wheels, and all the other "apparatus and paraphernalia of gambling and dissipation" could still be found there before the Civil War, even though the village charter outlawed gambling and the town fathers continued to enforce the ban. Although Saratoga Springs' gamblers remained fairly discreet, proprietors of several Virginia springs actually welcomed gambling at their establishments. According to the *Southern Literary Messenger*, "a considerable portion of the grounds at White Sulphur Springs are set off and appropriated to faro and billiard tables and other games, where regular professionals of the low art of gambling are regularly quartered." At Sweet Springs two professional gamblers plied their trade in "the best building on the premises." Business was good enough for admitted gambler Robert Bailey to make "several thousand dollars . . . on fair and honorable principles" from his faro banks at Berkeley Springs and Sweet Springs, two of Virginia's most prestigious resorts. English-American George Featherstonhaugh criticized springs proprietors for fostering an environment where "every direct encouragement is given to vice, and inducements held out to the vilest fellows in the country to flock to the place," but he found that few Virginians shared his disgust. As T. H. Breen has written, during the colonial period gambling constituted an acceptable activity in the lives of Virginia's planter class. Gambling at the nineteenth-century Virginia springs was not a vice, as Featherstonhaugh would have it, but rather "a celebration of leisured wealth" and a symbol of the Southern elite.[49]

Even so, the risks were great for the gamblers. Virginia laws had hardened since colonial times and by the early-to-mid-1800s viewed gambling unfavorably. Judges imposed "remarkably severe" penalties, including prison time, on gamblers. In this hostile climate, most gamblers preferred to play it safe and to be "very cautious in their movements." The Watson brothers operated a gambling enterprise at Sweet Springs during the 1823 season in a neatly appointed two-story house that appeared completely normal from the outside. They reportedly kept a billiard table on the second floor of the house and posted doorkeepers at the entrances "to refuse admittance to all, except the visitants who are known to be from a distance." Such precautions prevented local legal trouble but may have curtailed business. A decade later the card sharp (and nephew of Senator Henry Clay of Kentucky) Martin Duralde reported disappointedly that "at the Red [Sulphur Springs] I did not play a single card. No one seemed disposed to partake of that kind of enjoyment." Others worried that professional gamblers might "starve for want of trade, unless they meet more encouragement than the present water-drinking folks seem inclined to give them." But this reluctance to gamble lasted only a short time. When Duralde arrived at White Sulphur Springs a few days later, he found "a fine party playing" and urged his partner to "come over as soon as possible," predicting that "we can clear two or three hundred a day." Duralde's earnings paled in comparison to the lifelong successes of Robert Bailey, who estimated he earned "upwards of half a million" dollars by gambling. Bailey's secret was simple: "my orders to my dealers always was [*sic*] to suffer no person to bet but gentlemen, and to exclude all common persons." His dealers "were never to be suspected of unfairness in conducting the game, for I had much rather lose the whole bank, than any gentleman should be dissatisfied." Bailey's gambling operation conformed to the standards of refinement, gentlemanly conduct, and class homogeneity that ruled Virginia society.[50]

Other gamblers acted far less honorably. Springs resorts in both sections of the nation crawled with gentlemen "who bore the reputation of being rich, but it was far from so." Unlike the planters and businessmen who made their money in crops, slave trading, commerce, or manufacturing, "the club-room defrayed [professional gamblers'] expenses." Young "greenhorns" lost enough money to keep the experienced gamblers "in style as long as they pleased." The professionals seemed to one observer "like so many spiders setting their nets in different corners to catch the silly flies who buzz about on bank-note wings." Apparently the spiders caught their share: Mr. Lavin from Baltimore arrived at the springs in a splendid carriage but quickly "fell in amongst the gamblers." He eventually "lost so much that he is obliged to offer his equipage for sale." This predicament left his formerly stylish wife feeling "melancholy . . . they say she looks wretchedly."[51]

People objected to those gamblers who came to the springs "for the express purpose of preying upon the company who support this establishment," its wealthy visitors. Professional gamblers dressed flashily and possessed no connections to "known families." They merely stood by and looked for opportunities "of inveigling the young men away to rouge et noir." But many visitors at the springs enjoyed playing cards. John Briggs reported gambling after dinner for small stakes that "never exceeded I believe ¼th $." This diversion failed to interrupt his usual exercise, spring water drinking, or early rising. Briggs could safely say, "I have little fondness for cards." He saw cards as a necessary evil at the springs, "so remote from any large Town, and where so many idlers are collected." Others were far less ambivalent, calling gambling "a blot on the otherwise fair picture" at the springs and "a disgraceful and ignominious act." One visitor compared the professional gamblers with "*Vultures* + other birds of prey. They seem to me, continuous upon the watch, to entrap the young + thoughtless part of mankind who visit these places + who are possess'd of a quarter stock of *cash* + short of experience in the ways of the world." The problem was not so much the gambling but the fact that it occurred between social un-equals, which threatened to upset the delicate balance of Southern springs society. Virginia society winked at gambling, but only if the "deep play" was between people of equal social rank who faced no potential social loss from their actions.[52]

Despite the disapprobation of some, gamblers cut a popular figure at the springs. They sat at table with the most refined visitors, were "invited to all the pleasure parties, and assumed an air of importance" among the society. At Sweet Springs, the Watson brothers presented a "genteel appearance + modern + retiring manners." They were "very *modest* + unassuming amidst the crowd" and seemed to blend in with the hotel's other guests. Likewise, Robert Bailey attempted to transcend his reputation as a gambler by estab-lishing himself in the hotel business at Berkeley Springs. He "frequently gave parties over in the grove," which "were attended as heretofore by the most wealthy and respectable." These parties both increased his standing as a refined gentleman and brought "much custom to my bank." Eventually Bai-ley gained the management of balls at Berkeley Springs, an honor reserved for the most genteel members of society. But word reached the ladies that Bailey was a gambler, and they soon refused to dance with him. When even the newcomers declined his invitations to whirl about the hall, Bailey stormed into the ballroom, purchased the slave who played the fiddle for the dances, and hauled him out by the collar. Bailey demonstrated that in this instance money could, quite literally, buy refinement. Without a fiddler, the ladies could not display their accomplishments through dance. The next day several ladies addressed notes to Bailey asking for his (and his fiddler's) attendance at the ball that evening; he responded by insisting that he had in-jured his ankle and was unable to dance for the rest of the season. Bailey's complaint rose not from the ladies' refusal to dance with him but from their insistence on labeling him a "gambler." He declared that he was no such per-son, preferring to call himself a "sportsman." The difference lay in the fact that gamblers pursued gaming without honor or honesty with the goal of exploiting "subjects of prey." He, however, was a sportsman—which he

defined as "a high minded liberal gentleman, attached to amusements regardless of loss or gain." As a sportsman, and especially as a gentleman, Bailey guided his actions by honor. To prove his social position, Bailey fought
duels against men who accused him of being a mere gambler or welched on
their debts.[53] He had to assert and to fight for his status, something that a
true upper-class, refined gentleman would never do.

Although gambling was certainly present, and even prevalent, at other
springs, it never gained the open acceptance it enjoyed around the turn of
the century at Bailey's Berkeley Springs. The company of the Watson brothers, who attempted to meet social standards and eschewed controversy, was
something that "all seem to avoid" at Sweet Springs. People arranged their
seats at the dinner table far from the Watsons. Even when forced to sit directly opposite the gamblers, guests would "exchange no civilities whatever"
with the brothers. The hesitancy of many to associate with the Watsons was
part of a larger trend away from gambling and toward respectability at the
Virginia springs. Over the course of the nineteenth century, refinement
made gambling and potentially seedy characters such as the Watsons or
Robert Bailey increasingly unacceptable in polite society. Gambling changed
from a prevalent, open practice to something undertaken behind closed
doors with as much discretion as possible. As James Kirke Paulding wrote,
few gentleman-travelers carried their small bundle of clothes in saddlebags,
"as it is not customary to dress fine at the Springs, or elsewhere: those who
do, are apt to be taken for Black Legs, or Horse Jockeys." The mere mention
of a gambling habit could, by 1859, ruin a gentleman's reputation. A correspondent in the *Lexington (Va.) Gazette* wrote a detailed description of the
gambling practices of several Louisiana gentlemen at Red Sweet Springs but
spared their reputations by saying, "I could give the names, but forbear."
Others practiced no such discretion in their attempts to eradicate gambling
as early as 1838. That year J. W. Hevenson wrote a long, plaintive letter to
Col. Richard Singleton, the arbiter of society at White Sulphur Springs, regarding a "malignant + groundless aspersion" on his character. Anonymous
informants had accused Hevenson of cheating at cards, a charge he dismissed as "blackhearted + vile." He insisted that his "resolution of not
touching a card, has been preserved *inviolable.*" Hevenson was so desperate
to redeem his reputation that he proposed "a life hereafter intirely [*sic*] +
strictly free in all points from dissipation + *cards in any shape*" if Singleton
would refute the allegations and rehabilitate Hevenson's good name. During this time, a leading Southern journal urged springs proprietors to re-

move the "material stain" of gambling from their establishments and to concentrate on promoting the healthful benefits of the waters. Even inveterate gamblers such as Robert Bailey expressed remorse for their lives of turpitude. Yet despite his frequent efforts to reform his ways, Bailey continued to gamble. Always on the cusp of success, he won and lost several fortunes, "all of it gone from whence it came."[54] Gambling provided both a quick route to partial social success and a road to ruin. As such, it threatened the social order of established wealth that dominated springs society. It represented in the most obvious form the threat to established money and society that less scrutable and barely legitimate wealth posed. Whereas in the colonial period Virginians had tolerated gambling because it transpired only among equals, by the 1830s the social changes of the Market Revolution and the cotton booms allowed men of equal financial, but not social, rank to bet. In clamping down on gambling, Virginia's established elite attempted to solidify its position and to prevent the kind of social mobility that might undermine its status. Ironically, the supposedly more open society at Saratoga Springs lacked a major gambling house until the 1860s.

Despite the allure of gambling and the best efforts of springs proprietors and adventuresome guests to devise various amusements, James Kirke Paulding's statement that "Bathing, drinking the waters, eating, and sleeping, are the principal occupations; and for recreation, they sometimes dance" remained true. Daily life repeated "the same round of dissipation," "the same unvarying routine" of activities "ad libitum, ad infinitum." Paulding referred sarcastically to "an agreeable variety of eating, drinking, and sleeping—sleeping, eating, and drinking—and drinking, eating, and sleeping" at the springs. Another diarist complained, "I believe I might almost copy any one journal, and it would do for any other day. The same routine of walking to the spring, talking a little (or rather a great deal), frequently reading a little, and speaking to passing acquaintances, passes off the time." The problem was that in leading the repetitious, boring life that they desired at the springs, Americans went against their society's hectic pace. Referring to "Saratoga's idly busy throng," the author and social critic Clement Clarke Moore asked how they could

> . . . chase away . . . the horrors of ennui,
>   But for the three great epochs of the day,
>   The happy hours of Breakfast_Dinner_Tea?[55]

Many visitors could not have supplied Moore with an answer. They complained that they could "scarcely remember how the day was spent, in doing little or nothing." One guest recounted the long list of activities she engaged in during the day only to add that "when I get into my bed I can but think how the day has been spent." Time seemed "to pass very heavily" at the springs. Visitors described activities that succeeded in "driving 'dull care away,'" "wore away" time, or "beguiled the hours." The goal was not to find enjoyable, productive activities to fill the day but rather "to drive away the ennui that always must attend a residence at a fashionable watering-place." Many found the hunt for time-killing activities so pointless that they agreed with John Munford's assessment "of the unprofitable life I have lead" at the springs. In Abigail May's words, "we read, eat, drank, talk'd, walk'd, and went to bed at night one Day older, but very little if any wiser than we rose in the morning."[56]

Life at the springs was "unprofitable" because, in the opinion of Grace Fenton Hunter, "nothing could be more monotonous than the time here." Another observer considered the daily routine at Saratoga Springs "so unvarying, the scenes so little diversified + the conversation so stale, that one even tires of the execution." James Kirke Paulding was shocked by the "trouble people take sometimes to gain amusement, when they set out on purpose. I have known many, at these places, expressly set apart for the reception of people who don't know what to do with themselves, who actually took more pains to keep awake all day, than a poor man does to maintain his family." The strain of the effort showed: there was "nothing in the whole compass of yawns like a Saratoga yawn, if you hear one when a gaper is off his guard." Drowsiness seemed the "almost universal" state of being at the springs. Though society might occasionally appear jovial on the surface, upon closer examination "the people all look *ennuied,* nobody likes the place."[57]

Many guests criticized the springs as unproductive. With the constant round of walks, games, books, meals, and dances, people had no "trouble of thinking what shall be done with the *hour.*" Instead, "days weeks and months slip away imperceptibly." Clement Clarke Moore wrote that his routine at the springs made him feel

> *. . . like a squirrel cag'd, who, though he bound,*
> *And whirl about his wheel, yet ne'er advances.*

Many years earlier, Washington Irving had sarcastically described his time at the springs as "a delicious life of alternate lassitude and fatigue, of laborious dissipation, and listless idleness, of sleepless nights, and days spent in that dozing insensibility which ever succeeds them." This waste of leisure time troubled moralists such as Timothy Dwight, who feared that the annual gatherings at the springs "will contribute very little to the melioration of the human heart, or to the improvement of human matters." Others shared his concerns. While at Saratoga Springs, Catharine Maria Sedgwick heard a sermon instructing that "our leisure hours were precisely those for which we should be held to the strictest account," instructions that the "busy crowd of idlers" at Saratoga Springs ignored. They appeared to Sedgwick to be "throwing away the stuff that life is made of!" Unproductive, frivolous time lacked moral purpose. Sedgwick succeeded in expressing a deep-seated guilt among Americans about enjoying themselves, a sentiment that many at the springs shared. One woman felt dismay at "the distressing idea, that few, perhaps not one of the gay crowd here have performed the important duty for which life is bestowed." Her own ability to perform the "important duty," whether it was marriage, childbirth, spiritual salvation, or something entirely different, distressed the woman and drained her "enjoyment" of the springs. Dwight and Sedgwick spoke from their positions as cultural arbiters and members of an older social elite. They were troubled by the emerging order of Jacksonian America, where the ability to enjoy leisure time and to do nothing served as a mark of social status. Too many people now trifled away their time with no purpose, threatening the established elite that insisted upon productive leisure. Instead of building lyceums, museums, or public parks, the newer members of society established pleasure gardens, horse tracks, and tourist hotels; the contrast between the social purpose of leisure activities—to improve or to enjoy—was stark. The expansion of springs clientele beyond a small number of wealthy and influential individuals intensified this conflict.[58]

The new culture of idleness gained influence in early and mid-nineteenth-century America but was very much a contested idea that did not dominate society. Most Americans, insisted Alexis de Tocqueville, "want something productive and substantial in their pleasures; they want to mix actual fruition with their joy." Instead of pursuing moral improvement or better health (which was what the mineral springs were supposedly all about), people at the springs seemed to be "almost hurried to death" without actu ally doing anything. At resorts with no "court-house bells to summon the weary attorney to the halls of justice and litigation; no counting house duties or bank notices calling the jaded labourer from his domestic comfort," people still found reason for anxiety. Many hoped that "the mere release from business and care" would provide a relaxed atmosphere at the springs, but early nineteenth-century Americans felt restless with nothing to do.[59]

Visitors quickly grew "very tired" of springs life, whether in Virginia or New York State. They often wondered "how persons can pass more than one or two days here for I never saw such an idle place." Indeed, typical visits to the Virginia springs lasted about one week. The Virginia springs were part of a larger tourist circuit in the western part of the state, where travelers hopped from scenic spot to mineral spring and back again. Most diaries and letters, as well as the guidebooks that influenced them, trace a springs circuit that allowed fashionable travelers to stop at several resorts throughout the summer. Saratoga Springs constituted an even shorter stay for travelers, who followed the Northern Tour across the region. Brief visits, rather than extended vacations at a single spring, were the norm for antebellum tourists. Many travelers expressed an itch to move on and quickly tired of springs life. They might "want change" or "expect to go by the end of the week." Jane Caroline North found life at Sweet Springs "very dull here, and a change to a more lively place I shall hail with pleasure, as for *this* chiefly we are peregrinating, it is best to enjoy the 'gift while we may.'"[60] In either case the traveling bug kept North in the seat of a carriage instead of on the couch of a hotel parlor. Mobility, not immovability, marked one as a member of America's new social elite, the tourists.

The blessing and curse of the springs was their heterogeneous clientele. As one European visitor noted, at the springs "you see people of every opinion and of every kind. All America is represented here." Other observers such as Charles Latrobe were much less charitable in their descriptions of springs society. He called Saratoga Springs "a motley crowd of men and women of all degrees;—patricians, plebeians, first-rates, second-rates, third-rates: gentlemen whose manners savoured of the good old school, and others whose manners indicated their being copied from some new school, or— no school at all . . . men with name but little money; others who had money and no names." In most people's opinions, Saratoga Springs never equaled its reputation for fashion and high life. Disappointed in the society he found there, Henry McCall wrote, "Heaven help me for coming here for Aristocracy. For such a collection of Swills and Rowdies it has rarely been my chance to lay my eyes upon." By 1860 Saratoga Springs' reputation began to diminish its drawing power. So many people of dubious social status visited "that the old select circles are beginning to retire from the scene to more rural and quiet retreats." Even so, people still traveled for several days and spent thousands of dollars "to make the acquaintance of others from their own city ... [who], had they stayed at home, they would never have known."[61] But without going, they could never make an impression on society beyond their immediate circle. That was both the allure and revulsion of springs society: the ability to mix with people outside one's locality and social class. In the constant round of activities and competitions, springs visitors identified themselves: their dexterity in employing proper manners and displaying wealth demonstrated that they were either refined or rude, wealthy or middle class. Members of the elusive national elite used springs visits as an opportunity to define themselves but frequently could do so only in opposition to those classes under them. At the springs the national elite could see who they were not.

By eleven o'clock each night, life at the springs drew to a close. The band played its last note, the dancers twirled their last turn around the ballroom, the guests snuffed out the candles flickering in their rooms, and at last "sleep seals the drowsy eyes of the tired devotee of pleasure." When the sun rose the next morning, the springs awakened "again to go through its gay routine, till weariness, the desire to change, or the end of the season, puts a period to the scene." Yet in evaluating springs society, observers noted "a considerable hollowness in much of this gaiety." Some of the younger guests might find the springs a "paradise of delights," but many of the older visitors, who had tested the waters of fashionable society before, seemed to be "smiling at grief" instead of enjoying themselves. The experience of their years and a few seasons at the springs gave them the ability to see through the rituals of fashionable society and to agree with Washington Irving that at the springs "pleasure has taken an entire new signification, and at present means nothing but STYLE." Just being at the springs and competing with others in displays of style and refinement composed the object of a visit. Where Robert G. Shaw had endeavored to "make an effort to recruit," he found the same pressures of social status and class anxiety he thought he had left at home. To define the springs merely as "cities of play" where Americans suspended social conventions and "could express themselves in ways that would normally have been proscribed by external judgments or internal censors" renders them incomplete, devoid of class conflict, and one dimensional. Tocqueville was correct in his assertion that Americans preferred those amusements and resorts "that are like business and which do not drive business wholly out of their minds."[62] For many Americans, the business of the nineteenth century was conspicuous consumption, social display, and class formation.

Chapter 5

LOVE FOR SALE

*E*ach afternoon Saratoga Springs' fashionable guests arrayed their carriages in front of the grand hotels for the daily procession down Broadway to nearby Saratoga Lake. The order of this parade reflected the social hierarchy of Saratoga Springs—only the most prestigious visitors headed the line. During the summer of 1846, Madame Jumel—a woman with a stained reputation and the mistress and later wife of Aaron Burr, who had killed the prominent Federalist Alexander Hamilton in an 1804 duel—often led the procession. But some of Saratoga Springs' guests resented her efforts "by a magnificent equipage to dazzle" the crowd and disapproved of her relationship with Burr and her other past associations. On the afternoon of 26 August, Jumel set out in her coach and four-horse team, complete with footmen and an outrider, only to discover that she was not alone. Rather than being followed by the most select members of Saratoga Springs society, she saw that a carriage with two men "in ragged equipage" as footmen and a figure dressed much like herself pursued her. As was her custom,

Jumel had her carriage driven "slowly through Broadway, that the inhabitants might have a proper sense of their own insignificance." Meanwhile, in the carriage behind her, Tom Camel, a well-known local African American, "fanned himself with a large fan, and bowing and curtseying to the crowds which had gathered on every side." Madame Jumel soon discovered the ruse and "threatened, pleaded, and offered bribes" to stop the mockery, but to no avail. The carriages proceeded all the way to the lake and back with Camel mimicking Jumel's every move.[1]

Madame Jumel's humiliation highlights some of the key themes regarding gender roles at America's mineral spring resorts. She had stepped outside her prescribed role as a women of humble origins and had attempted to assume a position of social prestige. The leaders of Saratoga Springs society ensured that she would not receive their esteem, either by putting Tom Camel up to his charade or allowing it to transpire and approving of it with their laughter. Camel's mockery cut deeply not just because he blurred gender boundaries but also because as an African American he was on the lowest rung on Saratoga Springs' social ladder. His cross-dressing equated Madame Jumel with the basest members of society. By playing the part of Madame Jumel, Camel reduced that disreputable woman to his social level. She was no longer a refined lady but had been unmasked as a woman of common ancestry with a dubious past that included prostitution, a faked deathbed scene that convinced her first husband to wed, and association with a man whom few held in high esteem. All the while, Jumel pretended to be the most refined and high-bred lady. By not adhering to the accepted gender and social roles at Saratoga Springs, Jumel exposed herself to ridicule, humiliation, and the censure of the society she so desperately wanted to join and to dominate. Her mistake was not using the allure of sex to advance her social standing, which most at Saratoga Springs did, but by acting so brazenly. Society singled out Madame Jumel for reprobation because she threatened the stability of gender relations at the springs by pulling back the curtain of gentility that protected the interactions between men and women.[2]

During the late eighteenth and nineteenth centuries, Saratoga Springs and the Virginia springs served as an elite national marriage market, a place where members of America's upper classes could gather to evaluate each other and to negotiate the prospects of matrimony between their sons and daughters. There congregated "maidens in search of husbands, widows disconsolate, young men inclined to matrimony. . . . All have an object in view . . . and drinking the waters is with most of them quite secondary." For these "hosts of cheerful pretty faces of the softer sex, and hordes of young aspirants to their good graces," the only barrier between them and a poor match were manners, class boundaries, and "a very partial sprinkling of responsible matrons, and irresponsible old gentlemen, to keep them in order." In this ambiguous social setting, status, gender roles, and reputation were at stake. People came to the springs to both "marry + un-marry if they can." People visited not just to scout potential spouses but also to socialize, to flirt, or possibly even to engage in extramarital affairs. The normal rules of behavior, civic virtue, and interaction between the sexes were temporarily relaxed, which created a dangerous social situation. Making choices about potential spouses, evaluating one another's place in society, and deciding on a course of action and level of intimacy posed "a serious matter in a country where they have full liberty to bestow themselves where they wish." Thrown together in a heterogeneous, competitive society, men and women attempted to decode the external signifiers of each other's characters. Courtship was not a process of romantic love but a complex negotiation of the semiotics of flirtation. Every glance, every movement, every word, every article of clothing, every unuttered thought—all expressed coded messages in the language of love. Deciphering these messages tested the acumen, patience, and insightfulness of men and women at the springs. In a sense, the main task of springs life was to characterize and to categorize potential suitors. Most people reacted to this situation with the language and the logic of the marketplace—where everything from respectability to desirability was negotiable and for sale. Northern and Southern springs resembled, in the opinion of one visitor, "a good *exhibition room*, or (if you choose) a *market house*."[3]

The comparison of the springs to a marketplace was not unique to the United States. Seventeenth- and eighteenth-century English spas such as Bath, Tunbridge Wells, Epsom, and Cheltenham served as cultural models for American resorts, especially in the realm of gender relations. Those spas developed reputations as places of sexual adventure where the normal rules of etiquette and propriety were suspended. Men and women negotiated love and marriage in an environment that emphasized what David S. Shields has called "social play." Women used the newly developed social skill of wit to engage men and to fend off their advances, perhaps even deflecting marriage by demonstrating their conversational aplomb. Flirtation, poetry readings, and conversation enlarged women's socially accepted sphere of activity without actually surrendering their two most valuable assets, their single status and their virginity. At early English spas, sex and manners were intertwined in a way that liberated women by loosening social norms regarding contact between the sexes. As with their American successors, critics of English resorts pointed to the intrusion of market ideology into gender relations. In a passage that later American commentators echoed, the early eighteenth-century Grub Street pamphleteer Ned Ward wrote of Tunbridge Wells: "Maidenheads here bear an extravagant price."[4]

Shields describes a social setting that placed increased emphasis on appearance, manners, cultural sophistication, and performance. This "great project of civility" altered colonial British-American society. In coffeehouses, social clubs, and salons and at tea tables, British subjects learned the ways of polite society. The new standards of behavior stressed true feeling, sincerity, emotion, and proper manners. Adherents to the ideology of refinement and sensibility reacted powerfully to experience and were often carried away with compassion or gratitude. People measured character not solely by family name but by the quality of one's emotions. Displaying benevolence and feeling composed virtue; in many cases people engaged in "the pursuit of emotion for the sheer pleasure of feeling." Ideally, sincerity and sentimentalism in conduct were the mainstays of a culture that believed that the heart gave natural, visible responses to stimuli. Some, such as the diarist Abigail May, were "very observing of countenances—and affirm they are (generally speaking) the index of the Heart." This revolution in manners extended cosmopolitan manners and values beyond large urban centers. In seventeenth- and eighteenth-century England, London served as the metropolis, and in the colonies Philadelphia, New York, Boston, and Charleston played the part of cultural outposts whose citizens enjoyed the civilizing influence of polite manners. By the late eighteenth and early nineteenth centuries, these American outposts boasted a relatively sophisticated society. That society in turn exported the culture of civility and extended its influence into the hinterland, especially when members of the aspiring national elite gathered at American spas such as Saratoga Springs or the Virginia springs. Eventually, gentility came to rural people. At the springs Americans learned the lessons of polite society and began to form a culture of gentility in the United States.[5]

At the "market house" that was the American spa, ladies and gentlemen attempted to display their style—or their wares—to their advantage, thus maximizing their own value. Almost every activity and moment offered visitors an opportunity and an obligation to exhibit their fashion. Meals, with the "various styles of dress of both ladies and gentlemen," seemed "a good deal like a puppet show" to a White Sulphur Springs visitor in 1831. Dinners and evening balls offered an opportunity "for very brilliant and very lovely women to display their tastes, their jewels, and their fascinations." Even sitting in the hotel lobby waiting for a cabin or hotel room to be prepared was a moment of display—and one that many guests dreaded, having just stepped down from stages or trains in a disheveled, dusty state. Clothing presented an exterior image of whom visitors wanted to be and how they wished to be perceived. Thus clothes became an all-important part of the springs experience. A newspaper correspondent reported from Saratoga Springs in 1857 that "it does not 'do', you know, at a fashionable watering-place to allow yourself to appear twice during a season in the same garment."[6] Instead, women and men in both regions went to great lengths to assemble, don, and display the latest and most ornate fashions.

Simply wearing the latest style was not enough; the point was to distinguish oneself from the crowd. The competition to stand out was so fierce that women needed to remain on their guard lest their rivals steal their clothing or accoutrements, especially at the bathhouse. Fashionable rivalries reached such an excess at Saratoga Springs that a newspaper reporter termed it "A Novelty.—To see two women pass each other in the street without one or the other turning round to see what the other had on." In this competitive environment, women went to extremes to make themselves look beautiful. They "lost not pains in displaying themselves to the best possible advantage" by curling their hair into elaborate designs and adorning it with flowers or ribbons given to them by suitors. Some wore so much jewelry that it appeared "as if the contents of a jewel box had been scattered over her." Many New York City "millionaires' wives" satisfied the late nineteenth-century rage for diamonds by "carrying thousands upon their persons."[7]

Fashion reached its limits with the expanding size of the hoops inside ladies' dresses. Known as "bishops," these bustles extended a foot out from the woman's hips and bent "forward with a view to make them still more conspicuous," presenting "a serious inconvenience to all who are compelled to pass them." The outlandish size of these hoops may have served more than fashion; they "keep the beaux at a respectful distance." Merchants profited from the sale of dress hoops and hung them from posts and awnings on the sidewalk as an advertisement. Antebellum gentlemen embarrassed by the exhibition of ladies' undergarments had no choice "but to shut one's eyes and hasten forward." Women's inclination to "expose their arms and busts as well as their faces and hands" further shocked and offended. The ladies followed fashion in this practice, not the "ordinary ideas of delicacy and decency" of antebellum America. Reformers at Saratoga Springs lectured "on the destructiveness of tight lacing," but a woman who heard one such lecture did "not believe it caused one cord to be slackened."[8] Northern women, as well as Southerners at Saratoga Springs, ignored the call to simplify their dressing habits.

The insatiable appeal of fashion and competitive display created "a summer rush of silks" at American springs, "a moving to and fro of brocaded matrons and muslined virgins." Women both young and old could be seen "displaying and strutting with crinoline and high heel boots to a most alarming extent." It often seemed that "the ladies were dressed as if they were attending one of the finest assemblies in the Union." Although the everyday dress at the springs appeared "quite plain, and some hardly neat," grand balls, presidential visits, or the common agreement of the belles might shift daily dressing toward display and ornamentation. For these events "dresses, that had long been imprisoned, . . . were now brought out." These extravagant dresses used so much material that few women could actually move with ease. Just swinging an arm to the side proved "awkward" and not "graceful." One young lady of medium height wore one hundred and twenty-five yards of cloth in her dress and "looked like a white cloud made up of fringes . . . [and] multitudinous wavelets in which she was enveloped." Less ostentatious souls failed to see the point of such displays, a sentiment that was shared by some of the fancier dressers. After appearing in the ballroom, one preening woman lamented "how nicely I had dressed myself, just to undress again."[9]

In general, this level of display was confined to women. According to a Saratoga Springs men's clothier, his business was limited because "gentlemen do not care what they wear—anything will do. . . . Gentlemen do not talk about one another if their hats are not the most expensive, and their coats are not the newest fashion in the market." This gendered construction of fashion held that women, as objects of beauty and desire, needed to present themselves as favorably as possible, whereas men, who held a position of power in gender relations and selected from the carefully assembled belles, needed only to appear neat and clean. Indeed, some of Saratoga Springs' male guests strained convention when they arrived at table "in flannel shirts and dirty shoes, and altogether in a state unfit for ladies' company." This appearance only earned them the opprobrium of the women, who refused to dance with the ruffians. At the opposite extreme, only "dandies and fops," neither a respected nor desirable group in springs society, dressed to excess. They looked like "the prints in tailors' shops and their beauties as trim and graceful as their own bob-tail trotters." These men existed to model their wardrobe and "to display themselves to the best advantage in every suit." They saw little reason to jeopardize their appearance by dancing or walking with a lady lest they "Uncurl a whisker, rumple a cravat, / Disturb a curl that on fair forehead lies."[10] Few of the ladies, who dressed to impress the gentlemen, wanted to reverse their roles and become the admirers rather than the admired. Men need only appear respectable and dressed just well enough to suggest that they could provide a sufficient level of comfort. Anything more threatened the norms of gendered fashion.

Women's preparation and outlays for fashionable life at the springs were significant. James Kirke Paulding sarcastically recommended an extensive collection of necessary articles for a visit to the springs: six hats, two lace veils, four trunks of clothing, a dressing case, a trunk of hair curls, a dozen pair of shoes, and six dozen pair of hose. He omitted a pocketbook, "as papa (or his creditors) pays all, and young ladies ought never to know any thing about the value of money." The problem of overdressing was particularly egregious at Saratoga Springs but was also as old as the springs themselves. As early as 1800 ladies arrived "with a stock of clothes that will enable them to wear different dresses every day." By the late 1850s some women brought as many as fifteen trunks and one hundred and fifty dresses, enough to change outfits five times a day in one estimation, or even more often if they stayed a week. Yet even this plethora of clothing failed to meet some fashionables' needs. "There are cases of not unfrequent occurrence, when fifteen or twenty 'Saratoga trunks' . . . are barely sufficient to contain a lady's panoply of war." The reason lay not in the contents of their trunks but in those of their competitors. Many women came to the springs intent on "look[ing] better than Miss So-and-So," but after seeing their rivals' outfits, these women "were so dissatisfied with their clothing that they had a full wardrobe made up to suit the times."[11]

Such extravagance cost a pretty penny, which distinguished the truly desirable (i.e., wealthy) from the rest of springs society. One husband whose income barely topped two thousand dollars per year was hard pressed to keep his wife in style:

> Her morning dress cost twenty dollars; her embroidered skirt without which it cannot be worn, was fifteen or twenty, and the laces to match as many more. She has some eight or ten evening dresses, each of which cost from fifteen to twenty dollars; the embroideries to match are, at the lowest, two or three hundred. Her husband allows her twenty-five pairs of gloves and twenty-five pairs of gaiters a year, but these, she says, do not begin to last her. She would not be seen in a hat that costs less than ten or fifteen dollars, and she requires six in the course of a year.

At this rate the spendthrift spouse consumed about one-fourth of her husband's annual income. But he could never keep up or get ahead: "All these dresses will be out of fashion next year, and she will need a whole new set to be decent." Husbands and fathers faced enormous pressure, some of which came from their desire to display their accomplishments via their wives and daughters, to furnish a suitably fashionable wardrobe. According to Washington Irving, wives plundered shops and starved their families "to enable [themselves] . . . to make the Springs campaign in *style.*" The costs of making a fashionable mark at the springs were so high that "the lady of a southern planter will lay out the whole annual produce of a rice plantation in silver and gold muslins, lace veils, and new liveries, carry a hogshead of tobacco on her head, and trail a bale of sea-island cotton at her heels—while a lady of Boston or Salem will wrap herself up in the net proceeds of a cargo of whale oil, and tie on her hat with a quintal of codfish." Irving, in his usual sarcastic tone, seems to be exaggerating the problem, but his hyperbole points to the uneasiness many men, especially those from his elite social circle, felt toward women who spent their husbands' money in such an ostentatious manner. To do so contradicted the ideology of republican motherhood and simplicity that dominated the period when Irving visited and wrote about the springs, yet women still dressed elaborately. One female practitioner of conspicuous consumption at the Virginia springs was "said to have 19 trunks, and 75 dresses, though it is whispered that her father is not worth a dime, being bankrupt. Is it any wonder?" To another commentator at Saratoga Springs, such extravagance seemed like "a waste of . . . money!" But even critics such as Irving's friend James Kirke Paulding admitted the social power of clothes. They were social markers, "the *inten-*

sifiers—making vulgarity more vulgar; aristocracy more aristocratic." As Henry James wrote, "she is dressed for publicity. . . . To be so excessively dressed is obviously to give pledges to idleness."[12]

Ladies who spent exorbitantly and dressed ostentatiously visited Northern and Southern springs from the resorts' earliest days and grew in number over the course of the nineteenth century, but they never represented the only model of womanhood. More restrained, sober women often presented an admirable image that the ideology of republican motherhood encouraged women to emulate. The presence of these two feminine ideals speaks not only to the persistence—and weakness—of republicanism but also to the continual tension between the competition for status and traditional morality at the springs. As the social structure of early national and antebellum America changed, so too did gender roles, which led many social conservatives to criticize life at the springs. Whereas colonial women had enjoyed a visible role in public life, often participating in formal state events such as balls and dinners, the ideology and practice of republicanism in the early republic attempted to relegate women to the role of observers. Women were considered symbols and repositories of gentility in colonial America, but republican society abolished this role as it adopted a gender-based conception of citizenship that precluded women from taking a public role in official proceedings such as parades or court days. The concept of separate spheres relegated women to the domestic front, where their participation in public life was confined to gender-appropriate benevolent and reform associations. In republican ideology, women embodied virtue. The loving partnership between husband and wife was the ideal for political relationships, the perfect balance between vice and virtue. A woman's main tasks were to cultivate the home as a refuge from the strife of the public sphere and to raise her children to be virtuous citizens. But these traditional historiographical interpretations of gender in the early republic discount the power of politeness and the continued influence of the culture of civility in American life. Republicanism never replaced the metropolitan culture of civility that spread from England to America during the eighteenth century, and it offered no alternative to the negotiation of marriage in the marketplace. During the early republican period and throughout the nineteenth century, gender was still a contested category in American life, and men and women still battled over its definition within the logic of the prevailing force of the nineteenth century, the market, and its currency, politeness.[13]

One of the earliest and most eloquent accounts of life at the springs, the journal of Abigail May, a twenty-four-year-old woman who visited Ballston Spa, New York, during the summer of 1800, illustrates the competition and negotiation between men and women over appropriate gender roles. Throughout her diary May evaluates men and women based upon two key markers of character in her time, sentiment and refinement. May described Mrs. Western, an older woman she met at Ballston Spa, as possessing "an indefinable charm . . . her manners are the most elegant, her air the most graceful, her conversation the most clear and refined[,] her every look the most intelligent and prepossessing of any person I ever knew." Likewise, May singled out Mr. French for praise because of his "exquisite sensibility" and "delicate mind." May valued ladies and gentlemen who were "gentle and contrite" and could pass an evening in "interesting & rational Discourse." She rejected Mr. Baldwin, who "must hope for success, more from the powder on the outside of his head, than the Sentiment within." Among all the people May met and commented on, none equaled the young Catharine Maria Sedgwick: "She has a highly cultivated mind and a feeling heart. . . . [S]he is not so lovely but her mind—her mind, in the words of Lord Littleton 'to more than merely sense she joins the softening influences of female tenderness.'"[14]

May's ideal men and women possessed the qualities of sensibility, humility, affection, and refinement that skirted the edges of republican virtue as identified by historians of the early American republic. These qualities were closer to the characteristics of the civil society transferred from England to America in the colonial period. They are not specific to Abigail May in 1800 Ballston Spa but represent the values of a larger Anglo-American spa culture. During the 1830s, ladies at Virginia's White Sulphur Springs held gentlemen "in high estimation" for their "politeness." Even in the 1840s, people continued to value more than superficial appearance, preferring women such as "Miss S—— from lowland Virginia," who "does not strike you at first as being handsome, though the deathless intelligence, and sensibility, which illuminate her face, after a few hours' acquaintance, compensates [sic] for the want of regularity of features." Elite culture preferred a woman who appeared "perfectly unconscious of her beauty—so diffident and soft!" Ladies such as a mother and daughter from the Carolinas struck observers with their "truly elegant and polished manners; they are perfect specimens of what ladies should be—gentle and winning to all—charming the old and the young. Both intellectual, and highly accomplished, these gentle Carolinians seemed to please universally; for though their manners bespoke ladies, *usage-de-monde,* yet their hearts were seemingly untouched by the spirit of worldliness, that damper to all true nobleness of mind."[15] More than republicanism, civility continued to exert an influence on American attitudes and manners well after the colonial period.

The ideals of republican virtue and simplicity retreated before the advance of gentility and refinement in the late eighteenth and early nineteenth centuries. As evidence from mineral springs resorts shows, middle-class manners and worries about social hypocrisy emerged several decades before the Jacksonian era. This finding challenges Karen Halttunen's description of middle-class society, but the tensions she dates to the 1830s existed at the springs well before they entered polite parlors. The early republic's social arbiters criticized the new standards as manners that emphasized "the outside show of elegance and ease," attributes that were often "the result of study and of art." Gentility and refinement were easily manipulated principles that failed to separate the worthy from pretenders, as had been the case in the romanticized past of ordered society. The new manners were liberating because they conferred status based on accomplishments, not family connections or wealth. But by not defining objective standards of social status, they simultaneously created new social ills. The social mobility and masquerading that came with these new ideals threatened the position of social conservatives such as Clement Clarke Moore, who declared that "real worth alone can reach the heart." Echoing his sentiments, a reporter for the *Saratoga Springs (N.Y.) Whig* wrote in 1841: "Gentility is neither birth, wealth, manner, nor fashion,—but in mind. A high sense of honor—or a determination never to take a mean advantage of another—an adherence to truth, delicacy, and politeness towards those men with whom we have dealings—are the essential characteristics of a *gentleman.*" Manners did not gloss over a person's rough edges but reflected true feelings and "harmonize with nature and character."[16] When applied to affairs of the heart and the personal and family reputations at stake, definitions of gentility bore a great deal of significance.

The insistence by social conservatives on the importance of true feeling and inner worth, rather than outward appearances, was in part a longing for a romanticized golden age when a stable elite knew each other and maintained social order. By the 1850s writers such as Mary Jane Windle lamented that true gentlemen and ladies were part "of a school now nearly extinct." These vanishing men and women rejected the "empty vanities" of antebellum springs society in favor of "things more true to nature." But these true gentlemen and ladies discovered that the "manners, costumes, +c. of many of the fashionables, quite overpower[ed]" them. In 1853 some commentators expressed "surprise at the departure from the primitive and modest style of our mothers of the last century. We are now a fast people; and who can condemn a young belle or an undomestic married flirt for embracing everything in the ballroom that can show her to the best advantage." Critics lamented the passing of an idealized past, but that past had never really existed at the springs. The ideals and manners of the eighteenth century—the ways of the colonial gentry, Washington's court, and the waning Federalist elite—never held sway at the springs, where a competitive social reality predominated. As early as 1816, when James Kirke Paulding described sentimental ladies and blue stockings at the springs, fashionable modes of behavior governed society.[17] Lamentations for a waning golden age owed as much to the threat to the established social order from below as to the veracity of past societies. The old elite was simply attempting to solidify its cultural hegemony by invoking a more perfect past it purported to equal, while faced with challenges from less refined pretenders to social leadership.

As purveyors of this strain of cultural declension, critics such as Paulding and Windle belonged to a new group of social commentators in American culture. They wrote about travelers, resorts, and the social setting of the emerging leisure class. The act of writing created a new literary genre, the travel narrative, but also had larger cultural implications. Some of these authors, such as Paulding and Washington Irving, started their literary careers by dabbling in travel writing before moving on to weightier and ultimately more successful endeavors. Their successors in the next generation of American authors, George William Curtis and Charles Astor Bristed, also experimented in travel writing and social commentary as part of their larger literary endeavors. But others from the North and South, including the illustrator and author David Hunter Strother (Porte Crayon), the anonymous female columnist Netta, and Nathaniel Parker Willis, made a living by writing about the fashionable life led by tourists. Willis is a particularly important figure, and his writings played a significant role in the formation of a leisure culture. He was essentially the first professional writer to deal almost exclusively with leisure pursuits. He described a style of life that was available to all through social mobility and commercial endeavor. But Willis, a noted social climber, discovered that the leisure he described lacked the substance of hard work and striving that made him, as well as antebellum American society, successful. His writing displayed the social tension and unease that other, more aristocratic authors found in springs society.[18] When Irving or Bristed (the maternal grandson of the phenomenally wealthy John Jacob Astor II) railed against the incursion of the middle class into fashionable society, they were not just turning a phrase; they spoke as social authorities attacking the forces that created their own success and threatened the exclusivity of their social position.

Despite the attacks of elite social critics, the new class of "fast people" wasted little time on the imagined sentimentality of their grandparents. The gentlemen at Northern and Southern springs resembled "dandies, smothered in the envelope of cravats, sparkling with jewels, weighed with cables and rigged with ropes . . . a species of whiskered gentry, whose strength, like Sampson's, lay in their hair." Whenever possible, they "sauntered about, their hands in their pockets staring around them, with the most vainglorious air imaginable." Rather than cultivating sensibility or engaging in rational conversation with the ladies, this new breed of gentleman never went "to bed until after midnight, and rises at nine to breakfast at ten. He always is looking for a bath, and has apparently washed away every trace of any kind of character whatever." His reputation and image depended not on character but on "a fondly cared for mustache" and "hair of pomatum smoothness." The new standard of gentlemanly accomplishments in both the North and the South prized those "able to whiff a segar, use an eye glass, and say 'demmit' with a grace."[19]

The ladies were not much better. Their social graces emphasized the ability to "thump a piano, yawn over a novel, and turn up the nose at anything approaching to usefulness." Few followed the advice of conventional society to cultivate the qualities of republican mothers, preferring instead to perfect fashionable attributes such as witty repartee and the latest hairstyles. Springs visitors would have had to strain to overhear conversations regarding "domestic details," which were regarded as "the greatest possible bore to a mere fashionable casual drawing-room acquaintance." Banter that pleased gentlemen and made women look and sound younger dominated the springs. Despite the yearnings of critics for a return to a simpler time, women displayed the same type of social "wit" that David Shields discovered in his study of the Anglo-Atlantic world, especially at English spas. As did their English predecessors, American women at the springs emphasized surface accomplishments and cared little about internal worth. The New York City woman who "promenade[d] the piazza fashionably dressed, with the ladies and gentlemen, sometimes her arm resting on one of the latter" while her invalid husband sat inside the hotel was not simply a product of mid-nineteenth-century cultural declension; she had existed amid the fashionable display at the springs for decades.[20]

Abigail May described the paragon of the fashionable lady, Mrs. Amory of Boston: she is

> a *little twisted* and is proud . . . her riding dress shew her shape to every possible advantage, and every posture that could increase what (I suppose) she considered as Beauty was made use of. Nothing was quite good enough to go down her delicate throat at dinner, and it was with difficulty she could walk across the room, hanging on her husband. Added to all this, a supercilious and contemptuous dropping of the eye when any one passed, effectually disgusted our social party.

May's "disgust" came not solely from Mrs. Amory's behavior but also from Amory's ability to pull it off while sentimental ladies such as May sat to the side of the parlor, restrained by the tenets of republican simplicity from participating in such displays. Mrs. Amory's qualities were ubiquitous and extended to White Sulphur Springs, where in 1838 Mr. Stuart noticed the rich and "up-startish" Boggs girls parading around the ballroom. When he overheard their mother singing their praises, Stuart decided, "in conjunction with some ladies," to have some fun. Placing themselves near enough to Mrs. Boggs that she could hear their every word, the conspirators "began with the most extravagant exclamations of rapture" about one Miss Boggs's dancing. "'Look,' I cried, 'What inimitable grace!' &c &c until at length my transports surpassed the power of expression & I could only by gestures & countenance evince the wonder & admiration. All this while the old lady was sidling up nearer & nearer, so as not to lose a word, her countenance sparkling with delight, & the other ladies who were in the secret, almost convulsed with laughter!"[21]

Stuart and his accomplices exposed the main problem of springs society: many people tried too hard to achieve status—their "efforts were too *perceptible* to succeed." When social climbers such as the Boggs family made blatant efforts to advance their position, the established social order ensured that they were put back in their place with mockery. The goal was not to ridicule others but rather to ensure that only the most socially acceptable people gained entry to the bourse to negotiate marriage. Springs arbiters claimed to be able to spot a social fraud from afar. A gentleman might appear to be refined and polite but more often than not was "too much given to making pretty speeches." Those "full of pretension and folly" failed to impress most ladies. In one case Abigail May described Oliver Kain as "tall finely shap'd good eyes, and teeth—a very handsome man—what would you have more, alas! what a pity it is so fine a casket should be empty, or filled with trifles, as if nature clap'd on the cover and forgot to put in the brains." Such gentlemen possessed the "charm of manner" so valued by springs society but little else. Their refinement "is easily worn with its seamy side inward and fairest gloss outward." They might, as did "Capt. Fitzhugh of the navy, a gentleman of high polish and easy manners," meet all the requirements of refined, fashionable society, "except that he uses his fingers to his nose, instead of a handkerchief, and eructates rather too freely."[22]

Ladies tended to control their dyspepsia better than gentlemen but still lacked polish in the eyes of many observers. Their main fault was emotional shallowness and a lack of intellectual depth. As one Virginia gentleman noted, "With the Belles every thing is 'charming + sweet, or horrid.' . . . The other day I overheard a conversation of which the following is a sample. 'What a most charming, sweet breeze,' 'Yes Miss, a most splendid + nice air.'" Another woman, Miss Dulles of Philadelphia, seemed "a good specimen of a foolish, talkative girl, without discretion, or one interesting quality." Fashionable ladies such as Miss Dulles spent too much time on their appearances and not enough on other refinements such as intelligence, good conversational skills, and true feeling. Approached by a "fantastically dressed woman," Jane Caroline North noted that the woman "was inclined to be very sociable, but her distracted toilette discouraged any such feeling on my part." Those who reached the pinnacle of appearance, such as the celebrated "Waterford Beauty," fell short in other areas, being in this case "quite illiterate + uneducated."[23]

Too many ladies and gentlemen at the springs imitated style and civility well enough to earn "a reputation rather beyond . . . [their] merit." The springs produced people who, despite their surface appearances and "pretty talent for small talk," "purchased some of [their] most captivating qualities with [their] Barouch and pair." Foreign visitors noted that Americans had "a deficiency of taste and feeling" that marked them as inferior to their European colleagues. Americans lacked the intensity of love; enthusiasm for art, music, and literature; intelligence; sentiment; and subdued manners that James Silk Buckingham admired in his English countrymen and women.

The problem, according to one American, lay in the emphasis on external accomplishments. Good looks and a gloss of manners admitted "all sorts of people" to fashionable society. Men and women with newfound wealth circulated in the highest levels of springs society, but they lacked the "moral tone" that signified true status. Rather than improving one's moral condition, wealth and social station "too frequently exercise a deteriorating influence upon the character." As the novelist T. S. Arthur noted, "the consequence is . . . that they who are rich . . . are not always the ones whom we should most desire to mingle with."[24]

At the springs people spent the majority of their time in mixed company, whether in parlors, around the hotel grounds, or in other public spaces. These places provided countless opportunities to send and to receive the semaphore of courtship. A typical afternoon in the drawing room featured "a variety of amusements—Mr. Kain spouted poetry and sung. Mr. Cochran read aloud. Mr. Dupaster flattered. Mr. Rogers played back gammon and talked sentiment. Dr. Erving cut Miss Clarkes knotting. The ladies, knotted, netted, made tassels, fringe, cut watch papers—knit purses, wove watch chains, braided hair." This scene was seemingly innocuous, but who could foresee the results of Mr. Dupaster's flattery or Dr. Erving's attention to Miss Clarkes's knotting? The potential for flirtation and perhaps more existed. Seemingly boring games such as billiards allowed women to show "a fine form and hand and arm to the greatest advantage. Rising upon the Toes, the hand rais'd eyes fix'd and the exercise giving a fine glow to the cheeks, our Ladies really look'd quite killing." Gentlemen admired these skills with "a delightful sparkle" in their eyes. Bowling also afforded women "an opportunity of showing off a handsome arm, and sometimes a neat ankle." Several gentlemen at Rockbridge Alum Springs took display farther by bowling with their jackets off and neglecting to don them once several ladies arrived. Scandalized, one woman wondered "what business men have wearing sleeves to their *shirts*—pardon the name—I should have said *nether garments*," in front of ladies.[25] Whether plantation mistresses or Northern ladies, nabob planters or urban merchants, few early nineteenth-century Americans normally enjoyed such carefree, even intimate, physical interaction with the opposite sex on a daily basis.

When given the chance, Americans took advantage of the opportunity. After dinner most of Saratoga Springs' guests headed to the piazzas, where the gentlemen gazed upon "the fair votaries of fashion," whom they "commented on to their heart's content." The piazzas were a public space, a meeting place where people presumed the right to approach and to talk to one another; the piazzas might be considered the trading floors of the marriage market. Ladies often sat there in groups "in the most attractive negligee costumes, and with an *abandon* perfectly bewitching, with all the world to gaze at them . . . as utterly indifferent and unconscious as they would be in their own parlors." Men mingled, while passersby on the street looked on. One woman insisted that she could knit away "and never drop a stitch for the hour together, nor once look up, though I hear the creaking of boots at my side." She might blush at this moment or when she felt "some gentleman is gazing at me, and I cannot help myself from giving a sly glance at his feet, to see if they are handsome."[26]

Furtive exchanges on the porch were only the beginning of flirtation at the springs. According to the popular author George William Curtis, "Romance is the necessary association of watering-places, because they are the haunts of youth and beauty seeking pleasure." The young and old, wealthy and merely well-to-do, and beautiful and ugly mixed at the springs hoping to find a spouse or at least a temporary romance. Ballrooms and parlors served as "a sort of meeting ground" where young men and women "learn the ways of the world." Their most pressing task was to master the culture of flirtation that emphasized surface accomplishments, polite conversation, and endless flattery instead of true feeling and beauty. As a result, "the most distinguished flirts at all the houses are as ugly as the devil." Few people offered more than pleasantries; proper manners were a rarity. "The men," wrote one member of that sex to a female friend, "scarcely wear that deferential air, which is due from our sex to yours. They do not draw the line between familiarity + vulgarity." The young women assembled at the springs deserved "a better fate than they are likely to find among the throng of male associates who surround them."[27]

The gentlemen suitors ranged the gamut of desirability from pure dandies, who resembled "young roosters strutting about, with their standing collars, making love to the ladies," to those with a greater degree of polish. Jane Caroline North called Mr. Coles "the most romantic, Byronic, sentimental personage" and hoped to become "acquainted . . . much more!" Coles presented an image completely opposite that of another gentleman "who has relapsed into his old bachelor habits." Having withdrawn from the marriage market, "he smokes his Havana and wears his Panama (hardhearted creature) with an air of conscious victory." But even this specimen was not nearly as obsequious as an "American Beau Brummell," whose "sole ambition seems to be to make himself agreeable to ladies." Brummell, a reference to a contemporary English dandy and courtier, achieved popularity because he demanded neither romance nor the prospect of matrimony. When women needed an escort or a gentleman who "is not a candidate for matrimony, yet so kind that he is ready to offer himself, in order to give ladies the delectable privilege of once refusing an offer," Brummell was their man. "Ubiquity seems to be one of his endowments—it is impossible to find a place where he is not, at least, where he will not soon come. He is perfectly impregnable to insult; no lady accepts his company when she can find any other, but if he is scorned one day he is just as ready to subject himself to the same indignity the next—anything for the sake of basking an hour in a lady's smile—though he knows she despises him." Other than Brummell, the only improvement could come in the form of a gentleman of great wealth. Such a man found that "brilliant belles claim his acquaintance with nods and becks and wreathing smiles."[28] He was the ideal of most ladies.

Among the ladies "the greatest desideratum" was to be considered a belle with "charming beaux to wait on them." Visitors frequently expounded on the beauties of the ladies; one observer "never saw so large a proportion of handsome women in any assemblage." He claimed that for "any young gentleman on the look-out for a fashionable beauty, whether to flirt with or to make love to, I cannot imagine a more charming field for selection." Charles Griffin called a school mistress he saw at Saratoga Springs "a real smasher." Her eyes "shot an arrow . . . every time she looked towards me. But fortunate for me they didn't make my heart bleed. Her hair and eyes were black as charcoal and glistened so you could see your face in them. Her cheeks were plump, fresh and fair, and her manners very easy." His infatuation continued throughout the evening prayer meeting, where he "couldn't tell" why the woman continually snuck glances at him. That this exchange took place during a supposedly somber religious service speaks to the pervasiveness of flirtation at the springs. Young men and women seemed to obsess on the opposite sex and the prospect of romance.[29]

Simply seeing women drink from the spring enraptured some men. When the women arrived at the fountain, which habit dictated they do several times each day, gentlemen wasted no time in remarking "on the beauty of some fair drinker." At the fountain gentlemen seized the "opportunity of *dipping* themselves into the good opinion of the ladies; and it is truly delectable to see with what grace and adroitness they perform this ingratiating feat." Mark Pencil overheard one bystander remark as he watched one "surpassingly beautiful" woman:

She drinks—she drinks; behold the matchless dame;
To her 'tis water—but to us 'tis flame.

One poet grew "envious" of "the liquid she sips / Between her pulpy, swelling, ruby lips." If men could not enjoy the pleasure of physical contact with women, they could at least experience it vicariously. But the scene at the fountain was also a chance to glance

Her little feet and nice turned ancles shew,
Peeping from muslin petticoat below.[30]

Men admired women of means, as well as women of beauty. Two sisters attracted a crowd of suitors despite their "quite plain" looks. "But the magic of wealth dissipated every feature of uncomeliness, and they were accordingly sought after and courted very probably by those whose only aim was their fortune." These and other desirable women attracted "a multitude of little insects, in the shape of beaus, buzzing about" them.[31]

Romance seemed so pervasive that one commentator wrote, "Cupid is fluttering his wings in the transparent atmosphere." On the gravel walks of the Virginia springs, one could see belles and beaux "flirting, loudly laughing, sweetly talking." Women walked too and fro "under a shot of curious eyes" as the gentlemen surrounded them at every step. Eager gentlemen "spoil[ed] their cravats in their nervous efforts to tie them exquisitely." Ladies donned new dresses each day "in order to attract admirers." They then encouraged each of their suitors by accepting small gifts and kind words until one stood out as the favorite. Gentlemen gave ladies "their handkerchiefs, their gloves, even their slippers; it binds [the ladies] to nothing."[32] In short, almost every aspect of springs life related to romance.

The usual pattern of courtship required interest, investigation, and introduction. For example, several ladies were smitten with Elizabeth Ruffin's brother during Saratoga Springs' 1827 season. They initially assumed that the siblings were married because of the brother's "very attentive" behavior. One lady asked Ruffin directly if the gentleman was her husband, not "for her own gratification," but because "she had been frequently asked without being able to give satisfaction." Once word of the nonmarriage circulated,

Ruffin wrote that a group of women "most formally came forward for me to corroborate the report, great was their surprise when rightly informed and occasioned no little diversion among all hands." Almost instantly Ruffin's brother "excite[d] a great deal of curiosity among them." The ability to meet this newly available gentleman offered an opportunity that few ladies neglected. As had Abigail May years earlier in Ballston Spa, these ladies considered the introduction of new gentlemen at the springs an event "of consequence to set my Cap square."[33]

Introductions provided an opening to begin the courting process. But in an effort to regulate the "great summer-lottery of contact and acquaintance," Nathaniel Parker Willis's Committee of Management limited introductions at Saratoga Springs to men and women of legitimate and equal social rank. That way, the daughters of wealthy planters would not have to worry about flirting with the sons of middle-class lawyers and clerks or, even worse, canal workers. Willis's system imitated White Sulphur Springs' "Billing, Wooing and Cooing Society," established during the 1830s by Col. William Pope. As did Beau Nash at Bath, England, Pope presided over the ballroom, ensured proper matches between belles and beaux, and protected "the dear sweet young ladies from villains, and impostors, who deceive them at the Springs by an appearance of wealth." He posted rules for "the encouragement and promotion of marriage" and enrolled seventeen hundred gentlemen and ladies with proper pedigrees. With many parents either absent or unable to judge the character of suitors from beyond their immediate community and social network, families relied on this system of introductions to ensure appropriate matches and protect their daughters' virtue. The women who signed Pope's articles of flirtation, as well as their protectors, could check its regulations whenever they doubted a man's conduct, which "had a very beneficial effect on many young men." Although one gentleman had fallen "desperately in love" with a woman, propriety prevented him from declaring his attraction. As a friend noted, "His seat is nearly opposite to her at table so he has every facility for falling in love with her, but remember he *had not been introduced to her yet.*"[34]

Only after suitors secured a proper introduction to their mark did a "parade of finery, arranged with all the taste of a graceful Coquetry," begin. "Laughterloving" ladies were often attended by gentlemen "bending over them showing their eager attentions and whispering their graceful nonsense; all the time their hearts lifted up by the combined influence of wine, music and love as if they had inhaled a gallon and a quart of Nitrous Oxide."

Men and women at White Sulphur Springs. The caption reads, "Flirtation on the Lawn." From *Harper's New Monthly Magazine*, August 1886. Courtesy of the Albion College Library.

The pseudonymous poet Samuel Sombre described a scene "within the deep piazza's shade" at a Saratoga Springs hotel wherein a lady and her suitor

> *Enjoys what's called, I believe—flirtation;*
> *In other words,—that is to say,—*
> *She and a man make love, in play;*
> *Sigh, languish, simper, roll their eyes,*
> *And mumble out inanities.*

So ubiquitous and integral to springs society was this type of flirting that one commentator insisted "that there was no pleasure at a place of this sort without a little flirtation." Another agreed that his time at the springs "has been spent agreeably, but would not have been so much so had I not carried on a few *harmless* flirtations." Men and women in both Virginia and New York State often practiced their "arts of fascination" on friends or relatives for whom they felt little romantic love and who were therefore a safe subject. These surrogate suitors served as "a target upon which she shows her skill."[35]

Flirtation did not always imply romance or the possibility of sexual intercourse—more often flirtation served as a means of social intercourse, a negotiation between men and women over relationships, status, and intimacy. Intercourse here means business, not sexual, relations. Consider Charles Griffin, who lusted after a young woman he saw sitting in a bathhouse window every day and "hoped she wouldn't be the one to shower me" because he felt he would "be a bit bashful about it." When Griffin visited the bathing establishment, he confronted his fear. The woman he had fantasized about led him into a dark room and told him to take off his cloak. But as he nervously disrobed, the attendant disappeared, and Griffin took his bath without any sexual adventure. Even the breathless Samuel Sombre could only speculate that men and women "Squeeze hands,—perhaps go farther, too— / Who knows?—I don't—Pray friend, *do you!*" Extant sources reveal little evidence of people consummating their courtships but provide numerous examples of foreplay. In the age of the Market Revolution, gender relations resembled mercantile exchanges. Men and women bartered their identities and reputations on the open market of romance through the medium of flirtation, with a premium placed on a woman's—but not a man's—virginity. Actually engaging in sexual acts lowered the value of the product. A debased woman no longer commanded a high price on the marriage market, and no gentleman would court a woman whom society held in low esteem; if he slept with a woman, his market incentive—to secure a valued and protected commodity—was gone. For these reasons, as well as other social and religious considerations, most women and men delayed coitus until after marriage. For them pleasure came not from any sexual act, which may or may not have taken place, but from the negotiation, banter, and exchange of wit surrounding the possibility. Sex itself mattered little; the fun was in the chase. When Mary Murray observed that "G is flirting away at a fast rate with a little Miss W from the South who seems to understand the business as well as he does," she was not making an idle analogy. At the same time that marriages were increasingly based on sentiment and love, concepts of business and market exchange influenced gender relations at the springs.[36]

In the open market of springs society, the buyer controlled the exchange. Usually, women played the role of purchasers of flattery, whereas men offered their merchandise in the form of pleasantries. When Abigail May returned from an excursion up Lake George, which included a night spent camping on an island amid a raging thunderstorm, she "alighted amid a crowd of Beaus, who all flew to welcome me, and congratulate me on my escape from drowning." Here May controlled the supply of her affections, while the "beaus" provided an abundant demand for her attention. But she rebuffed their advances and acted like Miss Gamble, who upon departing the springs "was surrounded by Gentlemen, uniting in a common supplication to her, to have compassion on us; and procrastinate her stay, but our intreaties [sic] availed not!"[37] When outnumbered by eager suitors, women set the price for their friendship and controlled the negotiations.

Women were picky about the type of suitor and manner of courtship they preferred. The majority of flirters, whether male or female, preferred to flatter their targets. A British major at Saratoga Springs proved "*indispensable* to the ladies" because of his "increasing and interminable stock of agreeable nothings." Complimenting another's taste, dress, demeanor, or sensibility instantly ingratiated the giver of the compliment into his or her target's favor. In 1854 women at Red Sulphur Springs, Virginia, constantly pestered one gentleman by soliciting his "assistance in writing letters, a piece of flattery they think my vanity will not allow me to refuse." So persuasive was their praise that he consented. Flattery proved such a "benign, beguiling, be-everything" force that some considered it able to "smooth the wrinkles of care, and make even old age wear a smile."[38]

But many targets of this endless adulation caught onto its style and substance. The seemingly continuous "pompous speech" of Mrs. Bennett seemed "highly ridiculous" to Jane Caroline North. Similarly tired of the "thickly buttered compliments" directed toward his person and books, John Pendleton Kennedy "sought an early opportunity to terminate the conference" with a young lady in Virginia and snuck off to the hotel porch to smoke a cigar. But no one better classified the "profusion of fine speeches which actually infect the atmosphere we breathe" than Abigail May, who fumed: "buz, buz, our ears are assailed on every side with compliments . . . 'tis the *Ladies, must be flattered*— 'tis the part of the gentleman to administer the *soothing essence.*" May attributed these idle pleasantries to the British advice writer Lord Chesterfield, who "says, you may safely flatter a Woman from her understanding down to the exquisite taste of her fan, no flattery is either too high or too low for them." In May's opinion, too many men resembled the character Jessamy in Royall Tyler's 1787 play, *The Contrast*. A confirmed philanderer and dandy, Jessamy at one point calls another character a "Vulgar, horrid brute! Married, and above a hundred miles from his wife, and thinks that an objection to his making love to every woman he meets! He never can have read, no, he never can have been in a room with a volume of the divine Chesterfield." Determined to repel such admirers, May believed that she could "make some of our Jessamys acknowledge all women are not so weak as to swallow the dose however applyed."[39]

But when flattery failed, suitors possessed an arsenal of additional approaches to courtship. On an excursion through the Virginia mountains, a broad stream blocked a picnic party's route. "Miss J—— being somewhat timid, Mr. —————— gallantly caught her up in his arms, and bore her across, amid the bravos of the gentlemen, and the approving smiles of the ladies." Each acted his or her part exquisitely: Miss J—— as the frail lady and her gentleman as the gallant savior. Less noble individuals such as Mr. Morgan enchanted women with "some delightful observation upon the 'Heavens above and the Earth beneath', he spoke in so soft a voice, and look'd so much more than he said." Another of Abigail May's suitors, Mr. French, accompanied her on a walk to a nearby bridge, where he "produced paper and pencil—urging my taking a view so beautiful, it was vain to refuse." One requires little imagination to deduce that French wanted more than a quaint drawing. But his awkward attempts paled in comparison with those of Mr. K——, who "had exhausted his stock of ideas upon the ladies" and decided to pursue May. While strolling with her, Mr. K—— sprung his trap: "so taking hold of my arm he began quoting from Thompsons seasons with much theatric gesture and killing glances. We walked on and got to the centre of a bridge when he stop'd and began 'but happy they the happiest of their kind' he held me fast and went thro the passage with great correctness and emphatic display of feeling." Mr. K—— likely hoped that May would respond favorably to the poem, especially when he reached the conclusion, "the love that has been evoked in the loveliness of nature." Perhaps he thought that May would be overcome by emotion and fall into his arms. But she understood his intentions immediately and thwarted the plan. Looking at their companions, May "saw the girls and Erving laughing immoderately and could have join'd them nay for that matter I did."[40]

Men such as Mr. K—— were not the only ones who attempted to woo members of the opposite sex. Many ladies walked the public spaces of the springs with "their gaudy plumage proud" swinging "before th' admiring crowd." Indeed, many a belle

> Poses *herself, with studied grace,*
> *Just in a spot—(she knows the place)—*
> *And there, seductive, lies in wait,*
> *Where men are wont to congregate.*

Such women employed all their charms to hook "the fattest trout," posing as "a gay deceiver . . . an easy prize, a tempting bait." A woman could also project an air "of unconsciousness and indifference" in her everyday manner, often sitting on the hotel piazza in a state of melancholy. But when a favored admirer approached, "she wakes up with so much vivacity and joyousness that it is a great compliment to the person so received." Gentlemen were more likely to "gallantize the ladies" based upon their "invincible good humor and unfailing vivacity," a technique that frequently worked. Once they had established themselves as suitors, gentlemen relied on their physical appearance. They hoped that upon seeing and speaking to the ideal gentleman, women would remark as one did: "My bosom beats quick and my eyes start with tears."[41]

Even so, people's best attempts at courtship frequently fell short. When a gentleman visited her cabin "discussing very fluently + as he thinks very smartly," Laura Wirt simply picked up a book and then her pen and paper while others indulged the "great *Bore.*" While the "false fire" of the conversation flashed around her, Wirt wrote, "Heavens! man, hold your tongue. I cannot understand what I am writing." Many women lacked Wirt's ability to confront undesirable suitors, preferring instead to rely on more subtle expressions of indifference. Despite her best efforts to do "every thing to avoid it," Jane Caroline North could not prevent Mr. Riall from proposing to her. In her journal, she noted that her procrastination in halting Riall's "annoying behaviour . . . was only prolonging my own discomfort." Other women relied on their projected self-image to fend off suitors. Abigail May discovered that "the persecuting attention of Mr. Bowers quite vexed me— I thought myself secure from all, even civilities from him, as I had heard he 'detested ugly women' and thought a woman who pretended to sense and sentiment, the greatest bore in creation—as I make pretensions to all three—I placed my security there." In an attempt to rid herself of his atten-

tions, May apparently called Bowers "a sot and a deceiver," which not sur-
prisingly angered Bowers. He attempted to apologize to May for his behavior but fell short in his sincerity. May responded by saying, "Mr. Bowers the
next time you feel disposed to shew you within this way I hope you will be
treated as you deserve—with *silent contempt.*" Yet even this blunt threat did
not deter the intrepid Bowers from pursuing May. Several weeks later, he
again pressed his case, and May once again responded coolly: "I will tell you
Mr. Bowers, there are some gentlemen whom the less we know of them the
better. You happen to be one of that description."[42]

The problem with men such as Bowers, and springs society in general, lay
in the overreliance on "empty courtesies." Too many gentlemen moved beyond "the appearance of being well-dressed" and neglected "that deferential
air, which is due" ladies. They acted too casually and crudely around the
ladies. In general, these gentlemen sought not romance but social advancement. When suitors heard that two wealthy heiresses had arrived at White
Sulphur Springs, they lay "active siege to these fair *El Dorados.*" Left with few
options, the ladies, "to get rid of their tormentors, have caused to be circulated that they possess only a tumble-down plantation, mortgaged over the
rafters and roof, on the borders of a rice swamp." John Pendleton Kennedy
dispensed with a flirtatious woman by taking "the opportunity when she
turned her head to a lady on the other side of her . . . to elope which I did in
a manner that must have led her to think that I had fallen off the bench out
of the door."[43]

Flirting was not confined to the young. "Old Maids" enjoyed the revelry
as "the bloom of antiquated virginity." These "old Jezebels" often "dressed
like tragedy queens, made themselves the centers of groups whilst the bald
+ grey headed penniless old bubbles fly hover around the young ladies."
Many "old bachelors . . . lost their hearts" at the springs, not to older
women, but to pretty young maids. Even John Sylva Meehan, the Librarian
of Congress and "a queer looking old man with a yellow wig," fell in love. He
was seen "squiring" a young lady about Fauquier White Sulphur Springs in
1837 "with a grotesque gallantry which is quite amusing." However, the
transparent efforts of older suitors often failed. The "broken down belles"
rang hollow: their "efforts to convince the world that they are not *cracked* . . .
are truly ridiculous and absurd." They were "incapable of *ringing* any other
peals than those which would be the death knells of matrimonial peace and
happiness." Only foolish youths who knew no better answered their toll. Too
many of the old maids resembled Mrs. Rush of Philadelphia: "she is a large

coarse women rouged beyond all semblance to nature, & wears her dress so very décolleté as to be disgusting. . . . Her bust under the thin black covering looks very like an india rubber pillow when half filled with air." Such "spinsters" were "past the power of enchantment."[44]

But older women and widows made a significant mark on springs society. At White Sulphur Springs in 1812, two widows were said to "rule here with divided sway." Indeed, many of these "charming" bereaved women were thought to "stand among the most attractive of their sex." Gentlemen surrounded them "with daily tributes of worship and praise." When not being pursued by gentlemen, some widows joined the hunt themselves. Young ones strove exceptionally vigorously to reenter the state of matrimony. They often sat "buzzing like bees . . . maturing their plans for future conquest." Some old gentlemen widowers sent their grown-up daughters away for the season "that they might not stand in the way of a second engagement." Even a difference of thirty years raised few eyebrows: "that is nothing in our day; it is quite the fashion. . . . What if this gentleman *has* a few false teeth, and a well-combed wig; they become him. He is a man of fortune and talents, and the young lady will have agreeable companions in his youngest daughters." Even seventy-eight-year-old George W. Munford, suffering from an oozing sore on his leg the size of his palm, told the young ladies at Warm Springs "that it's a great pity that I have got so old, if I was a little younger what a delightful flirtation we could have." One widower of a scant three months asked his male cohorts to "pray tell me who that interesting-looking woman is . . . ? Her manner seems extremely winning. Mark that fascinating smile. How beautifully white her teeth are! Her lips are like two ripe cherries. And what a bust! Ah! there is indeed a woman!" Once they had finished grieving (presumably for a longer time and in a more sober style than the aforementioned gentleman), widows and widowers possessed an advantage over their younger, single, and inexperienced rivals. They knew the benefits of marriage, whether romantic, sexual, financial, or social, and understood the steps required to secure a new spouse. Encountering competition from widows such as the woman who "both gives and takes flattery like a woman of fifty campaigns," the naive belles faced a difficult path to marriage.[45]

To add to the young ladies' predicament, the atmosphere at American springs had "a most singular effect, that of passing off old married ones for single." In both Virginia and New York State, gentlemen at dances exhibited "a decided preference in favor of Married ladies, as they were all chosen, while the poor single ones were left as disconsolate wall flowers." Quite often husbands and wives took separate vacations, with interesting results. Louisa Collins felt obliged to tell her friend Mercie Harrison "of the *prodigious flirtation*" initiated with her by their mutual acquaintance at the White Sulphur Springs, Hill Carter, "in the absence of his beloved spouse, who is passing her recréation d'été most innocently in Alexandria." Taken aback by Carter's temerity, Collins declared his actions "most shocking, and *worthy of Penance.*" Some women did not share Collins's acute sense of propriety. One "beautiful and newly-married lady, with an old *rich husband*" carried on an affair at Saratoga Springs. Each weekend her husband visited her at the springs, but when his business called him away each Monday, "her weekly consolation in the shape of a favorite lover" arrived on the train. According to one wag, "It was curious to see the sober dress and quiet habits of the lady while the poor old husband was by; and the transition to gayety was just as curious when the husband was gone and the lover came." But the cuckolded old man never discovered the deception.[46]

Although many married women had "jealously-devoted husbands" who never left their sides, many more enjoyed spouses who kept "at a discreet distance, and only show themselves from business at proper times, about the end of the week, when virtue assumes to take the lead." Fashion permitted an even more brazen breach of marriage conventions. One married woman threw a dinner party for "her lover and a few female friends with *their* lovers" at the springs when their husbands were away, although the husband footed the bill. Many of these same ladies would "deign not to speak to their husbands in public, but are hanging eternally on the arm of some gentleman whom they court in public and who in our unsophisticated world would pass for their husbands." They had no conception of their "*criminality,* but act this from a principle of ton [i.e., fashion], which makes it impossible for them to take notice of each other in public!!" The commentator dreaded the future of a nation with such lax morals. But perhaps these permissive spouses knew something of springs society. Whatever the level of flirtation people engaged in while away from their husbands or wives, limits existed on the tolerable level of intimacy. Men and women might walk alone through the woods, talk in hushed tones, dance a dozen cotillions, laugh away the afternoon, even hold hands or exchange a kiss, but their diaries and letters reveal little evidence of illicit sexual liaisons or adulterous trysts at the springs. That type of activity fell outside the bounds of propriety in refined nineteenth-century society. The springs offered people the opportunity to escape the strictures of everyday marital and gender conventions and to relax. But the springs were not a boundless orgy of free love where normal standards vanished; limits to proper behavior forbade open adultery. Edwin Jeffres could enjoy chatting with the "accomplished and handsome" Mrs. Saunders without fear of scandal. He "informed her that I was a married man with four little daughters. She then informed me that she had no children. I remarked to her that I did not wonder at Mr. Saunders bringing her to the Springs & leaving her."[47]

From this perspective, marriage offered few positive attributes. The springs occupied the odd position of both marriage market and carnival-like setting, where normal social rules were temporarily suspended to allow for harmless social play. With examples of guiltless pleasure around them, few people opted for matrimonial bliss. But according to James Kirke Paulding, too many people at the springs, especially bachelors, "don't know when they are well off, and want to get married. . . . For my part, I think a man who goes to a watering-place to get a wife, deserves to be—married; a folly which . . . 'always brings with it its own punishment.'" Ever the crank, Paulding was not alone in his pessimism. Those who favored marriage saw it not as a romantic paradise but as a cure for social ills. Matrimony, wrote one newspaper critic, was "the surest cure for a passion for the gay circles of New York, Saratoga, and Washington." Once married, this critic hoped, the former belle might temper her enthusiasm for fashionable pursuits. Life at the springs proved otherwise. But in the end, most women adhered to the "culture of resignation" described by the historian Joan Cashin. Conservative authors such as Catharine Maria Sedgwick agreed upon "the prime necessity of woman's life, a male adjunct, who appeared as regularly as the knives and forks at meal times."[48]

Many women in the early republic and antebellum period attempted to carve out a niche for themselves as independent, single women. But the cultural pressures to marry and the financial hardship of living single were often too great to overcome. Young, single women frequently "felt the want of a male friend old enough to think of something better than flirtation and compliments." Surrounded by eager suitors and ambitious mothers, the woman alone "stood in need of something to strengthen her convictions and confirm her resolution against marrying for *convenience.*" Despite her best efforts to resist her parents' urgings to find a husband, which included repeated trips to the Virginia springs in the 1820s, Laura Wirt abandoned her efforts to establish her literary career and married Thomas Randall in

1827. Her case is indicative of the paucity of single women and prevalence of marriage among American women during her time.[49]

For most women, as well as men, marriage reduced itself to a quest for financial stability and success. Although historians have identified romantic love and companionate marriage as increasingly popular during the nineteenth century, at the springs financial concerns dominated. In his *New Mirror for Travelers; and Guide to the Springs,* James Kirke Paulding emphasized the importance of beauty, attention to fashion, vanity, the ability to strike a figure in public, and the dangers of women who are retiring, well read, or have a will of their own. But both the first and last point that Paulding made was that "money is absolutely essential to the patient endurance of the married state. The choice of a rich husband, or wife, supersedes, therefore, the necessity of all rules, as wealth secures to the successful adventurer all the happiness this world can give, so long as it lasts." Writing as a defender of his fellow Knickerbockers against the incursions of new money in New York State, Paulding attempted to delegitimize fashionable society by exposing it as the opportunistic marriage market it was. We could dismiss his remarks as the rants of a cantankerous snob or an isolated complaint, but other accounts of springs life back up Paulding's claims. Years later in Virginia, the gambler Martin Duralde reported that "many a marriage is made" at the springs, a place where "there never was a lady without riches." This atmosphere appealed to men such as George McDuffie of Abbeville, South Carolina, who was "determined to follow the footsteps of his patron, John C. Calhoun, in marrying a girl of fortune, that he may have leisure to devote himself to politics." The son of poor Scots immigrants to the Georgia backcountry, McDuffie clerked for members of the Calhoun family and eventually served in what was once a Calhoun congressional seat. In 1829 he married Rebecca Singleton, the daughter of the wealthy planter and White Sulphur Springs' social arbiter Col. Richard Singleton, and later served as a United States senator, a governor of South Carolina, and a successful lawyer. By means of his alliance with several of South Carolina's leading families through a marriage he secured at the springs, McDuffie rose high in the political structure of his adopted state. He exemplifies the possibilities for social mixing at the springs marriage market; in achieving his personal ambitions, he was a great success.[50]

Market values of self-fashioning, negotiation, exchange, and money above virtue suffused springs society. In his social satire *The Upper Ten*

Thousand, Charles Astor Bristed described a Saratoga Springs courtship where "'love had nothing to do with it.'"

The story's English narrator retorted, "'Well, I used to think that in your unsophisticated republican country, people married out of pure love; but now it looks as if the fashionables, at least, marry for money about as often as we do.'"

"'They don't marry for anything else,'" replied Bristed's character. As a leading figure in New York society, Bristed objected to those who sought to marry into the higher social orders. By criticizing the marriage market and its values, he defended his class against social climbers who would marry into it. Bristed's use of an English gentleman, the paragon of high society and refined manners in elite antebellum culture, as the astute observer of Saratoga Springs society further emphasized his disapproval of the new social reality where commoners dared to court the children of the aristocracy. James Kirke Paulding, Bristed's literary and social peer, reduced springs marriages to a simple formula: "If you have money you cannot be otherwise than happy."[51]

Despite the efforts of the literary elite to disparage springs society, a highly efficient system for negotiating marriages developed. Most prominent in this marketplace were the mothers of eligible daughters. Hoping to ensure the happiness and financial security of their daughters, mothers served as a type of marriage broker at the springs. Their purported purpose was "to shield [their daughters] from danger." Usually that meant standing "on alert to see that they don't fall in love with any body not well-established in business, or well to do in the world." Mothers made a spectacle of themselves at balls, always watching and "making all sorts of inquiries about the opposite sex; they come here to the ball, not to enjoy themselves but to look after their darling offspring." For these matron-brokers, "money is everything." Many took the quest for distinction and advancement to extremes. To one observer, the gallery of mothers surveying their daughters "resemble[s] climbing plants, who throw out their tendrils, and in their blindness are unable to distinguish a pillar of state from a decaying, worm-eaten post." Such parents lived "in a ferment of *finesse* for their children's advancement, passing their days in devising schemes of hymenial speculation."[52]

This speculation involved investigation, negotiation, risk, and sometimes reward. Young ladies displayed their wares, whether sentiment, style, or physical attractiveness, at every opportunity and dreamt "of the conquests they fancy they have made, and which they calculate will be followed up by a matrimonial alliance in the ensuing winter." They acted like the "Belle of the season" at the springs, "laughing through her bright, blue eyes, and no doubt the little coquette is laughing in her sleeve at some of the silly pretenders to her hand." To ensure the most illustrious match, belles toyed with their suitors,

> *She keeps the eager wretch at play,*
>   *And leads him on, from day to day,*
> *'Till, finding there is no bigger fishes*
>   *To meet her more aspiring wishes.*

Men were equally ruthless in their search for a mate. "A long legged lawyer" from Mississippi heard of a belle he thought "*might* suit him, and so came all the way from Natchez to offer himself." Arriving at Fauquier White Sulphur Springs only to find that the object of his affection was elsewhere, the lawyer convinced one of her friends to compose a letter outlining his intentions. "He had only a day to spare, and it would save time to apprise her in advance, of his business." The older man rushed to his beloved's house hundreds of miles from the springs, only to have a confused servant introduce him to his prospective bride as "her father. Down she ran, and met this grave gray headed stranger who handed her [the] letter. The same evening he took his departure."[53]

The Mississippi lawyer's speculation, which included the expense of traveling to Virginia and the blunt investigation of his intended's feelings, ended poorly. Some would have counted him lucky. One wealthy father sent his wife to Saratoga Springs with instructions to "find wealthy husbands for our girls this summer, otherwise we shall have to have an auction." Despite the wife's attempts to screen unworthy suitors, one of the daughters married "Captain Gun." Too late, her father arrived from home shouting, "I shall go to protest. Beggar! Beggar! Beggar!" Romance had triumphed over social class, and the father was obliged to support the couple. The desire for financial advancement and social prestige brought a gentleman in John Pendleton Kennedy's novel *Swallow Barn* "within an ace of getting yoked" to the daughter of "a preposterously rich old sugar planter from Louisiana." He made a "narrow escape ... by the non-committal principle" when the woman pressed the issue, and her family dropped the incipient courtship. Although Kennedy's character valued independence more than marriage or social advancement, what is most striking about this passage is the way that

Kennedy portrays the man as a ruthless schemer, who viewed courtship as a game of negotiation, not true romance. His character resembled the young, inexperienced bachelor who, in evaluating his marriage prospects, insisted that "the Lady must love him well enough to wait three years, for that he does not mean to turn out in the world without making up for some of his wasted time."[54]

In general, gentlemen were reluctant to marry, "never know[ing] their own minds till somebody helps them into daylight." Ladies did their best to illuminate men's minds and to brighten the prospects of marriage. But a gender gap existed between reluctant men and eager women: men gained companionship and a sexual partner, whereas women achieved financial support and social status, as well as sexual companionship. This disparity grew not only from the different rewards of marriage but also from society's expectations for men and women. A man could remain single and occupy a prominent place in society; an unmarried woman beyond her mid-twenties was generally considered an old maid and a family burden. With so much at stake for women and with such reluctant partners, advisors counseled young ladies to make quick decisions: "if you are asked in marriage, say, 'Yes!' for you may never be asked a second time."[55]

The trick was to not marry too early but to wait for a good match without either picking poorly or being duped by a rogue. Ladies at the springs observed many ill-fated courtships. In the springs' competitive environment, where men and women negotiated alliances and often obscured their true characters in the process, the risk of choosing poorly and the resulting embarrassment, humiliation, abandonment, or even pregnancy abounded. The marriage market at Saratoga Springs, like that described by the historian Paul Langford at Bath, England, in an earlier period, required a certain degree of freedom from societal and parental constraints to operate effectively. The liberal social atmosphere at the springs required men and women to trust each other. On both sides of the Atlantic, the results could prove disastrous. Women needed only to read sentimental fiction to find examples of the dangers of romance. American novels such as *The Coquette* or *Charlotte Temple* provided frightening case studies of women seduced by duplicitous men, and English novels hinted at similar depredations at the spas. Characters such as Jane Austen's Catherine Morland went to Bath unaware of the dangers posed by "the violence of such noblemen and baronets as delight in forcing young ladies away to some remote farm-house" where they practiced their "mischievousness."[56] In this dangerous setting, women needed to guard against duplicitous suitors who could ruin their virtue.

The threat of seduction was not an idle one, for the art of deception had many practitioners. Ladies sauntered about the hotels of Saratoga Springs in jewelry they borrowed or rented for the season to increase their social status. Elderly gentlemen went to the springs to seek their fortunes in a young bride as they teetered on the verge of bankruptcy. James Kirke Paulding witnessed "many instances of this fraud, which would be truly lamentable, did not the woman who sells herself in this manner deserve her fate." In Paulding's view, by seeking status these young women endangered themselves and stripped themselves of any moral certitude they might have otherwise enjoyed. By yearning for a wealthy, impressive husband, they exposed themselves to gentlemen such as the "'French Count'" at Saratoga Springs, who nearly won the hand of a fashionable, wealthy lady from New York City until her family "discovered that his 'head-quarters' was near the main entrance to one of our fashionable hotels." At the springs, men such as Willie P. Magnum, who registered at Saratoga Springs as the son of the North Carolina senator of the same name, could win the respect of refined gentlemen; be "flattered, admired, and courted by all the ladies"; and dance with the finest belle. Only when a steamboat captain entered the ballroom and saw Magnum "cutting it fat" on the dance floor was the ship's steward exposed by his employer. As the news of the masquerade circulated, the steward–senator's son "saw the captain and disappeared—the mortified Belle took the first stage and is now at home, deeply regretting that she met and admired the Senator's son!" According to Charles Astor Bristed, such young dandies sought not to advance their prospects of marriage but to "victimize an innocent *débutante,* and leave her more or less brokenhearted." That Bristed and Paulding appear yet again as critics of the marriage market should come as no surprise: as authors they recognized a good story, especially when it defended their social status and delegitimized the open marriage market at the springs. Yet their warnings went unheeded. By 1874 a Northern newspaper could scold, "the aristocracy represented by the old families is dying out; that of the slave-holding power no longer exists, and the new moneyed people have not the habits of a luxurious ancestry to assist them to struggle against the new elements of freedom and self-reliance which have been introduced into the life of women."[57] The social and gender control that came with class stability teetered on the edge of collapse throughout the nineteenth century.

These criticisms and a few disastrous courtships caused some people to overreact. The elite responded to social climbers by moving toward a stifled social atmosphere where "many well dressed ladies of the *ton* seem afraid to be social, lest their true position at home be inquired into and questioned; and many exquisitely-attired men of fashion decline social converse [*sic*], fearful, doubtless, of the laughter and contempt ignorance must ever provoke." Fear of exposure silenced the social climbers, whereas apprehension about the true characters of the individuals walking next to them on the piazza reduced the chances that members of the elite were willing to take. Writing about the Virginia springs, a poet warned fashionables about "the base, sordid elves" who sought not "virtues and charms," but whose "object is money."

> *Ye favored of fortune take care of yourselves*
>   *Ah! heed not their love tales, though melting as honey.*

But such caution eliminated too many possibilities. Hoping to find suitable spouses for their daughters without being duped, matrons exercised "the severest supervision" over their charges at Saratoga Springs, "for in such a crowd as is at the States [Hotel], though all wear the externals of fashion, it is not to be believed that all who look attractive, and may be so, are persons whom it is desirable . . . to ever know." Yet despite one aunt's rule that "'It takes one generation to make a gentleman, and two to make a lady,'" her niece acknowledged that her aunt "wisely makes many exceptions and so many that it can hardly be accepted as a proverb."[58] Caught between the desire to secure a suitable spouse and the dangers of the marriage market, most women at the springs made a cautious purchase and hoped for the best.

Correctly interpreting a suitor's intentions or a target's receptiveness proved exasperatingly difficult. Bill Crump and Betty Forbes shared a series of flirtations; eventually, "she thought she had him and began to trifle with him, whereupon he told her that she mistook the matter altogether; that he was not at all in love with her, and that he had only meant to be civil." Crump intended to continue his platonic relationship with Forbes and refused "to put up with any of the slighting airs that ladies practice to make sure of their game." Even though Crump saw that Forbes "meant to draw him on," the woman's sentiment won him over. His efforts to rebuke her advances backfired. She "was so penitent" in her response to his denials of affection that "the poor fellow's heart was quite softening, and . . . he soon found out that there was something new and strange the matter with him."

Against his firmest resolutions to the contrary, he had fallen in love with Forbes. Unable to negotiate the intricacies of courtship, Crump fell prey to the lady's charms. Still refusing to admit defeat, Crump swore to "never go near her again (a resolution she certainly does not mean him to keep, for she likes him)."[59]

Women such as Forbes exercised the final power in marriage negotiations—their refusals to agree could ruin the deal. Take, for example, the case of a British visitor to Saratoga Springs, Mr. Ashburton, who professed his love for Mrs. Harrison. She enjoyed flirting with gentlemen in her husband's absence and allowed Ashburton to enjoy her company. Dispassionate, Harrison "did not move a line in her face, or a muscle in her whole figure—not a fibre of her dress even stirred. If she had been a great block of white marble, she could not have shown less feeling." Knowing the business of courting, she replied that "It was better that he should go no further, as she had already understood quite enough. She was very sorry to give him pain—it was always unpleasant to give pain to any one. She was also very sorry that he had so deceived himself and so misapprehended her character, or misunderstood her conversation. He was very young yet, and had sense enough to get over this very soon." Harrison flirted, but only to a point. Once spurned, Ashburton swore off any more "experiments" on the character of American ladies. His experience with younger, single belles only reinforced his distrust of women. After unsuccessfully courting a number of women, both married and single, Ashburton "had become very skittish of mammas, and still more so of daughters. He regarded the unmarried female as a most dangerous and altogether to-be-avoided animal, and when you offered to introduce him to a young lady, looked about as grateful as if you had invited him to go up in a balloon."[60]

Misinterpreting the symbols and signals of courtship posed other perils as well. Ladies who paid too much attention to fashion, rather than relying on more sober standards, might end up with one of "the brainless, mustachioed fools, who in many cases hang around them." If, as a result of their preference for the dandies who dressed well and whispered sweet nothings in their ears, ladies "do not make a wise and happy choice, [they] will only have to blame for it their own lack of discernment." The overly status-conscious Ludlow sisters refused to attend Saratoga Springs when they learned that the neighborhood shopkeeper and his family planned to visit as well. When their own fortunes declined as their father's business faltered, they stayed home for the summer rather than suffer the embarrassment of not turning out in style. The family closed their shutters and ordered the servants not to answer the front door lest their rivals learn of the Ludlows' misfortune. When one of the daughters' suitors discovered while conversing with a mutual friend at Saratoga Springs that the Ludlows had abandoned their usual journey to the springs because of finances, he rushed back to the city, only to find that no one answered the Ludlows' door. The suitor met the girl's uncle on the street and discussed the situation, finally stating that "If she were such a slave to fashion and observance, she was not the woman for his wife." He quickly returned to Saratoga Springs and successfully courted the girl's friend and rival. For the Ludlows, following fashion and worrying about class cost them their primary objective, a well-established, accomplished, stylish husband for the eldest daughter. But trouble awaited even those who succeeded in snaring a fashionable spouse. Examples abounded of women who married for love without considering the more practical necessities of matrimony, such as money and social standing. Older women, once the great belles of the springs, sat "gazing and listening in the midst of scenes exactly like those she passed through so long ago—so long if reckoned by years, so much longer if reckoned by sorrow and suffering."[61] The consequences of conforming to fashion were nearly as dangerous as retreating into old maidism.

Losing face or falling short of society's esteem was horrid enough, but it was nothing like the fate of men and women entrapped by rakes and coquettes. As early as the 1790s, when the springs first began attracting a significant number of visitors, danger lurked in the form of duplicitous suitors. At Bath, Virginia, Ferdinand-Marie Bayard found "a young man in a sad plight." Once surrounded by a pretty woman and a host of slaves, he was now alone. "That fair lady, after having squandered [his] money, slaves, horses and carriage, continued on her way toward the north, and wished the young planter a successful crop." But these coquettes existed beyond the springs. "There are many of those loose women in America, who like migratory birds, visit the various states in the union, at certain times. . . . They are generally very pretty, rather decent, and do not lack education."[62]

But even if some women preyed on men, women faced greater risks: not only their reputation and wealth but also their virtue were at stake. As early as 1800, Abigail May reported the tale of the unfortunately named "Miss Kissam," who was enthralled by "a villian [sic]—by the name of Gillian, [who] has been here about a fortnight. He has paid very particular attention to Miss Kissam—she imprudently walk'd, rode and conversed with him frequently. He (as she says) offered himself to her—and was rejected—he told the gentlemen round, scandalous (I hope) falsehoods about her—and said he could have her whenever he chose, for she loved him to distraction." Gillian's flirtation and proposition were acceptable in springs society, but his bragging about it was not. His eagerness to boast that Miss Kissam did indeed kiss him crossed the line of respectability—he impugned Kissam's character and virtue, an unforgivable offense. Rensselaer Schuyler, a prominent local politician (and scion of one of New York's still-powerful patroon families) rescued the distressed damsel. May's introduction of this erstwhile savior is instructive: "set a rogue to catch a rogue may we not say the same of a rake?" Schuyler "told Miss Kissam [that Gillian] was a needy adventurer and that induced by her little paternal fortune he might perhaps marry her, but that he was a gamester, debauchee, and every thing that was bad—however Gillian still attended her." Schuyler relied on his power to solve the problem and "sent for an officer and put [Gillian] under arrest for £1,000 he owed him. And now Miss Kissam heard some plain truths. Tho! saved from one villainous plot, there *yet* remain'd *enough plotters*. She was urged to go to New York among her friends."[63] At the springs even some protectors acted from ignoble motives.

The trick was to walk a fine line between flirtation and folly, to court and to seduce while maintaining the veneer of propriety. Having read popular sentimental novels such as *The Coquette* and *Charlotte Temple,* women of the early republic knew the dangers of succumbing to the charms of rakes. No fashionable lady at the springs wanted to die giving birth to an illegitimate child, as Charlotte Temple did, or be abandoned at a roadside tavern after being seduced by a smooth gentleman, the fate of *The Coquette*'s protagonist, Eliza Wharton. As literary scholar Cathy Davidson has written, these novels provided a testing ground for the possibilities of courtship and romance. By reading these popular books, women discovered the dangers, rewards, and limits of courtship—valuable knowledge in an age that simultaneously valued status and sentiment. These cautionary tales persisted well into the Jacksonian era and antebellum period. Time-tested stalwarts such as *The Coquette* and *Charlotte Temple* continued to be published and read throughout the nineteenth century, and new versions appeared, as in 1841 when the *Saratoga Springs (N.Y.) Whig* printed a familiar story. A chance meeting at the fountain between a wealthy heiress and a British officer soon led to flirtation, courtship, and a quick marriage. The happy couple threaded their way south, stopping at romantic spots and spending a few days here and there in secluded cabins. Eventually their conversation shifted from the ambrosia of romance to their future prospects. The officer told his wife that having "made me the happy master of your person, it is time to give me the disposal of your fortune." But much to the officer's distress, his wife possessed "nothing in the world but what you see." He too was without means, having exhausted the proceeds of his gambling exploits on courting the fair lady and hiring their coach. The romance faded instantly. That evening the couple slept in separate chambers, and the officer paid for a seat on the midnight mail stage to New York. But his bride overheard the plot and awakened as the stage arrived, hopped aboard with her baggage, and rode to the city, "leaving the gallant Major to provide another conveyance, and a new wife at his leisure."[64]

To prevent frequent indiscretions or falls from grace, springs society relied on the power of condemnation. Social censure sought to ensure that scandalous behavior remained rare and a cause of great embarrassment. Decorum frowned upon a gentleman entering a ballroom drunk, breaking engagements to dance with ladies, or insulting gentlemen in the presence of a lady. But when a "salacious Caledonian" climbed through the window of the "Lodging Room of buxom Kate" at Berkeley Springs in 1775, "urged— he was compell'd, by the irresistible Call of renewed Nature," he met with little sympathy. At the springs "breaking Houses is breaking the Peace." Once inside he "was *unable* to make her *full*," punishment enough for the Scotsman's indecent behavior. For Philip Vickers Fithian, simply mentioning the incident provided sufficient censure, so outrageous was the conduct. But other actions demanded more specific denunciation. Two fashionable ladies, who sought "notoriety" at White Sulphur Springs during the summer of 1837, staged a race on the hotel lawn on which the gentlemen wagered. A number of ladies considered the exhibition "disgraceful" and closed their cabin doors to avoid the spectacle. Louisa Collins recalled that "one gentleman called out for them not to start until he had walked his *filly*, and after the race was over, the winner of the bet, proclaimed his to be, the *best bottomed nag!*" Such public discussion of sexuality was rare in polite society. The language shocked Collins, who asked a friend, "Did ever you hear the like! For my part, I think the appellation, '*lady*,' is inappropriate."[65]

For Louisa Collins and her correspondent, writing about the scandalous conduct censured the ladies' behavior and highlighted, by contrast, their own virtue. Most people, especially women, at the springs followed Collins's example of privately condemning questionable behavior. Gossip served as a check on unruly behavior and circulated rapidly at places where women "Retail, with zest, each trifling news." From her beauty salon in Saratoga Springs, Eliza Potter "often wished I could absent myself from conversations that I know ought to be confidential, and that I had no business to hear." But as a service worker, she "could not tell ladies to shut their mouths, and hence I was much oftener the receptacle of secrets than I desired to be." Many women saw it as their "imperative duty not only to tell all you know, but all you have heard, not failing to suggest probable circumstances" of love affairs and scandals. But often women pushed their desire for gossip to harmful levels. According to Abigail May, the springs were "a censorious place, and one cannot be too careful how they conduct, whatever we say goes to the other house, and vice versa. We frequently too are complimented with the credit of speeches we never made." Women could not afford to remain silent but had to strike a balance between prolixity and reticence, for "if a Lady is reserved, she is no company, they 'had as leaves sit by a mile stone[,]' if chatty and social, why 'how dearly she loves the men'—these very words have been used."[66]

Sometimes gossip served a suitor's purposes, as when one Southern gentleman took his belle on a stroll about Lover's Walk, the manicured garden at White Sulphur Springs. Just beyond a turn, they stopped and intensified their conversation. "Just then he heard a party approaching; his chance had come. The moment the party came in sight he suddenly kissed her. Everybody saw it. The witnesses discreetly turned back. The girl was indignant. But the deed was done. In half an hour the whole Springs would know it. She was compromised. No explanation could do away with the fact that she had been kissed in Lovers' Walk. But the girl was game, and that evening the engagement was announced in the drawing room." Similarly, at Saratoga Springs one jealous woman snared a much-desired gentleman from her rival by engaging the hotel's servants as spies. When the rival's male guardian visited early one morning to examine her letters, a servant burst into the room and reported to the proprietor that the gentleman had spent the entire night in the woman's chamber. Her reputation for virtue ruined, the woman returned home in shame, her prospects for marriage destroyed and her rival triumphant. At the springs women refused to confront a rival or enemy; instead they "slandered her behind her back, while to her face they were all kindness and love."[67] In this manner women used gossip to dispense with their fashionable competitors or to win suitors while retaining the veneer of politeness and refinement they so treasured.

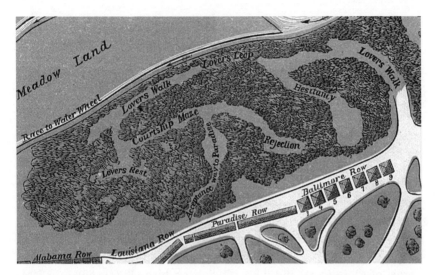

Detail of Lover's Walk, White Sulphur Springs. The path one took with a suitor supposedly predicted marital prospects. These trails did not appear on maps in the same author's previous publications. From John J. Moorman, *The Mineral Waters of the United States and Canada* (Baltimore, Md.: Kelly and Piet, 1867). Courtesy of the Saratoga Room, Saratoga Springs Public Library.

Women only managed to get away with such behavior because the springs were "the Paradise of pretty women; we do every thing that we please, and nothing can possibly go on without us." No matter to "what expense the gentlemen may go to change the state and tone of society, it is the ladies who give it its tone after all." Quite simply, in fashionable society "the ladies rule the day." Consider the case of Martin Van Buren, who visited Saratoga Springs in 1839 as the sitting eighth president of the United States. After "playing the gallant to the ladies" in the ballroom, he crossed the floor to shake hands with Mrs. DeWitt Clinton, the widow of one of Van Buren's principal rivals in New York State politics. Mrs. Clinton saw the president approaching, "folded her arms, gave him a scornful look, and turned off." But this behavior strained the limits of social convention a bit too far. Observers of Clinton's tantrum agreed that she had "behaved very ridiculously in refusing to shake hands with the President." Her actions fell outside the parameters of propriety. Philip Hone stated that "Mrs. Clinton's conduct has not been justified by any person whom I have heard speak of it." Even Van Buren's political enemies at the *New York Herald* "condemned her for it."[68]

Clinton violated one of the cardinal rules for women in springs society—
she exposed her personal pride and determination to right a past wrong.
Although Clinton's actions had nothing to do with flirtation, people's
responses indicate the fate that awaited women who stepped outside of accepted gendered norms of behavior. Failure to act like an alluring, demure
belle led to censure from one's rivals and neglect from the beaux. Overt political statements such as Clinton's or open sexual adventure such as that of
Madame Jumel were unacceptable. But even if women behaved properly,
they might fall prey to seduction and ruin at the hands of a rake. The
hothouse of springs society produced over-ripened gender roles that emphasized physical beauty, pleasing conversation, and an alluring, if decep-
tive, persona. "This mode of life," wrote James Silk Buckingham, "intro-
duces the young of both sexes much too early into public life." He felt that
"the gay season at Saratoga is a very unfavourable preparation for the discharge of those social and domestic duties which all are sooner or later
called upon to discharge." Flirting and acting as a seductive coquette or polished dandy contributed little toward productive life after the springs, especially if a belle or beau succeeded in finding a spouse. As one critic wrote,
"Youth, health, and beauty" were the holy trinity of the springs. "No old
belle ever returns. No girl who was beautiful and famous there . . . comes as
a grandmother to that gay haunt. The ghosts of her blooming days would
dance a direful dance around her." The values of springs society and the
characters they cultivated were worthless beyond the confines of its marriage market. George William Curtis could only wonder if the springs,
"where to be a belle was the flower of human felicity . . . had fulfilled its
promise?"[69]

Duped into believing that fashion was their ultimate achievement, women
stepped outside their prescribed social roles and failed to cultivate the polite accomplishments required of their gender. To elite social critics such as
Curtis, gender roles at Northern and Southern springs, with their incessant
emphasis on style, appearance, and marrying well, only served to undermine proper social order; the marriage market was too open. Members of
the elite preferred to keep the bourse closed and to only admit individuals
of equal social rank; these people were the kind who "'looked down upon
Washington Irving, don't you know, because he wrote.'"[70] But the reality of
American society differed from the elite's ideal. Just as Northern businessmen could not limit competition and Southern Tidewater planters could
not prevent the creation of a new planter class in the Southwest, social ar-

biters in both the North and the South failed to restrict access to the marriage market, and the competition for matrimony remained an open, negotiable process. Critics of nineteenth-century America railed in vain against the excesses of spa society; this struggle to preserve social exclusivity and passive roles for women was one that English spa society had lost centuries earlier. At the springs, the declension of gender and class went hand in hand.

Chapter 6

DRINKING THE SAME WATERS

Sectionalism at the Springs

*E*arly in the first reel of *Gone with the Wind*, Scarlett O'Hara complains to Mammy that she is not tired and would prefer not to take a nap in preparation for the evening's ball. Mammy replies that "Well-brought up young ladies takes naps at parties, and it's high time you started behaving yourself."

Scarlett is not convinced: "If we were at Saratoga, I wouldn't notice any Yankee girls taking naps."

"No, and you ain't gonna see no Yankee girls at the ball tonight, neither," retorts Mammy.[1] This exchange between Scarlett and Mammy crystallizes the key tension of springs society in antebellum America: the conflict of customs that occurred when people from North and South gathered together.

Yet out of this conflict, Americans came remarkably close to creating a national elite and a common culture at the springs. Before the Civil War, two distinct periods—characterized alternatively by success and failure—marked this experiment in creating a national culture. Between the beginning of the new nation and the late 1850s, springs in both Virginia and New York State shared a common culture in which visitors from all parts of the country felt welcome. The second stage of springs history began during the decade of the 1850s. The common springs culture continued during this era, but sectional politics stifled the convivial atmosphere and limited inter-regional exchanges. By the late 1850s, the common cultural and commercial interests that had united the springs dissolved amid sectional political rivalries.

From the earliest stages of springs society in the late eighteenth century, people noticed differences between visitors from various regions. Foreign observers, often the most perceptive and critical social commentators, noted that "a better spot can scarcely be selected for witnessing the different races and castes which constitute the heterogeneous population of the Union, and the different styles of beauty which its different latitudes produce." Besides commenting on the diversity of springs visitors, diarists felt the need to categorize them. Southern ladies and gentlemen dressed more elegantly than Northerners. Bostonians were much more reserved than New Yorkers. Guests from the Caribbean or Great Britain stuck out even more. According to the English visitor Anne Newport Royall, who observed life at the Virginia springs during the summer of 1826, "the northern people are reserved and distant; the Virginians frank, open and sociable." These differences were not superficial but "as great as between the natural growths and productions of the respective climate."[2]

But the great advantage of the springs between the end of the Revolution and the late 1850s was that these differences mattered little. Men and women from every state of the Union and every political persuasion danced, drank, and socialized at the springs "as if they were all members of one and the same family." In the congenial atmosphere of hotel parlors and shaded walks, men from North and South enjoyed conversations about such mundane topics as "the agriculture of the Southern states."[3]

In this era and social setting, men such as Henry Clay, the Kentucky politician and Washington insider, dominated. A Southerner by birth and persuasion, Clay was firmly a part of that culture while still promoting a national vision through his American System of internal improvements, high tariffs to boost manufactures and farm prices, and a strong national bank. Clay visited the Virginia springs nearly every summer between 1819 and his death in 1852, as well as Saratoga Springs on at least one occasion. Whether in the North or the South, Clay mingled effortlessly and was received with what appeared to be genuine cordiality and admiration. John J. Moorman, the longtime resident physician at White Sulphur Springs, who recorded his opinions on many prominent visitors, observed that he had "never seen a man of more easy, lofty and elegant volubility of tongue than Mr. Clay—or who could in his own peculiar and grandiloquent style say more agreeable and well timed things to his associates than he—and never one so happy in adapting his conversation to all sorts of conditions of persons." Always ready to please politicians, merchants, farmers, and especially ladies, Clay possessed a *"Natural Gallantry"* that won over those around him. During an 1845 visit to White Sulphur Springs, Clay easily outshone John Tyler, the former president of the United States from Virginia, who had opposed Clay's American System and had been read out of the Whig Party. Chagrined by the attention lavished on his political rival just months after Tyler had ended his term as president, Tyler packed his bags and rode away from the springs "at the very instant that a large crowd with a large band of music was surrounding Mr. Clay's cottage." Partisan politics and personal affinities, not state loyalties, guided springs society.[4]

At Saratoga Springs a similar reception awaited Clay. A procession met him outside of town with carriages, horses, and a band, while an artillery salute heralded his arrival. Gentlemen and ladies lined the streets and hotel piazzas to see the procession and to hear political speeches in honor of the guest; an invited few then proceeded to a dinner and grand ball in Clay's honor. That evening he bumped into his political opponent President Martin Van Buren, who courteously asked, "'I hope I do not obstruct your way.'" According to the diarist Philip Hone, Clay, "the veteran in politics and politeness," replied, "'Not here, certainly.'" Even in New York, a state dominated by the Democracy and hostile to Clay, he engaged the political heir of his arch rival, Andrew Jackson, with humor and congeniality. It was not that Clay refused to embrace political quarrels, for John Moorman insists that at the Virginia springs Clay readily took up the challenge when offered, but that he did so civilly and sought to resolve differences rather than to divide. The Great Compromiser concerned himself more with politeness than political posturing.[5]

Springs society followed his lead. Several Virginia springs named groups of cabins "Nullifier's Row" or "States Rights' Row" during the Nullification Crisis of Andrew Jackson's first term, and during the summer of 1835, one columnist overheard groups at the Virginia springs "denouncing the whole army of abolitionists and lamenting that Tappan and Thompson did not find it convenient to visit." Presumably, the Southerners had a few choice words to share with the noted abolitionists. But few took the threat seriously, referring to the Nullifiers as weak and sickly, a group of gentlemen whose chances of breaking up the Union seemed doubtful. Even male slaves singing love songs in front of white women failed to ignite real trouble. When this happened at Salt Sulphur Springs in 1835, the South Carolinians marched out of the room but "produced no effect for [the next] night there was a repetition" of the performance. During the 1830s slavery had not yet reached the status of a unifying issue that rallied Southerners to the banner of secession. South Carolinians might provide a revolutionary vanguard, but the rest of the South was not ready to follow. At the springs especially, slavery was not yet an inflammatory issue. One visitor from the Carolinas declared that Virginians cared very little about the institution and were "getting rid of this kind of property as fast as possible—and in a few years will have no interest in common with us on the subject."[6]

Only on rare occasions during the first period of springs history did interactions between visitors contain a hint of sectional tension. Instead of outright political hostility between Northerners and Southerners, commentators noticed an "odd sort of rivalship prevailing among the ladies of the different sections or states of the Union." The women studied, measured, and evaluated each other with "sly looks and glances . . . like strange gamecocks, in the same barn-yard." The rivalry existed as early as 1807, not a year known as a tense moment in sectional politics, when Washington Irving observed that Southern women retained an advantage in the fashionable contest at Northern springs. Conventional wisdom held that "it cannot be expected that a simple cit[izen] of the north can cope with them in *style*." These rivalries, however, never resulted in open conflict or hostility, perhaps because women in the early republic were not supposed to engage in politics. Instead, the competition may have actually led to greater understanding between the sections. James Skelton Gilliam's most troubling situation at Saratoga Springs in 1816 was not the topic of conversation but the fact that "I am the only person from the Southern states; of course I have a host of Yankees to contend with." But even when he found himself riding in a carriage with a Vermont delegate to the North's 1815 secessionist Hartford Convention, an occasion that would cause him to be "anethematised [*sic*]" at home, Gilliam "was vastly pleased however with the gentleman." During this early period of springs history, Americans still conceived of themselves as a single nation. They recognized the differences between people from various parts of the country but saw that diversity as a charming part of the nation's vastness, not an irrepressible conflict. For many elite Southerners, the chance to interact with their Northern compatriots and to enjoy the cultural offerings of Philadelphia, New York, and Saratoga Springs reinforced their conception that they belonged to a cosmopolitan, hierarchical aristocracy that transcended section.[7]

But larger social and economic changes had already begun to divide North and South. In 1833 the nation's third railroad, the Schenectady and Saratoga, shortened the travel time to New York's springs from days to hours. Where once a hodgepodge of sailboats and carriages transported visitors from the eastern seaboard to Saratoga Springs, by the 1830s an efficient system of steamboats and railroads whisked passengers to their destinations. Seasonal crowds now numbered in the thousands rather than the hundreds, and the quality of those guests changed as well. "Every would-be fashionable" could now afford the rail fare and needed only a few free days, rather than weeks, to visit the springs. One Southern springs promoter commented that "Saratoga Springs, from the very facility, and comparatively small expense, at which they can be visited, are no longer the same fashionable summer resorts they were wont to be." Instead of a select gathering of gentlemen and belles, visitors from "every class, colour, and condition in the state" arrived at Saratoga Springs hoping to enjoy the fashionable scene. Southerners were horrified to discover that "the fair daughters of the millionaire are not unfrequently vexed and mortified to find themselves rivaled, if not eclipsed, in the ball-room, by the blooming misses who lean on the arm of one with no prouder title than papa's tailor, or boot-maker." The same amusements, scenery, health-giving waters, and opportunity to meet powerful, rich, and famous people that attracted Southerners to Saratoga Springs created a heterogeneous crowd. A columnist for the *Southern Literary Messenger* declared that he passed his time pleasantly at the more exclusive Virginia springs but added that he would not "find it so at Saratoga, amid such an oppressive throng—such a rabble-route as that must be."[8]

Southerners insisted that life at the Virginia springs was different. Located on the nearly inaccessible western slope of the Allegheny Mountains, the Virginia springs were far less convenient than Saratoga Springs. Railroads did not reach the South's premier resort, White Sulphur Springs, until after the Civil War. As a result, the vast majority of visitors to the Virginia springs were Southerners from the wealthier strata of society. Only they had the time and money to make the extended journey to the springs. This isolation and homogeneity led one visitor to comment that "the general interchange of civilities exist [sic] to a greater degree among the company at these springs than at those of the North." A Northern writer agreed that "the free and easy air of every thing in and about the rural establishment, the haughty and erect stateliness of the men, and the abject suppleness of the servants, all formed a strong contrast, inexplicable in words, but instantly comprehended by the eye, between the modes of the South and the North, as compared with my remembrances of Saratoga."[9]

But these comparisons may have been overwrought. They did not square with many of the actions and intentions of visitors to the Virginia springs and the proprietors of those establishments. Social interactions at any Virginia spring rivaled Saratoga Springs for competitiveness, anxiety over social status, and pretension. And hotel proprietors in Virginia certainly wanted more, not less, business. Their building expansions, joint stock incorporations, advertising efforts, and involvement in road-building and railroad ventures spoke to a desire for an expanded clientele. On the same page that he lambasted Saratoga Springs for being too accessible, a guidebook author praised Fauquier White Sulphur Springs, near Fredericksburg, Virginia, and a rail spur, for being *"within three days of easy and comfortable travel from Boston."* Many Southerners described a much more diverse picture of life at the Virginia springs than some of Saratoga Springs' critics would have had their readers believe. Even William Burke, the tireless promoter of the Virginia springs over Saratoga Springs, wrote that "a hundred pictures might be drawn of oddities, absurdities, eccentricities, nonentities, ambitious mamas, anxious papas, fascinating misses, agreeable spinsters, delectable fops, twaddling gossips, and stupid book-makers" at White Sulphur Springs, which attracted a geographically and socially diverse clientele by the 1850s. Foreign commentators offered more stinging descriptions. The British traveler George Featherstonhaugh found "old sick men, young boys, husbands of charming wives, fathers of beautiful daughters, all in the same pickle together, mingling with the most extraordinary looking tobacco-chewing, expectorating, and villainous looking nondescripts" at the Virginia springs. The Old Dominion held no title to exclusivity.[10]

Southerners' discomfort with the social mixing that took place at both the Virginia springs and Saratoga Springs may have had less to do with social status than with the manner in which it was achieved. Status in the South grew from landholding, inherited wealth, and reputable family connections; these same bases existed in the North, but merchants, bankers, and professional men of means could enter the social elite much more easily at Saratoga Springs than at the self-consciously exclusive Virginia springs. The gossip writer Mary Jane Windle balked at the presence of "some few pious worshippers at the altar of mammon; human beings so gold-nurtured that poverty is to them the one evil of human life" at White Sulphur Springs. Elite Southerners recoiled at the introduction of new measures of status brought about by the Market Revolution and the infiltration of commerce (both long present in Southern society) into their bastion, the Virginia springs.[11] These criticisms composed less a reaction to a changing social situation than a yearning for a quickly fading, if not long gone, image of a more ideal South.

Saratoga Springs' visitors enjoyed a much more comfortable relationship with wealth and its creation. Affluence and family connections continued to influence entry into the "exclusives" of Saratoga Springs' society, but fashion was an "undeniable prerequisite." Most of Saratoga Springs' visitors came from the "honest citizens" of the nation who wore "the latest Parisian fashion" and mingled with the select. For these people, wrote George William Curtis, "Wealth will socially befriend a man at Newport or Saratoga, better than any similar spot in the world."[12]

Different economic systems and varying levels of acceptance of the emerging commercial society affected springs society. The more agrarian South and the more commercial North shared many economic assumptions, but they were moving at disparate paces; the Market Revolution spurred economic development in the North much faster than in the South. However, the South did not eschew the market or adhere to a precapitalist mentalité. As historian James Oakes has shown, Southern slaveholders were a highly mobile class who embraced the market and its potential for rapidly amassing fantastic wealth. Any planter who had made his money in the latest cotton boom—and many such planters from the Old Southwest attended the springs—benefited from the market economy.[13] But with the stories of success came tales of failure and economic ruin, which lent a healthy ambivalence to Southern views of the market. The North, although also unsure of the market's consequences, embraced its implications more enthusiastically than did the South.

Amid these increasing differences, springs promoters proclaimed the potential benefits of bringing the nation together at their resorts. They seemed determined to use the springs, which acted as both catalysts and products of the Market Revolution, to mitigate economically influenced sectional differences. As early as the 1830s, writers proposed that shared vacations at the springs would lead Americans "to disclaim the prejudices which had so long influenced their opinion against each other." Upon his return home, a visitor would "surrender a portion of that self-complacency which led him to claim a sectional superiority—the offspring of a circumscribed intercourse with the world." Comparatively isolated from the rest of the nation, Southerners acutely felt the need to mix with their Northern countrymen. Whereas Southerners journeyed north and discovered something of Northern society, few Northerners returned the favor. Observing what he thought was an increase in the number of Northern visitors to the Virginia springs in 1835, Charles Fenno Hoffman sounded an optimistic tone: "If the tour were more common with people of leisure from the north, it would tend much to root out the prejudices" between the sections. The "contact and collision" that resulted from meeting people from another section of the country made "a great deduction of that prejudice of opinion on local and peculiar points." Southerners benefited when Northerners better understood their section, its institutions, and customs, but interaction also improved the Yankees' lot, as "this action upon prejudice is reciprocal; the southerner meets his brother of the north, and forms an intimacy with and an attachment to him, that results necessarily in the production of the best feelings on both sides."[14]

Northern guidebook authors agreed with these sentiments in lauding "the most delightful and lasting intimacies" formed between the "distinguished men" who gathered at the springs. Mingling together in a purely social setting connected slaveholders and merchant capitalists in a way that politics or commerce never could. Dancing a reel, sharing a meal, and drinking the same putrid waters constituted a shared set of experiences, a common group of social expectations that transcended section. Only at the springs could a young woman from the North dance so well that she was considered "*quite good enough* to be a Southerner," something her Southern acquaintance said "was the highest compliment she ever paid a lady." These contacts, Southern writers hoped, contributed to a process "by which another link is added no doubt to the chains that bind this mighty union." Even slavery could be overcome if only Northern visitors could witness the "happy, smiling countenances of the African race" at the Virginia springs; Northerners would abandon their "former efforts to dissolve a relation fraught with so much happiness to the domestic."[15] Southerners claimed that their region differed from the caricatures in Northern prints and that if Yankees visited the South, social tensions would disappear. White, not black, relations mattered.

Instead, white connections made at Northern colleges, in Northern cities, and at other resorts provided the basis for forging a national elite. At such places the search for what Benedict Anderson calls "sociological solidity" was realized—elite Americans went beyond simply imagining that others shared their sociocultural outlook and class aspirations and encountered their fellow would-be aristocrats face to face.[16]

The desire for pleasant exchanges and unity had been a worthy project in the 1830s, but by the 1850s—the second phase of the springs' experiment in creating a national elite—the same pleas acquired a new sense of urgency. William Burke echoed the requests of his predecessors in his 1853 guidebook to the Virginia springs. Using a medical metaphor, Burke urged Northerners and Southerners to journey to "the social heart" of the republic, Virginia, and to visit its healing springs. He advised Americans that "If your [blood] streams have been rendered turbid by prejudice; if too much carbonic acid or unwholesome bile has mingled in their currents, she will urge you on to the healthy lungs in her parental bosom; she will oxygenize your *ill blood* in the pure atmosphere of her mountains; she will render it ruddy and healthy, and send it back bounding with impulse, inspiring fraternal affections and sympathies; and connecting the frame of our social and political Union by tissues that shall not decay, and ligaments that can never be loosened." In Burke's diagnosis, "Intercourse, free intercourse only, is necessary to make the two great sections appreciate each other, and to put an end to that pragmatical, offensive, fanatic meddling, which has served to alienate a generous, chivalric, and warm-hearted portion of this great family of republics." Simple contact between the sections would heal the festering wound of sectionalism.[17]

Northerners shared Burke's desire to avoid controversy and to mingle with citizens of their rival section. The travel writer George William Curtis hoped that by meeting at Saratoga Springs, Northerners and Southerners would "learn from contact and sympathy a sweeter temper and a more catholic consideration, so that the summer flowers we went to wreathe may prove not the garland of an hour, but the firmly linked chain of an enduring union." Curtis's language here is interesting. Unlike Burke, he opts not to capitalize "Union," as we might expect a Northerner to do. And his use of floral imagery seems to be an allusion to the myriad political compromises between North and South that wilted with time. But as did a Southern source cited earlier, Curtis conceives of the Union as a linked chain. Both Burke and Curtis sought to strengthen, not to weaken, that chain through the congregation of Americans at the springs. So important was the springs experience to the unity of the nation that Catharine Maria Sedgwick proposed that Saratoga Springs "be considered as a sort of Jerusalem, and an annual gathering there a national jubilee, when we are emancipated from something worse than political slavery,—for these sectional prejudices are chains and manacles to kindly feelings—dark prison houses to generous thought." Only on the "neutral ground" of Saratoga Springs could a situation exist when "the warmth and eloquence of the southerner melts the ice of the northern man, and finds and feels the generous current that flows beneath it." At Saratoga Springs "'sectional prejudice' vanishes." As Benedict Anderson has demonstrated, print culture served as an effective tool in constructing a national consciousness by allowing geographically scattered members of the elite to visualize each other through print. Sedgwick hoped that by reading about life at the springs and the unifying cultural forces at work there, Americans might forge a national culture. Even better, they might be inspired to visit the springs and further solidify the national elite.[18]

But the observation of social differences eventually crystallized into a belief that North and South were fundamentally different. By the second quarter of the nineteenth century, the South found itself at odds with the concerns and culture of the rest of the nation, as well as parts of itself. The social mobility that accompanied the expansion of slavery beyond the Tidewater and across the Old Southwest threatened the South's ruling aristocracy, who disapproved of the drive for power and money evident in so many of the nouveau riche planters from Louisiana, Alabama, or Mississippi; the coastal elite preferred family ties and personal virtue as the measure of social worth. The agrarian model touted by many long-established Southern families, who themselves engaged in market transactions, could not negate the capitalism at the heart of the Southern economy. In response to this challenge to their cultural hegemony, during and after the 1830s the South's leading intellectuals developed a sentimental literature of plantation novels that idolized the genteel planter of old in opposition to the greedy Yankee; they romanticized the past and provided a set of alternative cultural values that emphasized chivalry rather than ambition. Conversely, Northern authors began to criticize Southern society in works such as Harriet Beecher Stowe's *Uncle Tom's Cabin*, published in 1852. The cultural divide between the Southern idyll and brutal descriptions of the horrors of slavery increased during the antebellum period and furthered the distrust between the sections. Progressive Yankees and nostalgic Cavaliers looked to the golden age of the plantation South to justify their positions in the emerging order of democratic capitalism.[19] In this context, the efforts by many to promote the springs as a neutral ground seem quixotic and perhaps desperate. But by realizing that a cultural gap existed and attempting to bridge it, guidebook authors and social commentators sought to accomplish the one thing that they believed could unify the nation—to construct a national culture and a national elite based on their shared experience at the springs.

This task proved increasingly difficult. The rapidly developing industrial sector in the North created enough wealth for Northern merchant families to compete with Southern planters, who had long enjoyed a greater degree of relative economic prosperity, in ostentatious display. Cities such as New York and Philadelphia became centers of American fashion, and Northern ladies seized on the opportunity to eclipse their Southern rivals. By 1858 Eliza Potter could boast with confidence that the "great rivalry" between Southern and Northern fashion at the springs had shifted in favor of the North, an advantage the region "kept with unrivaled success." Such shifts in economic and sartorial power created tension and even outright competition at the springs, the nation's laboratory for sectional differences. During the summer of 1858, a negative review of Northern fashion appeared in a Washington newspaper and provoked a confrontation at the leading Virginia resort, White Sulphur Springs. Evidently, after reading the article, the Northern ladies apprehended "a prejudice against their dress and appearance" on the part of the Southern guests. In an attempt to draw out that opinion, the Yankee ladies held a fashion show. Whose dress was superior, that of the Northerners or the Southerners? To settle the dispute, a committee of ladies from both sections weighed the issue. A Northern member of the jury brought forth "involuntary reminiscences of Mr. Sumner" with her vilification of Southern style. Moving beyond a critique of fashion, she lambasted "the whole Southern country in general." Hoping to avoid further controversy, the committee "condemned to flames" the short "sketch" that started the entire conflagration and deemed the author in need of "reprimand and punishment." The conflict derived from changing fashion norms, but in the hypersensitive political climate of the late 1850s, even a newspaper column on dress styles carried sectional undertones.[20]

Such rivalries and confrontations developed at the springs not so much from the sections' diverging economic systems but from the growing belief that North and South were increasingly distinct. Foreign visitors first noticed the sectional differences, which they assessed in great detail, during the 1830s and 1840s. The result was an elaborate typology of American characters. By 1851 Eliot Warburton's analysis that Southerners were more "expensive in their mode of living, off-hand in their manner, but little nasal in their accent, gay and courteous—the northerns more moderate and tolerant, better informed and more sincere," sounded like a broken record. But only after years of such comments by George Featherstonhaugh, Frederick Marryat, Harriet Martineau, and countless others did Americans begin to place much significance on the differences between the sections. As late as 1859, Washington gossip columnist Mary Jane Windle, who presumably had seen her share of sectional types from her perch in the nation's capital city, pronounced herself "forcibly struck by the contrast" between representatives of the various parts of the country during a visit to White Sulphur Springs. Flummoxed, she asked, "*Why is this*? The blood of both, we presume, flows down to them from the Magna Carta." In her final analysis, Windle concluded that despite the common origins of Northerners and Southerners, their characters had diverged. She doubted whether Northern refinement still existed but confidently declared that "into whatever position in life a Southern gentleman may be thrown, the *gentleman* is apparent." Unlike his Northern counterpart, when a Southerner appeared in public, "the stamp of superiority is equally apparent." Americans had recognized their regional differences all along, but only in the glaring light of political conflict between the sections did these blemishes assume the character of scabrous sores instead of quaint beauty marks. Most agreed with Philadelphia lawyer Sidney George Fischer, who wrote in 1844 that "the union of the country is fictitious, and is becoming less real every day. . . . The difference exists in everything which forms the life of a people—in institutions, laws, opinions, manners, feelings, education, pursuits, climate & soil." But, he added four years later, "It is absurd to suppose that the South can succeed" outside the Union.[21]

During the early years of springs society, sectionalism and slavery posed little threat to the pleasant life there; they were instead topics for humorous observations. Not until the late 1850s, after King Cotton had united the South around the profitability of slavery, did sectional tensions divide springs visitors. By the late 1850s, slavery, far more than dress styles or political affili-ation, interrupted the relaxing atmosphere. New York's antikidnapping and personal liberty laws and the controversy surrounding the Fugitive Slave Act of 1850 combined to create a climate of fear and hostility.[22]

The example of Solomon Northup, a mixed-race freedman who was born near Saratoga Springs and worked in the United States Hotel there from 1834 to 1841, provided an excellent example of slavery's ills and Southerners' insecurity. Famed for his violin playing, Northup met two unscrupulous men who spirited him from Saratoga Springs to New York City under the premise of employment. They then lured him to Washington, where they drugged and beat Northup before selling him into slavery. Transported to a Louisiana sugar plantation, Northup lived the life of a slave for the next dozen years before a Canadian-born white working at the same plantation wrote a letter to the enslaved freedman's friends in New York. Benefactors soon arrived in Louisiana with affidavits attesting to Northup's free birth and thirty years of liberty before being captured, as well as an official re-quest for his return signed by New York's governor. Rescued and restored to freedom in New York, Solomon lived near Saratoga Springs until the early 1860s. A minor local celebrity who had published a narrative of his en-slavement that sold over thirty thousand copies and who had seen his kid-nappers prosecuted, Northup, by his presence, reminded abolitionists and proslavery advocates of the immediacy of slavery.[23]

Southerners must have taken notice of Northup's case, as it was men-tioned frequently in the *Saratoga Springs (N.Y.) Whig* throughout the mid-1850s. They might also have heard of—but probably not read—the aboli-tionist novel *Jamie Parker, the Fugitive,* about two female slaves who escaped their master while visiting Saratoga Springs. In this climate, Southerners hesitated to bring their personal slaves along on their summer excursions to the North lest those slaves be corrupted by abolitionists and convinced to flee their masters and to escape to freedom. Conversely, Northerners feared that free blacks or escaped slaves might be recaptured or sold into slavery, a variation on Solomon Northup's experience. A runaway slave such as Har-riet Jacobs could look forward to her trip "to the quiet of the country" at Saratoga Springs until she discovered herself "in the midst of a swarm of Southerners. I looked round me with fear and trembling," she noted, "dreading to see someone who would recognize me" and return her to slav-ery. The intrusion of the peculiar institution, here in the persons of the escaped slave Jacobs and her potential captors, as well as the political conflict generated by contradictory state and federal laws, upset the springs' pleasant society.[24]

More troublesome to the congenial atmosphere at the springs were the interactions between Southerners and free blacks in the North. Accustomed to servile African Americans, most Southerners were unprepared for the assertive behavior of Northern blacks. A perceived affront to a black waiter at Cape May, New Jersey, resulted in a general riot between Southern tourists and the resort's black waiters. Similarly, at Saratoga Springs a gentleman from Georgia "slit the nose of one of 'Africa's Sons' who was an impertinent waiter a few evenings since." To counter the boldness of the free black waiters, who dominated the profession at Saratoga Springs, one Virginian wished "that the South Carolinians had the insolent negroes of the North in their cotton fields for a term of months each year." Perhaps then Southerners would not have to face the discomforting prospect of comparatively unobsequious African Americans.[25] Whether the presence and actions of free black servants caused the social confrontations, or if such events occurred because of political battles, the situation was worsening.

But it was not only the rude waiters and domestics that irritated Southern visitors to Northern springs; a larger climate of hostility was emerging. During the summer of 1860, a parade of carriages, a brass band, and bonfires heralded the arrival of a Democratic candidate for president, Stephen Douglas, at Saratoga Springs. Such demonstrations were commonplace in American politics, but a speech calling "the people of the South a rabble, traitors, etc." was not.[26] If supporters of the conservative Democratic Party and the author of popular sovereignty had acted this way, Southerners probably assumed that the Northern, Free-Soil Republicans might have come close to rioting in a similar situation. There is no direct record of Southern reactions to this demonstration, but those still visiting Saratoga Springs must have been chastened.

Southern editors reacted quickly to the increasingly hostile climate, asking why slaveholders should "subject themselves to outrage and insult" in the North, "when their native mountains abound in such attractive places of resort?" Southern churches and students had already adopted the boycotting tactic. By the early 1850s, every major Protestant denomination had divided over the issue of slavery, and several Southern branches had formed their own colleges, presumably to be filled by Southern students who had started to abandon their Northern universities around the same time. If the hotel ledgers of two smaller Virginia springs are any indication,

Southern tourists echoed this trend. Almost 99 percent of visitors during the summers of 1857 and 1858 listed Southern places of residence. A Northern paper confirmed this homogeneity when it reported few Northern visitors at the Virginia springs. Southern visitors to Saratoga Springs likewise noted "very few here from the South" during their visits to that resort, but hotel records disagree.[27]

As Table 2 suggests, Northern tourists, not Southern tourists, heeded "the many threats contained in Southern prints" to stay at home. With a sizable number of Southern visitors at Saratoga Springs finding the company there "mostly a sociable + agreeable lot," many felt that "this great bug-a-boo of disunion is growing more and more ridiculous." Northerners and Southerners continued to mingle at Saratoga Springs with little incident and a charming level of enjoyment. Even a prominent proponent of Southern rights, Mississippi senator Jefferson Davis, could say in 1858, after touring Northern resorts, that "the difference [between the sections] is less than I had expected."[28] The view from Saratoga Springs was fairly benign on the questions of slavery and secession, with relatively little fear of disunion.

Opinion at the Virginia springs proved far different. There men such as Edmund Ruffin of Virginia—a prominent agricultural reformer, essayist, promoter of Southern nationalism and independence, and frequent Virginia springs visitor—"used every suitable occasion to express my opinion, & the grounds thereof, that the slave-holding states should speedily separate from the others, & form a separate confederacy." His initial efforts in the summer of 1856 met with little success, however, because many people agreed in principle that secession was necessary to ward off Northern attempts to "destroy our institution of slavery, & thus ruin the southern states" but were unwilling to express these feelings openly or to commit to actual rebellion. Yet Ruffin persevered, hoping "to be a worthy & efficient advocate of the cause." He devoted the next several years to traveling across the South dressed in a Virginia-made suit of homegrown cotton, filling sympathetic ears with talk of secession while publishing on the cause at every opportunity.[29]

Ruffin faced a difficult task in convincing Southerners of the wisdom and necessity of secession, especially during his visits to the springs. Even in 1860, when secession "furnish[ed] most of the subjects of conversation here among the men," Ruffin found himself "alone, as an avowed disunionist." But he continued to "avow that opinion upon every occasion." Perhaps the social scene at the Virginia springs was too relaxing for political turmoil. As

Table 2

Regional Origin of Springs Visitors, 1850s

Resort/Hotel	Slave States		Free States		Foreign		
	N	%	N	%	N	%	N[a]
Virginia							
Buffalo Lithia Springs, 1857	864	99.6	3	.4	0	0	867
Buffalo Lithia Springs, 1858	841	98.9	9	1.1	0	0	850
Yellow Sulphur Springs, 1857	719	98.8	7	1.0	2	0.3	728
Yellow Sulphur Springs, 1858	791	98.3	14	1.7	0	0	805
Saratoga Springs							
Union Hall, 1852	815	16.0	4,214	82.6	74	1.5	5,103
Clarendon Hall, 1860	271	26.0	735	70.4	37	3.6	1,043

Sources: Buffalo Lithia Springs register, 1857–58, VHS; Yellow Sulphur Springs register, 1857–58, VHS; Union Hall register, 1852, HSSSp; Clarendon Hall register, 1860, NMR.

[a]N = 9,396.

late as 1853, a slaveholder and abolitionist were observed debating "the subject of slavery—for three days together—without quarrelling." Rather than being dominated by radicals such as Ruffin, many at the springs agreed with the moderate John Pendleton Kennedy of Maryland, who called secessionism "a flame which must burn itself out." Even as late as 1860, some newspapers reported little talk of politics at the springs. Instead visitors seemed "more intent upon discussing the virtues of the waters and the excellencies of the table."[30]

Apparently the congenial atmosphere established by Henry Clay persisted. As the historian John McCardell has written, Southern nationalism and secession were not preordained but had to be created. North and South did not compose two distinctly different sections or peoples on the eve of the Civil War. They shared many assumptions about society, economics, politics, and thought, but slavery lent an ideological charge to these topics. Only when the South perceived that the nation's political system was failing to protect its interests, notably slavery, did secession gain credibility beyond a small minority of fervent nationalists. Few Southerners supported the idea of an independent Southern nation during the Jacksonian era. Only the efforts of radical seccessionists such as Ruffin and the growing inability of the national political system to solve the controversy over the westward expansion of slavery persuaded Southerners of the efficacy of secession and the viability of a separate nation.[31]

Against the majority of Southern opinion and despite little encouragement from those they met, Ruffin and his fellow fire-eaters continued to militate for secession. These Southern nationalists, especially the South Carolinians, were conspicuous for their "hostility to the Federal government." According to John Pendleton Kennedy, they were a group "distempered with nullification and Disunion" and a generation "educated in the most settled hatred of the United States." They eagerly and readily engaged the few Northerners still coming to the Virginia springs, as did one Democrat from South Carolina who bickered with a fellow Democrat from Maine, each getting in a number of "hard licks." Any controversy, however mild, served as ammunition for secessionist armaments. After its 1857 corporate reorganization, White Sulphur Springs offered land for the construction of a Protestant church. The Methodists quickly took up the offer, erecting a church under the auspices of the Baltimore Conference, which had remained in the Northern camp after the 1845 schism over slavery divided the denomination into Northern and Southern branches. Outraged that donors to the church's construction fund "were aiding to strengthen an abolitionist religious association," Edmund Ruffin and a few associates exposed the situation and "tried to excite and keep up this ferment." Eventually the two sides reached an amicable settlement that granted both branches of Methodism title to the building. The issue of controlling the church was "of but small amount" in Ruffin's opinion. Although he delighted in thwarting the advance of abolitionism, his larger goal was to draw "more attention to the strange & great abuse" Northern institutions inflicted on Southerners.[32] For Ruffin, the church issue was a stalking horse for proslavery arguments and secession. Few matched his efforts and achievements as an opportunistic political operative.

Few Northerners, especially politicians, dared to venture into such a tense situation during the 1850s. Those with the temerity to visit the Virginia springs generally fared poorly. President Millard Fillmore, a native New Yorker who had helped to pass the Compromise of 1850 but remained ambivalent on the extension of slavery, met with an "entirely tame & indifferent" reception at the White Sulphur Springs in 1851. Even when John Pendleton Kennedy, a well-respected Southern author, social arbiter, and fellow Whig, escorted the president into the ballroom, people greeted Fillmore with "no enthusiasm, no demonstration." The committee appointed to receive the president "seemed not to know what to do, they were afraid of being too attentive so fell into the opposite." As one woman put it, "Never was a man treated with less attention." The South Carolinians at the springs continued the "narrow absurd conduct." That state's ladies refused to attend the presidential ball, and of South Carolina's many male luminaries in attendance, "*not one* was introduced" to President Fillmore. The waiters alone, all of whom were African American and "decorated with cockades & streamers," marked the special occasion. A similar reception awaited the fifteenth president of the United States, James Buchanan. No matter that Buchanan was a Northern man with Southern principles and a signer of the controversial proslavery Ostend Manifesto. During his visit to White Sulphur Springs in 1857, "all the South Carolina gentlemen refused to hold any intercourse" with him. An observer stated the obvious: this rudeness revealed "a very bitter feeling in that state on the slavery question."[33]

Moving beyond confronting slavery's enemies, Southerners turned the springs into an advertisement for proslavery ideology. Slave laborers at the springs were happy, industrious, clean, and contented. Southern nationalists pointed to men such as the bath keeper at White Sulphur Springs, a free black and returned Liberian colonist, who "greatly prefers his present employment" to his service as a judge in the West African settlement. Another author wished that Harriet Beecher Stowe could see the "healthy . . . yet evidently not overworked or oppressed" slaves at the springs and the "noble representation of slave life in the South" they offered. Rather than being mistreated, slaves led a relatively pleasant life at the springs: the labor was supposedly light, whether waiting tables or cleaning rooms. The author of an earlier guidebook anticipated the proslavery panegyrics of George Fitzhugh: "there is more equality, good and kindly feeling, existing in the South between master and slave, or the whites and blacks, than between the master and his hired white servant, in the North." By contrast, one Southern apologist claimed, workers at Saratoga Springs labored in "subterranean stories for the better engenderment of damp, mildew, and malaria." Such abysmal conditions compelled "the menial occupants to retain a becoming sense of their semi-humanity, by existing in a state of semi-interment." In short, the author continued, "Nothing can exceed the dreariness of . . . servant life in the Northern watering-places." In reality, free African American men at Saratoga Springs enjoyed a degree of relative prosperity and comfort. They dominated the table-waiting and musical trades, where they commanded a limited degree of respect and decent pay. Many lived in boarding houses run by other free blacks or in the upper floors and out-buildings of hotels, not the "subterranean stories" described by Southern authors. The more miserable jobs at Saratoga Springs were allotted by sex, not race: laundresses and maids, whether they were Irish, French Canadian, or African American, lived at the bottom of the social order.[34] Southerners conveniently ignored these facts. They eagerly alerted Northerners to the hypocrisy of the free-labor system, in which wage laborers supposedly lived less comfortably than did Southern chattel.

Slavery disturbed the deceptively genial atmosphere of springs social life. It disrupted what writers envisioned as a cordial gathering of Americans forging nonpartisan, national bonds of unity. An English visitor found his American hosts pleasant and agreeable until they discussed "the black spot on the brightness of this country's Future . . . ; the cancer eating into the giant frame, deforming its beauty, withering its strength—the awful curse of SLAVERY." This subject could not be "quietly argued or reasoned upon—the very word rouses the angry passions like an insult." Tempers rose at the mere mention of the word, shattering the facade of politeness. Slavery even interrupted the springs' main business, courtship. When a "fair nullifier from South Carolina" attempted to introduce "an anti-slavery *beauty*" from New York to a Southern friend, she demurred. "He might be pro-slavery; and if so she should not be introduced to him."[35]

In this atmosphere, opinion swung eventually in favor of secessionists such as Edmund Ruffin. The Kansas-Nebraska Act—signed by the same Millard Fillmore snubbed at White Sulphur Springs—and the subsequent conflict in Bleeding Kansas convinced many Americans of exactly what Ruffin had been saying all along—that compromise was no longer possible. Even optimistic observers such as George William Curtis lost faith. Whereas a few years earlier he had lauded the potential of the springs to unite the nation, by 1856 he committed to radical abolitionism. In his speech "The Duty of the American Scholar to Politics and the Times," Curtis railed against the slave power and the inability of Northerners to counter its advances. Pointing to the beating of Senator Charles Sumner and the Kansas-Nebraska Act, he demanded action. "Brothers! the call has come to us," he told the audience at Wesleyan University. "I call upon you to determine whether this great experiment in human freedom, which has been the scorn of despotism, shall by its failure be also our sin and shame. I call upon you to defend the hope of the world." Curtis continued to remind his audience of their bleeding comrades on the Kansas plains and the heroic parallels to historic battles at Marathon and Lexington. In conclusion, he declared that "The fight is fierce; the issue is with God, but God is good." Having moved from his early optimism of uniting the Union to a more pessimistic position that required the defeat of the "slave power," Curtis's transformation represents the rapid escalation of tensions and the disintegration of civility at the springs and throughout the nation. The man who had once hoped that Americans would "learn from contact and sympathy a sweeter temper" now campaigned for the Free-Soilers and spoke to abolitionist audiences across the Northeast.[36]

Curtis's position was one that Edmund Ruffin would have welcomed because it radicalized and polarized the discourse over slavery and drove more Southerners toward Ruffin's cause. Indeed, Ruffin's own powers of persuasion seemed insufficient. During his 1856, 1858, and 1859 trips to the Virginia springs, Ruffin met few who supported him wholeheartedly. In his many discussions about slavery with various Southerners, Ruffin found only "contingent or conditional disunionists." Not until John Brown's October 1859 raid on the federal arsenal at Harper's Ferry did sentiment swing to secession. Ruffin capitalized on the event by obtaining one of the pikes with which Brown had intended to arm slaves for a planned insurrection and carried it wherever he went, presumably including his August 1860 visit to White Sulphur Springs. During that springs season, Ruffin happily claimed that all the gentlemen "from the cotton states, with whom I have conversed here, are for secession, in the event of Lincoln's election." Southerners, or at least those from the cotton-growing states of the Deep South, finally listened to Ruffin's persistent pleas that secession was the only way to preserve Southern interests. Events that he could not control—Brown's raid and Lincoln's election—brought Ruffin the success and acceptance he craved. He and others of his fierce secessionism were cheered by the sight of the Rockbridge Rifles, the county militia, camping and drilling on the grounds of Rockbridge Alum Springs during the summer of 1860.[37]

As Richard Arnold, Savannah's leading physician and a politician with connections among the coastal elite of both North and South, noted in September 1860, "the people of the North are a foreign and hostile people to us and I wish no alliance with them. We ask no favors, we ask simply to be let alone. This they refuse to do, and they threaten us now in our very households and carry their unholy meddling to our very hearthstones. I wish the affair would come to a point." Frustrated by political compromise and the growing social divisions between the sections, Arnold believed that "the only good thing for which we are indebted to the North is Ice, a fit emblem of their hearts and manners, which serves to temper our drinks to a proper temperature." He acknowledged the "complicated" ties that united the states but maintained that "the dissolution of this Union is inevitable."[38] By the fall of 1860, few on either side seemed willing to compromise.

This atmosphere of competition and hostility ended the dreams of springs promoters such as William Burke to strengthen the ties that connected the nation. Rather than bringing people together to realize their commonalties, the springs served to highlight their differences and eventually drove North and South apart. The annual congregation of wealthy tourists at mineral water resorts constituted a missed opportunity in American history. Here was a cultural impulse that appealed to a discrete, affluent, and politically powerful group of Americans. For much of the early nineteenth century, South Carolina planters and Boston abolitionists drank the same waters and placed their common social interests above political issues. From these experiences might have emerged a sense of shared interests and thence a class-based common culture of leisure and privilege. The springs may have been one of the few social institutions that united elite Americans during the early republic, as well as during the heightening political tensions of the 1850s. But political precepts and sectional identities, based primarily on the competing systems of organizing labor and social structure, disrupted the genteel sociability of springs life. Rather than crossing or redefining the boundaries of sectional identity, antebellum Americans reinforced the status quo.[39]

If the springs helped to create an aristocracy in colonial America, as Carl Bridenbaugh suggests, they could not fashion a similar class in the antebellum republic. Even though a fledgling national springs culture—albeit with regional variations—existed during the first half of the nineteenth century, that culture could not unite the nation. Over time, economic and social change resulted in political divisions that the springs, despite their reputed curative powers, could not heal. Elite Americans may have enjoyed the same springs experience, but on one crucial issue their politics differed. The optimistic predictions of springs promoters that interactions between Northerners and Southerners would "render the Union of the States *more perfect*" failed to come true.[40]

Sectional identities and tensions triumphed at America's mineral water resorts. Saratoga Springs' more heterogeneous clientele and free black wait-

ers moved toward national unity, whereas Virginia's springs and their in-
voluntarily enslaved workforce evolved into an increasingly homogeneous
society separate from the rest of the nation. Instead of spending the 1860s
dancing, drinking, flirting, and dining themselves into dissipation, springs
visitors either passed their summers at a diminished, sober resort such as
Saratoga Springs or echoed the diary entry of Mary Chesnut. Writing from
Fauquier White Sulphur Springs, Virginia, in 1861, she commented that
"Yesterday we had no mail—but heard cannon."[41]

Chapter 7

WAR, NOSTALGIA, AND ANOMIE, 1861–1896

*R*ather than an end, the Civil War marked the beginning of a new era for mineral springs based on nostalgia for a vanished past in Virginia and a celebration of the Union victory in Saratoga Springs. Although far fewer people visited the Virginia springs, and the number of Saratoga Springs' Southern clientele decreased during and immediately after the war years, springs society continued in an only slightly diminished form. In fact, the continuity of springs society and an apparent disregard of its members for the war—even as in Virginia troops fought nearby—indicates the distance of the springs' elite clients from the realities of the war that devastated the nation.

But the Civil War did affect American mineral springs. It altered the physical structure of several Virginia springs and made peoples' remembrance of their wartime experiences there far more personal, even as the basic social routine remained largely unchanged in both regions. Economic necessity forced the Virginia springs to search for new revenue and clients, either through promotion from guidebooks or through cooperation with railroad companies. Saratoga Springs not only survived but also became much grander and more opulent in the postwar period. The social structure changed in both regions: Saratoga Springs felt the leveling tendencies of American society more keenly, and the Virginia springs dealt with the incursion of a less genteel clientele. Although the Virginia springs continued to be more exclusive than Saratoga Springs, neither springs region retained its antebellum character without some modification. Wealthy visitors in Virginia and New York State responded to the challenge of a democratic society by quickening the pace of elite class formation and cultural nationalization in opposition to both middle-class incursions and racial and ethnic diversity. Together, Northern and Southern aristocrats created a nostalgic vision of national unity that placed class above race, section, or politics. All these processes had begun in the late eighteenth century, but the rapid changes of post–Civil War America accelerated their progress.

Breaking down local and regional identities and creating a sense of nation—of belonging to a larger community beyond village, county, state, or region—were the larger transformations that shaped postwar and late nineteenth-century American society. Whereas in 1861 America consisted of a series of "island communities" separated from each other by geographic and cultural distances, by 1896 the nation had united into an intricate web of transportation connections and social interactions. The isolated urban elites of various cities no longer remained unto themselves but gathered at resorts such as Saratoga Springs and White Sulphur Springs to articulate their shared values, their class unity, and their distinctiveness from the masses. By the 1890s Saratoga Springs and the Virginia springs seemed more alike than ever before, and their clientele included a self-conscious national elite that visited both resorts as part of a larger seasonal migration of the American aristocracy. That aristocracy was based not just on economic position, cultural conservatism, and political power but also on a reconciliationist ideology of "depoliticized memory" that saw the Civil War as a "heroic crisis survived." Cultural and historical amnesia allowed Americans to forget the struggle for emancipation and African Americans' role in the war and Reconstruction and also made the creation of a white, wealthy American elite possible.[1] The springs proved vitally important to the cultural and economic unification of late nineteenth-century America.

The Civil War affected the Virginia springs much more directly than it did Saratoga Springs because Virginia contained battlefields and contested regions. Fauquier White Sulphur Springs lay outside the main springs region along the Rappahannock River, less than twenty miles from the war's first battle at Bull Run, and experienced the fighting firsthand. One year after Mary Chesnut "heard cannon," an "intense fire of artillery for six or eight hours" erupted within sight of the hotel as Confederate troops drove Union forces north of the Rappahannock. Given the back-and-forth fighting in northern Virginia, eventually Union troops returned to Fauquier White Sulphur Springs in 1863. Surveying the previous year's damage, George Manning Fell described the hotel as a ruin "from turret to foundation stone. The massive granite pillars are still standing . . . begrimed with smoke + heat" from the battles and Union bombardment. Although he sampled and enjoyed the waters, Fell imagined the springs' antebellum purpose: "I suppose many a gay, hotheaded rebel has passed the Summer months away, cooling perhaps his fevered bun, and ruminating over the events then about to happen, and now progressing." Fell understood the spring's medical and social significance but wasted little sentiment on its destruction.[2]

To the west, the main springs region's strategic and political significance placed it at the center of fighting. Proximity to a key east-west turnpike and the western terminus of the Virginia Central Railroad ensured that both armies desired to control the region. In addition, residents of the mountainous areas of northwestern Virginia, which had fewer slaves and close commercial ties to the Ohio River valley, were less enamored of the proslavery argument and were reluctant to secede. In 1861 Union forces captured much of western Virginia, particularly along the Ohio and Pennsylvania borders, as well as several western springs and portions of the Baltimore and Ohio Railroad. But Confederate forces retained the strategic White Sulphur Springs and were garrisoned there until 1863. In August of that year, just a few months after West Virginia's creation and admission to the Union, Federal troops moved into Greenbrier County to claim the area, which had been included in the new state, and the Virginia State Law Library at Lewisburg. On 26 and 27 August a battle just two miles from the White Sulphur Springs hotel resulted in a Confederate victory and roughly three hundred combined casualties, perhaps the largest Civil War confrontation in West Virginia. Describing the engagement as "a right nice spot of fun upon the whole; although it looked right gloomy and rather dangerous sometimes when the balls were singing around us," Virginia officer Fielding R. Cornett added that "every thing is perfectly quiet here now, and will probably remain for some time." A nearby Union victory in November 1863 began the de facto Union control of most springs facilities west of the Alleghenies and sporadic guerrilla fighting throughout the region.[3]

Only one additional engagement involved the springs. During May and June 1864, General David Hunter raided deep into Virginia in an attempt to unite Federal forces in the Shenandoah Valley and southwestern Virginia, as well as to draw Confederate troops away from Richmond in anticipation of a Union attack there. The campaign proved an initial success; Hunter's army captured Staunton and Lexington before retreating from a defeat by Confederate troops at Lynchburg. Along the way, Union troops destroyed strategic resources such as the Virginia Military Institute. But as the Union soldiers retreated across the mountains into the springs region, they encountered more ambiguous military targets. At Warm Springs, the hotel manager and nearby Lewis family had aided Confederate guerrillas, which made their property ripe for burning. Soldiers plundered the hotel of "chairs, mattresses, and crockery" but found little else, as "the owner had run off and hid himself." Only the persuasion of Mrs. Lewis and the skepticism of staff aide Colonel David Hunter Strother "that men of their character would engage in such inglorious warfare" spared the resort. Strother, a Unionist from Berkeley Springs, Virginia, had visited the springs before the war and had written a humorous, if somewhat disparaging, account of the region under the pseudonym Porte Crayon. Common gentility may have induced Strother to help save Warm Springs, but he also valued the spa for its own qualities. He even bathed "in the ladies' pool, which was less crowded," the men's pavilion being filled with soldiers and "dirty with a green ooze." The next day the Union soldiers marched to White Sulphur Springs, which had been rendered "desolate and forlorn" by several years as a Confederate hospital. Strother "could not bring myself to quench my thirst with the mineral water" despite its fame and collapsed asleep on a sofa. Another officer, Captain Henry A. DuPont, lobbied General Hunter against burning the hotel despite its past use as a Confederate headquarters, barracks, and hospital. DuPont told Hunter, "if we have later to occupy and hold this country, the White Sulphur Springs will be the natural point for our principal station, as so many roads converge here. Such being the case, the buildings as they stand would furnish excellent winter quarters for at least a brigade of troops." DuPont won the argument, although the buildings were never used by either army after 1863. The new hotel building, completed in 1858, constituted White Sulphur Springs' basic housing stock after the war.[4]

During an earlier period, between 1861 and 1863, the hotel had served as the main Confederate military hospital in the west and also doubled as a troop barracks. At first invalids such as Virginia officer Randolph Harrison, whose "sore throat . . . though it interferes with me at meal times, doesn't affect my health or spirit at others," filled the hotel cum hospital. Pronouncing himself "as comfortable as possible since I've been here," Harrison stayed for several weeks, sometimes sleeping outdoors with his troops. In those moments when his throat bothered him, he pronounced that "a few nights sleeping in the hotel will put me right," and he rested there sporadically until his regiment moved westward in mid-August. As fighting intensified, more serious casualties trickled in, and by 1863 approximately 1,600 Confederate soldiers had received treatment at White Sulphur Springs, with 192 dying of their wounds or disease. Several Sisters of Mercy from Charleston assisted the physicians and nurses, of whom some of the latter were slaves. But as the main theater of operations shifted eastward, Montgomery White Sulphur Springs became the primary Confederate hospital in May 1862. Located east of the Allegheny Mountains yet both south and west of Virginia's battlefields, Montgomery White Sulphur Springs was far from the fighting but still near a railroad for easy transportation. Until it closed at the war's end in May 1865, the hospital held an average of 650 patients per month. Although some patients suffered from gunshot wounds, most afflictions were "Chronic Diseases such as liver and diseases of kidneys, dyspepsia +c." The springs might aid these complaints, but smallpox proved a more deadly threat.[5]

The hospitals at these and other springs, however, were far from dismal places. Despite the presence of so many wounded soldiers, some injured or ill officers sent for their wives during their convalescence. Suffering from "bowel complaints" and "the fatigue of camp life," Major John R. Bagby expressed "regret" that his wife did not join him at either Coyner's Springs or Allegheny Springs. The officer corps mixed with civilians, including entire families from Richmond, who visited the springs for the same reason as before the war—pleasure. Bagby, however, leavened his jealousy of "other officers here with their wives + children" with news of the wounded. The presence of a man shot at Seven Pines "about the center of his breast" with both an entry and exit wound, or of General Arnold Elzey of Maryland, his face tattered at Cold Harbor by a "ball entering the side of his face near his mouth breaking his jawbone + then passing around + coming out at the back of his neck," sobered the society. Although Bagby acknowledged that Elzey and others deserved to have their wives present, Bagby found "sufficient reason why we should deny ourselves this pleasure."[6]

The presence of soldiers' wives—and especially officers' wives—at hospitals and even at the front remained a common occurrence in nineteenth-century warfare, but the tone of springs society seemed contrary to that of a military hospital. Early in the war visitors to White Sulphur Springs found "pleasant companionship" with "nice people there, some real Southern families." One staff officer, Giles Buckner Cooke of the Army of Western Virginia, spent the summer of 1863 at four different springs and "enjoyed conversation" or played backgammon with a variety of ladies. His duties required him to escort dignitaries, to inspect the troops, and to carry information between different officers, but Cooke arranged to spend nearly every morning and afternoon between 8 July and 6 August flirting with "the ladies." Cooke's experience indicates the continuity of springs society at many resorts, even with the military present. Civilian accounts confirm the presence of "very kind and polite company increasing rapidly," and in 1863 Kittrell's Springs housed "over 300 at present, a good band of musick and dancing a plenty." Although wounded and ill soldiers subdued the social atmosphere, and the familiar complaints of "not any amusements," hard beds, dirty and smelly rooms, and cramped conditions limited people's enjoyment, the Virginia springs maintained a level of fashionable life. Warm Springs saw its overall volume of business decline between 1859 and 1863 (it did not enjoy the financial patronage of a Confederate hospital as did White Sulphur Springs or Montgomery White Sulphur Springs), but it continued to draw a significant number of visitors each season. Powhatan Ellis Sr. noted perhaps the biggest difference between antebellum and early Civil War crowds at Allegheny Springs: "The company's [sic] composed entirely of Southern gentlemen and ladies from Mississippi, Alabama and this state. Warm, and not a Northern man here, and I question whether one would be—ha ha ha ha." When the Confederate army arrived several days later, his humor probably subsided. Subsequent years revealed a much smaller and less festive gathering, but upper-class Southerners, and especially wealthy Virginians, continued their annual springs pilgrimages to those resorts that remained inside the Confederacy's borders. Somehow, they found disposable income amid the tightened economy of the wartime South.[7]

The story is much the same at Saratoga Springs, where historians' claims of a reduced Southern clientele seem logical but lack absolute proof. Theodore Corbett bases his claim that "during the Civil War, 1861 to 1865, the town lost population, a sign that the war interrupted the flow of visitors to the spa," on the departure of building trades workers for military service, not on visitation figures. To state that "Southerners abandoned Saratoga Springs and northern resorts in the 1850s as hostility to slavery became open, and they did not return in considerable numbers, even after the Civil War," ignores the seventy-nine guests from former slaveholding states, 8.1 percent of the total, at the Union Hotel in 1869. True, fewer Southerners visited Saratoga Springs in 1869 than in 1852 or 1860, when 16.0 and 26.0 percent, respectively, of the guests of two separate hotels listed Southern addresses, but they still constituted "considerable numbers." Although wartime depredations and difficult travel certainly limited Southerners' ability to visit Saratoga Springs, there is no direct evidence that Southerners abandoned the springs after the Civil War, just as claims that they avoided Saratoga Springs in the 1850s appear suspect. Although every major historical work on Saratoga Springs has repeated the claim "that the valuable Southern clientele was lost," the presence of what one contemporary called "the bitterest most unrepentant of Rebels" in 1865 suggests that the war represented a hiatus—or, to borrow a musical term, a ritard—rather than a conclusion to the Southern presence at Saratoga Springs.[8]

Much more solid evidence exists regarding the tenor of Saratoga Springs' society during the war. Most demonstrative are the activities of John Morrissey, an Irish immigrant famed as a bare-knuckle boxer, New York State political operative, and gambling entrepreneur. In 1863 Morrissey expanded his Saratoga Springs gambling interests into horse racing and organized a series of races on 3 August. Although horse racing existed in Saratoga Springs as early as 1847 and regained legality in New York State in 1854 under the guise of breed improvement, racing had not yet achieved prominence or social acceptability. Morrissey changed that by regularizing and controlling betting, organizing a racing association, and garnering Cornelius Vanderbilt's financial and social backing. The 1864 season featured additional racing and such luminaries as Mary and Robert Todd Lincoln, the president's wife and son, drawn in part by Saratoga Springs' newest attraction. One national newspaper pronounced that year's scene at the Union Hall "most attractive. . . . From the hotel itself come forth the most distinguished of men, the most world-famed of women; from its porch dash off equipages that have no match." Visiting another New York spa in 1864, Sidney George Fischer noted, "The beauty of the country, the delightful temperature, the comfortable living, the pleasant society . . . made my visit agreeable."

Notice that Fischer commented on springs life and his surroundings, not on political maneuverings or battlefield dispatches.[9]

The normalcy of the spa life that Fischer and others experienced allowed *Harper's Magazine,* noted for its coverage of Civil War battles, to publish an 1862 short story on young tourists courting their way across New York State's travel destinations: Trenton Falls, Niagara Falls, and Saratoga Springs. Perhaps the story was a form of literary escapism, but its characters seem completely oblivious to the death and destruction gripping many of their countrymen. For these individuals, springs society continued during the Civil War with little reduction in its vivacity. That wealthier male citizens could purchase a draft substitute and thereby avoid military service only removed one more limitation on Northern springs society. As in Virginia, the Civil War may have slowed life at Saratoga Springs, but it did not end, or even suspend, the springs experience. By 1865 society had recovered enough that a New York newspaper could write: "For a hard-working, tenacious and thrifty people just out of a great war, none throw money about with the same prodigality. Rapidly gathered, hastily squandered."[10]

But the war remained fresh in most springs visitors' memories. Sporadic visits by Confederate or Union troops, whether as invalids or pleasure seekers, reminded tourists that there was a war on. In its aftermath, people made conscious efforts to remember the conflict. On 19 April 1865 Saratoga Springs heard "Funeral services and tolling of bells. Places of business closed at 12n. on account of the tragical death of President Abraham Lincoln." This observance marked only the beginning of Saratoga Springs' remembrance of the Civil War. That summer "the bright stars of our armies," including General Ulysses S. Grant, gathered at Saratoga Springs for "grand celebrations of the Fourth." On other occasions specific military units held reunions at Saratoga Springs, and during July 1869 the Seventh New York Regiment dominated the Union Hotel, where 68.3 percent of the guests hailed from that state or unit. One newspaper called the "pleasure trip . . . the most interesting event of the season." Years later, in 1885, former president Ulysses S. Grant, bankrupt and long out of office, returned to the springs as an invalid. His friends and benefactors paid for the ailing general's stay in a cottage on the grounds of the Hotel Balmoral atop Mt. MacGregor, just outside Saratoga Springs. His stay ended sooner than expected when Grant succumbed to throat cancer 23 July. Remarkably, his body remained at the cottage until 4 August, when it began a solemn procession through Albany and New York City to Grant's temporary burial place in

Grand Ball at the Union Hotel Opera House, 4 July 1865. Most of Saratoga Springs' hotels held dances to honor Civil War veterans, who—along with the finely dressed women surrounding them—dominate the foreground of this image. From *Frank Leslie's Illustrated Newspaper*, 22 July 1865. Courtesy of the Saratoga Room, Saratoga Springs Public Library.

Riverside Park four days later. Chronicled with lengthy stories and full-page engravings in *Harper's Weekly* and *Frank Leslie's Illustrated Magazine,* Grant's death at Mt. MacGregor became part of the national myth surrounding his life. The Hotel Balmoral attempted to capitalize on the event by preserving Grant's cottage as a shrine, and Saratoga Springs hosted the "Annual Reunion of the Society of the Army of the Potomac." The construction of a Civil War monument in the middle of Broadway reified Saratoga Springs' commitment to the Union victory and the community's willingness to use it for business purposes.[11]

The Virginia springs lacked a great triumph to celebrate yet spared no effort in commemorating the war. Montgomery White Sulphur Springs held reunions for those who had stayed at the hospital, as well as a host of Confederate generals, officers, and politicians during the early 1870s, and other springs attracted veterans as well. But the South's premier resort, White Sulphur Springs, faced business difficulties that slowed its return to prominence. Several years of neglect and hard use by two armies had left the

Ulysses S. Grant and his family at Mt. MacGregor, Saratoga Springs. Grant died a few days later. From *Harper's Weekly*, 27 June 1885. Courtesy of the Saratoga Room, Saratoga Springs Public Library.

physical plant in disrepair, and the company had little money for renovations. The cash shortage extended back to William Calwell's early ownership and worsened in February 1861 when stockholders transferred title to six wealthy investors because the original investors faced "some difficulty . . . in negotiating said Bonds, on account of the size." Jeremiah Morton, a major investor both before and after the transfer, realized that "it will be impossible to raise loans" after secession and made arrangements to preserve his Northern accounts and property but had less success with the White Sulphur Springs Company. The Confederate government paid between $120,000 and $130,000 for rent, damage, supplies, and furniture during the 1861–63 hospital period, but it paid "in Confederate bonds, which proves a total loss." The future of the resort, which already faced a $600,000 debt at the war's outbreak, looked exceptionally bleak.[12]

But good fortune had placed the South's greatest hero and icon nearby. Robert E. Lee lived on the edge of the springs region as the president of Washington College in Lexington, Virginia, and he visited White Sulphur Springs several times in the late 1860s. Although twentieth-century opinion

Broadway scene, Saratoga Springs, ca. 1890. The statue of the Union soldier *(left)* was erected 21 September 1875. This photograph was taken from the southern end of Broadway, facing the Grand Union Hotel from Congress Park. Courtesy of the Saratoga Room, Saratoga Springs Public Library.

characterizes Lee's visits as three summers "surrounded by people eager to recapture happiness," his stated intention possessed more purpose. His wife, Mary Custis Lee, had long suffered from arthritis and rheumatism and had traveled to many Virginia springs in search of relief. When she chose White Sulphur Springs over her usual trips to Rockbridge Alum Springs, Warm Springs, Hot Springs, and the Rockbridge Baths in 1867 "merely on the ground," Robert E. Lee wrote, "that she has never tried those waters, and, therefore, they might be of service to her," Mr. Lee abandoned his usual practice of allowing his wife to venture into the springs region alone. This time he told his son, "I will endeavor to get her there with one of the girls, at least," and ended up joining the family entourage. Lee explicitly wrote that he made a "visit to the White Sulphur Springs for the benefit of Mrs. Lee's health." Each of the next two summers found Robert E. Lee at the springs with his wife or a daughter, and sometimes both. Only during his final trip to White Sulphur Springs in 1869 did he state: "I want to drink [the waters] for three or four weeks." Although other springs guests may have used Lee's visits as an opportunity to commiserate over their defeat, and Lee may have employed his wife's illness as an excuse for his own pleasure seeking, he at least felt the need to state that his reasons for visiting the springs were less political and less social. Unlike the romanticized accounts presented in modern assessments of Robert E. Lee's visits, health—first his family's and then his own—motivated his trips to the springs.[13]

As early as 1868 White Sulphur Springs' proprietors recognized the value of Lee's visits. Part-owner Jeremiah Morton wrote another investor requesting special treatment for another famous Confederate, Captain Matthew Fontaine Maury, the naval hero just returned from exile in Mexico and England. Maury's service as a naval administrator—he had wounded his leg decades earlier and was incapable of active service—paled in comparison to his efforts to raise funds and ships for the Confederacy while in England between 1862 and 1865, but his refusal to acknowledge defeat and his attempted colonization of Mexico by unrepentant Confederates earned him lasting fame among Southern partisans. Just returned to the United States in 1868, Maury held a professorship in meteorology at the Virginia Military Institute in Lexington. Morton seemed certain that Maury "will be invited to be the guest of other watering places, but I want the honour + profit to ensue, to the White Sulphur, where the Lion of the forest and the Leviathan of the deep (Lee + Maury) will tread a sod. . . . No two names, among the living, tower so high and shed such a luster upon the good old Commonwealth." Using the political appeal of the Confederacy's heroes, Morton declared that Maury's presence "will be valuable to the Springs." Maury's fellow Lexington resident Robert E. Lee held even more profit potential, especially after his death in October 1870.[14]

White Sulphur Springs' proprietors hit upon a brilliant scheme to attract visitors during the 1877 season. They announced a 15 August "Lee Monument Ball" to raise funds for an equestrian statue of Lee in the former Confederacy's capital, Richmond. The sixteen hundred guests who attended that year, and others in four subsequent events, raised over $90,000 for the statue. Remarkably, a Northern journalist called it "an occasion so memorable that it may be regarded as a notable event in the history of the springs." What the *Harper's New Monthly Magazine* correspondent found so notable was "the presence of crowds from every part of the country, visitors from the North seeming no less desirous than visitors from the South of aiding in the object of the ball." The *Richmond (Va.) Whig* agreed that "the great galaxy of beauty of nearly every state is represented," even if the vast majority of the ball's organizers listed Southern addresses. This confluence of opinions and the expressed desire for unity suggests a readiness to forget the war's hardships and nation's divisions, even in the wake of a hotly contested presidential election that surrendered many of the war's successes to Southern conservatives. An emerging consensus among wealthy springs visitors and social reporters from both North and South held that the antebellum dream—national unity based on the sections' mixing socially at the springs—had been realized in the postwar period. A twentieth-century retrospective and promotional pamphlet recollected Lee: "that gallant gentleman who daily, on the porches and in the parlor, drew the guests from the North into the general enjoyment was not simply dispensing Southern hospitality. A great heart was busy restoring the blessings of peace." Armed with this nostalgic portrait of a united nation and its virtuous fallen leader, devoid of soldiers' blood or slaves' suffering, the bulletin announced an August 1932 "Lee Week" to erect a "permanent shrine" in the cottage where Lee had stayed, the restoration of the Confederate cemetery, and days "filled with reminders of the beloved General and his times"—presumably not including the defeat of his rebellion against the United States.[15] Springs promoters recognized the lasting utility of the Lee legend and cultivated an image of their resorts as the final bastion of the Lost Cause and the last court of its monarch, the Gentleman General, Robert E. Lee.

Most early twentieth-century authors agreed with this romantic depiction of springs life during Reconstruction. Novelists portrayed the Virginia springs as places where Southerners come "to try to forget pain and to search for health and surcease of sorrow." Leading Southern politicians and Confederate officers strolled the grounds "uttering morning greetings or discussing happy subjects." The Virginia springs were populated by people with "unabated vehemence of our sympathy with the defeated wearers of the Gray" and "the portly 'Mammy'" of "caressing tones and deferential manners," who spoke in an obsequious dialect. Perceval Reniers, the Virginia springs' chief twentieth-century chronicler, described White Sulphur Springs and its guests as a "refuge. Here would be kin and kind, here they might perhaps find some scraps of their former gaiety and forget for a while that they were Saturday's children, ruled over by white rascals and their former slaves in the name of 'reconstruction,' an ignominy devised by the victorious Republicans because it served their political designs. Slowly, having heard that the Springs were open again, they were coming in." His depiction, however, seems more suited to a 1941 romanticized past than the social reality of 1870s society.[16]

White Sulphur Springs' longtime promoter and resident physician, John J. Moorman, described the resort this way: "here congregate the fairest of the fair from every State." His 1878 pamphlet sought to attract customers from beyond the South but contained both the desire and the reality of postwar springs visitors. As early as 1868, one Virginia spring included guests "from all parts of the country," and one year later another Southerner found "every style of beauty in which our wide-spread country exults—the golden locks and azure eyes of the northern blonde, and the raven hair and black eyes of the southern brunette," at White Sulphur Springs. Promoters at Allegheny Springs echoed Moorman's claim of a diverse clientele by including a three-page list of prominent guests from eighteen different states, including New York, Pennsylvania, Ohio, and Illinois. Even though the majority of guests hailed from Southern states—and included such luminaries as Virginia's lieutenant governor Jonathan J. Mayre and Senator J. W. Johnston, as well as the former Confederate general Joseph E. Johnston—by mentioning Northern visitors Allegheny Springs advertised its sectional diversity and its desire to attract more than unreconstructed Confederates. Powhatan Ellis Jr., whose family made seasonal visits to Warm Springs before and after the war, noted many visitors from Baltimore and Richmond as part of "a charming company here, from every quarter of the Union, and all seem pleased, and enjoying themselves." Again, "It was General Lee who was the embodiment of the distinctive beauty in the social atmosphere. . . . His whole soul was engaged in the work of reconstruction, and he lost no opportunity to promote it socially." Contrary to Reniers's depiction of grumbling Confederates licking their wounds, the Virginia springs attracted a national clientele.[17]

The springs' relatively placid antebellum social environment, which included Northern and Southern guests, took some time to return. At first, politicians such as Clement Claiborne Clay, the one-time Confederate governor of Alabama, who had been jailed at Fortress Monroe, Virginia, led the effort to reunite the nation. He and other Southern politicians joined their Northern counterparts at Bedford Alum Springs in 1867, where President Andrew Johnson was rumored to be visiting soon. This type of interaction led to an important Reconstruction political document, the 1868 White Sulphur Springs Manifesto. The Union general William S. Rosecrans initiated the communiqué and eventually convinced Robert E. Lee and thirty-one other leading Southern and Northern politicians and former officers visiting White Sulphur Springs to sign it. After endorsing the Democratic Party platform and presidential slate, the manifesto's signers agreed to lay "aside all differences that may heretofore have existed among us" and to reestablish the Union with one caveat: "The efforts of the Radicals in Congress to overthrow the constitution, change the form of government and establish negro supremacy in the South, cannot succeed without involving the country in another bloody and desolate war." David W. Blight has called the White Sulphur Springs Manifesto "peace and healing on Southern terms" and an end to Reconstruction without reconciliation. Although the "soldiers' peace" came a decade too early to achieve national consensus, it presaged a reconciliationist ideology that respected and perpetuated antebellum racial and class structures. The meeting's final resolution made the signers' intent clear: the proceedings were to be published in "Conservative papers throughout the country." Political leaders forgot sectional divisions when it came to preserving social and racial boundaries.[18]

In this context, Northerner Charles Pilsbury's account of a train trip from Washington to western Virginia seems typical: "Every mile of the journey is over historic ground. It is only necessary to mention the names of a few of the stations to call up memories of the bloody past, when the gray coated soldiers of the Confederacy and those in the Federal blue swarmed on the hillsides and swept over the plains below. In those days the smoke of battles obscured the now peaceful sky, and in the fields where the grain is ripening, the great reaper, Death, did his harvesting. No traces of the conflict now remain save a Federal burial-ground at one place, and here and there the ruins of an earthwork." Both sides seemed willing to perform the cultural work of forgetting the war by glossing over its causes and sanctifying its costs. Making the war about personal sacrifice and battlefield valor removed any unpleasant ideological associations and allowed the nation to focus on its common experience of suffering and loss. Northerners began flocking to the South as tourists intent on viewing the conquered Confederacy, but without the hard edge of partisanship that marked the war; they wanted to remember, not to relive, the war. The Virginia springs offered a cultural site for renegotiating nationalism. Stripped of sectional connotations, the springs were the ultimate nostalgia theme park: a replica of a bygone era of social simplicity deep in the mountains. By 1886 White Sulphur Springs had become a place where one could "see the whole Southern life there in

Robert E. Lee at White Sulphur Springs, August 1869. Former Confederate generals occupy the back row. Front row *(left to right)*: Turkish minister to the United States Blacque Bey, Lee, banker and philanthropist George Peabody, banker W. W. Corcoran, Virginia politician and former Confederate congressman Judge James Lyons. Courtesy of The Greenbrier.

August ... it's something new, picturesque—negroes, Southern belles, old-time manners. You cannot afford to neglect it."[19]

Nevertheless, reconciliation took time and negotiation. One North Carolinian recounted an 1873 stagecoach conversation during which someone he supposed to be a Virginian said, "'it was pleasant to travel about in this manner + to interchange thoughts and feelings with persons from different portions of our country. Here the South + the North + the great west meet on equal terms and formed better opinions of each other.' 'Yes,'" the man replied, "'I make it a special rule to cultivate, under such circumstances, all the individuals I meet with, whether they were from the West or the North.'" He concluded the exchange by saying "that I had occasion to admire some of them very much, but that I had never been able in my admiration of the individual to forget my dislike of the class." Only then did he realize that his companions resided in the West and North and that his comments offended them. Southerners talked one way about sectional interaction among themselves and in another way when meeting Northerners; uniting the nation sometimes proved a public posture. But journalists, especially those writing for Northern publications, reported a less ambivalent version of Southern sentiments. Ulysses S. Grant's 1875 visit to White Sulphur Springs caused a reporter for *Harper's New Monthly Magazine* to gush about "A singular commingling . . . the general-in-chief of the North and some of the hardiest fighters of the South, the men but yesterday sworn foes, and today familiar associates!" This 1878 account seems optimistic for the time but portrays the desire of many—especially Northerners—to forget the war and to find aspects of a unified culture. The Virginia springs' once primarily Southern clientele—a myth that applied only in the immediate antebellum and wartime period—now included delegations from around the country forcing the intimacy of reconciliation. The *Harper's* reporter asserted that "the war, first imbittering, has ended by, in a measure, unifying the sections," and White Sulphur Springs' sectionally mixed social environment would make it "the great watering place of the continent." In 1886 another correspondent for the same magazine still found minor sectional rivalries, this time over manners. This friendly competition echoed the mild disputes at resorts during the early republic and even in the early 1850s. As in the previous period, this amiability was "the result of increasing friendship between the representatives of the two geographical sections." Saratoga Springs' promoters seemed to agree with this assessment. Plagiarizing George William Curtis's antebellum call for national unity at Saratoga Springs, an 1871 guidebook declared, "Here party distinctions and local rivalries are forgotten. Here, too, men mingle and learn from contact and sympathy, a sweeter temper and a more catholic consideration, so that summer flower we went to wreathe may prove not the garland of an hour, but a firm link in the chain of our American Union." Several decades after the first calls for sectional unity at the springs, Northern and Southern promoters still advanced their cause; their prospects appeared brighter, even if achieving their goal proved to be no easy task.[20]

Achieving sectional amiability at the springs owed as much to the economic realities of the Reconstruction South as to ideological inclination. Many Southern families agreed with Virginia Tunstall Clay, who had spent much of 1865 lobbying President Johnson and Washington banker W. W. Corcoran to parole her husband, Clement Claiborne Clay. Although she visited White Sulphur Springs and Red Sweet Springs in 1866, she wrote her sister from home, "I am *so tired* of this dull country. Mr. Clay is very kind and tells me I may go *anywhere* I choose to go, but I am so awfully good, that I won't go *anywhere*, because he would have to borrow money." Her cousin, Jonathan Withers, felt that Clifton Springs in western New York State possessed adequate facilities and sufficient curative power to merit an extended residence. Besides being conveniently located on the New York Central Railroad, "we could live more economically here than at home." The spa's location in the Yankee heartland posed little problem to these one-time Confederates.[21]

One extended family felt the pinch of postwar economic change more acutely than the Clays. The Ellis family had visited Warm Springs and other Virginia resorts since the 1830s and had invested in Warm Springs. But by the 1880s the family's members had changed from wealthy tidewater planters and influential Virginia politicians to less affluent merchants and journalists. The second generation's leader, Powhatan Ellis Jr., served as a major in the Confederate army but struggled as a planter after the war and eventually made ends meet by writing political histories of Virginia. His brother-in-law, George W. Munford, was clerk of the Virginia House of Delegates until after the war, when he failed at farming and secured a clerkship in the U.S. Census Bureau. By 1881 Munford, then seventy-eight years old, still visited Warm Springs but believed that "this is my last trip to any place, where I am not able to pay my way without feeling under obligations which I have no way of repaying." Using his long-standing relationship with the hotel proprietor to his benefit, Munford agreed to write an account of a ball (his invalidism made him unable to attend) for the *Richmond (Va.) Dispatch*, which both earned Munford some cash and promoted Warm Springs. Similarly, Powhatan Ellis Jr. frequently sold copies of his books to fellow springs guests to pay his bills. Both men, and apparently the rest of the family, depended on the generosity of Thomas H. Ellis for much of their livelihood. Although he had attended the University of Virginia, had participated in Richmond's defenses during the Civil War, and had attempted to restore the family agricultural business after the war, Thomas H. Ellis left Virginia for Chicago in 1871. He succeeded in business well enough to assist his family members financially, especially after he secured a clerkship with the federal government and returned to Virginia in 1883. He seemed particularly willing to bankroll family visits to the Virginia springs and in 1881 fondly recalled dancing at Warm Springs forty years earlier when still a young man. He offered to transfer the family homestead there to Powhatan Ellis Jr. and paid to renovate a Richmond home for his invalid relative. For this once proud and prominent Virginia family, only the relative who moved to the North and prospered as a businessman could support the springs lifestyle they so dearly valued. The Tucker branch of the family, headed by former Confederate diplomat Nathaniel Beverley Tucker, pondered selling the family farm in tidewater Gloucester to purchase a summer home at Berkeley Springs, West Virginia. "We see no other way," wrote Jane Shelton Ellis Tucker, "in which we can ever see anything of our children and grandchildren. A healthy summer home in a cheap place is what we need, and we can secure it here, and have friends here who will be kind to us. Richmond is dearer than any other place, but it is too expensive and too hot in summer, and this place is more convenient to Mr. Tucker's business" in Washington. They simply could not afford to maintain a summer home, a permanent city residence, and a rural family seat. Virginia's great planter families adjusted their priorities in the postwar economy.[22]

Mineral springs resorts also faced new economic challenges. The one establishment that left extensive records, White Sulphur Springs, barely survived the war and its aftermath. Aside from the losses caused by converting its debts into Confederate war bonds, the White Sulphur Springs Company struggled to achieve a positive cash flow. Its $400,000 debt swelled to $1,200,000, and the resort went into court receivership after October 1869. Stockholders quarreled over complicated matters such as how best to service the debt and less complex issues such as when to meet. When William H. Calwell, a member of White Sulphur Springs' founding family and still an investor and player in the resort's management, refused to give Jeremiah Morton key financial information before the annual meeting, Morton angrily wrote, "As a stockholder and director of the company, I have the right to be informed; and I have a right to call on you to furnish such information, as it is presumed you have." Morton persisted in his insistence that the White Sulphur Springs Company provide a return on his investment, protesting the hotel's 1873 lease to A. J. Caperton, the company's largest shareholder. Caperton paid $25,000 in annual rent, but sources told Morton that the company could fetch twice that amount. If better managed, Morton insisted, White Sulphur Springs could command $80,000 in annual rent and "save every debt, and possibly the stock, and commend the confidence of the stockholders." In a letter marked "PRIVATE," fellow stockholder A. K. Philips theorized, "if we can hold on to the property 3 to 5 years we will be able to dispose of it at a price that will reimburse us for all our outlay and more." But Morton and Philips were not the only plotters. Morton confided to other investors that Calwell and Caperton intended "to keep the property, in that condition, that it will be going down, until this RR ring will be ready to swallow it with a single gulph [*sic*], they being taken care of." Rather than see his investment disappear while others reaped personal profits, Morton drafted a legal statement that accused the White Sulphur Springs Company of undercharging for yearly rents and creating an entity worth only half its $1.1 million debt. His plan would revive the springs, increase its revenue, and, most important, make its "stock more valuable." One year later a fire— "the work of an incendiary"—destroyed several springs buildings and dimmed the company's business prospects.[23]

But while Morton and other major shareholders battled over how best to save their investments, White Sulphur Springs' managers endeavored to balance the books. Agents posted "cards and circulars" along railroad lines in Virginia, Washington City, and Baltimore; debated stringing a telegraph wire to the hotel; considered hiring a New York firm to conduct on-site gambling; and negotiated with railroad companies for discount rates. When the Virginia Central Railroad refused to offer specially priced tickets or to carry springs employees at discounted prices, White Sulphur Springs looked to other lines for the same deals, arguing that any traffic "benefiting us, must benefit the RRs." In 1869 that synergy achieved completion when the Chesapeake and Ohio Railroad reached White Sulphur Springs, creating the resort's first rail link to eastern cities, the Virginia Tidewater, and the lower South. Manager William H. Peyton summarized the railroad's coming impact: "our company will then increase rapidly." White Sulphur Springs' managers anticipated the arrival and sent Peyton to New York City to recruit guests. He met newspaper editor Horace Greeley and "had a pleasant + satisfactory interview with him, he gave us good notice + I think will come to see us this summer." In addition, Peyton shipped one dozen cases of bottled water to New York City in hopes of boosting business. These trips, taken each May for several years, resulted in many arrivals from the North, including "persons I saw while in N. York and who had never been here before." Peyton expected "an early season, as well as a large one . . . the result of my trip north." Construction of the western portion of the Chesapeake and Ohio to Huntington, West Virginia, began the next year. When completed on 28 January 1873, the railroad offered a direct link from the Ohio River to White Sulphur Springs. Railroads eased transportation and brought the springs within the reach of a much larger clientele. Faced with the changing postwar economy, the Virginia Springs embraced rail travel's potential to attract new guests and to replace their declining Southern business, even if the visitors arrived from the North.[24]

Once again White Sulphur Springs established the trend that other Virginia springs followed as a new style of guidebook emerged. These books contained much of the same information on medical efficacy, accommodations, climate, and pleasant amusements that had been in their antebellum counterparts, but by the 1870s the new guides began to emphasize the "modern improvement in locomotion," rail travel. "Facility of access" mattered more than isolation or exclusive company as springs resorts battled for business. Guidebooks featured maps and extensive tables listing distances and travel times from various cities to different springs. Being "within easy access of the Atlantic seaboard" and "the first of all the Western springs reached by the traveler" constituted a major promotional advantage. As early as 1870, Rockbridge Alum Springs bragged that New York City lay within a twenty-four-hour journey and that guests could leave Baltimore or Washington in the morning and arrive at the springs in time for afternoon tea, a claim that several other resorts echoed. A Shenandoah Alum Springs brochure went so far as to place the resort's main attraction on its cover: "The Nearest Alum Springs to Washington, Baltimore, and the Northern Cities." Small railroads such as the Richmond and Allegheny issued detailed descriptions of hotels and attractions along their routes, and other railroads offered "Summer Excursion Tickets" that allowed unlimited stopovers. Agreements with individual springs to offer discounted fares during the springs season also increased business. Much the same story applied to Saratoga Springs, where rail connections had existed since the early 1830s, but improved networks and faster service after the Civil War boosted traffic. Guidebooks for Saratoga Springs included standard information on train routes, rates, and stops along the way, basically offering the same from-the-coach view of popular attractions as did Virginia's railroad guidebooks. The main difference emerged from the more developed rail network around Saratoga Springs that allowed publishers to include information on destinations as distant as Quebec and Niagara Falls, not just those along a specific railroad as in Virginia.[25]

The extension and integration of Southern railroads into a national rail network necessitated that the springs court new visitors. Old and respected resorts such as White Sulphur Springs or Sweet Springs benefited from easier travel and access to western markets via the Chesapeake and Ohio, but they also faced new competition. Places such as Blue Ridge Springs appeared almost overnight along rail lines and quickly rose to prominence, in part based on their claims of "No Staging" in transit. Railroads helped to create a second boom in the mineral springs business, as 20 percent of Virginia and West Virginia springs (sixteen of eighty establishments) began business in the forty years after the Civil War. The railroads, always on the forefront of economic change and business practices, enjoyed the increased passenger traffic so much that they began publishing their own guidebooks, frequently including handsome engravings or photographs. The business proved so attractive that in 1891 the syndicate that had purchased the Chesapeake and Ohio Railroad from Collis P. Huntington, having already built an extension from Covington to Hot Springs, bought three old spas isolated in the narrow valley where the line ran—Healing, Hot, and Warm Springs—in hopes of generating additional passenger traffic. Railroads and mineral springs now constituted a single tourist economy where transportation and lodging came as a package deal.[26]

The implications of improved rail travel and competition between new hotels were significant. Guests from around the country increased their presence throughout the late 1870s and 1880s, even at resorts such as Warm Springs, located six miles from a direct rail connection. People could get close to the springs, if not right to their doors, much more easily than a few years earlier. What jumps out from letters and promotional tracts is that guests came from farther and farther away. George W. Munford's 1881 list from Warm Springs is instructive: "They come from all parts of the Union—from Texas, Louisiana, South and North Carolina, Connecticut, Pennsylvania, New York, Boston, Delaware, Ohio, West Va, Kentucky + I know not where else. Virginia furnishes its quota and even Chicago is represented." A brochure from the same time and place lists guests from twenty-three states—including California, Indiana, and Illinois—and Canada. By 1896 White Sulphur Springs was truly a national resort, with guests from thirty-three different states and roughly equal numbers from Confederate, Union, and Border states. Although guests from Virginia continued to dominate the Virginia springs, nearly as many visitors came from Kentucky and Missouri as from Maryland, and Ohio ranked behind only Virginia and West Virginia in terms of total visitors. Transportation links to Cincinnati, St. Louis, and Chicago, the dream of canal and railroad promoters during the late eighteenth and early nineteenth centuries, connected the Virginia springs to the new market of western tourists, just as railroads before the

Table 3

Regional Origin of Springs Visitors after 1860

Resort/Hotel	Confederacy		Union		Border		
	N	%	N	%	N	%	N[a]
Virginia							
Old Sweet Springs, 1896	100	36.1	99	35.7	55	19.9	277[b]
White Sulphur Springs, 1896	237	35.0	176	26.0	261	38.6	677[c]
Saratoga Springs							
Union Hotel, 1869	33	3.4	868	88.4	46	4.7	975[d]

Sources: Old Sweet Springs Ledger, July 1896, VHS; Greenbrier White Sulphur Springs ledger, July 1896, UVa; Union Hotel register, 19–30 July 1869, SSPL.

[a]N = 1,929.

[b]Twenty-three traveling musicians and performers listed no state origin.

[c]One visitor each came from Colorado, Nebraska, and England.

[d]Twenty-eight registrants (2.9%) listed foreign origins, primarily Cuba (seventeen).

Civil War and during the 1860s and 1870s had brought the eastern seaboard closer to the springs. "The springs," wrote John Esten Cooke in *Harper's New Monthly Magazine*, "are losing their distinctive Southern character by the infusion of new elements. The North and the West have discovered the charm of the locality, and the change has begun. In 1877 large numbers of visitors came from these sections. Sectional lines are disappearing, and rapid transit by way of the Chesapeake and Ohio Railway from the East and the West has given a great impetus to summer travel in the direction of the Virginia mountains." The implications for the class dynamics of the Virginia springs, which had long claimed—if not realized—social exclusivity, would prove to be profound.[27]

Saratoga Springs experienced a much more rapid acceleration and expansion of tourism's social and economic setting during the postwar period. Ironically, this growth owed some of its success to several fires that destroyed the town's hotels. On 18 June 1865, diarist Daniel Benedict recorded a "Great fire. United States hotel and cottages, ball room, barber shop, club room, Marvin's row, Marvin House, livery stable, (Dexter's) Costigan House, Scribner's club room, etc., etc., destroyed." The next year, wood-framed Congress Hall burned in one hour after a late-night fire originated in the "ironing department" as maids scurried to prepare for the hotel's annual opening. The Columbian Hotel and Bedortha's Water-Cure also succumbed to fire within two years. Despite the hardships faced by these business owners and workers, these losses actually helped Saratoga Springs because the fires cleared valuable downtown real estate for redevelopment. After a few years of planning and fund-raising by developers, a new breed of hotel changed Saratoga Springs' character. The United States Hotel and the renovated Grand Union Hotel (formerly the Union Hotel) included 768 and 824 rooms, respectively, and greatly increased Saratoga Springs' guest capacity, as well as its level of luxury. These "monster" hotels included elaborate gardens, dining rooms that seated as many as twelve hundred guests, "vertical railroads" (elevators), parlors, ballrooms, running water and toilet facilities, and gas lighting. More than one account reported that the United States Hotel's million dollar renovations had made it "the finest hotel in the world." Another observer called the Grand Union Hotel, which had spent $500,000 on furniture alone, "the most beautiful scene in America."[28]

In essence, Saratoga Springs spent the Reconstruction period improving its facilities and creating an even grander scale of luxury. The city's resort economy boomed during the Civil War era, going from nine hotels in 1850 to twenty-six in 1870, while older hotels enlarged by "expanding their wings and adding room beyond room, till they cover acres of ground, and the halls and piazzas stretch out into miles." But Saratoga Springs did more than simply increase its total guest capacity. It seized upon the growing tourism trend and broadened its clientele beyond the elite visitors who had arrived during the early republic and antebellum periods. Saratoga Springs had certainly attracted a broad social spectrum of visitors during the 1840s and 1850s, but the town made a much more conscious effort to capture these visitors in the postwar period. Seneca Ray Stoddard, a prolific local photographer and guidebook author, noted Saratoga Springs' business philosophy: "Here are accommodations for the rich and the poor, the old and the young, steady and giddy, wise or foolish, fast or staid, rough or cultivated—all are welcome, for Saratoga is one vast caravansary, every house a hotel, and every resident glad to see the summer's company, for it is meat, drink, and clothing to them." More and more visitors noted the social diversity at Saratoga Springs, but even one of its harshest critics, Sidney George Fischer, admitted that "Saratoga has special attractions and will no doubt increase in size & improve in the style of its accommodations every year. . . . Probably, this will not be my last visit."[29]

Social commentators and guidebook authors constantly gushed about the opulent comforts at Saratoga Springs' new hotels, a significant change from their carping over antebellum accommodations. These hotels seemed to represent a cultural accomplishment—evidence of refinement and sophistication—"in a country so new as the United States." They represented "the growth of our country, and speak well for a Centennial of prosperity." The idea of a single establishment that housed, fed, and entertained hundreds of people simultaneously, without regard to any status but the ability to pay, appealed to the democratic and commercial values central to late nineteenth-century American life. Because of the "enterprise, wealth, and foresight," demonstrated by Saratoga Springs' developers, one commentator declared that "this watering place has no occasion to fear the future."[30]

The most significant change between antebellum and Reconstruction Saratoga Springs was the increasing diversity of its guests. The seventy thousand annual visitors still included those "from every part of the Union" as well as "Canada, Europe, Mexico, South America, and the West Indies," but interclass social mixing had intensified. Calling Saratoga Springs "cosmopolitan, complex," one guidebook noted that invalids, millionaires, flirters, and sportsmen all found a place at Saratoga Springs. But what most struck the author was how "Clergymen and merchants, bankers and lawyers, politicians and gentlemen, jostle against each other." Such contact constituted a type of social interaction usually seen only in America's cities, if at all. What made Saratoga Springs special was that "there gathers here a wonderfully variegated collection of people, each *sui generis,* and affording the rarest facilities for the study of human nature." The opportunity of "judging the manners and forming some estimate of the diversified character of our countrymen" fascinated reporters who rarely had the chance to do so. Saratoga Springs resembled a laboratory where combinations of regional, class, and political identities could be tested.[31]

Between the 1860s and 1890s, both springs regions attracted crowds similar to their antebellum constituencies—Saratoga Springs was socially mixed, whereas the Virginia springs catered to the upper class. Yet despite its economically diverse society, Saratoga Springs attracted the late nineteenth century's new elite: the richest Americans. The resort was visited by "more of the fashionable and wealthy classes, than any watering place in the United States" in 1866 and distinguished itself in part because "almost every other chief watering place in the land is but an infant in years compared with this ancient and time-honored resort." The usual complement of "senators, judges, governors, members of Congress" came to Saratoga Springs, but so did "millionaires in plenty." The presence of those millionaires is what separated postwar Saratoga Springs from its antebellum incarnation and its Virginia counterparts. When in 1874 *Frank Leslie's Illustrated Newspaper,* published by the eponymous owner of Saratoga Springs real estate and a nearby mansion, declared "Never were millionaires so plentiful, or magnates so thick as the autumn leaves," the Virginia springs lacked such a crowd. Even though one 1876 account refers to "educated, well bred people" at Warm Springs and another calls White Sulphur Springs "the fashionable resort of Southern society," few Southern accounts observe excessive wealth: "First and very agreeable" and filled with "the *elite* of the Southern States," but not millionaires. Springs promoter and resident physician John J. Moorman describes statesmen, men of letters, poets, beautiful women and their devotees, clergymen, doctors, lawyers, and judges before getting to "the man of commerce, the financier" as guests at White Sulphur Springs. Just after these types, he mentions "the thrifty planter, the sturdy farmer, and the retired man of wealth and ease." Moorman devalues businessmen by placing them so far down the list at "the Paris and Athens of America," not its London or Wall Street. The values he promoted placed little emphasis on commerce or the creation of wealth. Instead, at the Virginia springs guests met "old acquaintances." As one journalist wrote from White Sulphur Springs in 1880, "It is not uncommon to meet at this Spring ladies and gentlemen who have not missed a season for twenty or thirty years."[32]

White Sulphur Springs emphasized, as it had during the antebellum period, these repeat customers as one of its key drawing points "well calculated to promote social intercourse and to call out the kindliest feelings of our nature." This language, repeated in Moorman's publications and in company promotional pamphlets into the 1890s, bears a striking resemblance to the tone and syntax of Moorman's earlier editions on White Sulphur Springs. In saying that "Society seems here to meet on common ground, and the different shades of feeling influencing it at home are laid aside, while each individual promotes his own happiness by contributing to the happiness of others," he was evoking the supposedly carefree, socially homogeneous springs society that many Southerners, or at least springs promoters, recalled from the first half of the nineteenth century. In Moorman's view, White Sulphur Springs possessed "the freedom from care, the relaxation from bonds which have fettered us to the treadmill of business" that made the springs special. At the springs, "the amenities of social intercourse, relieved from those necessary but vexatious rules of etiquette which hem in fashionable life at home," did not exist. Moorman was echoing the claims of Southern partisans and springs promoters from decades earlier who had insisted that their society was different, that its homogeneity and static class structure allowed social freedom and easy interaction without fear of mingling with the lower classes.[33]

Saratoga Springs made similar claims to social ease and exclusivity. It was a place where "There is a freedom and ease about the place that will not be repressed. Ladies stroll from one hotel to another, or down the street, without troubling about hats, bonnets, or shawls. The streets resemble a flower show or fashionable pic-nic, while the rows of carriages standing all day opposite these great hotels resemble the outside of the opera on a gala night." Saratoga Springs and other "Cities of Play," writes historian Jon Sterngass, allowed people to abandon social norms, to enjoy created identities, and to pursue pleasure for its own sake. Although he oversimplifies Saratoga Springs' social setting, Sterngass emphasizes a carefree social atmosphere that is remarkably similar to that at the Virginia springs, even with Saratoga Springs' more heterogeneous society. Some visitors even questioned that quality: "there are not many poor people who can get two weeks at Saratoga for nothing." In one Southerner's opinion, Saratoga Springs was "the most expensive place in the country." There is evidence, in other words, that Northern and Southern springs possessed some similarities in terms of social setting during the postwar period. One 1883 guidebook to the Virginia springs went so far as to write that White Sulphur Springs was "the grand attraction among the southern springs, like Saratoga is among the springs of the north."[34]

A key distinction, however, set Saratoga Springs apart from its Virginia counterparts. As early as 1871, people described it as "by far the most varied and cosmopolitan of our watering places; resorted to by many bold adventurers of either sex, but also sought by many of the wise and good; entertaining hundreds of coarse parvenus, but the summer home of much of that wealth which acquired or inherited the grace of refinement." Philadelphia diarist Sidney George Fischer found Saratoga Springs much different in 1867 than during a visit eighteen years earlier, when it was "the chief watering place of the country & the resort of the best society from North & South." As the years passed, Fischer noted, "wealth increased & travelling became fast & cheap, [Saratoga] attracted the newly made rich & would be fashionable pleasure seekers, & lovers of show & vulgar aspirants to good society." Other resorts such as Newport and Long Branch diverted the best society, making Saratoga Springs "notorious for assembling the worst" society. The advent of horse racing at Saratoga Springs brought "pedestrians of every condition in life, from merchant prince . . . to merchant tailor; from gentleman gambler to the lowest order of pickpocket." By 1868 there clearly was "no such democratic institution as the turf. It levels all distinctions: nobody is any better than anybody else; and if you insist upon occupying a private box and making companions of elegant extracts, you will lock yourself up in your own room and put the key in your pocket."[35]

What wealthy visitors found amid the crowd astounded and shocked them. The assembly of "Wall-St. millionaires and Canal-St. milliners, the petted beauties of Fifth-Ave. and the sturdy Kansas farmer" created a "display of fine clothes, drapery, and adornments" that seemed "a milliner's paradise" in 1865. Almost thirty years later visitors still saw "groups of handsomely dressed men [with] full pockets and empty heads. Gorgeously bedecked women upholstered by Worth in Paris and Tiffany in New York at enormous outlay with tremendously wide hats some literally covered with many colored flowers until they look like a flower garden." Observers were troubled not by the ostentatious display but by the women who "look as if they had begun life at the washtub on the Bowery or Hogans Alley." Distraught by the scene, Daniel deJarnette Staples declared, "It is beyond a doubt the commonest looking crowd and the homeliest looking women I ever saw." In 1870 the essayist and novelist Henry James acknowledged that "the good old times of Saratoga, I believe as of the world in general, are rapidly passing away. The time was when it was the chosen resort of none but 'nice people.' At the present day, I hear it constantly affirmed, 'the company is dreadfully mixed.'" Hesitating to characterize the older Saratoga Springs, James determined to "confine myself to the dense, democratic, vulgar Saratoga of the current year." James left little doubt as to how he felt about Saratoga Springs. Another writer mused that if Saratoga Springs "is the highest and best blossoming of our culture and refinement," as other commentators intimated, "how much better are we than the untutored savages?"[36] The inclusion of nonelite tourists threatened the very roots of springs society but emerged from the same success and popularity that social arbiters lauded.

The myth of social exclusivity at Saratoga Springs and the Virginia springs differed from the reality of postwar tourism. Less wealthy, and even middle-class, travelers had been coming to Saratoga Springs for several years. But by the 1870s this changed because "the amount of room and the accommodations are so ample, that people of moderate means, even in the height of the season, can always be provided with rooms and board of good quality, and at moderate expense." Now Saratoga Springs was actively culti-vating the business of middle-class tourists. The Virginia springs recognized tourism's rapid expansion and embraced a market in which consumers searched for "'the greatest comfort at the least expense.'" Guidebooks tar-geted a less affluent clientele that desired "rates which can be paid without seriously affecting an average income." Virginia's resorts, many of which went into business in the years immediately before or after the Civil War, now solicited middle-class tourists. Jordan's White Sulphur Springs, Shenan-doah Alum Springs, and Allegheny Springs, to name just a few, gained rep-utations as comfortable and respectable establishments with "rates quite moderate." Fauquier White Sulphur Springs, renowned as a genteel spa be-fore wartime fighting burned its buildings to the ground, reopened in 1878 with a modified time-share plan—as White Sulphur Springs had done fifty years earlier—designed for "PERSONS OF MODERATE MEANS who desire to avoid the heat of the city, *permanent summer homes.*"[37]

That both the Virginia springs and Saratoga Springs sought middle-class business is no surprise. From their earliest inceptions, the springs aimed for as much business as possible from whatever quarter it came, primarily be-cause they belonged to a seasonal, fragile industry that could not afford to discriminate. The postwar tourism explosion both exacerbated this need— each resort needed to retain its clientele amid an expanding array of tour-ism options—and offered entrepreneurs the opportunity to start new springs and tourism businesses. The Virginia springs became more diverse and numerous as a whole and attracted a more diverse clientele. However, exclusive places such as White Sulphur Springs did not suddenly become bourgeois assemblages; quite the opposite. Springs that formerly held a rep-utation for exclusivity retained it. But now less prestigious, newer, or more pedestrian springs—especially those close to Richmond or Washington— could turn a profit by attracting a more modest clientele that could not stay for extended periods. The geographical dispersal of the Virginia springs permitted them to grow while they still retained their social distinctiveness. But economic transformations did not necessarily bring social change to the Virginia springs. At Saratoga Springs, it did. There social differentiation came not at the resort level but at each hotel. The Union Hotel attracted gamblers, fashionable tourists, and women with less than virtuous reputa-tions, whereas the Clarendon Hotel appealed to gentlemen and "the best company." In essence, "two classes" existed at Saratoga Springs: "quiet, respectable people who go to drink the waters & breathe the wholesome air, & a crowd of sporting men, fast men, gamblers and adventurers, the demi-monde in short, male & female, who attend the races together & gather together for their various objects of pleasure & profit." Saratoga Springs' coarseness, wrote one correspondent, was caused by "the difference between a group of three or four hotels and a series of cottages and villas." Although the author wrote of Newport, which possessed the reputation of being more exclusive than Saratoga Springs, he made a point that also applies to the Virginia springs: spatial arrangements affect social interactions. Because the Virginia springs were spread over hundreds of miles with dozens of individual establishments, they could differentiate into resorts that appealed to specific segments of the population. Saratoga Springs, with its clustered hotels of various costs, jumbled the rich and not-so-rich together. One newspaper celebrated this juxtaposition: "Saratoga perhaps deserves our greater homage, as being characteristically democratic and American; let us, then, make Saratoga the heaven of our aspiration, but let us yet awhile content ourselves with Newport as the lordly earth of our residence." Replace the name of Newport with those of the Virginia springs and the comparison holds.[38]

Part of Saratoga Springs' democratic nature came from the type of wealth it attracted, as Europeans noted. One French visitor claimed that "the men gather in the barroom and discuss business; the hotel is like a stock exchange for the use of brokers who come up from New York." An Englishwoman called Saratoga Springs "the meeting place of great men. . . . The railway kings of America meet here, part in pleasure, part in earnest. The wires are often woven here for many a political combination." The United States Hotel accommodated so many industrialists that its "Division Street piazza has always been known as 'millionaires' piazza,'" which provided a daily gathering spot for William H. Vanderbilt and his cronies. The men on "Vanderbilt Corner," wrote one reporter, "seat themselves on rude wooden chairs, speak in that low tone dramatists relegate to conspirators; ever and anon consult telegraphic slips or pocket-memoranda, whiffing the while cigars." These "sovereigns of the railroad met as usual to hold council and discuss the propriety of relieving poor embarrassed Europe through the medium of express-trains and elevators." These gatherings were more than a literary creation; Vanderbilt and others conducted real business on the porches, including the 1874 Saratoga Agreement that set grain rates and apportioned traffic among six railroads running west from New York City.

William H. Vanderbilt cutting a deal on the porch of the
United States Hotel. From *Frank Leslie's Illustrated Newspaper*,
30 August 1879. Courtesy of the Saratoga Room, Saratoga
Springs Public Library.

The agreements occurred almost yearly in the 1870s and 1880s, with limited
success in controlling prices.[39]

That wealthy men visited Saratoga Springs, which they had done for
decades, did not upset commentators as much as what those men did while
there. Even if "the tape of the stock telegraph is not watched with feverish
anxiety as it is in the city," men still conducted business at Saratoga Springs.
For these men, "It is indispensable that money shall be spent freely. It is a
kind of point of honor and good breeding among a lot of money-getters
and sharp business men, that however they may stickle and higgle for the
last cent in a bargain at home, they shall absolutely throw money away here.
Always get the most expensive article, and make no account of the filthy
lucre." The values of nineteenth-century corporate America and its con-

spicuous consumption did not fit some critics' conception of the social atmosphere of Saratoga Springs or proper upper-class behavior. Ever curmudgeonly and ready to defend the elite, Sidney George Fischer wrote from Saratoga Springs, "I thought the tone of the party, its general effect, was deficient in refinement, in dignity, in short it was rather vulgar. And why not? *Business people* are now in society, here as in New York. A refined society with such materials is impossible."[40]

More than the presence of businessmen and their pecuniary ways rankled springs critics. An English visitor remarked that "Saratoga appeared to greet its well-dressed guests with 'eat, drink, and be merry,' and they in turn seemed wild to obey the summons." The ferocity and alacrity with which tourists pursued pleasure lacked the reserve and dignity expected of English gentlemen but also seemed extreme for Americans. Despite visitors' "much more persistent than successful" quest for amusement, "There seemed a restless, and there undoubtedly was a very pretentious . . . air about the crowd at Saratoga. . . . Never, in the whole course of my life, had I seen such manifest signs of the general possession of wealth accompanied by such a wide-spread lack of refinement." The effort of seeking pleasure mitigated its achievement. The crowd "in spite of all the splendour, and the show . . . looked singularly jaded and apathetic, and seemed to be playing at enjoying themselves rather than actually doing so. One seldom heard a downright merry laugh, and there was a half listless, half fierce look on many a face, which neither music, nor dancing, nor dishes appeared to have power to dispel." Visitors and commentators pondered the cause of such disappointment amid wealth and luxury, devising only one answer. In 1868 a writer for *McBride's Magazine* declared: "Once Saratoga was a whited sepulchre: now, it is a sepulchre without any whitewash whatever. Once, the fashion of New York, Philadelphia and the South met here and gave tone to the life: now, the *crème de la crème* is a bad quality of skimmed milk, and Saratoga is a huge caldron, bubbling over with vice and frivolity." Elite society lacked the luster it had once possessed as more individuals demanded admittance. One Southerner neatly summarized the distinction between wealth and class in an 1870 letter from Saratoga Springs: "on a whole I do not think the ladies dressed prettily, there were a great many Shoddies here who wore handsome silks + jewelry but dressed void of taste." Lacking the refinement that previous guests possessed, by the 1890s Saratoga Springs had become "the most wicked and immoral place in the U.S."[41]

But Saratoga Springs did not instantly become a middle-brow resort completely lacking in refinement. People still tended to socialize with their own kind, and "different sets and cliques" existed. Saratoga Springs may have admitted various classes, ethnic groups, and regional types, "But betwixt the uncongenial sorts are established here as elsewhere those impalpable but unscalable dividing lines which rise in society everywhere. All these various elements here mingle, moving together yet separate." Americans seemed to recognize that even if they believed in equality in opportunity, there should be "a refining process" to separate the merely rich from the genteel. In 1871 one newspaper observed that "a considerable faction of what has been satirically called our 'aristocracy of wealth' . . . has begun to be dissatisfied with itself and its attainments, and to be ashamed of its former modes of display." The efforts of some nouveau riche socialites to limit their ostentatious display encouraged the columnist to remark, "I firmly believe . . . there may yet be an American aristocracy which shall set the world an example of modesty, refinement, purity, and grace." Saratoga Springs resisted the debasement of class only because its lengthy history "distinguished it from the herd of new places whose mushroom growth is like that of the gentility which they harbor."[42]

Tradition and a smaller business class insulated the Virginia springs from the large-scale infusion of different classes affecting Saratoga Springs. Although observers at the Virginia springs withheld the harsh censure of Saratoga Springs' critics, they still witnessed a similar declension from proper society. The "daily panorama of elite, elegance, money, beauty" at Allegheny Springs in 1868 impressed Clement Claiborne Clay. Even so, "it had a smack almost too prononcé, for me, of the mad search after society + excitement that characterizes the pleasure resort of Europe and the East." The increasing similarity between Southern and Eastern—or Northern—manners demonstrates the integration of the Virginia springs into the national tourist culture and economy. One North Carolinian attributed the increase in invalids at Hot Springs to "the number of persons who are from distant States. The Hot Springs have more reputation abroad, + the whole of a wealthy family, on account of one or two invalids amongst them, will come + spend a month or two + then go to some Northern resort or the White Sulphur." Several such families were at Hot Springs in 1873, but "only two or three who are not shoddy." Even the apogee of Southern manners, White Sulphur Springs, faced "the presence both of the *nouveau riche* class and of Messrs. Tag, Rag, and Bobtail." The "Old White" retained "the same air of high-breeding and rational relaxation for the sake of relaxation" despite "the fast and somewhat pretentious and 'shoddy' existence of the present time." In

1878, a scant thirteen years after the Confederacy and its slave-based hierarchy fell, a Northern commentator praised the White's "ancient *regime,* before the modern spirit of democracy had levelled every thing to so distressing a uniformity." The author recognized democracy's benefits and the Old
South's shortcomings, but he still reminisced over "a grace in social intercourse, a freedom from self-assertion, and a natural, unpretending ease,
springing from true simplicity and refinement, which made society delightful." The idealized past of social homogeneity and cultural grace and simplicity still seduced many; romanticized visions of antebellum springs society continued to influence people's vision of the postwar springs.[43]

Once again, Virginia's springs proprietors seized on this nostalgia, reinforced by an almost exclusively African American workforce. As in the antebellum period, visitors' "colored Servants" paid half price for room and
board. Northern author Charles Dudley Warner believed that African
American waiters and servants created an "easy-going pace" at White Sulphur Springs. "The presence of the coloured brother in force distinguished
this from provincial resorts at the North, even those that employ this color
as servants. The flavor of Old Virginia is unmistakable, and life drops into
an easy-going pace under this influence. What fine manners, to be sure! The
waiters in the dining-room, in white ties and dress-coats, move on springs,
starting even to walk with a complicated use of all the muscles of the body,
as if in response to the twang of a banjo; they do nothing without excessive
motion and flourish. The gesture and good-humored vitality expended in
changing plates would become the leader of an orchestra." Warner made
this acceptable role of the physical, emotive, and dramatic African American even more vivid in his account of "A fine specimen of the 'Richmond
darky' of the old school—polite, flattering, with a venerable head of gray
wool, was the bar-tender, who mixed his juleps with a flourish as if keeping
time to music." These individuals entertained springs visitors and harkened
back to a time before emancipation when African Americans occupied one
role in the South—servant. Warner romanticized life and the anachronistic
race relations that prevailed at White Sulphur Springs, yet other resorts
attempted to redefine racial roles among their staff. Although Jordan Rockbridge Alum Springs declared that "in organizing [the] corps of attendants,
the majority will be white, and trained for the position they may occupy,"
the more popular Warm Springs charged "White Servants, according to
accommodations required." This disincentive to bring white maids and but-
lers favored the continued racial division between workers and guests at the
Virginia springs.[44]

Nostalgic portrayal of an African American waiter at White
Sulphur Springs. The caption reads, "'Haven't I Waited on
You Befo', Sah?'" From *Harper's New Monthly Magazine*,
August 1886. Courtesy of the Albion College Library.

Saratoga Springs proved equally willing to reinforce racial stereotypes of
servile African Americans by employing "an army of waiters and attendants,
all of whom are black." These jobs were unstable, however, and provided
only seasonal employment and sometimes difficult working conditions in
hot kitchens and laundries, crowded dining rooms, and cramped hotel
rooms and stables. At least one African American worker, Emma Waite,
worked at three different hotels during the 1870 season, feeling "almost
burnt up" after three days at Congress Hall and having been "discharged
from the Union Hall today on account of their getting white help." Historian Myra Beth Young Armstead has ably documented the autonomy of
black culture and agency that resort workers enjoyed at Saratoga Springs,
something their Virginia counterparts did not possess to the same degree.
Even so, late nineteenth-century culture depicted "Negro waiters of watering-places,—a class full of rare and grotesque characters admirably fitted

for stage illustration." Apparently wealthy Northerners and Southerners shared a desire to be served by African Americans who fit their conception of proper racial roles.[45]

Northerners and Southerners also disliked another ethnic group. When Southerners disapproved of a particular resort, they used blunt language to denigrate it: Hallie Donaghe described Capon Springs as "the most unsociable, lonely, disagreeable, and *Jewish* place I ever saw." Similarly, Daniel deJarnette Staples said of Saratoga Springs, "Half of these people are Jews and the other half snobs: our party is the most aristocratic one in the lot." When newspaper writers wanted to censure John Morrissey's gambling house, they described the players as "a rakish, ugly, coarse looking set, as a rule, the Hebrew type appearing very frequently." This equating of Jewishness with disreputable society reveals a new strain of social thought at the springs: those who were discernibly different in ethnicity should be excluded. There is little evidence of anti-Semitism at Saratoga Springs before the Civil War, and Salomon de Rothschild, a prominent European Jew, made no mention of difficulties during his 1860 visit. But by 1873 the *Daily Graphic* newspaper felt the need to advocate the acceptance of Jews at Saratoga Springs, and the question of whether to admit Jews there came to a head in 1877 with what became known as the Seligman affair.[46]

Joseph Seligman, a German-born Jew, had made a fortune as a merchant, prominent banker, and wartime supplier. His banking house, J. and W. Seligman and Company, sold United States war bonds in Germany when few in France or England would purchase them and handled the conversion and refunding of the American government's debts during the 1870s. An influential advisor and financier for the Grant and Hayes administrations, Seligman seemed the embodiment of the self-made man and an American success story. But when he attempted to check into the Grand Union Hotel in 1877, the desk clerk told him that Jews were not permitted. Seligman's exclusion became a national scandal played out in newspapers across the country. He and his backers—including Henry Ward Beecher, who preached a sermon advocating tolerance, and Bret Harte, who wrote a poem about the incident—alleged outright discrimination, but the case was more complex. The Grand Union Hotel had come under the control of Judge Henry Hilton in 1876 upon the death of retail tycoon A. T. Stewart, whose estate Hilton managed. Stewart and Seligman had been less than friendly commercial rivals for years, and Hilton may have been trying to gain a business edge for his client's estate. On the other hand, Stewart's company had shifted most of its funds from Seligman's bank before the incident occurred, and Seligman may have been attempting to embarrass the Grand Union Hotel and to harm its business in retaliation. Most telling are the political implications. Hilton rose to prominence as a Tweed Ring operative, turning his legal skills and connections into a minor fortune. Seligman had long been active in New York City and State Republican Party politics and was a member of the Committee of Seventy, which eventually disbanded the Tweed Ring. Both Seligman's charges of blatant anti-Semitism and Hilton's rebuttals that he only acted because his Christian guests requested that he exclude Jews seem less than genuine, although prejudice was certainly the language with which they engaged their rivalry.[47]

In this specific case Hilton probably discriminated not because Seligman was Jewish but because he and other Jews represented all that Hilton and his friends construed as wrong with American society. In a letter to the *New York Times,* Hilton wrote that he opposed "Seligman Jews" who "brought the public opinion down on themselves by a vulgar ostentation, a puffed-up vanity, an overweening display of condition, a lack of those considerate activities so appreciated by good American society, and a general obtrusiveness that is frequently disgusting and always repulsive to the well bred." Seligman, in other words, was offensive because he was a particular type of Jew and a particular type of American. This controversy was part of a larger battle between old and new money for social control in 1870s America. Hilton appealed to the social standards of the traditional American aristocracy—which was predominantly conservative, Protestant, and English in its culture—as a means of keeping out those who did not share its values. Social critic Charles Dudley Warner's 1886 line that Saratoga Springs "has reached the point where it cannot be killed by the inroads of Jew or Gentile" spoke to a social maturation and cultural development among the American springs-going elite that could withstand ethnic or class difference. But the Seligman affair was also part of a contest between members of the nouveau riche (to distinguish themselves and to gain acceptance) and members of the old elite (to exclude them). Hilton, a man of recent wealth and humble origins, perhaps wanted to show his hotel's guests that he too knew the difference between the true aristocrats and the social pretenders, as represented by the stock "Jewish" character. Ethnic and religious identity provided a clear distinction among the self-made millionaires in 1870s America, and many proved perfectly willing to use their identity as white Protestants to separate themselves from and to elevate themselves above their

Cartoon depicting the Seligman affair. The caption reads:
"CLERK. 'I am very sorry, but my orders are ————'
TOURIST. 'Yesh, yesh, I know all about your orters; but how
voz it dot you knowed I vozn't a Ghristian.'" Although the
cartoonist seems to mock the tourist's stereotypical Jewish
speech and appearance, an accompanying editorial
condemned hotels' exclusion of Jewish guests. From *Harper's
Weekly*, 28 June 1877. Used by permission of HarpWeek, LLC.

cohorts. Discrimination at Saratoga Springs' hotels and at other resorts
continued into the twentieth century and sometimes intensified, leading in
part to the creation of distinct Jewish hotels and resorts across America.[48]

The rapid rise of new money—and its stereotypically "Jewish" qualities—
belonged to a larger transformation of class in America. During the early
nineteenth century, the appearance of less wealthy tourists and the easy attainability of status was more an odd occurrence worthy of note than a
wholesale social trend. By the late 1860s, what had begun as a few isolated
instances of confusing class dynamics turned into a larger transformation
of American society. As in the antebellum period, European observers were
among the first to notice this shift. In 1865 the French traveler Ernest Du-

vergier de Hauranne wrote an account of his visit to the United States and Saratoga Springs that shocked his sensibilities. "You cannot imagine how much the Americans adore aristocracy," he said. "They are for the most part self-made men, builders of their own fortunes, parvenus who have seldom enjoyed wealth and position for more than a single generation; they have a superstitious respect for anything which can boast of having existed for a while." De Hauranne could not imagine how society functioned without hierarchical structures, even those based on recently accumulated wealth. To him, American society lacked Europe's established aristocracy. The only exception was the South, where "Slavery served to support aristocratic pretensions." Problematically, "it is about to disappear, but the old moneyed families will not on that account show any more indulgence to the newly rich of today. To assert their claim to aristocracy they keep their distance from public affairs and call themselves partisans of the South." The new definition of class revolved around not economic means but cultural practice and political belief. Rather than admit the nouveau riche to the inner circles, Southerners created a definition of class that excluded many people on a basis that wealth could not purchase.[49]

Henry James echoed some of de Hauranne's points in an 1870 essay that appeared first in *The Nation* and later as part of *Portraits of Places*. His description of "worthy sons of the great Republic" lounging on the Union Hotel porch is illuminating:

> They come from the uttermost ends of the continent—from San Francisco, from New Orleans, from Duluth. As they sit with their white hats tilted forward, and their chairs tilted back, and their feet tilted up, and their cigars and toothpicks forming various angles with these various lines, I imagine them surrounded with a sort of clear achromatic halo of mystery. They are obviously persons of experience—of somewhat narrow and monotonous experience certainly; an experience of which the diamonds and laces which their wives are exhibiting hard by are, perhaps, the most substantial and beautiful result; but, at any rate, they are men who have positively actually lived. For the time, they are lounging with the negro waiters, and the boot-blacks, and the news-venders; but it was not in lounging that they gained their hard wrinkles and the level impartial regard which they direct from beneath their hat-rims. They are not the mellow fruit of a society impelled by tradition and attended by culture; they are hard nuts, which have grown and ripened as they could. When they talk among themselves, I seem to hear the mutual cracking of opposed shells.

This society valued something other than family name, its longevity in this country, one's place of residence, or one's removal from the griminess of labor. The men on Saratoga Springs' porches valued hard work and treasured personal achievement, however attained. At Saratoga Springs, James wrote, there was a "wholesale equalization of the various social atoms." Saratoga Springs' wealthy could talk with "the negro waiters, and the bootblacks, and the news-vendors" without shame, for they may have once occupied similar social, if not racial, positions. At Saratoga Springs, "a man in a 'duster' at a ball is as good as a man in irreproachable sable; a young woman dancing with another young woman is as good as a young woman dancing with a young man; a child of ten is as good as a woman of thirty; a double negative in conversation is better than a single." Yet for all of this society's democratic potential, James despaired for the "splendid social isolation" he found. There were too many people at Saratoga Springs "who know no one—who have money and finery and possessions, only no friends." James yearned for something more substantial, for some sense of connectedness and social relation, amid the anomie he witnessed on Saratoga Springs' porches.[50]

This disjunction and social confusion distinguished Saratoga Springs and the Virginia springs. In recounting his protagonists' movements from Bar Harbor to Saratoga Springs to Niagara Falls to White Sulphur Springs to Newport, Charles Dudley Warner paused to describe what he saw as the distinctive society at the latter destination, "the only watering-place remaining in the United States where there is what may be called an 'assembly,' such as might formerly be seen at Saratoga or at Ballston Spa in Irving's young days." The formal balls, introductions, carefully arranged dinner seating, and pleasant exchanges on White Sulphur Springs' tree-shaded lawn created what Warner's character Stanhope King called "'the only place left where there is a congregate social life.'" Undaunted, his cousin Mrs. Glow replied, "'You mean provincial life. Everybody knows everybody else.'" Although a Northerner found this sort of familiarity disturbing, Southerners reveled in it. White Sulphur Springs was dominated by women such as the former belle Mrs. Farquhar, who "was related to everybody in Virginia—that is, everybody who was anybody before the war—and she could count at that moment seventy-five cousins, some of them first and some of them double-cousins, at the White Sulphur." Her connections proved beneficial to King, who, having been thwarted in his courtship of Irene Benson, gained Farquhar's patronage and blessing. "Mrs. Farquhar's remark meant that all these cousins and all their friends the South over would stand by Miss Benson socially from that moment." Even though King's family objected to his eventual engagement to Benson, whose family came from Ohio, Mrs. Farquhar's imprimatur, as well as the Benson family's substantial fortune, eventually convinced King's relatives to sanction the relationship. Money mattered at Saratoga Springs, but family counted at White Sulphur Springs.[51]

The ostentation and social display at Saratoga Springs, as well as its vast dining rooms and hectic social life, provided "a contrast" to the "family sort of life" and "happy-go-lucky service and jollity of the White Sulphur." Even so, by the 1880s commentators found the Virginia springs to be "less distinctively a Southern resort" than during the antebellum period, largely because of the influx of Northerners via railroads. This significant development altered the basic tenets of Southern society. As Mrs. Farquhar noted, "'Since you Yankees upset everything by the war, it is really of no importance who one's mother is.'" Northern society emphasized attainment, whereas Southern society valued heredity. The difference created friction. Twenty years before Mrs. Farquhar spoke in the pages of Warner's serialized story, Richard Arnold, a much more serious (and nonfictional) student of class and sectional relations, had written of the Civil War's consequences: "The revolution of our Social fabric is too great, the entire upheaval & overthrow of all the foundations of our Society too universal, not to affect every body & to place persons in an almost entirely new status." He insisted that the South would welcome "any Gentleman or Lady who observes the courtesies of Society" but not those "Jacobins" who sought to overturn Southern society. He even attributed "the elements of the bitter hatred and vindicative [sic] malignity of the majority of the Northern people against the South" to "the superiority of our general Social state. In one word we were too feudal to suit codfish aristocracy, Petroleum wealth, or Shoddy Show."[52]

But with the Confederacy's defeat, Arnold and other aristocratic Southerners had no choice but to accommodate newly minted Northern wealth, something they may have done with more alacrity than their letters indicate. By aligning along class lines, wealthy Northerners and Southerners could protect against the dangerous rumblings from below that threatened their status. In addition, class unity lent them a common identity that owed nothing to the struggles over emancipation and black civil rights that had dominated the 1860s and 1870s. Economics united the nation in a way that politics never could. The 1891 purchase of one of the South's oldest social rendezvous, Warm Springs, by Northern investors connected with the Chesapeake and Ohio Railroad and that railroad's 1910 acquisition of the mecca of Southern society, White Sulphur Springs, after a series of investors had failed to turn a profit demonstrated the South's dependence on Northern capital. Now the trains brought not just visitors from the Yankee cities but also Northern business practices and social values. William Calwell's dream of building a financially profitable grand resort reached fruition only when his successors adopted the same tactic that Gideon Putnam's protégés had followed at the century's outset: build as large an institution as possible, develop efficient and inexpensive transportation links, and appeal to a socially broad clientele.[53]

During the 1890 season, Mrs. William Grant, a wealthy Southerner, wrote her husband from White Sulphur Springs of a Mr. Fairfax, a son of Virginia's ancient Fairfax family, who captured the eyes and imagination of the belles. His father had been "immensely wealthy" and owned vast tracts of land. The Civil War and "high living" had cost the father his property and wealth, but the son "went to work when he finished his college course, took large contracts in Texas, made three hundred thousand dollars, returned + bought back the estates + homestead of his father." Fairfax represented a success story for late nineteenth-century Virginians because of his business acumen, as well as his dedication to family and property. Southern values had shifted to a point at which Mrs. Grant could define "the best people" as those "who own the homes, the estates, and the businesses upon which is based the pleasure of this and every other place." The first two qualities had existed during the antebellum period, but the third dominated society in the 1890s. By that decade business had become crucial to Virginia's economic—and especially social—well-being. In 1896 a special overnight train, the FFV Limited, whisked the "First Families of Virginia" from their homes to White Sulphur Springs in time for breakfast. The train's origin and intermediate stops illustrate the integration of the Virginia aristocracy into the national elite and the nation's new centers of power and money: New York City, Philadelphia, Baltimore, and Washington. Indeed, visitors from the former Confederate states represented a minority at White Sulphur Springs during the 1896 season. The springs were now part of a national tourism economy and their visitors part of an American elite.[54]

Notes

ABBREVIATIONS

WORKS FREQUENTLY CITED ARE IDENTIFIED
BY THE FOLLOWING ABBREVIATIONS.

Duke:	Manuscripts and Special Collections, Perkins Library, Duke University, Durham, North Carolina
FH:	Consulted copy in the collections of Field Horne, Saratoga Springs
GBA:	Greenbrier Archives, White Sulphur Springs, West Virginia
HSSSp:	Historical Society of Saratoga Springs
LoV:	Library of Virginia, Richmond
MdHS:	Maryland Historical Society, Baltimore
MHS:	Massachusetts Historical Society, Boston
NMR:	National Museum of Racing, Saratoga Springs
N-YHS:	New-York Historical Society, New York City

NYSHA: New York State Historical Association, Cooperstown

NYSLA: Manuscripts Division, New York State Library and Archives, Albany

SCHS: South Carolina Historical Society, Charleston

SHC: Southern Historical Collection, University of North Carolina–Chapel Hill

SLM: *Southern Literary Messenger*

SSCH: Saratoga Springs City Historian's Office

SSPL: Saratoga Room, Saratoga Springs Public Library

SWM: Manuscripts Department, Swem Library, College of William and Mary, Williamsburg, Virginia

USC: South Caroliniana Library, University of South Carolina, Columbia

UVa: Manuscripts and Special Collections, Alderman Library, University of Virginia, Charlottesville

VHS: Virginia Historical Society, Richmond

WVU: West Virginia Collection, West Virginia University, Morgantown

INTRODUCTION

1. Carl Bridenbaugh, "Baths and Watering Places of Colonial America," *William and Mary Quarterly,* 3d. ser., 3 (April 1946): 151–81.

2. Yellow Sulphur Springs ledger, 1857–58, VHS; Buffalo Lithia Springs ledger, 1857–58, VHS; Clarendon Hall register, 1860, NMR; Union Hall register, 1852, HSSSp; J. Calvin Smith, *The Illustrated Hand-Book, A New Guide for Travelers Through the United States of America* (New York: Sherman and Smith, 1847), 54; James Drew diary, 21 August 1846, N-YHS; *Six Weeks in Fauquier* (New York: Samuel Colman, 1839), 33; A. M. Maxwell, *A Run Through the United States* (London: Henry Colburn, 1841), 190.

3. Mark Pencil, Esq. [Mary Hagner], *The White Sulphur Papers, or Life at the Springs of Western Virginia* (New York: Samuel Colman, 1839), 40; Dandridge Spotswood diary, 23 July 1848, VHS; John Rutherfoord to John C. Rutherfoord, 23 August 1854, John Rutherfoord Papers, Duke; St. George Coalter Tucker to John Randolph Bryan, 25 August 1836, Brown, Coalter, Tucker Papers, SWM; Thomas Gordon Pollock to Mother, 3 August 1860, Abram David Pollock Papers, SHC; White Sulphur Springs ledger, 1816, GBA; *Springs, Water-Falls, Sea-Bathing Resorts, and Mountain Scenery of the United States and Canada* (New York: J. Disturnell, 1855), 67; Anne Newport Royall, *Sketches of History, Life, and Manners in the United States, by a Traveler* (New York: Johnson Reprint Corporation, 1970 [1826]), 72; Sans Souci Register, 1825–26, Brookside Museum, Ballston Spa, N.Y.

4. Robert Wiebe, *The Opening of American Society: From the Adoption of the Constitution to the Eve of Disunion* (New York: Knopf, 1984), chaps. 1–3, 190–93; Gordon S. Wood, *The Radicalism of the American Revolution* (New York: Knopf, 1991), 241–43, 271–86.

5. Stuart M. Blumin, *The Emergence of the Middle Class: Social Experience in the American City, 1760–1890* (New York: Cambridge University Press, 1989); Edward Pessen, *Riches, Class,*

and Power before the Civil War (Lexington, Mass.: D. C. Heath, 1973); Robert F. Dalzell Jr., *Enterprising Elite: The Boston Associates and the World They Made* (New York: W. W. Norton, 1987); Ronald Story, *The Forging of an Aristocracy: Harvard and the Boston Upper Class, 1800–1870* (Middletown, Conn.: Wesleyan University Press, 1980); Douglas T. Miller, *Jacksonian Aristocracy: Class and Democracy in New York, 1830–1860* (New York: Oxford University Press, 1967); Frederic Cople Jaher, *The Urban Establishment: Upper Strata in Boston, New York, Charleston, Chicago, and Los Angeles* (Urbana: University of Illinois Press, 1982), 7, 727–30.

6. James Sterling Young, *The Washington Community, 1800–1828* (New York: Columbia University Press, 1966), 16, 65–73, 88–109, 123–42, 251–53; Daniel P. Kilbride, "The Cosmopolitan South: Privileged Southerners, Philadelphia, and the Fashionable Tour in the Antebellum Era," *Journal of Urban History* 26 (July 2000): 563–90; Daniel P. Kilbride, "Cultivation, Conservatism, and the Early National Gentry: The Manigault Family and Their Circle," *Journal of the Early Republic* 19 (summer 1999): 221–56; Bertram Wyatt-Brown, *The House of Percy: Honor, Melancholy, and Imagination in a Southern Family* (New York: Oxford University Press, 1994), 80, 87–103.

7. Henry James, *Hawthorne* (New York: AMS Press, 1968 [1887]), 42–44; Paul Langford, *A Polite and Commercial People: England, 1727–1783* (Oxford: Clarendon Press, 1989), 102–16; Peter Dobkin Hall, *The Organization of American Culture, 1700–1900: Private Institutions, Elites, and the Origins of American Nationality* (New York: New York University Press, 1982).

8. Bridenbaugh, "Baths and Watering Places of Colonial America," 152; Jonathan Paul De-Vierville, "American Healing Waters: A Chronology (1513–1946) and Historical Survey of America's Major Springs, Spas, and Health Resorts Including a Review of Their Medicinal Virtues, Therapeutic Methods, and Health Care Practices" (Ph.D. diss., University of Texas–Austin, 1992); Francis J. Scully, *Hot Springs, Arkansas, and Hot Springs National Park* (Little Rock: Hanson Co., 1966).

9. On the origins of nationalism, see Benedict Anderson, *Imagined Communities: Reflections on the Origin and Spread of Nationalism* (London: Verso, 1991), 7; and Drew Gilpin Faust, *The Creation of Confederate Nationalism: Ideology and Identity in the Civil War South* (Baton Rouge: Louisiana State University Press, 1988). Henry James, "Saratoga," *The Nation* 11 (11 August 1870): 88.

10. William Burke, *The Virginia Mineral Springs* (Richmond: Ritchies and Dunnavant, 1853), 43; Alexis de Tocqueville, *Democracy in America* (New York: Knopf, 1994 [1838]), 2:95–99, 136, 172.

11. Tocqueville, *Democracy in America,* 2:171, 217–20. Tocqueville never actually visited the springs in either New York or Virginia. See George Pierson, *Tocqueville in America* (Gloucester, Mass.: Peter Smith, 1969); http://www.tocqueville.org (consulted October 1998). Linda Kerber, *Federalists in Dissent: Imagery and Ideology in Jeffersonian America* (Ithaca, N.Y.: Cornell University Press, 1970), viii; James Kirby Martin, *Men in Rebellion: Higher Government Leaders and the Coming of the American Revolution* (New Brunswick, N.J.: Rutgers University Press, 1973), 183; Wood, *The Radicalism of the American Revolution,* 195; Richard L. Bushman,

The Refinement of America: Persons, Houses, Cities (New York: Knopf, 1992), xix, 81, 182, 183, 404; Jan Lewis, *The Pursuit of Happiness: Family and Values in Jefferson's Virginia* (Cambridge, England: Cambridge University Press, 1983), 217; John F. Kasson, *Rudeness and Civility: Manners in Nineteenth-Century America* (New York: Hill and Wang, 1990), 59–69.

12. Tocqueville, *Democracy in America*, 2:100; Clement Clarke Moore, "A Trip to Saratoga," 1844, Clement Clarke Moore Papers, N-YHS. See Stephen Nissenbaum, *The Battle for Christmas* (New York: Knopf, 1996), 65–71, 88–89; James I. Robertson, *Stonewall Jackson: The Man, the Soldier, the Legend* (New York: Macmillan, 1997).

13. E. P. Thompson, *The Making of the English Working Class* (New York: Vintage, 1966), 9–11; Thorstein Veblen, *The Theory of the Leisure Class* (New York: Penguin, 1979 [1899]), 38–52.

14. Cindy S. Aron, *Working at Play: A History of Vacations in the United States* (New York: Oxford University Press, 1999); Orvar Löfgren, *On Holiday: A History of Vacationing* (Berkeley: University of California Press, 1999); Lynne Withey, *Cook's Tours and Grand Tours: A History of Leisure Travel, 1750–1915* (New York: William Morrow, 1997); Dona Brown, *Inventing New England: Regional Tourism in Nineteenth-Century America* (Washington, D.C.: Smithsonian Institution Press, 1995); John Sears, *Sacred Places: American Tourist Attractions in the Nineteenth Century* (New York: Oxford University Press, 1989); Dean MacCannell, *The Tourist: A New Theory of the Leisure Class* (Berkeley: University of California Press, 1999); Charlene Marie Lewis, *Ladies and Gentlemen on Display: Planter Society at the Virginia Springs, 1790–1860* (Charlottesville: University Press of Virginia, 2001); Margaret Gail Gillespie, "Havens for the Fashionable and Sickly: Society, Sickness, and Space at Nineteenth Century Southern Springs Resorts" (Ph.D. diss., University of North Carolina–Chapel Hill, 1998); Jon Sterngass, *First Resorts: Pursuing Pleasure at Saratoga Springs, Newport, and Coney Island* (Baltimore: Johns Hopkins University Press, 2001), 146–47; Theodore Corbett, *The Making of American Resorts: Saratoga Springs, Ballston Spa, and Lake George* (New Brunswick, N.J.: Rutgers University Press, 2001); Kenneth M. Stampp, "The Irrepressible Conflict," in *The Imperiled Union: Essays on the Background of the Civil War* (New York: Oxford University Press, 1980), 191–45.

1. COMMERCIALIZING LEISURE

1. Stan Cohen, *Historic Springs of the Virginias: A Pictorial History* (Charleston, W.Va.: Pictorial Histories Publishing Company, 1981); Frederick Chambers, *Map of the Village of Saratoga Springs, Saratoga County, New York* (Philadelphia: Richard Clark, 1858), SSCH.

2. Cohen, *Historic Springs of Virginia*, 56, 113, 164; Edward F. Grose, *Centennial History of the Village of Ballston Spa* (Ballston Spa, N.Y.: Ballston Journal, 1907), 55–58.

3. J. H. Plumb, "The Commercialization of Leisure in Eighteenth-Century England," in *The Birth of a Consumer Society: The Commercialization of Eighteenth-Century England*, ed. Neil McKendrick, John Brewer, and J. H. Plumb (Bloomington: Indiana University Press,

1982), 265–85; R. S. Neale, *Bath, 1680–1850: A Social History* (London: Routledge and Kegan Paul, 1981); Donald Yacovone, "A New England Bath: The Nation's First Resort at Stafford Springs," *Connecticut Historical Society Bulletin* 41 (January 1976): 2–3; Samuel Peters, 1782, as quoted in Carl Bridenbaugh, "Baths and Watering Places of Colonial America," *William and Mary Quarterly,* 3d. ser., 3 (April 1946): 153.

4. Mary S. McDuffie to Uncle, 15 July 1854, Singleton Family Papers, USC; Gabriel Manigault diary, 20 December 1777, Manigault Family Papers, USC; Elkanah Watson, Journal B, 20 November 1782, Elkanah Watson Papers, NYSLA.

5. Elkanah Watson, Journal B, 15 September 1790, Elkanah Watson Papers, NYSLA; Diary of a Scot Touring the Eastern United States, June 1824, N-YHS; Amelia M. Murray, *Letters from the United States, Cuba, and Canada* (New York: G. P. Putnam, 1856), 368; Ferdinand-Marie Bayard, *Travels of a Frenchman in Maryland and Virginia . . . during the Summer of 1791,* trans. and ed. Ben C. McCary (Ann Arbor, Mich.: Edwards Brothers, 1950 [1798]), 39–40; Elkanah Watson, "Mixed Medley," 20 August 1805, Elkanah Watson Papers, NYSLA.

6. Barbara Carson, "Early American Tourists and the Commercialization of Leisure," in *Of Consuming Interest: The Style of Life in the Eighteenth Century,* ed. Cary Carson, Ronald Hoffman, and Peter J. Albert (Charlottesville: University Press of Virginia, 1994), 400; Dona Brown, *Inventing New England: Regional Tourism in Nineteenth-Century America* (Washington, D.C.: Smithsonian Institution Press, 1995), 3–40; Cindy S. Aron, *Working at Play: A History of Vacations in the United States* (New York: Oxford University Press, 1999), 15–34; John Sears, *Sacred Places: American Tourist Attractions in the Nineteenth Century* (New York: Oxford University Press, 1989), 9–11; Olive Blair Graffam, "The Commercialization of Leisure at the Antebellum Springs of Virginia: Studies of Hot Springs and Fauquier White Sulphur Springs" (master's thesis, George Washington University, 1988); William Burke, *The Mineral Springs of Western Virginia: With Remarks on Their Use, and the Diseases to Which They are Applicable* (New York: Wiley and Putnam, 1842), 287. Although Brown, Aron, and Sears date the commercialization of leisure to the 1820s, Carson's argument that the process began in the eighteenth century agrees with this work's evidence and argument. The most important synthetic of work on this period—Charles Sellers, *The Market Revolution: Jacksonian America, 1815–1846* (New York: Oxford University Press, 1991)—makes little mention of the springs, tourism, or the commercialization of leisure.

7. Roger Haydon, ed., *Upstate Travels: British Views of Nineteenth-Century America* (Syracuse, N.Y.: Syracuse University Press, 1982), 27; Brown, *Inventing New England,* 28–31; *The Tourist, or Pocket Manual for Travellers* (New York: Harper and Brothers, 1838), 85.

8. Gideon Miner Davison, *The Fashionable Tour: Or, A Trip to the Springs, Niagara, Quebeck, and Boston, in the Summer of 1821* (Saratoga Springs, N.Y.: G. M. Davison, 1822). Two major guidebooks appeared before *The Fashionable Tour,* but neither achieved the same level of commercial success or widespread use: S. S. Moore and T. W. Jones, *The Traveler's Directory; or, A Pocket Companion: Shewing the Course of the Main Road from Philadelphia to New*

York, and from Philadelphia to Washington . . . From Actual Survey (Philadelphia: n.p., 1802); George Temple, *The American Tourist's Pocket Companion, or, a Guide to the Springs and a Trip to the Lakes* (New York: D. Longworth, 1812). Quoted in Gideon Miner Davison, *The Fashionable Tour; A Guide to Travellers Visiting the Middle and Northern States, and the Provinces of Canada* (Saratoga Springs, N.Y.: G. M. Davison, 1830), xvii.

9. Theodore Dwight, *The Northern Traveller* (New York: Wilder and Campbell, 1825), iv; *The Tourist, or Pocket Manual for Travellers,* i; S. DeVeaux, *The Travelers' Own Book, to Saratoga Springs, Niagara Falls and Canada* (Buffalo: Faxon and Reed, 1841); Gideon Miner Davison, *The Traveller's Guide Through the Middle and Northern States and the Canadas* (Saratoga Springs, N.Y.: G. M. Davison, 1840), xv.

10. In 1840 Davison changed his book's title from *The Fashionable Tour* to *The Traveller's Guide Through the Middle and Northern States, and the Provinces of Canada.* Dwight also tinkered with his *Northern Traveller* title by adding new information on the Pennsylvania coal region, New England, and the Virginia springs.

11. Henry Huntt, *A Visit to the Red Sulphur Spring of Virginia, During the Summer of 1837* (Boston: Duton and Wentworth, 1839); Mark Pencil, Esq. [Mary Hagner], *The White Sulphur Papers, or Life at the Springs of Western Virginia* (New York: Samuel Colman, 1839), vii; Burke, *The Mineral Springs of Western Virginia.*

12. Burke published three editions, and Moorman issued six; John J. Moorman, *The Virginia Springs with Their Analysis and some Remarks on their Character* (Philadelphia: Lindsay and Blakiston, 1847), iv; Robert Cowan, *A Guide to the Virginia Springs* (Philadelphia: Thomas, Copperthwait, 1851), xi.

13. Larkin Newby to Cecilia Newby, 25 June 1823, Larkin Newby Papers, SHC.

14. See Nancy Goyne Evans, "The Sans Souci, a Fashionable Resort Hotel in Ballston Spa," *Winterthur Portfolio* 6 (1970): 111–26; Graffam, "The Commercialization of Leisure at the Antebellum Springs of Virginia"; Charlotte Lou Atkins, "Rockbridge Alum Springs: A History of the Spa, 1790–1974" (master's thesis, Virginia Polytechnic Institute and State University, 1974).

15. Robert S. Conte, *The History of the Greenbrier: America's Resort* (Charleston, W.Va.: Pictorial Histories Publishing Company, 1989), 1–5; William Olcott, *The Greenbrier Heritage* (Netherlands: Arindt, Preston, 1980), 11–14; additional information in Greenbrier County Record Books, notes in GBA; George Waller, *Saratoga: Saga of an Impious Era* (Englewood Cliffs, N.J.: Prentice-Hall, 1966), 52–54; Nathaniel Bartlett Sylvester, *History of Saratoga County, New York* (Philadelphia: Everts and Ensign, 1878), 228; Grace Maguire Swanner, *Saratoga: Queen of Spas* (Utica, N.Y.: North Country Books, 1988), 103–5; Hugh Bradley, *Such Was Saratoga* (New York: Doubleday, 1940), 19–36.

16. Timothy Dwight, *Travels in New England and New York,* ed. Barbara Miller Solomon (Cambridge, Mass.: Belknap Press, 1969), 3:293; Winslow C. Watson, ed., *Men and Times of the Revolution; or, Manners of Elkanah Watson* (New York: Dana, 1856), 290; Dr. Nathan Fish, 1801, as quoted in Cornelius E. Durkee, *Reminiscences of Saratoga* (Saratoga Springs, N.Y.: Reprinted

from the *Saratogian,* 1927–28), 87; William L. Stone, *Reminiscences of Saratoga and Ballston* (New York: R. Worthington, 1880), 77–78; Philip Vickers Fithian, *Journal, 1775–1776,* ed. Robert Greenhalgh Albion and Leonard Dodson (Princeton, N.J.: Princeton University Press, 1934), 145; "Lewis Summer's Journal of a Tour from Alexandria, Virginia to Gallipolis, Ohio in 1808," *Southern Historical Magazine* 2 (February 1892): 57–58; Thomas Jefferson, *Notes on the State of Virginia,* ed. William Peden (New York: Norton, 1954 [1787]), 35.

17. James Calwell to Polly Bowyer Calwell, 9 August 1816, Calwell Letters, GBA; Olcott, *The Greenbrier Heritage,* 16–17; Conte, *The History of the Greenbrier,* 7–9; Greenbrier County Deed Books, GBA.

18. Deeds: 1791–1812, Putnam Collection, NYSHA; Durkee, *Reminiscences,* 63; Stone, *Reminiscences,* 55–62, 64.

19. For example, the Hot Springs Tavern in Virginia took in 80 percent of its annual revenues during the peak springs season from late June to early October ("Cash Rec'd at the Hot Springs Tavern," 1816–17, Daggs Family Business Records, LoV). Rockwell Putnam, the son of Gideon Putnam most active in the Saratoga Springs real estate and mineral springs business, transacted 65 percent of his bank deposits during the summer months (Folders 1831–34, 1835–39, Box 1, Putnam Collection, NYSHA); Town of Saratoga Springs Chattel Mortgages, 1833–60, SSCH. The mean length of stay for springs visitors was 9.5 days (data from Table 1 ledgers); Graffam, "The Commercialization of Leisure at the Antebellum Springs of Virginia," 65–67.

20. James Kirke Paulding, *Letters from the South, Written During an Excursion During the Summer of 1816* (New York: James Eastburn and Company, 1817), 1:231; Abigail May diary, 24 May 1800, NYSHA; Helen Beall Lewis, ed., "Journal of Alexander Dick in America, 1806–1809" (master's thesis, University of Virginia, 1984), 276, 296; Warm Springs and Harrisonburg Turnpike Toll Collection Book, 1838–53, LoV; Mary Thompson to Mrs. Frances M. Lewis and Mrs. Mary Neale, Conway Whittle Family Papers, SWM.

21. *Virginia Gazette,* 21 July 1768; Bath County Petitions, 9 and 21 December 1811, 7 December 1827, 17 December 1828, 16 January 1832, 10 February 1837, LoV; George Rogers Taylor, *The Transportation Revolution, 1815–1860* (Armonk, N.Y.: M. E. Sharpe, 1951), 23, 49, 88, 92, 99–101, 320–22, 382; data taken from John W. Williams, comp., *Index to Enrolled Bills of the General Assembly of Virginia, 1776 to 1910* (Richmond: Davis Bottom, 1911); Lana Martindale, "Highways to Health and Pleasure: The Antebellum Turnpikes and Trade of the Mineral Springs in Greenbrier and Monroe Counties, Virginia" (unpublished paper, 1994), 13–19, VHS; Minutes of the James River and Kanawha Company, 16 December 1835, GBA; data from Williams, *Index to Enrolled Bills.* Few companies incorporated during the economic panics of 1819–20, 1837, 1839–43, or 1857.

22. John Rossen to Clara, 1 August 1849, GBA; Philip St. George Cocke diary, 1853, Elliot-Cocke Collection, UVa; Williams, *Index to Enrolled Bills;* Kenneth W. Noe, *Southwest Virginia's Railroad: Modernization and the Sectional Crisis* (Urbana: University of Illinois Press, 1994), 12–28, 32–35, 55–66; Robert C. Black, *The Railroads of the Confederacy* (Wilmington, N.C.:

Broadfoot, 1987 [1952]), 2; Carter Goodrich, *Government Promotion of American Canals and Railroads, 1800–1890* (New York: Columbia University Press, 1960), 87–120; map attached to Moorman, *The Virginia Springs: Comprising an Account of all the Principal Mineral Springs of Virginia, with Remarks on the Nature and Medical Application of Each* (Richmond: J. W. Randolph, 1857); Montgomery White Sulphur Springs Broadside, 1856, SWM.

23. Taylor, *The Transportation Revolution,* 57–59; Dwight, *The Northern Traveller,* 6; Haydon, *Upstate Travels,* 11, 20 (the 1824 U.S. Supreme Court decision *Gibbons v. Ogden,* which held that the federal government possessed the power to regulate interstate commerce, facilitated the breakup of the Livingston-Fulton steamboat monopoly); *The Tourist,* 43, 95. The canal route took twelve to fourteen hours versus only two to three hours via excellent turnpike roads.

24. Taylor, *The Transportation Revolution,* 75–77; Durkee, *Reminiscences,* 7–8, 89–90, 173; Grose, *Centennial History,* 112; Stone, *Reminiscences,* 180–81; Daniel Benedict diary, 1831–32 entries, SSCH (Benedict served as the ticket agent and station master of the Schenectady and Saratoga Railroad); DeVeaux, *The Travelers' Own Book,* 16; Durkee, *Reminiscences,* 13.

25. Benedict diary, 3 June and 13 August 1833, SSCH; data from tables of "Arrivals at the Springs" published in the *Saratoga Springs (N.Y.) Whig,* July and August 1840.

26. J. E. Snow to "Bro and Sist Snow," 7 August 1851, SSPL; Davison, *The Traveller's Guide* (1833), 150–51; O. L. Holley, ed., *The Picturesque Tourist* (New York: J. Disturnell, 1844), 89.

27. Saratoga and Washington Rail-Road Company Papers, 1847–49, NYSLA; *Lexington (Va.) Gazette,* 18 September 1835.

28. Carol Sheriff, *The Artificial River: The Erie Canal and the Paradox of Progress, 1817–1862* (New York: Hill and Wang, 1996), 6.

29. Carson, "Early American Tourists and the Commercialization of Leisure," 389; Lottery ticket, 10 June 1793, Homestead Archives, Hot Springs, Va. See Jean Graham McAllister, *A Brief History of Bath County, Virginia* (Staunton, Va.: McClure Press, 1920), 21; J. T. McAllister, *Historical Sketches of Virginia Hot Springs, Warm Sulphur Springs, and Bath County, Virginia* (Salem, Va.: Salem Printing, 1908), 8; Oren F. Morton, *Annals of Bath County, Virginia* (Staunton, Va.: McClure Press, 1917), 48; Perceval Reniers, *The Springs of Virginia: Life, Love, and Death at the Waters, 1775–1900* (Chapel Hill: University of North Carolina Press, 1941), 56; Conte, *The History of the Greenbrier,* 13. Relevant financial records are part of the Singleton Family Papers, USC and SHC; quotations from James Calwell to Richard Singleton, 10 September 1827 and 1 October 1831, USC.

30. Erasmus Stribling, 16 December 1834 petition, Augusta County Petitions, LoV; data from *Acts and Joint Resolutions of the General Assembly of the Commonwealth of Virginia* (Richmond: William F. Ritchie, various years), as listed in Williams, *Index to Enrolled Bills* (see Thomas A. Chambers, "Fashionable Dis-Ease: Promoting Health and Leisure at Saratoga Springs, New York, and the Virginia Springs, 1790–1860" [Ph.D. diss., College of William and Mary, 1999], 352–53). Sweet Springs was chartered in 1836 and 1856; Tazewell White Sulphur

Springs in 1840 and 1842; Fauquier White Sulphur Springs in 1836 and 1854; Hot Springs in 1840, 1848, and 1856; Red Sulphur Springs in 1837 and 1838; and White Sulphur Springs in 1834, 1845, 1853, and 1854. Several leading Virginia families held stock in various springs (Charlene Marie Lewis, "Ladies and Gentlemen on Display: Planter Society at the Virginia Springs, 1790–1860" [Ph.D. diss., University of Virginia, 1997], 142–43).

31. Jane H. Pease argues that the conspicuous consumption of wealthy Southerners, especially on their trips to spas and Northern resorts, limited the amount of capital available for investment. The expansion of springs businesses in the antebellum period and the activities of Richard Singleton suggest that this was not the case. See Jane H. Pease, "A Note on Patterns of Conspicuous Consumption among Seaboard Planters, 1820–1860," *Journal of Southern History* 35 (August 1969): 381–93.

32. Gavin Wright, *Old South, New South: Revolutions in the Southern Economy since the Civil War* (New York: Basic Books, 1986), 11, 20–33; Harry L. Watson, "Slavery and Development in a Dual Economy: The South and the Market Revolution," in *The Market Revolution in America: Social, Political, and Religious Expressions,* ed. Melvyn Stokes and Stephen Conway (Charlottesville: University Press of Virginia, 1996), 44–68.

33. Town of Saratoga Springs Chattel Mortgages, 1833–60, SSCH.

34. J. G. McAllister, *A Brief History of Bath County,* 5; J. T. McAllister, *Historical Sketches of Virginia Hot Springs,* 27; Sylvester, *History of Saratoga County,* 12; Grose, *Centennial History,* 113. On the growth of springs towns, see Christopher Edwin Hendricks, "Town Development in the Colonial Backcountry—Virginia and North Carolina" (Ph.D. diss., College of William and Mary, 1991), 277–89.

35. Gideon Putnam, "Rules and Regulations, 1811," Putnam Collection, NYSHA; Chandos Michael Brown, *Benjamin Silliman: A Life in the Young Republic* (Princeton, N.J.: Princeton University Press, 1989), 130, 206–10, 230–35, 238–48, 250–58; Stone, *Reminiscences,* 162, 296; Donald Tucker, *Collector's Guide to the Saratoga Type Mineral Water Bottle* (North Berwick, Maine: Donald and Lois Tucker, 1986), 1, 31, 85; E. J. Huling, "Some Reminiscences of Life and Times Since 1828," 25, SSPL.

36. Durkee, *Reminiscences,* 5, 148; Stone, *Reminiscences,* 293; Bernhard C. Puckhaber, *Saratogas: A History of the Springs, Mineral Water Bottles Which are Known as 'Saratogas,' Bottling Plants and Glass Works of Saratoga County, New York, from 1823 to 1889* (Ballston Spa, N.Y.: Journal Press, 1976), 14–16; John H. Steel, *An Analysis of the Congress Spring, with Practical Remarks on its Medical Properties* (New York: William W. Rose, 1856), 21; *Peck's Tourist Companion to Niagara Falls, Saratoga Springs, the Lakes, Canada, Etc.* (Buffalo, N.Y.: William B. and Charles E. Peck, 1845), 168; *Saratoga Springs (N.Y.) Whig,* 14 July 1840.

37. Pencil, *The White Sulphur Papers,* 159; "Statement of Receipts and Expenditures for the White Sulphur Springs Hotel for the Season of 1860," Philip St. George Cocke Papers, UVa; *The Bedford Alum Springs, Near New London, Virginia, P. Echols, Proprietor* (Lynchburg, Va.: Virginian Job Printing Establishment, 1854), 9; advertisements ran weekly in the *Lexington*

(Va.) Gazette, June–September, 1854; William Frazier, *The Rockbridge Alum Springs Case: A Historical Narrative* (*Staunton [Va.] Spectator,* 1883), 29; "A statement of the quantity of Alum Water shipped . . .," Rockbridge Alum Springs Papers, Leyburn Library, Washington and Lee University, Lexington, Va.; Porte Crayon [David Hunter Strother], *Virginia Illustrated: Containing a Visit to the Virginia Canaan, and the Adventures of Porte Crayon and His Cousins* (New York: Harper and Brothers, 1857), 176.

38. Agents were located in Richmond, Baltimore, Washington City, Philadelphia, New York City, Albany, Boston, Petersburg (two agents), and Louisville (John J. Moorman, *Water From the White Sulphur Springs, Greenbrier County, Virginia* [1840 pamphlet], 1–2, italics in original). "Congress Water," advertisement in Steel, *An Analysis of the Congress Spring,* facing p. 34.

39. Chambers, "Fashionable Dis-Ease," 352–53; Mary Jane Windle, *Life in Washington, and Life Here and There* (Philadelphia: J. B. Lippincott and Company, 1859), 215; *Memoirs of an Emigrant: The Journal of Alexander Coventry, M.D., In Scotland, The United States, and Canada during the period 1783–1831,* 24 September 1802, NYSLA; entry for Thomas Lewis, 7 September 1829, Hot Springs Tavern Ledger, 1829–31, Daggs Records, LoV.

40. Peregrine Prolix [Philip Holbrook Nicklin], *Letters Descriptive of the Virginia Springs* (Philadelphia: H. S. Tanner, 1835), 29; Jonathan Berkeley Grimball diary, 9–11 July 1835, SHC; James Johnston Pettigrew to James Cathcart Johnston, 14 August 1855, Pettigrew Family Papers, SHC.

41. John Pendleton Kennedy to wife, 26 July 1851, John Pendleton Kennedy Papers, WVU; Stephen Allen Memoirs, 12 August 1841, N-YHS; Lewis, "Ladies and Gentlemen on Display," 169, 188–89; Graffam, "The Commercialization of Leisure at the Antebellum Springs of Virginia," 35–36; Dorothy Gilchrist, "The Virginia Springs: A Mirror of Ante-Bellum Society" (master's thesis, University of Virginia, 1943), 52–53.

42. Indenture, White Sulphur Springs Company, 24 December 1858, UVa; Allen Memoirs, White Sulphur Springs, 12 August 1841, N-YHS; George William Featherstonhaugh, *Excursion Through the Slave States, from Washington on the Potomac to the Frontier of Mexico; with Sketches of Popular Manners and Geological Notices* (London: John Murray, 1844), 1:70–71; Conte, *The History of the Greenbrier,* 14; Olcott, *The Greenbrier Heritage,* 20; Greenbrier County Deed Book 12, 5 September 1832, from notes in GBA. The cottage purchasers included five from Louisiana, one from Mississippi, and eight from Virginia.

43. The exact figure is 28.4 percent ("Statement of Receipts and Expenditures," Philip St. George Cocke Papers, UVa); J. Lynah to Mrs. Francis M. Lewis, 28 March 1857, Conway Whittle Family Papers, SWM; Mary C. Lynn and William Fox, comps., "The 1850 Census of Saratoga Springs: A Numerical Listing," 1991, SSPL; Lynn and Fox, "The 1860 Census of Saratoga Springs: A Numerical Listing," 1991, SSPL. See also Theodore Corbett, *The Making of American Resorts: Saratoga Springs, Ballston Spa, and Lake George* (New Brunswick, N.J.: Rutgers University Press, 2001), chaps. 8–9; and Myra B. Young Armstead, *"Lord, Please Don't Take Me in August": African Americans in Newport and Saratoga Springs, 1870–1930* (Urbana: University of Illinois Press, 1999), chap. 1.

44. Lewis, "Ladies and Gentlemen on Display," 145–51; Christian Weber to John Green, 19 March 1842, Keith Family Papers, VHS.

45. Data from hotel ledgers listed in Table 1; J. Humphreys to Jeremiah Morton, 11 December 1860, Halsey Family Papers, UVa; Helen Grinnan to John Gray, [1843], Keith Family Papers, VHS; Lewis, "Ladies and Gentlemen on Display," 152–55.

46. Reniers, *The Springs of Virginia*, 61; Conte, *The History of the Greenbrier*, 43; William Bolling diary, 19 August 1841, VHS; Trant diary ("Journal of a Trip to the White Sulphur Springs, August 1836" [typed mss.]), 29 August 1836, GBA; Featherstonhaugh, *Excursion Through the Slave States*, 1:71–72; details of the sale are in sections 3, 5, and 12, Stuart Family Papers, VHS; Jeremiah Morton to J. J. Halsey, 13 July 1860, Halsey Family Papers, UVa. The operating deficit for 1860 was $62,724.58 on $144,625.60 in gross receipts, a negative balance of 43.7 percent ("Statement of Receipts and Expenditures," Philip St. George Cocke Papers, UVa).

47. Putnam Collection, NYSHA; R. L. Allen, *Hand-Book of Saratoga, and Strangers' Guide* (New York: W. H. Arthur, 1859), 25–26.

48. *Lexington (Va.) Gazette*, 25 August 1859.

2. SELLING THE SETTING

1. Gideon Miner Davison, *The Fashionable Tour; A Guide to Travellers Visiting the Middle and Northern States, and the Provinces of Canada* (Saratoga Springs, N.Y.: G. M. Davison, 1830), xvii.

2. John Conron, *American Picturesque* (University Park: Pennsylvania State University Press, 2000), xvii–xix, 19–27; Leo Marx, *The Machine in the Garden: Technology and the Pastoral Ideal in America* (New York: Oxford University Press, 1964), 3–9, 85–87, 365; Perry Miller, "The Romantic Dilemma in American Nationalism and the Concept of Nature," in *Nature's Nation* (Cambridge: Harvard University Press, 1967), 197–207. Other useful works include Barbara Novak, *Nature and Culture: American Landscape and Painting, 1825–1875* (New York: Oxford University Press, 1980), 159–60, 226–27; Angela Miller, *Empire of the Eye: Landscape Representation and American Cultural Politics, 1825–1875* (Ithaca, N.Y.: Cornell University Press, 1993), 11–17; Roderick Nash, *Wilderness and the American Mind* (New Haven, Conn.: Yale University Press, 1973), chaps. 4–6; Neil Everndon, *The Social Creation of Nature* (Baltimore: Johns Hopkins University Press, 1992), chap. 6; Elizabeth R. McKinsey, *Niagara Falls: Icon of the American Sublime* (New York: Cambridge University Press, 1985); Carol Sheriff, *The Artificial River: The Erie Canal and the Paradox of Progress, 1817–1862* (New York: Hill and Wang, 1996), 26, 60–62; Patricia Anderson, *The Course of Empire: The Erie Canal and the New York Landscape, 1825–1875* (Rochester, N.Y.: Memorial Art Gallery of the University of Rochester, 1984), 16–19; Stephen Daniels, *Fields of Vision: Landscape Imagery and National Identity in England and the United States* (Princeton, N.J.: Princeton University Press, 1993); and John R. Stilgoe, *Common Landscape of America, 1580–1845* (New Haven, Conn.: Yale University Press, 1982).

3. Henry Howe, *Historical Collections of Virginia* (Charleston, S.C.: W. R. Babcock, 1845), 343; [Samuel Mordecai], *Description of the Album of Virginia: or, The Old Dominion, Illustrated* (Richmond: Virginia State Library, 1980 [1858]); Theodore Dwight Jr., *The Northern Traveler and Northern Tour* (New York: John P. Haven, 1841), 219; "Montgomery White Sulphur Springs," broadside, 1 June 1856, Duke; F. Stone to Thomas D. Stone, 25 August 1857, GBA; Robert Cowan, *A Guide to the Virginia Springs* (Philadelphia: Thomas, Copperthwait, 1851), 27; Edward Beyer, *Album of Virginia* (Richmond: Virginia State Library, 1980 [1857]); Mordecai, *Description of the Album of Virginia,* 37.

4. *Springs, Water-Falls, Sea-Bathing Resorts, and Mountain Scenery of the United States and Canada* (New York: J. Disturnell, 1855), 123; Gideon Miner Davison, *The Traveller's Guide Through the Middle and Northern States and the Canadas* (Saratoga Springs, N.Y.: G. M. Davison, 1840), 42; Cowan, *A Guide to the Virginia Springs,* 18; John Esten Cooke, "The White Sulphur Springs," *Harper's New Monthly Magazine* 57, no. 339 (1878): 343, 345.

5. *Saratoga Springs (N.Y.) Whig,* 27 July 1841; see also S. DeVeaux, *The Travelers' Own Book, to Saratoga Springs, Niagara Falls and Canada* (Buffalo: Faxon and Reed, 1841), 89; Davison, *The Traveller's Guide* (1840), 42; *The Tourist, or Pocket Manual for Travellers* (New York: Harper and Brothers, 1838), 85; Reuben Sears, *A Poem, on the Mineral Waters of Ballston and Saratoga, with Notes Illustrating the History of the Springs and Adjacent County* (Ballston Spa, N.Y.: J. Comstock, 1819), 14; "Saratoga," *Knickerbocker* 54 (Sept. 1859): 241–56.

6. *The Traveler's Guide for Montreal, Quebec and Saratoga Springs* (Montreal: Printed for the Publisher, 1859), 26.

7. Dona Brown, *Inventing New England: Regional Tourism in Nineteenth-Century America* (Washington, D.C.: Smithsonian Institution Press, 1995), 4–5, 34–38; John Sears, *Sacred Places: American Tourist Attractions in the Nineteenth Century* (New York: Oxford University Press, 1989), 3–10; Roger Haydon, ed., *Upstate Travels: British Views of Nineteenth-Century America* (Syracuse, N.Y.: Syracuse University Press, 1982), 8–9.

8. Thomas Cole, "American Scenery," *Northern Light* 1 (May 1841); "White Sulphur Springs" pamphlet, 1881, SHC; Marx, *The Machine in the Garden,* 88–89, 228; Conron, *American Picturesque,* 10–11.

9. James Skelton Gilliam diary, 29 July 1816, LoV; Abigail May diary, 7 June 1800, NYSHA; Sears, *Sacred Places,* 14–16, 49–71.

10. John H. Steel, *An Analysis of the Mineral Waters of Saratoga and Ballston* (Albany, N.Y.: D. Steele, 1817), 16–17. Steel's erroneous tale became the standard history of Saratoga Springs' discovery well into the late twentieth century. See, for example, R. L. Allen, *A Historical, Chemical and Therapeutical Analysis of the Principal Mineral Fountains at Saratoga Springs* (Saratoga Springs, N.Y.: B. Huling, 1853), 12–13; Nathaniel Bartlett Sylvester, *History of Saratoga County, New York* (Philadelphia: Everts and Ensign, 1878), 149; George Waller, *Saratoga: Saga of an Impious Era* (Englewood Cliffs, N.J.: Prentice-Hall, 1966), 3. The editor of the Sir William Johnson Papers pointed out this discrepancy, based on a close reading of Johnson's letters, but the revised date did not appear in print until 1988 (Grace Maguire Swanner, *Saratoga: Queen of*

Spas [Utica, N.Y.: North Country Books, 1988], 103). See Milton W. Hamilton to Evelyn Barrett Britten, 23 April 1953, SSCH. Robert E. Berkhofer, *The White Man's Indian: Images of the American Indian from Columbus to the Present* (New York: Vintage Books, 1979), 86–96.

11. "Journal of a Trip to the Mountains, Caves and Springs of Virginia," *SLM* 4 (March 1838): 199–200.

12. Philip J. Deloria, *Playing Indian* (New Haven, Conn.: Yale University Press, 1998), 3–5, 40–69.

13. Daniel Shepherd, *Saratoga: A Tale of 1787* (New York: W. P. Fetridge, 1856), 360; "Letter of a Virginian," *Albany (N.Y.) Statesman,* 6 September 1820.

14. *Banco; or, The Tenant of the Spring: A Legend of the White Sulphur* (Philadelphia: C. Sherman, 1839), 18–27.

15. Cole, "American Scenery"; Sears, *Sacred Places,* 4–6; Henry Dilworth Gilpin, *A Northern Tour* (Philadelphia: H. C. Carey and I. Lea, 1825), 2; William Burke, *The Mineral Springs of Western Virginia: With Remarks on Their Use, and the Diseases to Which They are Applicable* (New York: Wiley and Putnam, 1842), 13; Conron, *American Picturesque,* 7–10. On English desires for a rural golden age, see Raymond Williams, *The Country and the City* (New York: Oxford University Press, 1973).

16. C. O. Lyde diary, 5 July 1841, Duke. Generally the Virginia springs stuck to the more traditional Greek revival architectural style until the mid-1850s. Only then did they begin adopting the more modern Gothic and Italianate styles. John Gibson Worsham Jr., "'A Place so Lofty and Secluded': Yellow Sulphur Springs in Montgomery County," *Virginia Cavalcade* 26 (summer 1977): 31; Charlene Marie Lewis, "Ladies and Gentlemen on Display: Planter Society at the Virginia Springs, 1790–1860" (Ph.D. diss., University of Virginia, 1997), 90–100, 113; Robert Cowan, *A Guide to the Virginia Springs* (Philadelphia: Thomas, Copperthwait, 1851), 20; Howe, *Historical Collections,* 288; Jonathan Berkeley Grimball diary, 22 August 1835, SHC; John J. Moorman, *The Virginia Springs with Their Analysis and some Remakes on their Character* (Philadelphia: Lindsay and Blakiston, 1847), frontispiece maps; Burke, *The Mineral Springs of Western Virginia,* 126; "Virginia Springs," *SLM* 3 (May 1837): 282.

17. "Visit to the Virginia Springs, During the Summer of 1834," *SLM* 1 (May 1835): 474–76; Edmund Randolph to Marianne O'Meade, 4 August 1840, Edmund Randolph Papers, VHS; Frontispiece of Moorman, *The Virginia Springs* (1847); Beverly Tucker to Lucy Ann Tucker, 21 August 1837, Tucker-Coleman Collection, SWM; Beyer, *Album of Virginia,* 18; John W. Jarvis diary, 9 July 1849, UVa.

18. "Virginia Springs," 282; Mary Jane Windle, *Life in Washington, and Life Here and There* (Philadelphia: J. B. Lippincott and Company, 1859), 208; Edmund Randolph to Marianne O'Meade, 4 August 1840, Edmund Randolph Papers, VHS; *Six Weeks in Fauquier* (New York: Samuel Colman, 1839), 15; Susan Bradford Eppes to Pa, 1 August 1847, Susan Bradford Eppes Papers, SHC; Windle, *Life in Washington,* 166; Angela Miller, *Empire of the Eye: Landscape Representation and American Cultural Politics, 1825–1875* (Ithaca, N.Y.: Cornell University Press, 1993), 11–14; Nash, *Wilderness and the American Mind,* 40–42.

19. Susan Bradford Eppes to Pa, 1 August 1847, Susan Bradford Eppes Papers, SHC; "Journal of a Trip to the White Sulphur Springs," 23 August 1836, GBA; Nash, *Wilderness and the American Mind,* 40–42; Mona Domosh, *Invented Cities: The Creation of Landscape in Nineteenth-Century New York and Boston* (New Haven, Conn.: Yale University Press, 1996); Henry W. Lawrence, "Southern Spas: Source of the American Resort Tradition," *Landscape* 27, no. 2 (1983): 46; Lewis, "Ladies and Gentlemen on Display," 73–76, 94, 104–6, 113–14; Marx, *The Machine in the Garden,* 102.

20. Charles A. Pilsbury, "A Southern Watering-Place," *Potter's American Monthly* 15 (1880): 258–64; White Sulphur Springs pamphlet, 1881, SHC.

21. J. Scott, "A Map of a number of building Lots and Buildings near the Congress Spring the property of Gideon Putnam as the same was Surveyed in June 1808," Putnam Collection, NYSHA; Mosette Glaser Broderick, "History in Towns: Saratoga Springs, New York, the Queen of American Resorts," *Magazine Antiques* 128 (July 1985): 96, 107; Stephen S. Prokopoff and Joan C. Siegfried, *The Nineteenth Century Architecture of Saratoga Springs* (New York City: New York State Council on the Arts, 1970); Lawrence, "Southern Spas," 3; "The Fashionable Tour, or, A Journal kept in the Summer of 1834," 194, N-YHS; Henry Tudor, *Narrative of a Tour in North America* (London: J. Duncan, 1834), 190; Davison, *The Traveller's Guide* (1840), 141; Watson, "Mixed Medley," 19 August 1805, Elkanah Watson Papers, NYSLA.

22. May diary, 28–29 June 1800, NYSHA; J. B. Dunlop, "Diary of a British Traveller in the United States," 23 August 1811, N-YHS; Andrew Reed and James Matheson, *A Narrative of a Visit to the American Churches by the Deputation from the Congregational Union of England and Wales* (London: Jackson and Walford, 1836); *The Diary of George Templeton Strong,* ed. Allan Nevins and Milton Halsey Thomas (New York: MacMillan, 1952), 30 July 1841, 1:166. On the cultivation of English landscape, see Michael Reed, *The Georgian Triumph, 1700–1830* (London: Routledge and Kegan Paul, 1983); and Daniels, *Fields of Vision.*

23. Reed and Matheson, *A Narrative of a Visit to the American Churches;* "Letter of a Virginian."

24. "Saratoga," *Knickerbocker,* 249; Resolutions for 1 April 1843, 13 December 1843, 22 April 1845, 11 April 1846, and 23 April 1853, Village Board of Trustees Minutes, SSCH; "Saratoga—Opening of the Season," *New York Tribune,* 13 June 1842; Mary Thompson to Mrs. Frances M. Lewis, 27 July 1854, Conway Whittle Family Papers, SWM; Act Incorporating the Village of Saratoga Springs, 17 April 1826, SSCH.

25. Phyllis Hembry, *The English Spa, 1560–1815: A Social History* (London: Athlone Press, 1990), 114–30; Lewis, "Ladies and Gentlemen on Display," 101–4; Marx, *Machine in the Garden,* 228–37; William R. Taylor, *Cavalier and Yankee: The Old South and American National Character* (New York: Anchor Books, 1963); David Bertelson, *The Lazy South* (New York: Oxford University Press, 1967), chaps. 10–13; C. Vann Woodward, "The Southern Ethic in a Puritan World," *William and Mary Quarterly,* 3d. ser., 25 (July 1968): 343–70; Conron, *American Picturesque,* 171–73.

26. H. P. Tompkins to W. P. Smith, 21 September 1832, William Patterson Smith Papers, Duke; Mr. Cummings, "Guide/Jumble of Advice for Summer's Journey," 25 July 1805, Mackay-Stiles Papers, SHC; P. G. to Elizabeth Greene, 7 July 185[?], GBA.

27. Helen Beall Lewis, ed., "Journal of Alexander Dick in America, 1806–1809" (master's thesis, University of Virginia, 1984), 268–69; *Six Weeks in Fauquier,* 22; Stephen Allen Memoirs, 12 August 1841, N-YHS.

28. Levin Smith Joynes letter, 21 August 1856, Joynes Family Papers, VHS; John Rossen to Sister, 12 August 1849, GBA.

29. George William Featherstonhaugh, *Excursion Through the Slave States, from Washington on the Potomac to the Frontier of Mexico; with Sketches of Popular Manners and Geological Notices* (London: John Murray, 1844), 1:55–56, 65.

30. John H. B. Latrobe, "Odds and Ends" journal, 1832–35, John H. B. Latrobe Family Papers, MdHS; Francis Scott Key, "Lines on the White Sulphur Springs," GBA. Printed versions of the poem distributed at 1950s celebrations of Robert E. Lee Week at the Greenbrier Hotel, White Sulphur Springs, omitted this line.

31. Latrobe, "Odds and Ends" journal, MdHS; Key, "Lines on the White Sulphur Springs," GBA. Again, these lines were excluded from the official Greenbrier version of the poem. Peregrine Prolix [Philip Holbrook Nicklin], *Letters Descriptive of the Virginia Springs* (Philadelphia: H. S. Tanner, 1835), 31, 51; Featherstonhaugh, *Excursion Through the Slave States,* 1:55.

32. Porte Crayon [David Hunter Strother], *Virginia Illustrated: Containing a Visit to the Virginia Canaan, and the Adventures of Porte Crayon and His Cousins* (New York: Harper and Brothers, 1857), 160; Levin Smith Joynes to Mother, 9 August 1856, Joynes Family Papers, VHS; W. J. Nivison to John Nivison, 26 August 1813, Skipwith-Wilmer Papers, MdHS; Featherstonhaugh, *Excursion Through the Slave States,* 1:54; Pilsbury, "A Southern Watering-Place," 258.

33. Basil Hall, *Travels in North America in the Years 1827, 1828* (London: Codell and Com, 1829), 2:25; Charles J. Latrobe, *The Rambler in North America* (New York: Johnson Reprint Corporation, 1970 [1832]), 130; "Saratoga Springs, May, 1856," Broadside, Putnam Collection, NYSHA. The Beechers advised that all of life's public activities could be easily carried out in two 25 by 16 foot rooms (Catharine E. Beecher and Harriet Beecher Stowe, *The American Woman's Home; Or, Principles of Domestic Science* [Hartford, Conn.: The Stowe-Day Foundation, 1985 (1869)], 26); Cornelius E. Durkee, *Reminiscences of Saratoga* (Saratoga Springs, N.Y.: Reprinted from the *Saratogian,* 1927–28), 69; Union Hall Inventory, 12 October 1848, Putnam Collection, NYSHA; Northern Hotel Inventory, 18 May 1844, SSCH; Nathaniel Parker Willis, *American Scenery; or, Land, Lake, and River* (London: George Virtue, 1840), 1:21; James Silk Buckingham, *America, Historical, Statistical, and Descriptive* (London: Fisher, Son and Company, 1841), 2:443–44; Allan Nevins, ed., *The Diary of Philip Hone, 1828–1851* (New York: Arno Press, 1970), 1:407; James Kirke Paulding, *The New Mirror for Travellers; and Guide to the Springs. By an Amateur* (New York: G. and C. Carvill, 1828), 223; Hall, *Travels in North America,* 24; "Saratoga Springs," *The Ariel* 4, no. 11 (18 September 1830): 84.

34. Ellen Bond diary, 29 July 1850, NYSLA; Latrobe, "Odds and Ends" journal, MdHS.

35. P. G. to Elizabeth Greene, 7 July 185[?], GBA; Featherstonhaugh, *Excursion Through the Slave States,* 1:55; Mordecai, *Description of the Album of Virginia,* 19; William Burke, *Red Sulphur Springs* (Wytheville, Va.: D. A. St. Clair, 1860), 5.

36. "Virginia Springs," 282; "Journal of a Trip to the Mountain, Caves and Springs of Virginia," *SLM* 4 (April 1838): 261; "Journal of a Trip to the White Sulphur Springs," 29 August 1836, GBA.

37. Beverly Tucker to Lucy Ann Tucker, 21 August 1837, Tucker-Coleman Collection, SWM; Willis, *American Scenery,* 1:20.

38. "Pre-Raphaelites at Saratoga," *McBride's Magazine* 2 (September 1868): 256; Cooke, "The White Sulphur Springs," 342; Bertelson, *The Lazy South,* 178–86; Woodward, "The Southern Ethic in a Puritan World"; Nash, *Wilderness and the American Mind,* 60–61. On the larger question of Americans' conflicted ideals about vacations and leisure, see Cindy S. Aron, *Working at Play: A History of Vacations in the United States* (New York: Oxford University Press, 1999).

39. George William Curtis, *Lotus-Eating; A Summer Book* (New York: Harper and Brothers, 1852), 12–13; Edward Strutt Abdy, *Journal of a Residence and Tour in the United States of North America* (London: John Murray, 1835), 2:262–63; Daniel T. Rodgers, *The Work Ethic in Industrial America, 1850–1920* (Chicago: University of Chicago Press, 1978), 94–106, 124; Conron, *Picturesque America,* xviii; Henry James, "Saratoga," *The Nation* 11 (11 August 1870): 88–89.

3. THE DEMOCRATIZATION OF AMERICAN MEDICINE

1. Valentine Seaman, *A Dissertation on the Mineral Waters of Saratoga* (New York: Samuel Campbell, 1793), v–vi.

2. G. Turner, "Description of the Chalybeate Springs, Near Saratoga," *The Columbian Magazine or Monthly Miscellany* 1 (1787): 306; Samuel Tenney, "An Account of a Number of Medicinal Springs at Saratoga in the State of New York," *Memoirs of the American Academy of Arts and Sciences* 2, pt. 1 (September 1783): 43–61. Other early accounts include Benjamin Rush, *Directions for the Use of Mineral Water and Cold Baths at Harrowgate near Philadelphia* (Philadelphia: Melchior Steiner, 1786); Benjamin Rush, *Experiments and Observations on the Mineral Waters of Philadelphia, Abington, and Bristol* (Philadelphia: James Humphreys, 1773); and John de Normandie's 1769 lecture on Bristol Springs, Pennsylvania, to the American Philosophical Society in 1769, perhaps the first such analysis in the United States (Jonathan Paul DeVierville, "American Healing Waters: A Chronology [1513–1946] and Historical Survey of America's Major Springs, Spas, and Health Resorts Including a Review of Their Medicinal Virtues, Therapeutic Methods, and Health Care Practices" [Ph.D. diss., University of Texas–Austin, 1992], 63).

3. Seaman, *A Dissertation on the Mineral Waters of Saratoga,* i–x. On the utilitarian emphasis of American science, see John C. Greene, *American Science in the Age of Jefferson* (Ames: Iowa State University Press, 1984), 3–6; and Brooke Hindle, *The Pursuit of Science in Revolutionary America* (Chapel Hill: University of North Carolina Press, 1956), 353–54.

4. Seaman, *A Dissertation on the Mineral Waters of Saratoga,* 16–29; Peter Vandervoort, *A Tretis on the Analisis of Ballston Mineral Spring Water* (Johnstown, N.Y.: Jacob Dockstader, 1795), 3; William Meade, *An Experimental Enquiry in the Chemical Properties and Medicinal Qualities of the Principal Mineral Waters of Ballston and Saratoga, in the State of New York* (Philadelphia: Harrison Hall, 1817), xv.

5. [Robert Livingston], "A Review of a Dissertation on the Mineral Waters of Saratoga," *Medical Repository,* Second Hexade, 5 (1808): 241–15, 253–56. For a full account of the controversy surrounding the various analyses of Saratoga Springs' waters, see Henry E. Sigerest, "The Early Medical History of Saratoga Springs," *Bulletin of the History of Medicine* 13 (May 1943): 540–84; John Harley Warner, *The Therapeutic Perspective: Medical Practice, Knowledge, and Identity in America, 1820–1885* (Princeton, N.J.: Princeton University Press, 1997), 12–16; and Valentine Seaman, *A Dissertation on the Mineral Waters of Saratoga. Including an Account of the Waters of Ballston,* 2d. ed. (New York: Collins and Perkins, 1809), 72–78.

6. Review of Seaman in *The New York Medical and Philosophical Journal and Review* 1, no. 2 (1809): 286–90; Sigerest, "The Early Medical History of Saratoga Springs," 572–74; Valentine Seaman, "An Examination of 'A Review of a Dissertation on the Mineral Waters of Saratoga,'" *Medical Repository,* Third Hexade, 1, no. 2 (August, September, October, 1809): 210–16; *New-York Medical and Philosophical Journal and Review* 2, no. 1 (1810): 142–44, 176–75; "A Partial View of the operation of the Combined Powers, as drawn up in the Appendix to the last number of the *Medical and Philosophical Journal and Review,*" *Medical Repository* 13 (1809–10): 1–8; Greene, *American Science in the Age of Jefferson,* 91–106, 172; Alexandra Oleson and Sanborn C. Brown, eds., *The Pursuit of Knowledge in the Early American Republic: American Scientific and Learned Societies from Colonial Times to the Civil War* (Baltimore: Johns Hopkins University Press, 1976). See especially the articles by John C. Greene, Nathan Reingold, and James H. Cassedy.

7. Sigerest, "The Early Medical History of Saratoga Springs," 583; John H. Steel, *An Analysis of the Mineral Waters of Saratoga and Ballston* (Albany, N.Y.: E. and E. Hosford, 1817).

8. Steel, *An Analysis of the Mineral Waters of Saratoga and Ballston,* 13, 16–22, 24, 37–41, 92–94.

9. Steel, *An Analysis of the Mineral Waters of Saratoga and Ballston* (1819); Milo N. North, M.D., A Resident Physician, *Saratoga Waters, or the Invalid at Saratoga* (New York: M. W. Dodd, 1840); R. L. Allen, M.D., Resident and Consulting Physician, *A Historical, Chemical, and Therapeutical Analysis of the Principal Mineral Fountains at Saratoga Springs.* See, for example, John J. Moorman, M.D., Resident Physician at the White Sulphur Springs, *A Directory for the Use of the White Sulphur Waters; with Practical Remarks on Their Medical Properties, and Ap-*

plicability to Particular Diseases (Philadelphia: T. K. and P. G. Collins, 1839); Thomas Dent Mütter, *The Salt Sulphur Springs, Monroe County, Virginia* (Philadelphia: T. K. and P. G. Collins, 1840); Warner, *The Therapeutic Perspective*, 19–20; Lamar Riley Murphy, *Enter the Physician: The Transformation of Domestic Medicine, 1760–1860* (Tuscaloosa: University of Alabama Press, 1991), 15–23, 70–71.

10. For Saratoga Springs, at least nine guidebooks, nine travel accounts, one periodical, and three gazetteers included medical information on the springs. Five periodicals, six promotional broadsides, five travel accounts, and two gazetteers from Virginia did the same. Numerous advertisements and articles in local and regional newspapers also contained this information; see, for example, *Saratoga Springs (N.Y.) Whig*, 2 June 1840; *Lexington (Va.) Gazette*, 13 July 1859.

11. Editions of John H. Steel, *An Analysis of the Congress Spring, with Practical Remarks on its Medical Properties* (Saratoga Springs, N.Y.: G. M. Davison, 1847 and following), SSPL; Richard D. Brown, *Knowledge Is Power: The Diffusion of Information in Early America, 1700–1865* (New York: Oxford University Press, 1989), chaps. 8–9.

12. The earliest such account is Isaac Weld, *Travels Through the States of North America* (New York: Johnson Reprint Corporation, 1968 [1807]), 1:277; Robert Mackay to Eliza, 23 July 1816, Mackay-Stiles Family Papers, SHC; William Bolling diary, 9 September 1842, VHS.

13. David Hosack, *Observations on the Use of the Ballston Mineral Waters* (New York: n.p., 1811), 3–7; Meade, *An Experimental Enquiry*, 107; Steel, *An Analysis of the Mineral Waters of Saratoga and Ballston* (1819), appendix.

14. Mary Jane Windle, *Life at the White Sulphur Springs; or, Pictures of a Pleasant Summer* (Philadelphia: J. B. Lippincott and Company, 1857), 44–45; Guy Hinsdale, "John Jennings Moorman, M.D.: A Biographical Note," *Annals of Medical History* 6 (July 1934): 354; John J. Moorman, *Some Notes on a Portion of a Work by William Burke, Entitled "The Mineral Springs of Western Virginia"* (Philadelphia: Merrihew and Thompson, 1843), 20 (italics in original).

15. Anonymous diary, 14 August 1825, NYSLA (italics in original); Larkin Newby diary, 14 July 1823, Larkin Newby Papers, SHC.

16. John Bell, *On Baths and Mineral Waters* (Philadelphia: Henry H. Porter, 1831); John Bell, *The Mineral and Thermal Springs of the United States and Canada* (Philadelphia: Parry and McMillan, 1831). The exceptions were an imprint by Saratoga Springs' local newspaperman and springs publisher Gideon Davison and two 1850s studies of the Virginia springs published by a newspaper/printing office in the western part of the state, both located in important subregional centers (see Thomas A. Chambers, "Fashionable Dis-Ease: Promoting Health and Leisure at Saratoga Springs, New York, and the Virginia Springs, 1790–1860" [Ph.D. diss., College of William and Mary, 1999], 348–51).

17. *Acts and Joint Resolutions of the General Assembly of the Commonwealth of Virginia. For the Years 1834–1835* (Richmond: William F. Ritchie, 1835), 157. Only springs incorporated be-

tween 1835 and 1850 were required to publish chemical analyses (data from John W. Williams, comp., *Index to Enrolled Bills of the General Assembly of Virginia, 1776 to 1910* [Richmond: Davis Bottom, 1911], and *Acts and Joint Resolutions* for various years); William Barton Rogers, *Report of the Progress of the Geological Survey of the State of Virginia for the Year 1841,* in *A Reprint of Annual Reports and Other Papers on the Geology of the Virginias* (New York: Appleton, 1884), 549–66.

18. Rev. Thornton Stringfellow, *Two Letters on Cases of Cure at Fauquier White Sulphur Springs; Embracing, Also, Mineral Waters in General* (Washington: Union Office, 1851), 3; Samuel Tenney, "An Account of a Number of Medicinal Springs at Saratoga in the State of New York," *Memoirs of the American Academy of Arts and Sciences* 2, pt. 1 (September 1783): 43–61; Moorman, *A Directory for the Use of the White Sulphur Waters,* 30–35. Almost every medical guidebook for both Saratoga Springs and the Virginia springs that I have located includes several of these testimonials.

19. *The Bedford Alum Springs, Near New London, Virginia* (Lynchburg, Va.: Virginian Job Printing, 1854), 11 (italics in original). On female patients in England, see Victoria Louise Masten, "Taking the Waters: Elite Women in English Spa Towns, 1700–1800" (master's thesis, California State University–Long Beach, 1993), 25–36; and Sarah Stage, *Female Complaints: Lydia Pinkham and the Business of Women's Medicine* (New York: W. W. Norton, 1979).

20. Steven M. Stowe, "Seeing Themselves at Work: Physicians and the Case Narrative in the Mid-Nineteenth-Century American South," *American Historical Review* 101 (February 1996): 41–43, 55–63; Warner, *The Therapeutic Perspective,* 37–57; Stephanie Browner, "Ideologies of the Anesthetic: Professionalism, Egalitarianism, and the Ether Controversy," *American Quarterly* 51 (March 1999): 108–43.

21. Laurel Thatcher Ulrich, *A Midwife's Tale: The Life of Martha Ballard, Based on Her Diary, 1785–1812* (New York: Vintage, 1990); Warner, *The Therapeutic Perspective,* 19–20; Murphy, *Enter the Physician,* 15–23, 70–71.

22. James E. Cassedy, *Medicine in America: A Short History* (Baltimore: Johns Hopkins University Press, 1991), 35–38; Ronald G. Walters, *American Reformers, 1815–1860* (New York: Hill and Wang, 1978), 146–56. On the water-cure, see Susan E. Cayleff, *Wash and Be Healed: The Water-Cure Movement and Women's Health* (Philadelphia: Temple University Press, 1987); Harry B. Weiss and Howard R. Kemble, *The Great American Water-Cure Craze: A History of Hydrotherapy in the United States* (Trenton, N.J.: Past Times Press, 1967); Jane B. Donegan, *"Hydropathic Highway to Health": Women and Water-Cure in Antebellum America* (New York: Greenwood, 1986); Laura Beveridge, "The Water-Cure Days: Coping with Cultural Change at Wesselhoeft's Hydropathic Establishment in Brattleboro, Vermont" (master's thesis, University of Vermont, 1994); and Harvey Green, *Fit for America: Health, Fitness, Sport, and American Society* (New York: Pantheon, 1986), 56–67.

23. Warner, *The Therapeutic Perspective,* 58–72; Browner, "Ideologies of the Anesthetic:

Professionalism, Egalitarianism, and the Ether Controversy," 110, 130; George D. Kersley, *Bath Water: The Effect of the Waters on the History of Bath and of Medicine* (Bath, England: Victor Morgan Books, 1973).

24. Meade, *An Experimental Enquiry,* 109; Steel, *An Analysis of the Mineral Waters of Saratoga and Ballston* (1817), 25, 44–78 (italics in original).

25. The earliest and briefest was George Hayward, *Remarks on Some of the Medicinal Springs of Virginia* (Boston: D. Clapp, 1839); William Burke, *Red Sulphur Springs* (Wytheville, Va.: D. A. St. Clair, 1860), 9; Henry Huntt, *A Visit to the Red Sulphur Spring of Virginia, During the Summer of 1837* (Boston: Duton and Wentworth, 1839); Henry Huntt, *Observations on a Change in Climate in Pulmonary Consumption* (Washington, D.C.: Jacob Gideon, 1834).

26. Warner, *The Therapeutic Perspective,* 11–12, 17–19; Cassedy, *Medicine in America,* 24–25; see the entry for "Aqua" in George B. Wood, M.D., and Franklin Bache, M.D., *The Dispensitory of the United States of America* (Philadelphia: Gregg and Elliot, 1843), 112–16; Phillip R. Shriver, ed., *A Tour to New Connecticut in 1811: The Narrative of Henry Leavitt Edwards* (Cleveland, Ohio: Western Reserve Historical Society, 1985), 85. The average dose seems to be around twelve glasses per day, still a significant amount.

27. Christopher C. Jenkins to Mrs. Jenkins, 13 July 1826, Christopher C. Jenkins Papers, Duke; St. George Tucker Coalter to Judith Coalter, 29 July 1836, Brown, Coalter, Tucker Papers, SWM; *Wilson's Illustrated Guide to the Hudson River* (New York: H. Wilson, 1848), 58; "Edwin + Laura: A Poem in Two Cantos," 1825, sextet 76, Duke.

28. Jonathan Berkeley Grimball diary, early July 1835, SHC; Porte Crayon [David Hunter Strother], *Virginia Illustrated: Containing a Visit to the Virginia Canaan, and the Adventures of Porte Crayon and His Cousins* (New York: Harper and Brothers, 1857), 134; William L. Stone, *Reminiscences of Saratoga and Ballston* (New York: R. Worthington, 1880), 295.

29. William G. Rothstein, *American Physicians in the Nineteenth Century: From Sects to Science* (Baltimore: Johns Hopkins University Press, 1985), 26, 38; Richard Shryock, *Medicine and Society in America, 1660–1860* (Ithaca, N.Y.: Cornell University Press, 1962), 28; Hugh Grigsby Blair diary, 1 July 1842, VHS; Edward Eccles to Mother, 11 July 1843, Eccles Family Papers, SHC. For an English comparison, see David Harley, "A Sword in a Madman's Hand: Professional Opposition to Popular Consumption in the Waters Literature of Southern England and the Midlands, 1570–1870," *Medical History* Supplement 10 (1990): 50–55.

30. Charles William Ashby to Sarah Elizabeth Ashby, 9 and 24 July, 6 and 17 August 1860, Charles William Ashby Papers, VHS; Cyrel Carpenter to Alvin Carpenter, 14 March 1839, NYSLA; Edwin Bedford Jeffres diary, 3 September 1852, VHS.

31. Seaman, "A Method of Making an Artificial Mineral Water, Resembling in Every Respect that of Saratoga," in *A Dissertation on the Mineral Waters of Saratoga,* 38–40; Chandos Michael Brown, *Benjamin Silliman: A Life in the Young Republic* (Princeton, N.J.: Princeton University Press, 1989), 200–210, 230–64; Seaman, *A Dissertation on the Mineral Waters of Saratoga* (1809), 124–31.

32. Cornelius E. Durkee, *Reminiscences of Saratoga* (Saratoga Springs, N.Y.: Reprinted from the *Saratogian*, 1927–28), 5; Stone, *Reminiscences*, 293. A bitter quarrel erupted between John Moorman and William Burke, the resident physicians at White Sulphur and Red Sulphur Springs, Virginia, respectively, over the medical utility of bottled water that blurred the distinction between medicine and commerce at the springs. See Burke, *The Mineral Springs of Western Virginia*, 107–9, 112–13; and Moorman, *Some Notes on a Portion of a Work by William Burke*, 4–5, 7–8, 13, 15, 20.

33. *Lexington (Va.) Gazette*, 1 July 1852 and 1 June–24 August 1839. This advertisement ran in each weekly edition throughout the summer; *Saratoga Springs (N.Y.) Whig*, 10 August 1841; "Carpenter's Saratoga Powders" advertisement, 1832, SSPL; Steel, *Analysis of the Congress Spring*, 22.

34. K. David Patterson, "Disease Environments of the Antebellum South," in *Science and Medicine in the Old South*, ed. Ronald L. Numbers and Todd L. Savitt (Baton Rouge: Louisiana State University Press, 1989), 152–65; Lawrence Fay Brewster, *Summer Migrations and Resorts of South Carolina Low-Country Planters* (Durham, N.C.: Duke University Press, 1947), 3–7; Marshall S. Berdan, "The Pestilence that Walketh in Darkness: The Cholera Epidemic of 1832," *Virginia Cavalcade* 43 (summer 1993): 14–23; Charles E. Rosenberg, *The Cholera Years: The United States in 1832, 1849, and 1866* (Chicago: University of Chicago Press, 1962).

35. John Knight to Frances Beall, 11 June 1834, John Knight Papers, Duke; Julia Porcher to Catherine R. Porcher, 1 August 1828, Porcher-Dinnies Family Papers, SCHS. The Virginia General Assembly moved its meeting to Fauquier White Sulphur Springs from Richmond from June through August of 1849 to avoid the cholera epidemic in Richmond (Frederick William Franck, "The Virginia Legislature at the Fauquier Springs in 1849," *Virginia Magazine of History and Biography* 58 [1950]: 66–83).

36. James Kirke Paulding, *Letters from the South, Written During an Excursion During the Summer of 1816* (New York: James Eastburn and Company, 1817), 1:231; Friherre Axel Klinkowström, *America, 1818–1820*, trans. and ed. Franklin D. Scott (Evanston, Ill.: Northwestern University Press, 1952 [1824]); *Some Account of the Medicinal Properties of the Hot Springs, Virginia* (Richmond: Chas. H. Wynne, 1857), 9; *Bedford Alum Springs*, 4; Daniel Drake, *The Northern Lakes: A Summer Resort for Invalids of the South* (Cedar Rapids, Iowa: Torch Press, 1954 [1842]); Brewster, *Summer Migrations and Resorts of South Carolina Low-Country Planters*.

37. Gideon Miner Davison, *The Traveller's Guide Through the Middle and Northern States and the Canadas* (Saratoga Springs, N.Y.: G. M. Davison, 1840), xv; Reuben Sears, *A Poem, on the Mineral Waters of Ballston and Saratoga, with Notes Illustrating the History of the Springs and Adjacent County* (Ballston Spa, N.Y.: J. Comstock, 1819), 36.

38. E. M. Grosvenor to Charlotte and Sarah Holcomb, 5 June 1833, George Holcomb Papers, NYSLA; Viator, "The White Sulphur Springs," *New England Magazine* 3 (September 1832): 226; Charles Ellis, Senior, to Charles Ellis, Junior, 22 July 1832, Munford-Ellis Family Papers, Duke; Dandridge Spotswood diary, 15 July 1840, UVa, George Munford to Laura Taylor,

26 August 1828, Munford-Ellis Family Papers, Duke; Linda J. Borish, "The Robust Woman and the Muscular Christian: Catharine Beecher, Thomas Higginson, and Their Vision of American Society, Health, and Physical Activities," *International Journal of the History of Sport* 4 (1987): 129–54.

39. Rambler, "Glances at Men and Things," *The New-Yorker* 7, 23 (24 August 1839): 366; George William Featherstonhaugh, *Excursion Through the Slave States, from Washington on the Potomac to the Frontier of Mexico; with Sketches of Popular Manners and Geological Notices* (London: John Murray, 1844), 1:55; Roberta P. Burwell to Mrs. Josiah Tidball, 12 August 1840, Louise Anderson Patten Papers, VHS; Mark Pencil, Esq. [Mary Hagner], *The White Sulphur Papers, or Life at the Springs of Western Virginia* (New York: Samuel Colman, 1839), 21; Jane Caroline North diary, 13 August 1852, Pettigrew Family Papers, SHC; Martin Duralde to George W. Ferms, 4 July 1846, Martin Duralde Papers, LoV; Grimball diary, 6 August 1835, SHC.

40. Data taken from eighty-one diaries and letters where invalids expressed an opinion on the waters' effects (thirty-seven favorable, twenty-four mixed, and twenty negative). For extensive examples of treatment at the springs over an extended period of time, see St. George Tucker Coalter's letters from the Virginia springs for the years 1833, 1836, and 1838 in the Brown, Coalter, Tucker Papers, SWM; Richard D. Burroughs Correspondence and Papers, Duke; Israel Wilson journal, 1837–44, Lilly Library, Indiana University, Bloomington; and Abigail May diary, May–August 1800, NYSHA.

41. Levin Smith Joynes to Mother, 9 August 1856, Joynes Family Papers, VHS; Robert Mackay to Eliza, 22 July 1816, Mackay-Stiles Family Papers, SHC; William Wirt to Elizabeth Wirt, 12 August 1825, William Wirt Papers, MdHS.

42. Thomas R. Joynes to Levin S. Joynes, 31 August 1837, Joynes Family Papers, VHS; Herman Melville, *The Confidence-Man: His Masquerade* (New York: Penguin Classics, 1990 [1857]), 94–102.

43. George Munford to Lucy Taylor, 16 August 1828, Munford-Ellis Family Papers, Duke. The biblical reference is to Jeremiah 8:22, a lamentation by the prophet Jeremiah that the health of his daughter Judah had not been cured by the famous resin from a tree in Transjordan believed to cure all ailments. See also Jeremiah 46:11.

44. May diary, 28 July 1800, NYSHA. See also Genevieve M. Darden, ed., "A Visit to Saratoga: 1826," *New York History* 50 (July 1969): 283–301; "Journal of a Trip to the White Sulphur Springs," August 1836, GBA.

45. One report estimated that 3 in 150 guests were invalids (*Memoirs of an Emigrant*, 25 July 1822, NYSLA), whereas another claimed a half dozen visitors out of several hundred suffered from an actual ailment ("Journal of a Trip to the White Sulphur Springs," 22 August 1836, GBA); Washington Irving, "Style at Ballston," *Salmagundi* 16, Thursday, 15 October 1807, in *Salmagundi*, ed. Bruce I. Granger and Martha Hartzog (Boston: Twayne, 1977), 256.

46. Stone, *Reminiscences*, 7; James Silk Buckingham, *America, Historical, Statistical, and Descriptive* (London: Fisher, Son and Company, 1841), 2:435; Timothy Dwight, *Travels in New*

England and New York, ed. Barbara Miller Solomon (Cambridge, Mass.: Belknap Press, 1969), 3:293; Clement Clarke Moore, "A Trip to Saratoga," 1844, Clement Clarke Moore Papers, N-YHS; Sigmund Diamond, trans. and ed., *A Casual View of America: The Home Letters of Salomon de Rothschild, 1859–1861* (Palo Alto, Calif.: Stanford University Press, 1961), 66.

47. Thomas Gordon Pollock to Mother, 3 August 1860, Abram David Pollock Papers, SHC; Cindy S. Aron, *Working at Play: A History of Vacations in the United States* (New York: Oxford University Press, 1999), 6–10, 15–24, 42–44.

48. Paulding, *Letters from the South,* 2:231, 240; Mayo Cabell to Briscoe G. Baldwin, 16 June 1845, Stuart-Baldwin Papers, UVa; John Edwards Caldwell, *A Tour Through Part of Virginia, in the Summer of 1800,* ed. William M. E. Rachal (Richmond: Dietz, 1951 [1809]), 5.

49. Robert E. Lee to Charles Lee, 2 August 1836, Robert E. Lee Collection, UVa; Charlene Marie Lewis, "Ladies and Gentlemen on Display: Planter Society at the Virginia Springs, 1790–1860" (Ph.D. diss., University of Virginia, 1997), 259–316; Janice Zita Grover, "Luxury and Leisure in Early Nineteenth-Century America: Saratoga Springs and the Rise of the Resort" (Ph.D. diss., University of California–Davis, 1973), 132–68.

4. SOCIETY OF FASHION

1. George William Curtis, *Lotus-Eating; A Summer Book* (New York: Harper and Brothers, 1852), 113; "Letter of a Virginian," *Albany (N.Y.) Statesman,* 6 September 1820; Robert G. Shaw to Jacob Townsley, 16 August 1838, Shaw Family Papers, MHS, FH; Clement Claiborne Clay to Father, 17 September 1854, Clement Claiborne Clay Papers, Duke; *Our Summer Retreats: A Hand Book to All the Chief Waterfalls, Springs, Mountain and Sea-side Resorts, and other Places of Interest in the United States* (New York: T. Nelson and Sons, 1858), 30; Janice Zita Grover, "Luxury and Leisure in Early Nineteenth-Century America: Saratoga Springs and the Rise of the Resort" (Ph.D. diss., University of California–Davis, 1973), 3–4; David S. Shields, *Civil Tongues and Polite Letters in British America* (Chapel Hill: University of North Carolina Press, 1997), 40–54; Phyllis Hembry, *The English Spa, 1560–1815: A Social History* (London: Athlone Press, 1990).

2. "Notes Beside the Steam Engine," *New York Herald,* 21 August 1847; "Letter of a Virginian"; "Saratoga Springs," *New York Mirror,* 3 August 1839; S. DeVeaux, *The Travelers' Own Book, to Saratoga Springs, Niagara Falls and Canada* (Buffalo: Faxon and Reed, 1841), 90; Elihu Hoyt, "Journal of a Tour to Saratoga Springs," 9 August 1827, SSCH.

3. Most visitors in 1853 and 1854 to the Tip Top House, in New Hampshire's White Mountains, came from the upper fifth of wealth, even if others were decidedly middle class; see Peter B. Bulkley, "Identifying the White Mountain Tourist, 1853–1854: Origin, Occupation, and Wealth as a Definition of the Early Hotel Trade," *Historical New Hampshire* 35 (1980): 106–62; *Springs, Water-Falls, Sea-Bathing Resorts, and Mountain Scenery of the United States and Canada* (New York: J. Disturnell, 1855), 67; Henry Dilworth Gilpin, *A Northern Tour* (Philadelphia: H.

C. Carey and I. Lea, 1825), 66; Rambler, "Glances at Men and Things. Saratoga Springs," *The New-Yorker* 7, no. 23 (24 August 1839): 366; James Silk Buckingham, *America, Historical, Statistical, and Descriptive* (London: Fisher, Son and Company, 1841), 2:435; Eliot Warburton, ed., *Hochelaga; or, England in the New World* (New York: Wiley and Putnam, 1851), 22.

4. James Skelton Gilliam diary, 26 July 1816, LoV; William Elliott to Mother, 9 August 1830, Elliott-Gonzales Papers, SHC; Elizabeth Ruffin diary, 14 August 1827, Harrison-Cocke Family Papers, SHC; DeVeaux, *The Travelers' Own Book,* 90; "Saratoga Springs," *New York Mirror,* 3 August 1839; see John F. Kasson, *Rudeness and Civility: Manners in Nineteenth-Century America* (New York: Hill and Wang, 1990), 70–98.

5. William Burke, *The Virginia Mineral Springs* (Richmond: Ritchies and Dunnavant, 1853), 51; *Six Weeks in Fauquier* (New York: Samuel Colman, 1839), 32; Mark Pencil, Esq. [Mary Hagner], *The White Sulphur Papers, or Life at the Springs of Western Virginia* (New York: Samuel Colman, 1839), 40.

6. Pencil, *White Sulphur Papers,* 40; Dandridge Spotswood diary, 23 July 1848, VHS; John Rutherfoord to John C. Rutherfoord, 23 August 1854, John Rutherfoord Papers, Duke; St. George Tucker Coalter to John Randolph Bryan, 25 August 1836, Brown, Coalter, Tucker Papers, SWM; Thomas Gordon Pollock to Mother, 3 August 1860, Abram David Pollock Papers, SHC; Anne Newport Royall, *Sketches of History, Life, and Manners in the United States, by a Traveler* (New York: Johnson Reprint Corporation, 1970 [1826]), 72; Edward Beyer, *Album of Virginia* (Richmond: Virginia State Library, 1980 [1857]), 28; Burke, *The Virginia Mineral Springs,* 42 (italics in original); *Lexington (Va.) Gazette,* 25 August 1850. According to Charlene Lewis, the exclusivity of the Virginia springs was their greatest attraction; see Charlene Marie Lewis, "Ladies and Gentlemen on Display: Planter Society at the Virginia Springs, 1790–1860" (Ph.D. diss., University of Virginia, 1997), 320–23. Patricia C. Click interprets social competition at the springs as an aspect of class definition (*The Spirit of the Times: Amusements in Nineteenth-Century Baltimore, Norfolk, and Richmond* [Charlottesville: University Press of Virginia, 1989], 7, 90–93, 103–4). Viewed in comparison with Saratoga Springs, the Virginia springs appear far less exclusive than Lewis posits and the scene of a significant level of social display, competition, and class negotiation, albeit within a relatively homogeneous group.

7. William Burke, *The Mineral Springs of Western Virginia: With Remarks on Their Use, and the Diseases to Which They are Applicable* (New York: Wiley and Putnam, 1842), 12–13, 22; H. P. Tompkins to William P. Smith, 21 September 1832, William Patterson Smith Papers, Duke; Burke, *The Virginia Mineral Springs,* 25; *The Tourist, or Pocket Manual for Travellers* (New York: Harper and Brothers, 1838), 85, 105. On class rivalries in public places and their implications, see Kasson, *Rudeness and Civility,* 2–7, 70–146, 215–45.

8. William Elliott to Mrs. Elliott, 16 July 1839, 17 August 1828, Elliott-Gonzales Papers, SHC; John Howell Briggs, "Journal of a Trip to the Sweet Springs," 15 August 1804, VHS.

9. Nathaniel Parker Willis, "Manners at Watering Places," in *Hurry-Graphs; Or, Sketches of*

Scenery, Celebrities and Society, Taken From Life (New York: Scribner, 1851), 294–95; J. Lynah to Mrs. Francis M. Lewis, 28 March 1857, Conway-Whittle Family Papers, SWM; Hembry, *The English Spa, 1560–1815*, 135–44.

10. J. Mackay to Mother, 6 September 1842, Mackay-Stiles Family Papers, SHC; John C. Rutherfoord to Wife, 25 September 1860, John Rutherfoord Papers, Duke; Mary Thompson to Mrs. Frances M. Lewis and Mrs. Mary Neale, [1848], Conway-Whittle Family Papers, SWM; Thomas Smith to William P. Smith, 1 September 1826, William Patterson Smith Papers, Duke; John Rossen to Sister, 12 August 1839, GBA; James Alexander Seddon to Charles Bruce, 12 August 1858, Bruce Family Papers, VHS.

11. Lynne Withey, *Cook's Tours and Grand Tours: A History of Leisure Travel, 1750–1915* (New York: William Morrow, 1997); Dona Brown, *Inventing New England: Regional Tourism in Nineteenth-Century America* (Washington, D.C.: Smithsonian Institution Press, 1995), 3–4, 15–16; John Sears, *Sacred Places: American Tourist Attractions in the Nineteenth Century* (New York: Oxford University Press, 1989), 3–5; Roger Haydon, ed., *Upstate Travels: British Views of Nineteenth-Century America* (Syracuse, N.Y.: Syracuse University Press, 1982), 1–29; Barbara Carson, "Early American Tourists and the Commercialization of Leisure," in *Of Consuming Interest: The Style of Life in the Eighteenth Century*, ed. Cary Carson, Ronald Hoffman, and Peter J. Albert (Charlottesville: University Press of Virginia, 1994), 404; Pencil, *White Sulphur Papers*, 13; Charles J. Latrobe, *The Rambler in North America* (New York: Johnson Reprint Corporation, 1970 [1832]), 126; Gilpin, *A Northern Tour*, 66; Hoyt, "Journal of a Tour to Saratoga Springs," 6 August 1827, SSCH.

12. "James Morrell's Trip in August, 1813," *Pennsylvania Magazine of History* 39 (1915): 431; Elkanah Watson, "Mixed Medley," 19 September 1805, Elkanah Watson Papers, NYSLA; James Kirke Paulding, *Letters from the South, Written During an Excursion During the Summer of 1816* (New York: James Eastburn and Company, 1817), 1:227. Paulding refers here to the Schuylkill River, which bisects Philadelphia. "Saratoga—Opening of the Season," *New York Tribune*, 13 June 1842.

13. John Pendleton Kennedy, *Swallow Barn; Or, A Sojourn in the Old Dominion* (Baton Rouge: Louisiana State University Press, 1986 [1831]), 34; Peregrine Prolix [Philip Holbrook Nicklin], *Letters Descriptive of the Virginia Springs* (Philadelphia: H. S. Tanner, 1835), 24–25; Levin Smith Joynes to Mother, 9 August 1856, Joynes Family Papers, VHS; P. G. to Elizabeth Greene, 7 July 18[??], GBA; John Rutherfoord to John, 17 August 1859, John Rutherfoord Papers, Duke (italics in original).

14. Frederick Marryat, *A Diary in America with Remarks on Its Institutions* (New York: Knopf, 1962 [1839]), 74; Alexander Mackay, *The Western World; or, Travels in the United States in 1846–1847*, as quoted in Roger Haydon, ed., *Upstate Travels: British Views of Nineteenth-Century America* (Syracuse, N.Y.: Syracuse University Press, 1982), 109; T. S. Arthur, "Going to the Springs; or, Vulgar People," in *Heart-Histories and Life-Pictures* (New York: n.p., 1853), 155–56; Shields, *Civil Tongues and Polite Letters in British America*, 47–53; Michael Zucker-

man, "Tocqueville, Turner, and Turds: Four Stories of Manners in Early America," *Journal of American History* 85 (June 1998): 13–42; James Kirke Paulding, *The New Mirror for Travellers; and Guide to the Springs. By an Amateur* (New York: G. and C. Carvill, 1828), 235.

15. *Our Summer Retreats,* 30; Philip Vickers Fithian, *Journal, 1775–1776,* ed. Robert Greenhalgh Albion and Leonard Dodson (Princeton, N.J.: Princeton University Press, 1934), 126; *The Tourist,* 94 (italics in original); Hoyt, "Journal of a Tour to Saratoga Springs," 8 August 1827, SSCH; *New York Mirror,* 3 August 1839; Lewis, "Ladies and Gentlemen on Display," 388–93.

16. "Diary of a Tour of New York and Canada," 1834, N-YHS; Netta, "First Impressions of Saratoga, No. 2," *National Era* 13, no. 659 (18 August 1859): 1; *Memoirs of an Emigrant,* 25 July 1822, NYSLA; Marryat, *A Diary in America,* 234; Pencil, *White Sulphur Papers,* 140.

17. Latrobe, *The Rambler in North America,* 128; Mary Jane Windle, *Life in Washington, and Life Here and There* (Philadelphia: J. B. Lippincott and Company, 1859), 210; Charles Richard Weld, *A Vacation Tour in the United States and Canada* (London: Longman, Brown, Green, and Longmans, 1855), 22; Netta, "No. 2," 1; Hoyt, "Journal of a Tour to Saratoga Springs," 7 August 1827, SSCH; Pencil, *White Sulphur Papers,* 140; Anonymous diary, 14 August 1825, NYSLA.

18. Pencil, *White Sulphur Papers,* 142; Nathaniel Parker Willis, *American Scenery; or, Land, Lake, and River* (London: George Virtue, 1840), 1:21; Ellen Bond diary, 30 July 1850, NYSLA; Gideon Miner Davison, *The Traveller's Guide Through the Middle and Northern States and the Canadas* (Saratoga Springs, N.Y.: G. M. Davison, 1840), 134; J. B. Dunlop diary, 1810–11, N-YHS; Jonathan C. Rutherfoord to Ann, 13 September 1856, Jonathan Rutherfoord Papers, Duke; John Henry Strobia, "Journal of an Excursion to the North and East," 28 August 1817, VHS.

19. Robert McCoskry Graham diary, 30 July 1848, N-YHS; Spotswood diary, 17 July 1848, VHS; Roberta P. Burwell to Mrs. Josiah Tidball, 12 August 1840, Louise Anderson Patten Papers, VHS; Buckingham, *America, Historical, Statistical, and Descriptive,* 2:442; Paulding, *Letters from the South,* 1:196; Patrick Shirreff, *A Tour Through North America; Together With a Comprehensive View of the Canadas and United States* (Edinburgh, Scotland: Oliver and Boyd, 1835), 57.

20. Latrobe, *The Rambler in North America,* 130; Thomas Low Nichols, *Forty Years of American Life, 1821–1861* (New York: Stackpole Sons, 1937, [1864]), 192; Charles Astor Bristed, *The Upper Ten Thousand: Sketches of American Society* (New York: Stinger and Townsend, 1852), 115.

21. Pencil, *White Sulphur Papers,* 23; Latrobe, *The Rambler in North America,* 130; Mackay, *The Western World,* as quoted in Haydon, *Upstate Travels,* 111–12; John H. B. Latrobe, "Odds and Ends" journal, 1832–35, John H. B. Latrobe Family Papers, MdHS (italics in original).

22. Pencil, *White Sulphur Papers,* 18, 29; Prolix, *Letters Descriptive of the Virginia Springs,* 19; Larkin Newby diary, 15 August 1823, SHC; Hembry, *The English Spas, 1560–1815,* 202.

23. Robert Mackay to Eliza, 22 July 1816, Mackay-Stiles Family Papers, SHC; Pencil, *White Sulphur Papers,* 48; George William Featherstonhaugh, *Excursion Through the Slave States, from Washington on the Potomac to the Frontier of Mexico; with Sketches of Popular Manners and Geological Notices* (London: John Murray, 1844), 1:76; C. O. Lyde diary, 7 July 1841, Duke.

24. Mackay, *The Western World,* as quoted in Haydon, *Upstate Travels,* 112; Windle, *Life in Washington,* 61; Buckingham, *America, Historical, Statistical, and Descriptive,* 2:442; Samuel Sombre [James Watson Gerard], *Aquarelles: Or Summer Sketches* (New York: Stanford and Delisser, 1858), 36.

25. James Alexander Seddon to Charles Bruce, 12 August 1858, Bruce Family Papers, VHS; Edward Allen Talbott, *Five Years Residence in Canada, Including a Tour of America in the Year 1823* (London: Longman, 1824), 349; J. E. Snow to "Bro and Sist-Snow," 7 August 1851, SSCH; Lewis, "Ladies and Gentlemen on Display," 340; Weld, *A Vacation Tour in the United States and Canada,* 23; Jane Caroline North diary, 25 and 30 August 1852, SHC (italics in original). The 1850 Federal Census lists twelve black, five mulatto, and two white waiters, aged nineteen and seven (Mary C. Lynn and William Fox, comps., "The 1850 Census of Saratoga Springs: A Numerical Listing," 1991). See also Myra B. Young Armstead, *"Lord, Please Don't Take Me in August": African Americans in Newport and Saratoga Springs, 1870–1930* (Urbana: University of Illinois Press, 1999).

26. Loren Schweininger, ed., *From Tennessee Slave to St. Louis Entrepreneur: The Autobiography of James Thomas* (Columbia: University of Missouri Press, 1984), 128; Strobia, "Journal of an Excursion to the North and East," 6 August 1817, VHS; *Memoirs of an Emigrant,* 25 July 1882, NYSLA; William Bolling diary, 19 August 1841, VHS (italics in original); "Another Visit to the Virginia Springs, or the Adventures of Harry Humbug," *SLM* 1 (September 1835): 774; Sombre, *Aquarelles,* 37; Bristed, *The Upper Ten Thousand,* 122–23; Latrobe, "Odds and Ends" journal, MdHS.

27. John Rossen to Sister, 12 August 1849, GBA; Bolling diary, 19 August 1841, VHS; Martin Duralde to Uncle [Henry Clay], 1 July 1846, LoV; P. G. to Elizabeth Greene, 7 July 18[??], GBA; Watson, "Mixed Medley," 20 August 1805, Elkanah Watson Papers, NYSLA (italics in original); Roberta P. Burwell, to Mrs. Josiah Tidball, 12 August 1840, Louise Anderson Patten Papers, VHS.

28. *Memoirs of an Emigrant,* 25 July 1822, NYSLA; Shirreff, *A Tour Through North America,* 57; "Ann Overton Price's Book at the White Sulphur Springs," 14 August 1828, GBA; Latrobe, "Odds and Ends" journal, MdHS; Buckingham, *America, Historical, Statistical, and Descriptive,* 2:442; Abigail May diary, 6 June 1800, NYSHA; Sombre, *Aquarelles,* 38; Windle, *Life in Washington,* 173; Pencil, *White Sulphur Papers,* 43, 56; Louisa M. Collins to Mercie Harrison, 21 September 1837, Byrd Family Papers, VHS.

29. Netta, "First Impressions of Saratoga, No. 3," *National Era* 13, no. 660 (25 August 1859): 1; "Diary of a Tour of New York and Canada," N-YHS; Hoyt, "Journal of a Tour to Saratoga Springs," 7 August 1827, SSCH; Latrobe, *The Rambler in North America,* 133; John Edwards Caldwell, *A Tour Through Part of Virginia, in the Summer of 1800,* ed. William M. E. Rachal (Richmond: Dietz, 1951 [1809]), 32; Netta, "No. 3," 1; Curtis, *Lotus-Eating,* 115–16.

30. Edward Strutt Abdy, *Journal of a Residence and Tour in the United States of North America* (London: John Murray, 1835), 2:314; Paulding, *Letters from the South,* 1:232; James Alexander Seddon to Charles Bruce, 12 August 1858, Bruce Family Papers, VHS (italics in orig-

inal); Mary Thompson to Mrs. Frances M. Lewis, 26 August 1850, Conway Whittle Family Papers, SWM; anonymous diary, 14 August 1825, NYSLA; Ellen Tazewell (Wirt) Vass McCormick to H. Coalter Cabell, 23 September 1833, Cabell Family Papers, VHS.

31. Thomas Hamilton, *Men and Manners in America* (New York: Augustus M. Kelley, 1968 [1833]), 2:379; J. K. L. to Charles, 5 September 1854, Carrington Family Papers, VHS; Buckingham, *America, Historical, Statistical, and Descriptive,* 2:445; Sarah Virginia Hinton diary, 25 September 1860, SWM; Briggs, "Journal of a Trip to the Sweet Springs," 1 August 1804, VHS; May diary, 29 July 1800, NYSHA.

32. Grace Fenton Garnett Hunter diary, 1 August 1838, UVa; Lyde diary, 12 July 1841, Duke; Mary Murray, "Journal kept on a Jaunt to Ballston + Saratoga," 7 August 1825, N-YHS.

33. May diary, 2 August 1800, NYSHA; Pencil, *White Sulphur Papers,* 37; Paulding, *Letters from the South,* 1:203; St. George Tucker to Mrs. Judith H. Coalter, 21 and 24 July 1833, Coalter, Tucker Papers, SWM.

34. Saratoga Springs Social Library record book, 1808–34, SSCH; Davison, *The Traveller's Guide* (1840), 144; Red Sweet Springs Broadside, 1856, VHS (italics in original).

35. William Reynold diary, 25 July 1841, WVU; Montgomery White Sulphur Springs Broadside, 1856, SWM; Red Sweet Springs Broadside, 1856, VHS; St. George Tucker to Mrs. Judith H. Coalter, 18 July 1833, Brown, Coalter, Tucker Papers, SWM; Lewis, "Ladies and Gentlemen on Display," 374–85; Newby diary, 19 August 1823, SHC; St. George Tucker Coalter diary, 15 August 183[?], Brown, Coalter, Tucker Papers, SWM (italics in original); Briggs, "Journal of a Trip to the Sweet Springs," 20 August 1804, VHS; *Lexington (Va.) Gazette,* 20 August 1846.

36. "Rail Road Saloon" advertisement, *Saratoga Springs (N.Y.) Whig,* 27 July 1841; Weld, *A Vacation Tour in the United States and Canada,* 23; DeVeaux, *The Travelers' Own Book,* 93; Marc Friedlander et al., eds., *Diary of Charles Francis Adams* (Cambridge, Mass.: Harvard University Press, 1986), 7:49; "From Saratoga," *New York World,* 25 August 1860.

37. Una Pope-Hennessy, ed., *The Aristocratic Journey: Being the Outspoken Letters of Mrs. Basil Hall Written during a Fourteen Months' Sojourn in America, 1827–1828* (New York: G. P. Putnam's Sons, 1931), 60–61; Marianne Finch, *An Englishwoman's Experience in America* (New York: Negro Universities Press, 1969 [1853]), 115–17; North diary, 26 August 1852, SHC. See Todd DeGarmo, "Indian Camps and Upstate Tourism" (paper presented at the Conference on New York State History, Saratoga Springs, N.Y., 6 June 1997), and *New York Folklore Newsletter* (summer 1993): 4–10.

38. Pencil, *White Sulphur Papers,* 40, 146–47; Charles Colbert, *A Measure of Perfection: Phrenology and the Fine Arts in America* (Chapel Hill: University of North Carolina Press, 1997).

39. "Journal of a Trip to the Mountains, Caves and Springs of Virginia," *SLM* 4 (April 1838): 302; "Visit to the Virginia Springs, During the Summer of 1834," *SLM* 1 (May 1835): 476; Netta, "No. 2," 1; Theodore Corbett, *The Making of American Resorts: Saratoga Springs, Ballston Spa, and Lake George* (New Brunswick, N.J.: Rutgers University Press, 2001), 185–207.

40. "Journal of a Trip to the Mountains, Caves and Springs of Virginia," 386; Netta, "No.

2," 1; St. George Tucker to Mrs. Judith H. Coalter, 21 July 1833, Brown, Coalter, Tucker Papers, SWM; May diary, 2 and 15 June 1800, NYSHA (italics in original). On the social implications of religious revivals and denominations, see Rhys Isaac, *The Transformation of Virginia, 1740–1790* (Chapel Hill: University of North Carolina Press, 1982); and Nathan O. Hatch, *The Democratization of American Christianity* (New Haven, Conn.: Yale University Press, 1989).

41. Genevieve M. Darden, ed., "A Visit to Saratoga: 1826," *New York History* 50 (July 1969): 290; Trant diary ("Journal of a Trip to the White Sulphur Springs, August 1836" [typed mss.]), 23 August 1836, GBA; Eliza Law to William Law, 14 August 1835, William Law Correspondence, Duke.

42. Pencil, *White Sulphur Papers,* 29–30; Willis, *American Scenery,* 1:21.

43. Bristed, *Upper Ten Thousand,* 128; Stephen Allen Memoirs, 13 August 1828, N-YHS.

44. "Journal of a Trip to the Mountains, Caves and Springs of Virginia," 262; Pencil, *White Sulphur Papers,* 108; Briggs, "Journal of a Trip to the Sweet Springs," 15 August 1804, VHS; Allan Nevins, ed., *The Diary of Philip Hone, 1828–1851* (New York: Arno Press, 1970), 1:406; Beverly Tucker to Lucy Ann Tucker, 21 August 1837, Tucker-Coleman Collection, SWM; Willis, *American Scenery,* 21.

45. Willis, *American Scenery,* 21; *Lexington (Va.) Gazette,* 12 August 1836; Pencil, *White Sulphur Papers,* 63.

46. Mary Jane Windle, *Life at the White Sulphur Springs; or, Pictures of a Pleasant Summer* (Philadelphia: J. B. Lippincott and Company, 1857), 33–34; *Lexington (Va.) Gazette,* 12 August 1836.

47. May diary, 21 July and 22 August 1800, NYSHA; Sombre, *Aquarelles,* 43–44.

48. Eliza Potter, *A Hair-Dresser's Experience in High Life* (New York: Oxford University Press, 1991 [1859]), 72; William Elliott diary, 6 August 1823, Elliott-Gonzales Papers, SHC; Watson, "Mixed Medley," 19 August 1805, NYSLA (italics in original); Viator, "The White Sulphur Springs," *New England Magazine* 3 (September 1832): 226; Windle, *Life in Washington,* 188; *Lexington (Va.) Gazette,* 12 August 1836.

49. Ferdinand-Marie Bayard, *Travels of a Frenchman in Maryland and Virginia . . . during the Summer of 1791,* trans. and ed. Ben C. McCary (Ann Arbor, Mich.: Edwards Brothers, 1950 [1798]), 51; Burke, *The Mineral Springs of Western Virginia,* 24; Edmund Randolph to Marianne O'Meade, 4 August 1840, Edmund Randolph Papers, VHS; "Visit to the Virginia Springs," 545; Briggs, "Journal of a Trip to the Sweet Springs," 15 August 1804, VHS; Graham diary, 31 July–2 August 1848, N-YHS; Henry L. Pierce to Edward L Pierce, 5 July 1844, Pierce Family Papers, MHS, FH; DeVeaux, *The Travelers' Own Book,* 93; "Letters from the Country," *New York Mirror* 8, no. 6 (14 August 1830): 44; Phillip R. Shriver, ed., *A Tour to New Connecticut in 1811: The Narrative of Henry Leavitt Edwards* (Cleveland, Ohio: Western Reserve Historical Society, 1985), 85; "Act Incorporating the Village of Saratoga Springs," SSCH; see, for example, Village Board of Trustees Minutes, 5 April 1860, SSCH; "Journal of a Trip to the Mountains, Caves and Springs of Virginia," 386; Newby diary, 19 August 1823, SHC; Reynold

diary, 25 July 1841, WVU; *The Life and Adventures of Robert Bailey, from his Infancy up to December, 1821* (Richmond: J. and G. Cochran, 1822), 69, 212; Featherstonhaugh, *Excursion Through the Slave States*, 1:79; T. H. Breen, "Horses and Gentlemen: The Cultural Significance of Gambling among the Gentry of Virginia," *William and Mary Quarterly*, 3d. ser., 34 (April 1977): 239–42; Ann Fabian, *Card Sharps, Dream Books, and Bucket Shops: Gambling in 19th-Century America* (Ithaca, N.Y.: Cornell University Press, 1990), 13.

50. Newby diary, 19 August 1823, SHC; Martin Duralde to Henry, 20 July 1846, LoV; Caldwell, *A Tour through Part of Virginia*, 26; Martin Duralde to Colonel Z. N. Oliver, 25 July 1846, LoV; *The Life and Adventures of Robert Bailey*, 64, 215; Breen, "Horses and Gentlemen," 256–57.

51. Potter, *A Hair-Dresser's Experience in High Life*, 81; Edmund Randolph to Marianne O'Meade, 4 August 1840, Edmund Randolph Papers, VHS; Jonathan Berkeley Grimball diary, 15 July 1835, SHC.

52. Featherstonhaugh, *Excursions Through the Slave States*, 1:79–80; Briggs, "Journal of a Trip to the Sweet Springs," 1 and 15 August 1804, VHS; "Journal of a Trip to the Mountains, Caves and Springs of Virginia," 386; Newby diary, 19 August 1823, SHC (italics in original). See Breen, "Horses and Gentlemen," 256–57; Fabian, *Card Sharps, Dream Books, and Bucket Shops*, 2–4, 40; and Clifford Geertz, "Deep Play: Notes on the Balinese Cockfight," in *The Interpretation of Cultures* (New York: Basic Books, 1973), 412–53.

53. Bayard, *Travels of a Frenchman*, 51; Newby diary, 19 August 1823, SHC (italics in original); *The Life and Adventures of Robert Bailey*, 64–75, 212. On the social stigma of gambling, see Lewis, "Ladies and Gentlemen on Display," 334–36, 462; and Fabian, *Card Sharps, Dream Books, and Bucket Shops*, 18–23, 37.

54. Newby diary, 19 August 1823, SHC; Paulding, *Letters from the South*, 1:39; *Lexington (Va.) Gazette*, 4 August 1859; J. W. Hevenson to Richard Singleton, 1 August 1838, Singleton Family Papers, USC (italics in original); "Journal of a Trip to the Mountains, Caves and Springs of Virginia," 386; *The Life and Adventures of Robert Bailey*, 215.

55. Paulding, *Letters from the South*, 1:232; Gilliam diary, 2 August 1816, LoV; Nichols, *Forty Years of American Life*, 192; Bristed, *Upper Ten Thousand*, 127; Paulding, *Letters from the South*, 1:167; Hunter diary, 6 August 1838, UVa; Clement Clarke Moore, "A Trip to Saratoga," 1844, Clement Clarke Moore Papers, N-YHS.

56. Hunter diary, 26 July 1838, UVa; Sarah Rutherfoord to John Rutherfoord, 12 July 1811, John Rutherfoord Papers, Duke; Windle, *Life in Washington*, 198; Louisa M. Collins to Mercie Harrison, Virginia, 21 September 1837, Byrd Family Papers, VHS; Robert Carter Berkeley diary, 2 August 1826, VHS; "Visit to the Virginia Springs," 545; Elizabeth Ruffin diary, 22 August 1827, SHC; Fauquier White Sulphur Springs broadside, 1857, SWM; May diary, 7 June, 20 August 1800, NYSHA; Gilpin, *A Northern Tour*, 64; Windle, *Life in Washington*, 177.

57. Hunter diary, 19 and 24 July 1838, UVa; Gilliam diary, 16 August 1816, LoV; Paulding, *Letters from the South*, 1:172, 2:241; Caroline Gilman, *Poetry of Traveling in the United States* (New York: S. Colman, 1838), 86; F. Stone to Thomas D. Stone, 25 August 1857, GBA; Louisa

Elizabeth (Cabell) Carrington to Henry Carrington, 3 September 1831, Carrington Family Papers, VHS (italics in original).

58. May diary, 8 August 1800, NYSHA (italics in original); Moore, "A Trip to Saratoga," N-YHS; Irving, "Style at Ballston," 259; Timothy Dwight, *Travels in New England and New York*, ed. Barbara Miller Solomon (Cambridge, Mass.: Belknap Press, 1969 [1821–22]), 3:294; Catharine Maria Sedgwick, "Leisure Hours at Saratoga," *United States Magazine and Democratic Review* 1 (January 1838): 199–200; Mary Grey Bidwell to Barnabas Bidwell, 20 July 1803, Bidwell Letters, Bidwell House, Monterey, Mass., FH. On the conflict between work and leisure, see Bruce C. Daniels, *Puritans at Play: Leisure and Recreation in Colonial New England* (New York: St. Martin's Griffin, 1995); Daniel T. Rodgers, *The Work Ethic in Industrial America* (Chicago: University of Chicago Press, 1974), xi–xv, 94–124; Sandra Tomc, "An Idle Industry: Nathaniel Parker Willis and the Workings of Literary Leisure," *American Quarterly* 49 (December 1997): 781–84; and Cindy S. Aron, *Working at Play: A History of Vacations in the United States* (New York: Oxford University Press, 1999), 6–9, passim.

59. Alexis de Tocqueville, *Democracy in America* (New York: Knopf, 1994 [1838]), 2:221; May diary, 8 July 1800, NYSHA; *Lexington (Va.) Gazette*, 29 August 1850; "Virginia Springs," 282.

60. Sarah to A. A. Lawrence, 13 July 1841, A. A. Lawrence Papers, MHS, FH. Ledgers from several Virginia springs provide the following statistics: mean length of stay 9.5 days, median stay 7.0 days (see Table 1 ledgers). Spotswood diary, 28 July 1848, VHS; William Elliott to Mrs. Elliott, 11 August 1836, Elliott-Gonzales Papers, SHC; North diary, 10 September 1852, SHC (italics in original).

61. Sigmund Diamond, trans. and ed., *A Casual View of America: The Home Letters of Salomon de Rothschild, 1859–1861* (Palo Alto, Calif.: Stanford University Press, 1961), 66; Latrobe, *The Rambler in North America*, 127–28; Henry McCall Jr. to Peter McCall, 13 August 1843, Cadwalader Papers, Historical Society of Pennsylvania, Philadelphia, FH; Potter, *A Hair-Dresser's Experience in High Life*, 60, 77–78.

62. "Journal of a Trip to the Mountains, Caves and Springs of Virginia," 306; Latrobe, *The Rambler in North America*, 129; Irving, "Style at Ballston," 256; Robert G. Shaw to Jacob Townsley, 16 August 1838, Shaw Family Papers, MHS, FH; Jon Sterngass, *First Resorts: Pursuing Pleasure at Saratoga Springs, Newport, and Coney Island* (Baltimore: Johns Hopkins University Press, 2001), 4; Tocqueville, *Democracy in America*, 2:221.

5. LOVE FOR SALE

1. Daniel Benedict diary, 26 August 1846, SSCH; Cornelius E. Durkee, *Reminiscences of Saratoga* (Saratoga Springs, N.Y.: Reprinted from the *Saratogian*, 1927–28), 144; William L. Stone, *Reminiscences of Saratoga and Ballston* (New York: R. Worthington, 1880), 218–20. Tom Camel was a 55-year-old illiterate, married black laborer (Mary C. Lynn and William Fox, comps., "The 1850 Census of Saratoga Springs: A Numerical Listing," 1991, SSPL).

2. The motivations for Camel's demonstration are mixed. Benedict claims that the charade was gotten up by workers disgruntled by their experience on a project at Jumel's property (Benedict diary, 26 August 1846, SSCH), whereas Stone and Durkee suggest that social leaders "determined to administer [Jumel] a lesson" (Stone, *Reminiscences,* 219; Durkee, *Reminiscences,* 144); William Cary Duncan, *The Amazing Madame Jumel* (New York: A. L. Burt, 1935). See also John F. Marszalek, *The Petticoat Affair: Manners, Mutiny, and Sex in Andrew Jackson's White House* (New York: The Free Press, 1997); and Kirsten E. Wood, "'One Woman So Dangerous to Public Morals': Gender and Power in the Eaton Affair," *Journal of the Early Republic* 17 (summer 1997): 237–75.

3. "Saratoga Springs," *New York Mirror,* 3 August 1839; Charles J. Latrobe, *The Rambler in North America* (New York: Johnson Reprint Corporation, 1970 [1832]), 128; Elkanah Watson, "Mixed Medley," 19 September 1805, Elkanah Watson Papers, NYSLA; Ernest Duvergier de Hauranne, *A Frenchman in Lincoln's America. Huit Mois en Amérique: Lettres et Notes de Voyage, 1864–1865,* trans. and ed. Ralph H. Bowen (Chicago: R. R. Donnelley and Sons, 1974 [1866]), 1:137–38; Levin Smith Joynes to Mother, 21 August 1856, Joynes Family Papers, VHS (italics in original).

4. [Edward "Ned" Ward], *The London Spy,* ed. Kenneth Fenwick (London: Folio Society, 1955), quoted in David S. Shields, *Civil Tongues and Polite Letters in British America* (Chapel Hill: University of North Carolina Press, 1997), 40–46, 49.

5. Shields, *Civil Tongues and Polite Letters in British America,* xiii–xix, 36–38, 302–7; Phyllis Hembry, *The English Spa, 1560–1815: A Social History* (London: Athlone Press, 1990); R. S. Crane, "Suggestions toward a Genealogy of the 'Man of Feeling,'" in *The Idea of the Humanities and Other Essays, Critical and Historical* (Chicago: University of Chicago Press, 1967), 1:197; Richard L. Bushman, *The Refinement of America: Persons, Houses, Cities* (New York: Knopf, 1992), 83; Paul Langford, *A Polite and Commercial People: England, 1727–1783* (Oxford: Clarendon Press, 1989), 461–518; John F. Kasson, *Rudeness and Civility: Manners in Nineteenth-Century America* (New York: Hill and Wang, 1990), 147–81; Karen Halttunen, *Confidence Men and Painted Women: A Study of Middle-Class Culture in America, 1830–1870* (New Haven, Conn.: Yale University Press, 1982), xvi. Halttunen dates the emergence of middle-class politeness to the 1830s, but evidence from the springs suggests that the culture of civility made its way to America from English spas around the close of the eighteenth century. Abigail May diary, 26 July 1800, NYSHA.

6. Susanah Isham (Harrison) Blain to Mrs. Mary Harrison, 24 August 1831, Harrison Family Papers, VHS; Eliza Potter, *A Hair-Dresser's Experience in High Life* (New York: Oxford University Press, 1991 [1859]), 58; *A Trip to the Virginia Springs, or the Belles and Beaux of 1835. By a Lady* (Lexington, Va.: R. H. Glass, 1843), 21–22; "Life at Saratoga," *Harper's Weekly,* 8 August 1857.

7. James Kirke Paulding, *Letters from the South, Written During an Excursion During the Summer of 1816* (New York: James Eastburn and Company, 1817), 1:113; *Saratoga Springs (N.Y.) Whig,* 15 June 1841 (italics in original); James Skelton Gilliam diary, 7 August 1816, LoV; C. O.

Lyde diary, 6 August 1841, Duke; Julia Gardiner Tyler to Juliana McLachean Tyler, 10 August 1845, Tyler Family Papers, SWM; M. Davenport, *Under the Gridiron: A Summer in the United States and the Far West* (London: Tinsley Brothers, 1876), 123.

8. Benjamin Temple to Lucy L. Temple, 4 September 1837, Harrison Family Papers, VHS; William Radford to G. W. Munford, 11 August 1842, Munford-Ellis Family Papers, Duke; "Saratoga and Newport," *New York Daily Times*, 15 August 1856; "Saratoga: the Celebrities There—Balls, Amusements, etc.," *New York Daily Times*, 18 August 1856; Barnes F. Lathrop, ed., "A Southern Girl at Saratoga Springs, 1834," *North Carolina Historical Review* 15 (April 1938): 160.

9. "From Saratoga," *New York World*, 20 July 1860; Willis R. Williams to Suppie, 22 August 1858, Willis R. Williams Papers, SHC; "James Morrell's Trip in August, 1813," *Pennsylvania Magazine of History* 39 (1915): 425–43; Beverly Tucker to Lucy Ann Tucker, 21 August 1837, Tucker-Coleman Collection, SWM; Mark Pencil, Esq. [Mary Hagner], *The White Sulphur Papers, or Life at the Springs of Western Virginia* (New York: Samuel Colman, 1839), 103; Netta, "First Impressions of Saratoga, No. 4," *National Era* 13, no. 661 (1 September 1859): 1; Netta, "First Impressions of Saratoga, No. 7," *National Era* 13, no. 664 (22 September 1859): 1; Jane Caroline North diary, 2 September 1851, SHC.

10. Minnie Myrtle, "A Loiterer's Gleanings at Saratoga," *New York Daily Times*, 31 July 1854; Charles Astor Bristed, *The Upper Ten Thousand: Sketches of American Society* (New York: Stinger and Townsend, 1852), 85–86; Edmund Randolph to Marianne O'Meade, 4 August 1840, Edmund Randolph Papers, VHS; Elizabeth Ruffin diary, 11 and 22 August 1827, SHC; Clement Clarke Moore, "A Trip to Saratoga," 1844, Clement Clarke Moore Papers, N-YHS.

11. James Kirke Paulding, *The New Mirror for Travellers; and Guide to the Springs. By an Amateur* (New York: G. and C. Carvill, 1828), 84–85; May diary, 12 July 1800, NYSHA; Thomas A. Chambers, "Seduction and Sensibility: The Refined Society of Ballston, New York, 1800," *New York History* 78 (July 1997): 245–72; "Life at Saratoga," *Harper's Weekly*, 8 August 1857; Potter, *A Hair-Dresser's Experience in High Life*, 61–62, 90.

12. Myrtle, "A Loiterer's Gleanings at Saratoga"; Washington Irving, "Style at Ballston," *Salmagundi* 16, Thursday, 15 October 1807, in *Salmagundi*, ed. Bruce I. Granger and Martha Hartzog (Boston: Twayne, 1977), 257 (italics in original); Levin Smith Joynes letter, 21 August 1856, Joynes Family Papers, VHS; Netta, "No. 7," 1; Paulding, *New Mirror*, 304 (italics in original); Henry James, "Saratoga," *The Nation* 11 (11 August 1870): 87.

13. Cynthia A. Kierner, "Genteel Balls and Republican Parades: Gender and Early Southern Civic Rituals, 1677–1826," *The Virginia Magazine of History and Biography* 104 (spring 1996): 185–210; Cynthia A. Kierner, "Hospitality, Sociability, and Gender in the Southern Colonies," *Journal of Southern History* 72 (August 1996): 449–80; Jan Lewis, "The Republican Wife: Virtue and Seduction in the Early Republic," *William and Mary Quarterly*, 3d. ser., 44 (October 1987): 689–721; Shields, *Civil Tongues and Polite Letters in British America*, 308–19.

14. May diary, 7–8 and 16 June 1800, 10 and 14 August 1800, NYSHA.

15. Barbara Welter, "The Cult of True Womanhood, 1820–1860," in *Dimity Convictions:*

The American Woman in the Nineteenth Century (Athens: Ohio University Press, 1976), 41; Nancy Cott, *The Bonds of Womanhood: "Woman's Sphere" in New England, 1780–1835* (New Haven, Conn.: Yale University Press, 1977); Linda Kerber, *Women of the Republic: Intellect and Ideology in Revolutionary America* (New York: Norton, 1986); Lewis, "The Republican Wife"; Shields, *Civil Tongues and Polite Letters in British America,* 308–19; St. George Tucker to Mrs. Judith H. Coalter, 21 July 1833, Brown, Coalter, Tucker Papers, SWM; *A Trip to the Virginia Springs,* 30–31, 45 (italics in original).

16. Halttunen, *Confidence Men and Painted Women;* Moore, "A Trip to Saratoga," N-YHS; *Saratoga Springs (N.Y.) Whig,* 8 June 1841 (italics in original); George William Curtis, *Lotus-Eating; A Summer Book* (New York: Harper and Brothers, 1852), 107; Bushman, *The Refinement of America,* xiv–xv; Kasson, *Rudeness and Civility.*

17. Mary Jane Windle, *Life in Washington, and Life Here and There* (Philadelphia: J. B. Lippincott and Company, 1859), 358, 198, 167; "To Kate," 10 August 1860, Meade Family Papers, VHS; E. W. to Mrs. Bulloch, 9 August 1839, Bulloch Family Papers, SHC; "The Watering Places," *New York Herald,* 22 August 1853; Paulding, *Letters from the South,* 2:227–28.

18. Sandra Tomc, "An Idle Industry: Nathaniel Parker Willis and the Workings of Literary Leisure," *American Quarterly* 49 (December 1997): 780–805; David Henry Ellderbrock, "Limited Engagements: The Traveler as Subject and Social Critic in Nineteenth Century American Literature" (Ph.D. diss., University of California, Berkeley, 1995).

19. *A Trip to the Virginia Springs,* 37; North diary, 30 August 1852, SHC; John Pendleton Kennedy to "Dear," 26 July 1851, John Pendleton Kennedy Papers, WVU; *Saratoga Springs (N.Y.) Whig,* 28 September 1841.

20. *Saratoga Springs (N.Y.) Whig,* 28 September 1841; Bristed, *The Upper Ten Thousand,* 160; Shields, *Civil Tongues and Polite Letters in British America;* Susannah Caroline Warwick, "Journey to Saratoga Springs," 7 August 1829, John W. Daniel Papers, UVa.

21. May diary, 2 July 1800, NYSHA; S. to Wife, 26 July 1838, Stuart Family Papers, VHS.

22. Potter, *A Hair-Dresser's Experience in High Life,* 62 (italics in original); North diary, 1 September, 16 August 1851, SHC; May diary, 12 August 1800, NYSHA; Windle, *Life in Washington,* 167–68; William Radford to G. W. Munford, 11 August 1842, Munford-Ellis Family Papers, Duke.

23. G. M. to Lucy T., 9 September 1828, Munford-Ellis Family Papers, Duke; North diary, 7 and 11 August 1851, SHC; Gilliam diary, 29 July 1816, LoV.

24. North diary, 31 August 1852, SHC; Mary Murray, "Journal kept on a Jaunt to Ballston + Saratoga," 6 August 1825, N-YHS; James Silk Buckingham, *America, Historical, Statistical, and Descriptive* (London: Fisher, Son and Company, 1841), 2:437–39; T. S. Arthur, "Going to the Springs; or, Vulgar People," in *Heart-Histories and Life-Pictures* (New York: n.p., 1853), 158, 162.

25. May diary, 5, 18, and 20 August 1800, NYSHA; Bristed, *The Upper Ten Thousand,* 117; *Lexington (Va.) Gazette,* 20 August 1846 (italics in original).

26. Potter, *A Hair-Dresser's Experience in High Life,* 54; Netta, "First Impressions of Saratoga, No. 1," *National Era* 13, no. 658 (11 August 1859): 1.

27. Curtis, *Lotus-Eating,* 105; John Rossen to Sister, 12 August 1849, GBA; Philip English Mackey, ed., *A Gentleman of Much Promise: The Diary of Isaac Mickle, 1837–1845* (Philadelphia: University of Pennsylvania Press, 1977), 2:466; J. Lynah to Mrs. Francis M. Lewis, 28 March 1857, Conway Whittle Family Papers, SWM; "Notes Beside the Steam Engine," *New York Herald,* 21 August 1847.

28. Potter, *A Hair-Dresser's Experience in High Life,* 80; North diary, 17 August 1851, SHC; Myrtle, "A Loiterer's Gleanings at Saratoga"; Windle, *Life at the White Sulphur Springs,* 48, 61.

29. J. K. L. to Charles, 5 September 1854, Carrington Family Papers, VHS; Levin Smith Joynes, 21 August 1856, Joynes Family Papers, VHS; Charles Griffin, "A Trip to Saratoga," 16 May 1833, SSPL.

30. Pencil, *White Sulphur Papers,* 142–43; Irving, "Style at Ballston," 259 (italics in original); "On Seeing Miss *** at the Ballston Springs," as quoted in Edward F. Grose, *Centennial History of the Village of Ballston Spa* (Ballston Spa, N.Y.: Ballston Journal, 1907), 141.

31. Stephen Allen Memoirs, 16 August 1841, N-YHS; George Evelyn Harrison to Mrs. Ann H. Byrd, 11 September 1828, Byrd Family Papers, VHS.

32. Mary Jane Windle, *Life at the White Sulphur Springs; or, Pictures of a Pleasant Summer* (Philadelphia: J. B. Lippincott and Company, 1857), 46; *A Trip to the Virginia Springs,* 18; Laura Wirt to Caroline Wirt, 22 August 1826, William Wirt Papers, MdHS; Sigmund Diamond, trans. and ed., *A Casual View of America: The Home Letters of Salomon de Rothschild, 1859–1861* (Palo Alto, Calif.: Stanford University Press, 1961), 66.

33. Elizabeth Ruffin diary, 15 August 1827, SHC; May diary, 22 June 1800, NYSHA.

34. Nathaniel Parker Willis, "Manners at Watering Places," in *Hurry-Graphs; Or, Sketches of Scenery, Celebrities and Society, Taken From Life* (New York: Scribner, 1851), 290–96; *A Trip to the Virginia Springs,* 28–29; Hembry, *The English Spa, 1560–1815,* 135–47; Pencil, *White Sulphur Papers,* 138–39; Susan Bradford Eppes to Pa, 1 August 1847, Susan Bradford Eppes Papers, SHC (italics in original).

35. "Dagger's Springs," *Lexington (Va.) Gazette,* 12 August 1836; Samuel Sombre [James Watson Gerard], *Aquarelles: Or Summer Sketches* (New York: Stanford and Delisser, 1858), 40; Mary Murray diary, 13 August 1817, N-YHS; R. C. Rust to C. C. Clay, 14 September 1858, Clement Claiborne Clay Papers, Duke (italics in original); Netta, "No. 4," 1.

36. Charles Griffin, "A Trip to Saratoga," 16 May 1833, SSPL; Sombre, *Aquarelles,* 40 (italics in original); Lewis, "The Republican Wife," 715; Shields, *Civil Tongues and Polite Letters in British America,* 43–45; Murray diary, 12 August 1817, N-YHS; Ellen Rothman, *Hands and Hearts: A History of Courtship in America* (New York: Basic Books, 1984).

37. May diary, 20 July 1800, NYSHA; John Howell Briggs, "Journal of a Trip to the Sweet Springs," 29 August 1804, VHS.

38. "Letter From the Country," *New York Mirror* 8, no. 6 (14 August 1830): 44; J. K. L. to Charles, 5 September 1854, Carrington Family Papers, VHS; May diary, 4 June 1800, NYSHA.

39. North diary, 20 September 1851, SHC; John Pendleton Kennedy diary, 23 July 1851, West Virginia Collection, WVU; May diary, 20 August 1800, NYSHA (italics in original). Philip Dormer Stanhope, Lord Chesterfield was the recognized authority on the necessary social accomplishments of eighteenth-century gentlemen. His *Letters to His Son* and *Principles of Politeness* (both published in 1778) instructed his illegitimate son on the best ways to become a respected gentleman and to seduce women. Royall Tyler, *The Contrast* (New York: American Manuscript Society, 1970 [1787]), 58; May diary, 12 August 1800, NYSHA.

40. Pencil, *White Sulphur Papers,* 105; May diary, 7 June, 11 July, 17 August 1800, NYSHA. This passage is the opening line (1113) of the final section of "Spring" (James Thomson, *The Seasons and the Castle of Indolence,* ed. James Sambrook [Oxford: Clarendon Press, 1984 (1726–30)], 33).

41. Sombre, *Aquarelles,* 22–23, 38 (italics in original); Netta, "No. 4," 1; Paulding, *Letters from the South,* 2:242; "A Supposed Letter by a Lady from Ballston," as quoted in Grose, *Centennial History,* 141.

42. Laura Wirt to Catherine Wirt, 9 August 1826, William Wirt Papers, MdHS (italics in original); North diary, 15 September 1851, SHC; May diary, 20 and 22 July 1800, 15 August 1800, NYSHA (italics in original).

43. "My Dear Anne," 1 September 1836, GBA; J. Lynah to Mrs. Francis M. Lewis, 28 March 1857, Conway Whittle Family Papers, SWM; Windle, *Life in Washington,* 168 (italics in original); John Pendleton Kennedy to wife, 24 July 1851, John Pendleton Kennedy Papers, WVU.

44. Elizabeth Ruffin diary, 14 and 27 August 1827, SHC; Emmie to Sister, 28 July 1859, Elliott-Gonzales Papers, SHC; *Six Weeks in Fauquier* (New York: Samuel Colman, 1839), 33; Beverly Tucker to Luce Tucker, 7 August 1839, Tucker-Coleman Collection, SWM; "High Life at the White Sulphur," *Lexington (Va.) Gazette,* 14 September 1854 (italics in original); North diary, 27 August 1852, SHC.

45. Peyton Randolph to Maria, 6 August 1812, Peyton Randolph Papers, Colonial Williamsburg Foundation Library, Williamsburg, Va.; Windle, *Life in Washington,* 189; Windle, *Life at the White Sulphur Springs,* 61; Paulding, *Letters from the South,* 2:233; George W. Munford to Lizzie, 4 September 1881, Munford-Ellis Papers, Duke; William Burke, *The Virginia Mineral Springs* (Richmond: Ritchies and Dunnavant, 1853), 47–48 (italics in original); John Pendleton Kennedy to wife, 26 July 1851, John Pendleton Kennedy Papers, WVU.

46. Elizabeth Ruffin diary, 18 August 1827, SHC; Lyde diary, 22 July 1841, Duke; Louisa M. Collins to Mercie Harrison, 21 September 1837, Byrd Family Papers, VHS (italics in original); Potter, *A Hair-Dresser's Experience in High Life,* 63–64 (italics in original).

47. "Life at Saratoga," *Harper's Weekly,* 8 August 1857; Potter, *A Hair-Dresser's Experience in High Life,* 67 (italics in original); William Elliott to Mrs. William Elliott, 17 August 1828, Elliott-Gonzales Papers, SHC (italics in original); Edwin Bedford Jeffres diary, 11 August 1852, VHS.

48. Mikhail Bakhtin's idea of the carnival offers a useful perspective. See *Rabelais and His World,* trans. Helene Iswolsky (Bloomington: Indiana University Press, 1984); and *Problems of Dostoevsky's Politics,* trans. R. W. Rotsel (Ann Arbor, Mich.: Ardis, 1973). Paulding, *Letters from the South,* 1:172; Netta, "No. 7," 1; Joan Cashin, ed., *Our Common Affairs: Texts from Women in the Old South* (Baltimore: Johns Hopkins University Press, 1996), 2–26; Catharine Maria Sedgwick, "Leisure Hours at Saratoga," *United States Magazine and Democratic Review* 1 (January 1838): 200.

49. Beverly Tucker to Lucy Ann Tucker, 1 September 1839, Tucker-Coleman Collection, SWM (italics in original); Anya Jabour, "'It Will Never Do For Me To Be Married': The Life of Laura Wirt Randall, 1803–1833," *Journal of the Early Republic* 17 (summer 1997): 193–236.

50. Rothman, *Hands and Hearts,* 5–66; Paulding, *New Mirror,* 277–81; Martin Duralde to father, 27 July 1846, LoV; William Wirt to Elizabeth Wirt, 31 August 1825, William Wirt Papers, MdHS; *Dictionary of American Biography* (New York: Charles Scribner's Sons, 1928), 12:34–36.

51. Bristed, *The Upper Ten Thousand,* 119; Paulding, *New Mirror,* 280–81.

52. Allen Memoirs, 16 August 1841, N-YHS; Paulding, *New Mirror,* 229; *Frank Leslie's Illustrated Newspaper,* September 1859, SSPL; Netta, "No. 7," 1; Windle, *Life in Washington,* 185 (italics in original).

53. C. D. Arfwedson, *The United States and Canada, in 1832, 1833, and 1834* (London: Richard Bentley, 1834), 2:271; Burke, *The Mineral Springs of Virginia,* 49; Sombre, *Aquarelles,* 24; Beverly Tucker to Mrs. L. A. Tucker, 25 August 1844, Tucker-Coleman Collection, SWM.

54. "Cupid Triumphant," *Harper's Weekly* Supplement (15 July 1871): 660; John Pendleton Kennedy, *Swallow Barn; Or, A Sojourn in the Old Dominion* (Baton Rouge: Louisiana State University Press, 1986 [1831]), 336–37; Beverly Tucker to Lucy Ann Tucker, 11 September 1839, Tucker-Coleman Collection, SWM.

55. Netta, "First Impressions of Saratoga, No. 6," *National Era* 13, no. 663 (15 September 1859): 1; "Advice to Young Ladies," *Saratoga Springs (N.Y.) Whig,* 21 September 1841.

56. Langford, *A Polite and Commercial People,* 113–15; Hannah Webster Foster, *The Coquette; or, The History of Eliza Wharton; A Novel; Founded on Fact* (New York: Oxford University Press, 1986 [1797]); Susanna Rowson, *Charlotte Temple: A Tale of Truth* (New York: Oxford University Press, 1986 [1794]); Jane Austen, *Northanger Abbey* (New York: Penguin Classics, 1985 [1818]), 41.

57. Potter, *A Hair-Dresser's Experience in High Life,* 54, 67; Paulding, *Letters from the South,* 2:232–33; Viator, "Our Saratoga Correspondence," *Harper's Weekly,* 3 September 1859; "Life at the Springs," *Springfield (Mass.) Hampden Post,* 17 November 1847, SSPL; Bristed, *The Upper Ten Thousand,* 111; "Saratoga in Season," *The Daily Graphic,* 14 July 1874.

58. "Watering Places," *New York Herald,* 22 August 1853; "Ode to the White Sulphur Springs," 1835, GBA; Netta, "No. 4," 1.

59. Beverly Tucker to Lucy Ann Tucker, 15 and 25 August 1839, Tucker-Coleman Collection, SWM.

60. Bristed, *The Upper Ten Thousand,* 189–90, 201.

61. "Notes Beside the Steam Engine," *New York Herald,* 21 August 1847; Arthur, "Going to the Springs," 158–74; "People and Things at Saratoga—Sketches of Life," *New-York Daily Times,* 15 August 1856.

62. Ferdinand-Marie Bayard, *Travels of a Frenchman in Maryland and Virginia . . . during the Summer of 1791,* trans. and ed. Ben C. McCary (Ann Arbor, Mich.: Edwards Brothers, 1950 [1798]), 52.

63. May diary, 22 July 1800, NYSHA (italics in original).

64. Cathy N. Davidson, *Revolution and the Word: The Rise of the Novel in America* (New York: Oxford University Press, 1986), 110–50; *Saratoga Springs (N.Y.) Whig,* 20 July 1841.

65. Philip Vickers Fithian, *Journal, 1775–1776,* ed. Robert Greenhalgh Albion and Leonard Dodson (Princeton, N.J.: Princeton University Press, 1934), 127–28 (italics in original); Louisa M. Collins to Mercie Harrison, 21 September 1837, Byrd Family Papers, VHS (italics in original).

66. Sombre, *Aquarelles,* 21; Potter, *A Hair-Dresser's Experience in High Life,* 68; *A Trip to the Virginia Springs, or the Belles and Beaux of 1835. By a Lady* (Lexington, Va.: Printed at the "Gazette" Office, R. H. Glass, Printer, 1843), 20–21; May diary, 4 August 1800, NYSHA.

67. Charles Dudley Warner, "Their Pilgrimage," *Harper's New Monthly Magazine* 73, 435 (August 1886): 442; Potter, *A Hair-Dresser's Experience in High Life,* 75–77.

68. "Life at Saratoga," *Harper's Weekly,* 8 August 1857; Potter, *A Hair-Dresser's Experience in High Life,* 60, 62; Allan Nevins, ed., *The Diary of Philip Hone, 1828–1851* (New York: Arno Press, 1970), 1:411; E. W. to Mrs. Bulloch, 9 August 1839, Bulloch Family Papers, SHC.

69. Buckingham, *America, Historical, Statistical, and Descriptive,* 2:441, 452; Curtis, *Lotus-Eating,* 117, 122.

70. Warner, "Their Pilgrimage," *Harper's New Monthly Magazine* 73, no. 436 (September 1886): 595.

6. DRINKING THE SAME WATERS: SECTIONALISM AT THE SPRINGS

1. *Gone with the Wind,* Metro-Goldwyn-Mayer, 1969 (Selznick International Pictures, 1939).

2. Alexander Mackay, *The Western World; or, Travels in the United States in 1846–1847* (Philadelphia: Lea and Blanchard, 1849), 2:213–16, as quoted in Roger Haydon, ed., *Upstate Travels: British Views of Nineteenth-Century America* (Syracuse, N.Y.: Syracuse University Press, 1982), 109, 111; Abigail May diary, 1800, NYSHA; Anne Newport Royall, *Sketches of History, Life, and Manners in the United States, by a Traveler* (New York: Johnson Reprint Corporation, 1970 [1826]), 32; Solomon Mordecai to Ellen Mordecai, 17 August 1817, Mordecai Family Papers, SHC.

3. *Six Weeks in Fauquier* (New York: Samuel Colman, 1839), 33; *Memoirs of an Emigrant: The Journal of Alexander Coventry, M.D., In Scotland, The United States, and Canada during the period 1783–1831,* 25 September 1802, NYSLA.

4. Perceval Reniers, *The Springs of Virginia: Life, Love, and Death at the Waters, 1775–1900*

(Chapel Hill: University of North Carolina Press, 1941), 70–73, 166–68. Clay visited 20–23 July 1817 (White Sulphur Springs Ledger, 1817–19, GBA). He visited Saratoga Springs in 1839 to boost his political prospects (Allan Nevins, ed., *The Diary of Philip Hone, 1828–1851* [New York: Arno Press, 1970], 1:412–17); Bernard Mayo, ed., "Henry Clay, Patron and Idol of White Sulphur Springs: His Letters to James Calwell," *Virginia Magazine of History and Biography* 55 (October 1947): 301–17; John J. Moorman, "People and Incidents at the White Sulphur Springs," 26–28, 37, VHS; *Lexington (Va.) Gazette,* 11 September 1845.

5. Nevins, *The Diary of Philip Hone,* 1:412–18.

6. St. George Tucker Coalter to Mrs. J. H. Coalter, 8 August 1833, Brown, Coalter, Tucker Papers, SWM; "Another Visit to the Virginia Springs, or the Adventures of Harry Humbug," *SLM* 1 (September 1835): 774; John Pendleton Kennedy to Peter Hoffman Cruse, 4 August 1832, Peter Hoffman Cruse Papers, VHS; Jonathan Berkeley Grimball diary, 28 July 1835, SHC.

7. James Kirke Paulding, *Letters from the South, Written During an Excursion During the Summer of 1816* (New York: James Eastburn and Company, 1817), 2:236–37; Washington Irving, "Style at Ballston," *Salmagundi* 16, Thursday, 15 October 1807, in *Salmagundi,* ed. Bruce I. Granger and Martha Hartzog (Boston: Twayne, 1977), 256–60; James Skelton Gilliam diary, 10 and 28 July 1816, LoV; Michael O'Brien, "On the Mind of the South and Its Accessibility," in *Rethinking the South: Essays in Intellectual History,* ed. Michael O'Brien (Baltimore: Johns Hopkins University Press, 1988), 19–37; Daniel P. Kilbride, "The Cosmopolitan South: Privileged Southerners, Philadelphia, and the Fashionable Tour in the Antebellum Era," *Journal of Urban History* 26 (July 2000): 563–90; Bertram Wyatt-Brown, *The House of Percy: Honor, Melancholy, and Imagination in a Southern Family* (New York: Oxford University Press, 1994), 87–124.

8. *Six Weeks in Fauquier,* v–vi; "Red Sulphur Springs," *SLM* 9 (July 1843): 423.

9. Mark Pencil, Esq. [Mary Hagner], *The White Sulphur Papers, or Life at the Springs of Western Virginia* (New York: Samuel Colman, 1839), 42; Viator, "The White Sulphur Springs," *New England Magazine* 3 (September 1832): 226.

10. Patricia C. Click, *The Spirit of the Times: Amusements in Nineteenth-Century Baltimore, Norfolk, and Richmond* (Charlottesville: University Press of Virginia, 1989), 92–93, 98–99; Charlene Marie Lewis, "Ladies and Gentlemen on Display: Planter Society at the Virginia Springs, 1790–1860" (Ph.D. diss., University of Virginia, 1997), 8, 16, and chap. 6, "A Competitive Community of Elite Southerners"; *Six Weeks in Fauquier,* viii (italics in original); William Burke, *The Virginia Mineral Springs* (Richmond: Ritchies and Dunnavant, 1853), 50; Robert S. Conte suggests a more diverse clientele by the 1850s ("The Celebrated White Sulphur Springs of Greenbrier: Nineteenth-Century Travel Accounts," *West Virginia History* 42 [1981]: 210–11); George William Featherstonhaugh, *Excursion Through the Slave States, from Washington on the Potomac to the Frontier of Mexico; with Sketches of Popular Manners and Geological Notices* (London: John Murray, 1844), 1:38.

11. Mary Jane Windle, *Life in Washington, and Life Here and There* (Philadelphia: J. B. Lip-

pincott and Company, 1859), 168; Jan Lewis, *The Pursuit of Happiness: Family and Values in Jefferson's Virginia* (Cambridge, England: Cambridge University Press, 1983), 107–15, 163–65.

12. "Letters from the Country," *New York Mirror* 8, no. 6 (14 August 1830): 44; George William Curtis, *Lotus-Eating; A Summer Book* (New York: Harper and Brothers, 1852), 176.

13. James Oakes, *The Ruling Race: A History of American Slaveholders* (New York: Vintage, 1982).

14. "Virginia Springs," *SLM* 3 (May 1837): 281; Charles Fenno Hoffman, *A Winter in the West. By a New Yorker* (Ann Arbor, Mich.: University Microfilms, 1966 [1835]), 2:294; "Journal of a Trip to the Mountains, Caves and Springs of Virginia," *SLM* 4 (August 1838): 516.

15. *The Tourist, or Pocket Manual for Travellers* (New York: Harper and Brothers, 1838), 85; C. O. Lyde diary, 29 July 1841, Duke (italics in original); as quoted in E. Lee Shepard, ed., "'Trip to the Virginia Springs': An Extract from the Diary of Blair Bolling, 1838," *Virginia Magazine of History and Biography* 96 (April 1988): 201; "Virginia Springs," 281.

16. Benedict Anderson, *Imagined Communities: Reflections on the Origin and Spread of Nationalism* (London: Verso, 1991), 26–35.

17. Burke, *The Virginia Mineral Springs*, 292–93 (italics in original).

18. Curtis, *Lotus-Eating*, 121–22; Catharine Maria Sedgwick, "Leisure Hours at Saratoga," *United States Magazine and Democratic Review* 1 (January 1838): 202; Anderson, *Imagined Communities*, 37–46, 74–80.

19. William R. Taylor, *Cavalier and Yankee: The Old South and American National Character* (New York: Anchor Books, 1963), pt. 2: "The Sustaining Illusion."

20. Eliza Potter, *A Hair-Dresser's Experience in High Life* (New York: Oxford University Press, 1991 [1859]), 37–42. Apparently one of Windle's gossip columns, which she wrote for a Washington newspaper, ignited the controversy.

21. Eliot Warburton, ed., *Hochelaga; or, England in the New World* (New York: Wiley and Putnam, 1851), 25; Windle, *Life in Washington*, 164 (italics in original); Nicholas B. Wainwright, ed., *A Philadelphia Perspective: The Diary of Sidney George Fischer Covering the Years 1834–1871* (Philadelphia: Historical Society of Pennsylvania, 1967), entries for 28 April 1844 and 11 June 1848, 162–63, 211.

22. The extensive historiography on this question includes Kenneth M. Stampp, "The Irrepressible Conflict," in *The Imperiled Union: Essays on the Background of the Civil War* (New York: Oxford University Press, 1980); Michael F. Holt, *The Rise and Fall of the American Whig Party* (New York: Oxford University Press, 1999); Michael F. Holt, *The Political Crisis of the 1850s* (New York: Wiley, 1978); Bruce Levine, *Half Slave and Half Free: The Roots of Civil War* (New York: Hill and Wang, 1992); Richard H. Sewall, *A House Divided: Sectionalism and Civil War, 1848–1865* (Baltimore: Johns Hopkins University Press, 1988); Peter B. Knupfer, *The Union as It Is: Constitutional Unionism and Sectional Compromise, 1787–1861* (Chapel Hill: University of North Carolina Press, 1991); and Michael Morrison, *Slavery and the American West: The Eclipse of Manifest Destiny and the Coming of the Civil War* (Chapel Hill: University

of North Carolina Press, 1997). For a more complex interpretation that emphasizes intrasectional rivalries, the possibility of compromise, and conflicts besides slavery, see David M. Potter, *The Impending Crisis, 1848–1861* (New York: Harper and Row, 1976); J. Mills Thornton III, *Politics and Power in a Slave Society: Alabama, 1800–1860* (Baton Rouge: Louisiana State University Press, 1978); William E. Gienapp, *The Origins of the Republican Party, 1852–1856* (New York: Oxford University Press, 1990); and William H. Freehling, *The Road to Disunion: The Secessionists at Bay* (New York: Oxford University Press, 1990).

23. Solomon Northup, *Twelve Years a Slave,* ed. Sue Eakin and Joseph Logsdon (Baton Rouge: Louisiana University Press, 1968 [1853]), ix–xxiv, 3–20.

24. Emily Catharine Pierson, *Jamie Parker, the Fugitive* (Hartford, Conn.: Brockett, Fuller, and Company, 1851), 61–65, 122–28; Harriet A. Jacobs, *Incidents in the Life of a Slave Girl, Written by Herself,* ed. Jean Fagan Yellin (Cambridge: Harvard University Press, 1987), 175–76; John Hope Franklin, *A Southern Odyssey: Travelers in the Antebellum North* (Baton Rouge: Louisiana State University Press, 1976), 131–39; James Oakes, *Slavery and Freedom: An Interpretation of the Old South* (New York: Vintage, 1990), 170–72.

25. *Lexington (Va.) Gazette,* 15 August 1850; P. H. Aylett to Mother, 24 August 1845, Aylett Family Papers, VHS; Franklin, *A Southern Odyssey,* 148–49.

26. Sigmund Diamond, trans. and ed., *A Casual View of America: The Home Letters of Salomon de Rothschild, 1859–1861* (Palo Alto, Calif.: Stanford University Press, 1961), 66.

27. *Lexington (Va.) Gazette,* 29 August 1850; John M. McCardell, *The Idea of a Southern Nation: Southern Nationalists and Southern Nationalism, 1830–1860* (New York: W. W. Norton, 1979), 178–226; Buffalo Lithia Springs register, 1857–58, VHS; Yellow Sulphur Springs register, 1857–58, VHS; Franklin, *A Southern Odyssey,* 205–6; "Scenes in the Old Dominion," *New York Weekly Mercury,* 18 August 1860; John C. Ehringhaus letter, 21 July 1850, Hayes Collection, SHC.

28. Buffalo Lithia Springs register, 1857–58, VHS; Yellow Sulphur Springs register, 1857–58, VHS; Union Hall register, 1852, HSSSp; Clarendon Hall register, 1860, NMR; John C. Ehringhaus letter, 21 July 1850, Hayes Collection, SHC; "Saratoga and Newport," *New York Daily Times,* 15 August 1856; as quoted in Dunbar Rowland, ed., *Jefferson Davis, Constitutionalist: His Letters, Papers, and Speeches* (New York: J. Little and Ives, 1923), 3:356.

29. William Kaufman Scarborough, ed., *The Diary of Edmund Ruffin: Volume I, Toward Independence. October, 1856–April, 1861* (Baton Rouge: Louisiana University Press, 1972), "Introduction to the Attempt," 1856, 1:16; Betty L. Mitchell, *Edmund Ruffin: A Biography* (Bloomington: Indiana University Press, 1981); Eric H. Walther, *The Fire-Eaters* (Baton Rouge: Louisiana University Press, 1992), 228–69.

30. Scarborough, *The Diary of Edmund Ruffin,* 25 August 1860, 1:450; Marianne Finch, *An Englishwoman's Experience in America* (New York: Negro Universities Press, 1969 [1853]), 328; John Pendleton Kennedy diary, 29 July 1851, West Virginia Collection, WVU; *Lexington (Va.) Gazette,* 2 August 1860.

31. McCardell, *The Idea of a Southern Nation,* 3–9, 318–20, 336; Walther, *The Fire-Eaters,* 1–7, 297, 301; Kenneth M. Stampp, *America in 1857: A Nation on the Brink* (New York: Oxford University Press, 1990).

32. Kennedy diary, 29 July and 1 August 1851, WVU; Charles William Ashby to wife, 24 July 1860, Charles William Ashby Papers, VHS; Scarborough, *The Diary of Edmund Ruffin,* 5 September 1860, 1:338–39; Mitchell Snay, *Gospel of Disunion: Religion and Separatism in the Antebellum South* (Cambridge, England: Cambridge University Press, 1993).

33. Jane Caroline North diary, 11 and 29 August 1851, Pettigrew Family Papers, SHC (italics in original); F. Stone to William B. Stone, August 1857, GBA.

34. Scarborough, *The Diary of Edmund Ruffin,* 22 August 1860, 1:332–33; Mary Jane Windle, *Life at the White Sulphur Springs; or, Pictures of a Pleasant Summer* (Philadelphia: J. B. Lippincott and Company, 1857), 32–33; *Six Weeks in Fauquier,* 51–52; Mary C. Lynn and William Fox, comps., "The 1850 Census of Saratoga Springs: A Numerical Listing," 1991, SSPL; Myra B. Young Armstead, *"Lord, Please Don't Take Me in August": African Americans in Newport and Saratoga Springs, 1870–1930* (Urbana: University of Illinois Press, 1999).

35. Warburton, *Hochelaga,* 8; Windle, *Life in Washington,* 366.

36. As quoted in Edward Cary, *George William Curtis* (New York: Houghton, Mifflin, and Company, 1894), 111–17; Curtis, *Lotus-Eating,* 121–22.

37. Scarborough, *The Diary of Edmund Ruffin,* 29 August 1859, 12 and 25 August 1860, 1:336, 448, 450; Walther, *The Fire-Eaters,* 297–98; *Lexington (Va.) Gazette,* 2 August 1860.

38. Richard H. Shryock, ed., *Letters of Richard D. Arnold* (New York: AMS Press, 1929), 67, 98.

39. Franklin, *A Southern Odyssey,* xvi, 205, 259–61. On the social and cultural similarities between the sections, see Peter S. Onuf, "Federalism, Republicanism, and the Origins of American Sectionalism," in Edward L. Ayers, Patricia Nelson Limerick, Stephen Nissenbaum, and Peter S. Onuf, *All Over the Map: Rethinking American Regions* (Baltimore: Johns Hopkins University Press, 1996), 11–15; Edward Pessen, "How Different from Each Other Were the Antebellum North and South?" *American Historical Review* 85 (December 1980): 1119–49; Potter, *The Impending Crisis;* David M. Potter, *The South and the Sectional Conflict* (Baton Rouge: Louisiana State University Press, 1968); Richard L. Bushman, "A Poet, a Planter, and a Nation of Farmers," *Journal of the Early Republic* 19 (spring 1999): 1–14; James Tice Moore, "Of Cavaliers and Yankees: Frederick W. M. Holliday and the Sectional Crisis, 1845–1861," *The Virginia Magazine of History and Biography* 99 (July 1991): 351–88. For a starkly different view, see James M. McPherson, "Antebellum Southern Exceptionalism: A New Look at an Old Question," *Civil War History* 29, no. 3 (1983): 230–44; and Grady McWhiney, "North versus South: A Clash of Cultures," *Journal of Confederate History* 11, no. 1 (1989): 5–25.

40. Carl Bridenbaugh, "Baths and Watering Places of Colonial America," *William and Mary Quarterly,* 3d. ser., 3 (April 1946): 151–81; Peregrine Prolix [Philip Holbrook Nicklin], *Letters Descriptive of the Virginia Springs* (Philadelphia: H. S. Tanner, 1835), 37 (italics in original).

41. C. Vann Woodward and Elisabeth Muhlenfeld, eds., *The Private Mary Chesnut: The Unpublished Civil War Diaries* (New York: Oxford University Press, 1984), 11 July 1861, 93.

7. WAR, NOSTALGIA, AND ANOMIE, 1861–1896

1. Robert H. Wiebe, *The Search for Order, 1877–1920* (New York: Hill and Wang, 1967); Sarah H. Gordon, *Passage to Union: How the Railroads Transformed American Life, 1829–1929* (Chicago: Ivan R. Dee, 1996); David W. Blight, *Race and Reunion: The Civil War in American Memory* (Cambridge, Mass.: Harvard University Press, 2001), 383–85.

2. C. Vann Woodward and Elisabeth Muhlenfeld, eds., *The Private Mary Chesnut: The Unpublished Civil War Diaries* (New York: Oxford University Press, 1984), 11 July 1861, 93; Benjamin Lyons Farinholt diary, 25–27 August 1862, VHS; George Manning Fell to George O. Manning, 25 August 1863, UVa.

3. Robert S. Conte, *The History of the Greenbrier: America's Resort* (Charleston, W. Va.: Pictorial Histories Publishing Company, 1989), 59–63; Fielding R. Cornett to Rosemond, 5 September 1863, UVa.

4. Cecil D. Eby, ed., *A Virginia Yankee in the Civil War: The Diaries of David Hunter Strother* (Chapel Hill: University of North Carolina Press, 1961), 271–73; Henry A. DuPont, *The Campaign of 1864 in the Valley of Virginia* (New York: National Americana Society, 1925), 88–90.

5. Randolph Harrison to Elizabeth Williamson Harrison, 28 July 1861, 6 and 14 August 1861, Randolph Harrison Papers, VHS; Shirley M. Gilkeson, "Robert E. Lee at White Sulphur Springs," *United Daughters of the Confederacy: Its Magazine* [*UDCMag*] 59, no. 4 (April 1996): 19–20; Shirley P. Thomas, "Montgomery White Sulphur Springs," *UDCMag* 60, no. 3 (March 1997): 25–26; Dorothy H. Bodell, *Montgomery White Sulphur Springs: A History of the Resort, Hospital, Cemeteries, Markers, and Monument* (Blacksburg, Va.: Pocahontas Press, 1993), 7–33; Roderick McMillan to Alexander McMillan, 23 July 1863, Alexander McMillan Papers, Duke.

6. Randolph Harrison to Elizabeth Williamson Harrison, 28 July and 6 August 1861, Randolph Harrison Papers, VHS; John R. Bagby to Betty, 5 and 28 July 1862, 12 August 1862, John R. Bagby Letters, LoV.

7. Recollections of Josephine Cleary Wimsatt, UVa; Giles Buckner Cooke diary, 1863, VHS; "Dear Emaline + Mag" letter, 29 July 1863, Michael Turrentine Papers, Duke; Emily to Josey, 6 August 1862, Joseph S. Williams Papers, Duke; Warm Springs Hotel Daybook, 1859–63, UVa; Powhatan Ellis Sr. to Charly, [1861], Munford-Ellis Family Papers, Duke.

8. Theodore Corbett, *The Making of American Resorts: Saratoga Springs, Ballston Spa, and Lake George* (New Brunswick, N.J.: Rutgers University Press, 2001), 60, 134, 238–41. Footnotes for these pages do not offer any direct evidence, and his strongest assertion, on page 239, is undocumented. Numbers from Union Hotel Register, 19–30 July 1869, SSPL; Union Hall Register, 1852, HSSp; Clarendon Hall Register, 1860, NMR; Grace Maguire Swanner, *Saratoga:*

Queen of Spas (Utica, N.Y.: North Country Books, 1988), 139; *New York Daily Tribune,* 9 August 1865. Jon Sterngass repeats this myth, even though his own evidence proves a substantial Southern presence (*First Resorts: Pursuing Pleasure at Saratoga Springs, Newport, and Coney Island* [Baltimore: Johns Hopkins University Press, 2001], 27–28, 146, 168). See Table 3.

9. Edward Hotaling, *They're Off! Horse Racing at Saratoga* (Syracuse, N.Y.: Syracuse University Press, 1995), 26–61; "Union Hall, Saratoga," *Frank Leslie's Illustrated Newspaper,* 9 July 1864, 253; Nicholas B. Wainwright, ed., *A Philadelphia Perspective: The Diary of Sidney George Fischer Covering the Years 1834–1871* (Philadelphia: Historical Society of Pennsylvania, 1967), 30 September 1864, 482.

10. "The Chiropodist: A Story of the Watering Places," *Harper's Magazine* 24, no. 142 (March 1862): 460–66; "Saratoga Races," *New York Daily Tribune,* 9 August 1865.

11. Daniel Benedict diary, 19 April 1865, SSPL; *New York Daily Tribune,* 10 July 1865; Union Hotel Register, July 1869, SSPL; *Frank Leslie's Illustrated Newspaper,* 7 August 1869, 325, 25 June 1887, 304; O. P. Clarke, *General Grant at Mount MacGregor* (Saratoga Springs, N.Y.: The Saratogian Press, 1906).

12. J. Humphreys to Jeremiah Morton, 30 December 1860, 1 and 3 January 1861; Stockholders Resolutions, 22 February 1861; Jeremiah Morton, "Statement," 25 October 1873; all in Halsey Family Papers, UVa.

13. *General Robert E. Lee at White Sulphur Springs, 1867–'68–'69* (White Sulphur Springs, Va.: The Greenbrier, 1932), 3; Robert E. Lee to William H. F. Lee, 8 June and 29 October 1867, 30 June 1869, as quoted in Robert E. Lee Jr., *Recollections and Letters of General Robert E. Lee* (New York: Doubleday, Page and Co., 1904), 260, 269, 359; Gilkeson, "Robert E. Lee at White Sulphur Springs," 20.

14. Jeremiah Morton to William T. Sutherlin, 18 July 1868, William T. Sutherlin Papers, SHC.

15. Conte, *The History of the Greenbrier,* 84–85; John Esten Cooke, "The White Sulphur Springs," *Harper's New Monthly Magazine* 57, no. 339 (1878): 356; *Richmond (Va.) Whig,* 17 August 1877; *General Robert E. Lee at White Sulphur Springs,* 3, 8–9.

16. John S. Wise, *The Lion's Skin: A Historical Novel and a Novel History* (New York: Doubleday, Page, 1905), 258–59; Christina Bond, *Memories of General Robert E. Lee* (Baltimore: Norman, Remington, 1926), 14, 17–18; Perceval Reniers, *The Springs of Virginia: Life, Love, and Death at the Waters, 1775–1900* (Chapel Hill: University of North Carolina Press, 1941), 208.

17. John J. Moorman, *White Sulphur Springs, Greenbrier County, West Virginia* (Baltimore: Sun Book and Job Printing Office, 1878), 26; Slaughter to Lou, 16 August 1868, Kidd Family Papers, LoV; *Legends of the South. By Somebody who Desires to be Nobody* (Baltimore: William K. Boyle, 1869), 6; *The Allegheny Springs* (Philadelphia: Merrikew and Son, 1874), 58–60; Powhatan Ellis Jr. to Charles Ellis, 13 and 25 August 1878, 14 August 1879, Powhatan Ellis Papers, VHS; Bond, *Memories of General Robert E. Lee,* 22–23.

18. 20 August 1867, Clement Claiborne Clay Papers, Duke; *Richmond (Va.) Whig,* 6 August 1868; Conte, *The History of the Greenbrier,* 67–68; Blight, *Race and Reunion,* 103–6.

19. Charles A. Pilsbury, "A Southern Watering-Place," *Potter's American Monthly* 15 (1880): 259; Blight, *Race and Reunion,* 154; Charles Dudley Warner, "Their Pilgrimage," *Harper's New Monthly Magazine* 73, no. 435 (August 1886): 427.

20. Father to Nellie [Johnson], 12 August 1873, Griffith John McRee Papers, SHC; Cooke, "The White Sulphur Springs," 337, 353; Warner, "Their Pilgrimage," 442; R. R. Dearborn, *Saratoga and How to See It* (Albany, N.Y.: Albany News Co., 1871), 73; see George William Curtis, *Lotus-Eating; A Summer Book* (New York: Harper and Brothers, 1852), 121–22.

21. Virginia Tunstall Clay diary, 1866, 112, 117; Mrs. Clay to Sister, 15 June 1867 (italics in original); Jonathan Withers to C. C. Clay, 29 July 1868, to Jennie, 9 August 1868; all Clement Claiborne Clay Papers, Duke.

22. George W. Munford to Lizzie, 31 July 1881, 28 August 1881; Thomas H. Ellis to Mrs. E. T. Munford, 13 August 1881; all Munford-Ellis Family Papers, Duke; Jane Shelton Ellis Tucker to Powhatan Ellis Jr., 27 August 1880, Powhatan Ellis Papers, VHS.

23. Conte, *The History of the Greenbrier,* 64–65, Jeremiah Morton to William H. Calwell, 30 October 1873; Morton to R. B. Bolling and R. N. Dulaney, 12 November 1873; A. K. Philips to Jeremiah Morton, 10 October 1873; Morton, "Statement," 25 October 1873; A. N. Wallford to Jeremiah Morton, 8 August 1874; all Jeremiah Morton Papers, UVa.

24. William H. Peyton to William T. Sutherlin, 8 and 29 May 1868, 6, 16, and 24 June 1869, William T. Sutherlin Papers, SHC; A. W. Hamilton, "Chesapeake & Ohio Railway Extension," Charles Austin Goddard Papers, VHS; Conte, *The History of the Greenbrier,* 75–76.

25. *The Allegheny Springs* (Philadelphia: Merrikew and Son, 1874), 3; *Analysis of the Rockbridge Alum Springs in Virginia* (Baltimore: Kelly, Piet, and Co., 1870), 3; *Shenandoah Alum Springs* (Peoria, Ill.: J. W. Franks and Sons, 1882); "Rates and Routes to the Health and Pleasure Resorts . . . by the Richmond & Allegheny Railroad," 1886 pamphlet, VHS; for just one example, see John B. Bachelder, *Popular Resorts, and How to Reach Them* (Boston: Bachelder, 1875).

26. "Blue Ridge Springs, The Celebrated Dyspepsia Water," 187[?] pamphlet, VHS; Stan Cohen, *Historic Springs of the Virginias: A Pictorial History* (Charleston, W.Va.: Pictorial Histories Publishing Company, 1981); *B and O Summer Book: A Graphic Description of the Pittsburgh Division and Main Line Resorts* (Pittsburgh, Pa.: Baltimore and Ohio Railroad, 1883); Fay Ingalls, *The Valley Road* (Cleveland, Ohio: World Publishing, 1949), 42–66.

27. George W. Munford to Lizzie, 11 September 1881, Munford-Ellis Papers, Duke; "The Warm Springs, Bath County, Virginia," 1881 pamphlet, VHS; Greenbrier White Sulphur Springs ledger, July 1896, UVa; Cooke, "The White Sulphur Springs," 350.

28. Daniel Benedict diary, 18 June 1865, SSPL; *Harper's Weekly,* 23 June 1866, 397; *Faxon's Illustrated Handbook of Travel* (Boston: C. A. Faxon, 1874), 19; "The City of Medicine Waters," *The Daily Graphic,* 15 August 1878, SSPL; Sterngass, *First Resorts,* 156.

29. Corbett, *The Making of American Resorts,* 93–136; *Saratoga Illustrated: The Visitor's Guide of Saratoga Springs* (New York: Taintor Brothers, 1887), 15; S. R. Stoddard, *Saratoga*

Springs (Albany, N.Y.: Van Benthuysen, 1881), 1; Wainwright, ed., *A Philadelphia Perspective,* 1867, 531.

30. Thursty McQuill, *The Hudson River by Daylight* (New York: Gaylord Watson, 1876), 122.

31. C. C. Dawson, *Saratoga: Its Mineral Waters, and their use in Preventing & Eradicating Disease, and as a Refreshing Beverage* (New York: Russell Bros., 1868), 16; *Faxon's Illustrated Handbook of Travel,* 54 (italics in original); "Saratoga Springs," *Harper's* 53, no. 315 (August 1876): 399.

32. *The Uses and Value of Congress, Empire, and Columbian Water of Saratoga Springs* (New York: Hotchkiss' Sons, 1866), 5; "Summer Life at Saratoga," *Every Saturday,* 9 September 1871, 257; M. Davenport, *Under the Gridiron: A Summer in the United States and the Far West* (London: Tinsley Brothers, 1876), 118; *Frank Leslie's Illustrated Newspaper,* 30 August 1874, 427; Charles Ellis to Powhatan Ellis, 24 July 1876, VHS; Davenport, *Under the Gridiron,* 45; George Munford to Elizabeth T. Munford, 14 August 1881, Duke; Pilsbury, "A Southern Watering-Place," 258–64 (italics in original); John J. Moorman, *White Sulphur Springs, Greenbrier County, West Virginia* (Baltimore: Kelly, Piet and Co., 1873), 24–25.

33. "White Sulphur Springs, Greenbrier County, West Virginia," 1881 pamphlet, 11, SHC; see also Moorman, *White Sulphur Springs* (1873), 24; "Greenbrier White Sulphur Springs, West Virginia," 1896 pamphlet, 6–7, SHC.

34. Davenport, *Under the Gridiron,* 119; Sterngass, *First Resorts,* passim; Daniel deJarnette Staples to Mary Staples, 14 and 17 July 1896, Staples and Persinger Family Papers, UVa; *B and O Summer Book,* 114.

35. "Summer Life at Saratoga," *Every Saturday,* 261; Wainwright, ed., *A Philadelphia Perspective,* 1867, 530; "Pre-Raphaelites at Saratoga," *McBride's Magazine* 2 (September 1868): 256–61.

36. "Saratoga Races"; "From Saratoga," *New York Daily Tribune,* 14 August 1865; Daniel deJarnette Staples to Mary Staples, 14 July and "Monday" 1896, Staples and Persinger Family Papers, UVa; Henry James, "Saratoga," *The Nation* 11 (11 August 1870): 87–89.

37. *Faxon's Illustrated Handbook of Travel,* 15; "Rates and Routes to the Health and Pleasure Resorts," 1886 pamphlet, VHS; J. G. Panghorn, *Mountain and Valley Resorts on the Picturesque B and O* (Chicago: Knight and Leonard, 1884), 20–26; *The Fauquier White Sulphur Springs, An Old Popular Watering Place* (Washington: Morrison, 1878), 13 (italics in original).

38. Wainwright, ed., *A Philadelphia Perspective,* 1867, 531; *The Nation,* 15 September 1870, 171.

39. Ernest Duvergier de Hauranne, *A Frenchman in Lincoln's America. Huit Mois en Amérique: Lettres et Notes de Voyage, 1864–1865,* trans. and ed. Ralph H. Bowen (Chicago: R. R. Donnelley and Sons, 1974 [1866]), 1:132; H. Hussey Vivian, *Notes of a Tour in America. From August 7th to November 17th, 1877* (London: Edward Stanford, 1878), 35; *Saratoga Guide, Illustrated* (Saratoga Springs: Cozzens and Mingay, 1886), 34; "Summer Life at Saratoga," *Frank Leslie's Illustrated Newspaper,* 30 August 1879, 427; Albro Martin, *Railroads Triumphant: The Growth, Rejection, and Rebirth of a Vital American Force* (New York: Oxford University Press, 1992), 208–9.

40. "Summer Life in Saratoga," *Daily Tribune,* 27 June 1878; Wainwright, ed., *A Philadelphia Perspective,* 1 February 1866, 508–9 (italics in original).

41. "Society at Saratoga," *Tinsley's Magazine* 34 (1884), 240–41; "Pre-Raphaelites at Saratoga," 261 (italics in original); "To Sister," 2 August 1870, Creagh Family Papers, SHC; Daniel deJarnette Staples to Mary Staples, 17 July 1896, Staples and Persinger Family Papers, UVa.

42. Ellen Hardin Walworth, "Saratoga as an Institution," *Chatauquan* 15 (September 1892): 735; "Saratoga as it is," *Saratogian,* 9 August 1871; "Summer Life at Saratoga," *Every Saturday,* 257, 261.

43. Clement Claiborne Clay to Auntie, 8 September 1868, Clement Claiborne Clay Papers, Duke; Father to Nellie and Sam [Johnson, children], 24 July 1873, Griffith John McRee Papers, SHC; Cooke, "The White Sulphur Springs," 349 (italics in original).

44. Warner, "Their Pilgrimage," 429–30; *The Jordan Rockbridge Alum Springs* (Charlottesville, Va.: Chronicle Steam Printing House, 1873), 16; Header of Warm Springs stationery, 1881, Munford-Ellis Family Papers, Duke.

45. Davenport, *Under the Gridiron,* 118; Emma Waite diary, June 14 and 17, NYSLA; Myra B. Young Armstead, *"Lord, Please Don't Take Me in August": African Americans in Newport and Saratoga Springs, 1870–1930* (Urbana: University of Illinois Press, 1999); "Town-Talk: An American Play," *Every Saturday,* 11 (March 1871): 257.

46. Hallie R. Donaghe to Virginia [(Bagby) Taylor], 29 July 1881, Taylor Family Papers, VHS (italics in original); Daniel deJarnette Staples to Mary Staples, 23 August 1895, Staples and Persinger Family Papers, UVa; "Summer Life at Saratoga," *Every Saturday,* 261; "Saratoga," *Daily Graphic,* 1873, SSPL.

47. Lee Livney, "Let Us Now Praise Self-Made Men: A Reexamination of the Hilton-Seligman Affair," *New York History* 75 (January 1994): 66–98.

48. "Sensation at Saratoga," *New York Times,* 19 June 1877; Warner, "Their Pilgrimage," 589; Livney, "Let Us Now Praise Self-Made Men," 90–93; Cindy S. Aron, *Working at Play: A History of Vacations in the United States* (New York: Oxford University Press, 1999), 216–18.

49. De Hauranne, *A Frenchman in Lincoln's America,* 1:138–39.

50. James, "Saratoga," 87–89.

51. Warner, "Their Pilgrimage," 434, 437, 594.

52. Warner, "Their Pilgrimage," 434, 594; Pilsbury, "A Southern Watering-Place," 263; as quoted in Richard H. Shryock, ed., *Letters of Richard D. Arnold* (New York: AMS Press, 1929), 128, 138, 160.

53. Ingalls, *The Valley Road,* 42–66; Conte, *The History of the Greenbrier,* 95.

54. Mrs. William Grant to Husband, 15 and 24 August 1890, Mrs. William Grant Papers, UVa; "Greenbrier White Sulphur Springs," 1896 pamphlet, 13, SHC; Confederate states represented 35.0 percent of all visitors during July (Greenbrier White Sulphur Springs ledger, 1896, UVa). See Table 3.

Index